Peddlers of Crisis

Peddlers of Crisis

The Committee on the Present
Danger and the Politics of Containment

Jerry W. Sanders

South End Press   **Boston, MA**

Library of Congress Card Catalog Number: 83-060176
ISBN 0-89608-181-8 paper
ISBN 0-89608-182-6 cloth
Cover design by Ann L. Raszmann
First published in the United States by
South End Press
302 Columbus Ave
Boston, MA 02116
First published in Great Britian by
Pluto Press
The Works
105a Torriano Ave
London, England

For my sons,
and their generation

CONTENTS

ACKNOWLEDGEMENTS

Peddlers Of Crisis has passed through many seasons. The original investigation began with the founding of the Committee on the Present Danger (CPD), became a doctoral dissertation as the Committee's campaign spurred a shift to the right in the late 1970s, and finally, when the CPD took power with one of their own as president in 1980, this book followed. As I watched these events unfold from vantage points as scattered as Berkeley, Hawaii, and New York City — where various of these chapters were written — many persons shared my rapt fascination and dread trepidation, listened patiently to roughhewn interpretations and offered insights of their own, that made the book what it is. A note of gratitude is in order, though hardly adequate to the magnitude of their contribution.

While in Washington my research was furthered immensely by the staff of the Center For Defense Information. I would especially like to thank the Center's director Admiral Gene LaRocque, and research director David T. Johnson, for the collegial spirit with which they shared their knowledge and resources. Others who provided important help along the way were Michael T. Klare, Banning Garrett, the late Ambassador to the United Nations Charles W. Yost, and Robert Tannenwald. The most important yet difficult acknowledgement given the conclusions reached herein, must go to the members of the CPD who were quite willing — indeed gracious — in consenting to be interviewed for this project.

Deserving of special mention are Paul Nitze, Jeane Kirkpatrick, Richard Allen, Norman Podhoretz, Charles Tyroler II, Max Kampelman, Charles Burton Marshall, Chalmers Johnson, Seymour Martin Lipset, and Ralph Strauss. Other enlightening interviews were provided by Elbridge Durbrow of the American Security Council, General Daniel O. Graham, chairman of the Coalition For Peace Through Strength, and Joshua Muravchik of the Coalition For A Democratic Majority.

Financial support is a scarce resource when it comes to an inquiry into the politics of militarism. I was fortunate in this regard to have been the recipient of a Kent Fellowship from the Danforth Foundation which judged the subject to be of vital scholarly importance. An additional note of institutional appreciation is extended to the staff of the Alexander Library at Rutgers University for their assistance in making accessible the 2000 pages of unpublished letters and memoranda on the activities of the first Committee on the Present Danger in the early 1950s. I would also like to express my thanks to Fred Warner Neal who, many years before becoming a well-known spokesman for arms control, had served as a staff member of the original CPD. The informative interview he granted added invaluable perspective to my archival research.

During the writing of the Ph.D. dissertation at the University of California at Berkeley, I benefitted from the comments of numerous persons, among them the members of my dissertation committee William Kornhauser, David Matza, and Peter Dale Scott, as well as from the Inter-University Committee — Jonathan Cobb, Howard Dratch, Madeline Duckles, Todd Gitlin, David Gold, Vivian Gold, Jon Livingston, Will Riggan, Charles Schwartz, and Carol Wolman. For their keen interest and research assistance I am grateful to William Bryan Godbe III and Jon Vaught. Thanks also to Bill Salomon of the Berkeley Journal of Sociology for his editorial suggestions early on, and to Margaret Henderson for her diligence in typing the dissertation manuscript. Finally, John Dombrink's sage humor was a contribution that cannot be measured, as was the friendship of Charles Belkin who monitored my existence from start to finish.

Turning a dissertation into a book is no small task and is also something one does not accomplish alone. I will always be deeply indebted to Richard Barnet, Richard Falk, and Daniel Ellsberg for their advice and encouragement. In Hawaii, Louis Warsh and the Peace Studies students gave much support when it was sorely needed. Sherle Schwenninger, my colleague at the World Policy Institute where I completed the final chapters, provided the careful reading and stimulating discussion which made me regret he had not been around throughout the enterprise. John Schall, my editor at South End Press, deserves much credit for offering constructive suggestions in the nick of time and making this process an occasion of celebration besides.

In the end, I owe the most profound debt to two persons without whom *Peddlers Of Crisis* would not have been realized — Alan Wolfe and Mercedes Guerrero Sanders. Over the course of this work Alan was at various times my co-author, editor, and friend. The exemplar of C. Wright Mills' ideal of intellectual craftsmanship, Alan's willingness to share the lore of his craft was a source of education and inspiration which I could never repay. Finally, Mercedes, my wife, always reminded me in the difficult periods why I had embarked upon such a long and often tortuous journey, and explained to others its meaning at times when I had lost sight of the forest for the trees. The energy that went into this work was hers as well as mine. A last word of gratitude must go to our sons, Che Jeremy and Zachariah Octavio. I can only hope that someday they will find lessons in these pages that partially make up for the weekends and evenings from which their father was absent from frog-catching and baseball.

New York City
January 10, 1983

Foreword
to
PEDDLERS OF CRISIS
Alan Wolfe

During the late 1970s, when most of the U.S. economy was in decline, the business of expounding the Soviet threat became a growth industry. Latter-day Paul Reveres rode through the land, warning of an immediate danger to American security from an ever-expanding Soviet Union and proclaiming that unless the response was quick, thorough, and vigilant, the United States would find itself at the mercy of its implacable antagonist. Hard times demand easy answers, and the notion that America could be made right again through patriotic fervor in no small part contributed to the election in 1980 of a politician who had, in his entire career, never been known to underestimate the Soviet threat.

To be bullish on defense, one must be bearish on America. When Ronald Reagan announced in April 1982 that the Soviet Union had achieved a definite margin of strategic superiority over the United States — the first time in American history that this most dubious proposition of the new right had been endorsed by an incumbent president — he inadvertently revealed the public relations flaw in the Soviet threat campaign: the systematic downplaying of one's own strength. The pro-military lobby in the United States operates by cultivating fear. When the fear becomes too great, the effect, if I may cite the advice of government-made civil defense films from the 1950s, is to duck and cover. Irresponsible talk about nuclear war from supposedly responsible politicians contributed greatly to the fear that propelled the Nuclear

1

Freeze Campaign of 1982. As the Reagan Administration learned, bellicosity backfires against its advocates.

Fear, at least in a society as safe and secure as the United States, is not a spontaneous emotion. To convince the citizens of the world's most powerful state that they are helpless and weak requires careful planning and systematic effort. Jerry Sanders' *Peddlers of Crisis* is one of the most original and thought-provoking attempts to examine the merchandising of fear in the United States. Sanders and those like him are the genuine Paul Reveres, warning us against those who warn us against others. The American way of life is threatened, but from bloated military budgets, attempts to curtail civil liberty, and the regimentation of civilian institutions in the name of national security.

Twice in the experience of one generation has the selling of fear dominated the political consciousness of the United States. At the end of World War II, decision makers in Washington, faced with a choice between global accomodation with the Russians and an opportunity to use their monopoly of nuclear weapons as a political instrument, chose to interpret negatively every Soviet act, and thereby contributed substantially toward the creation of the Cold War. Once the *realpolitik* of wartime cooperation with the Russians was dropped in favor of a messianic anticommunism, the pieces of both international and domestic hysteria fell into place like a jigsaw puzzle. The Soviet threat was vigorously sold to the American people, and while the sale was taking place, an Atlantic alliance and free trade network of intercapitalist relations was created by a superpower which had, in its recent past, been isolationist and even antimilitarist.

Nothing lasts forever, and to the dismay of the Soviet threat lobby, the desire of the American people for peace and a relaxation of global tension made its appearance. No matter how hard the cold warriors tried, ordinary Americans time and again refused to be "educated" to the chiliastic vision of a world under siege. The Cold War inevitably waned, and when Richard Nixon, one of the architects of anticommunist hysteria, endorsed detente, a new chapter in postwar U.S. foreign policy seemed to open up. America, finally, was about to put its obsessions behind itself and to act like the mature power it claimed to be.

Detente was hardly a radical idea. In the mind of Henry Kissinger, in fact, detente suggested a forthright conservatism. The world, Kissinger maintained, was constantly in turmoil. Big powers, whatever their ideology, are conservative powers, for they invariably try to protect the status quo that keeps them big. Therefore the United States and the Soviet Union, both superpowers and obvious rivals, nevertheless had a common interest in working together to establish the rules of international behavior. Kissinger was aware that in the past American foreign policy had swung wildly back and forth from a Wilsonian commitment to ideological goals to a power-broker *realpolitik* that defended the national interest. Idealism and rhetoric were fine for election campaigns, where it was necessary to simplify matters for ordinary folk, but in the world of statecraft, big power diplomacy was the only way to run a foreign policy. Detente, to Nixon and Kissinger, represented the coming of age of American foreign policy under genuinely conservative auspices.

The same globalist foreign policy establishment that oversaw the cold war in the 1940s slowly came around to an endorsement of detente in the 1970s, primarily because of the transformation of both the American and the world economy. As Europe and Japan narrowed the gap between themselves and the United States, and as America itself began to feel the inflationary effects of military spending in Vietnam, the worldview of a simple-minded anticommunism no longer seemed to make sense. Let us join together with our economic allies in Western Europe and Asia, the dominant sentiment ran, and create a Trilateral world in which economic, not military, competition with the East would ensure the cohesion of the West. Just as the original Cold War impetus of the late 1940s was bipartisan, detente had its *realpolitik* advocates like Kissinger and its Trilateralist supporters like Cyrus Vance. When Jimmy Carter followed the Republican ascendency in 1976, most observers expected a smooth transition in foreign policy. Detente would continue, the SALT II treaty would be completed, and Trilateralist plans for global power sharing would be advanced.

As we now know, and as Jerry Sanders documents in this book, the ruling class lost control of its own foreign policy. Halfway through the Carter presidency, sentiment radically shifted in the United States back toward the Cold War sentiment of the 1940s. To some degree, of course, the Soviet Union helped matters along by invading Afghanistan, but it was clear well before that act, specifically when the U.S. Senate expressed its unwillingness to ratify the SALT II treaty, that American domestic politics had become more receptive to negative perceptions of the Soviet threat. In retrospect, this shifting of ground was not a natural phenomenon like an earthquake. The Carter years witnessed the political triumph of a group of dissident national security managers who had never accepted detente and who were prepared to use their expertise and experience to put the United States back on the track of the Cold War.

Peddling crisis is not an especially complicated business. One of the most telling aspects of Sanders' story is the automatic ease with which the cold war lobby slipped into a script written some time in the past. One first gathers the required number of "experts" from the vast network of think-tanks, universities, corporations, and scientific associations involved with military matters to coordinate the positions to be taken. Then one constructs the appropriate slogan — bomber gap, missile gap, window of vulnerability — designed to arouse the fear that THEY are ahead of US. Tapping anticommunist and rightwing funding sources, one then mounts a full-scale propaganda effort involving direct-mail, op-ed pieces, talk shows, seminars for policymakers, films, and all the other paraphernalia of fear. As public opinion responds, leading to increases in military spending, the Soviet Union inevitably responds as well, leading to a reassertion of the fear all over again. In a world dominated by nuclear weapons, fear is a reality, and those who exploit it with vivid imagery often have an initial advantage over those who try to talk calmly and rationally.

The Committee on the Present Danger, created to lobby Jimmy Carter as soon as he became president, lost the battle but won the war. Carter initially turned to the Trilateral Commission for advice, spoke of reducing the military budget, and warned America of an "inordinate fear of communism." But politicians understand that they must move which-ever way the wind blows, and throughout the Carter years, it became obvious that the wind was not blowing in the Trilateralist direction. By the election of 1980, groups like the Committee on the Present Danger had established the terrain of debate in the United States. The question was no longer whether the military budget would be rapidly expanded; the question now was by how much.

Ronald Reagan's election in 1980 brought the Committee on the Present Danger directly into the government. The immediate effect was a sharp increase in bellicose language, a repudiation of even the appear-ance of detente, and close to automatic approval for every weapons system being considered by the Pentagon. Thirty-five years after its initial formulation in the Truman Administration, a foreign policy oriented toward what Jerry Sanders calls Containment Militarism be-came the basis, not only of election rhetoric, but of actual foreign policy.

No sooner did the Committee on the Present Danger have a blank script on which to write its play — combined with an unlimited checking account to finance it — then did the Cold War vision of aggressive Soviet expansion begin to crumble. First and foremost, the Europeans, who accepted cold war programs in the late 1940s, politely refused to join the general denunciation of Soviet meddling. Indeed among peace groups and socialists in Europe, strong enough to influence government policy in Holland, Denmark, and Belgium, the perception began to grow that the United States was as untrustworthy as the Soviet Union. Second in line in their refusal to take the Soviet threat seriously were U.S. farmers, facing hard times at home and determined to continue to sell wheat to their most reliable overseas customer. By placing the farm vote ahead of a consistent anticommunism, Ronald Reagan indicated that the Soviet threat was a matter of convenience, not necessity, there to be addressed or ignored as politics demanded.

But without question the most unexpected turn about on the question of Cold War hysteria was manifested by the American people themselves. Two years after indicating their desire to build more weapons, polls began to show that Americans wanted to cutback spending on defense. All of a sudden, fear of nuclear war began to dominate the public consciousness, and notions of a weapons freeze became so powerful that even Soviet threat politicians like Senator Henry Jackson couched their plans for a weapons buildup in the rhetoric of a freeze. In response, President Reagan no longer spoke of the Russians as liars and cheats but proposed arms reductions talks with them. Even if the administration is not serious about such talks, and its planning for nuclear war goes on as if such talks were not happening, it is now clear that the same public sentiment which had prepared the way for the Committee on the Present Danger had turned once more.

Why is it that opinions and attitudes toward the Cold War change so often in the United States? The rightwing answer is that Soviet aggression leaves the United States little choice but to respond. The Russians, in fact, are hardly a peace-loving power, but not even the Reagan administration really believes what it says about Soviet intentions, for why would it continue to abide by the SALT II treaty if that treaty, as Reagan and the Committee on the Present Danger publically claim, gives the Russians an advantage? Very few people, including the Europeans who live next door to the red army, believe any more that the Russians are responsible for all the contours of the Cold War.

On the left the opinion has been offered that the Cold War dominates America because an overloaded military budget is fundamental to the operations of advanced capitalism. Yet it seems to be the case now, although it may not have been in the late 1940s, that a program of reinvigorated military spending could destroy the competitiveness of U.S. capitalism compared to West Germany and Japan, who are less burdened by the distorting effects of military production. True, certain companies in the United States are awash in funds due to the military buildup, but the role of the state in a capitalist economy is to protect the interests of the capitalist class as a whole, and military spending is doing the exact opposite. Military needs, at this point in time, represent a form of capitalist suicide.

I believe that another answer to the persistency of the Cold War needs to be offered, and that Jerry Sanders offers a convincing one. The Cold War, he argues, needs to be understood politically. The Committee on the Present Danger was successful because it understood basic American ideology and how to manipulate it. The Cold War provides a source of unity in a divided society, and when that society is experiencing its most difficult periods, it seeks the familiar and most easily digestible nostrums to relieve its anxiety.

But something which begins politically can end politically. In *Peddlers of Crisis* there is a message for peace and disarmament activists in the United States that should never be forgotten. That message is simple: the cold warriors kept their hopes alive through difficult times because they had a sense of mission and basic organizing skills. The Left needs both if it is to make the nuclear freeze something more than a fad. The Committee on the Present Danger has done an effective job of peddling crisis and fear. The question is whether others will be able to make a case for hope and reason. Good intentions are not enough. Effective political savvy, of the kind described in this book, is needed as well.

ALAN WOLFE

INTRODUCTION

The Omnipresent Danger

The lesson we should draw from the experience of the last ten years is that the United States, its allies, and all other nations which cherish peace should return to the containment policy pursued between Truman's time and the American withdrawal from Vietnam.

Eugene V. Rostow, co-founder and chairman,
Committee on the Present Danger [1]

Providing for the common defense now requires the kind of priority that it had in 1950, and it is a disservice to the American people to pretend that this can be accomplished without a major adjustment in national priorities.

Paul H. Nitze, co-founder and chairman of Policy Studies, Committee on the Present Danger [2]

Such men as these are crackpot realists: in the name of realism they have constructed a paranoid reality all their own.

C. Wright Mills, *The Power Elite* [3]

7

Within days of Ronald Reagan's election, three of his top national security advisers appeared on the evening news to warn that the United States must begin a massive military buildup.[4] The earnest Reagan spokesmen — Eugene Rostow, Paul Nitze, and William Van Cleave — represented the brain trust of the Committee on the Present Danger (CPD), a group eschewed by Carter four years before and snubbed in succeeding White House councils on foreign policy. When appointments to the Reagan Administration were announced, thirty-two of its members had emerged in key posts. One year into Reagan's term, a high-ranking State Department official underscored the Committee's hold on ideas as well as numbers, declaring: "The Administration seems to be espousing their (CPD) views lock, stock, and barrel." [5] Thus ended a most remarkable odyssey from political exile back to the pinnacle of power, an extraordinary tale of elite intrigue and mass manipulation, one with grave implications for this nation and the world.

From its founding on the heels of Carter's 1976 victory, the CPD's goal has been unequivocal: to resurrect a militarized doctrine of containment as the cornerstone of U.S. foreign policy. Reagan's campaign pledge to "rearm America," the diversion of the nation's resources to that end, interventionist posturing, and talk of "nuclear war-fighting," bear witness to the Committee's success as well as to the macabre stakes of militarism in the contemporary era.

The turn of events should have come as no surprise. In his bid for the presidency, Reagan himself was baptized into the CPD, much as his predecessor had affiliated with the Trilateral Commission. Significantly, the latter was a group Reagan attacked during the campaign even after it had long since abandoned the detente-like views it was accused of harboring by right wing tormenters. In contrast to Carter's Trilateral-laden Administration, Reagan brought in CPD chairman Rostow to head the Arms Control and Disarmament Agency (ACDA), a mismatch of philosophy and agency rivalled only by James Watt as Secretary of the Interior. Nitze, the CPD's director for policy studies and with Rostow co-founder of the Committee, was named to the sensitive post of Chief Negotiator for Theater Nuclear Forces in Europe, despite his uncompromising opposition to serious arms control dating back to the late 1940s.

Other Committee members appointed to prominent positions included National Security coordinator Richard Allen, later ousted for shady financial dealings, but not before accusing Europe of embracing a 'better Red than dead' philosophy; Richard Pipes, billed as chief Kremlinologist in the Reagan Administration, who warned that avoidance of nuclear war depended on the Soviet Union changing its system of government; Jeane Kirkpatrick, U.S. Ambassador to the United

Nations, who attracted Reagan's attention with her morally bankrupt and intellectually vacuous distinction between authoritarianism and totalitarianism, one now used to ignore 'human rights' in the Third World; and William Casey,who after managing Reagan's campaign became director of the CIA, an individual whose recent cloak-and-dagger experience included a game of hide-and-seek with the Security and Exchange Commission (SEC) investigating his financial records.

One could go on and on, citing the cameo roles in which the committee's members have been cast. Basking in the CPD's success, Director Charles Tyroler II — himself now a member of the Intelligence Oversight Board — chortled: "It happened so fast that we're almost amazed ourselves." [6] Washington lobbyist Charls E. Walker, a member of Reagan's Economic Policy Advisory Board added: "I thought we had come of age before, but in terms of the public, I guess now we've really made it." [7]

As architects and engineers of Reagan's foreign policy then, the CPD deserves the same scrutiny accorded the Trilateral Commission when Carter rode into Washington to take over the reins of power with its stamp of approval four years earlier.

The feature that stands out about the CPD is the familiarity of message and bearer. Considering many of them were "present at the creation," in the phrase chosen by Secretary of State Dean Acheson to lionize the founding of the post war containment doctrine, the CPD's call to arms was hardly newsworthy. Faithful soldiers in the postwar global crusade, the Soviet Threat had been their gospel and litany for a generation. Indeed anything less from the likes of Nitze and Rostow would have caused those gathered for the CPD's christening to sit up and take notice.

While the CPD would be the last to purposefully dust off the adage that "history repeats itself: the first time as tragedy, the second as farce," Marx's observation loomed like one of his portraits over the proceedings at the National Press Club the day the group announced its intentions. Here was Rostow, Vietnam hawk and diehard interventionist, calling for a return to policies that had led to the destruction of Southeast Asia and defeat for the United States besides, a figure thoroughly discredited only a few short years before. Flanking Rostow was Nitze, veteran leader of apocryphal threats, gaps, and other assorted hysterias, opening a new house of mirrors this time featuring a "window of vulnerability."

The ubiquitous Nitze has been a force to contend with through nine presidential administrations spanning a period of forty years, a record of durability that even the politburo must envy. Nitze in fact masterminded a major shift in the doctrine of containment in 1950. Outlined in a secret policy paper known as NSC-68, his world view served as America's official Cold War Manifesto until the political fallout over its implementation in Vietnam. After thirty years and military expenditures approaching $3 trillion, Nitze's ideas have changed little. In the campaign to defeat the Second Strategic Arms Limitation Treaty (SALT II) for instance, he argued:

> To have the advantage at the utmost level of violence helps at every lesser level. In the Korean War, the Berlin blockade, and the Cuban missile crisis, the U.S. had the strategic edge because of our superiority at the strategic nuclear level. That edge has slipped away. [8]

The consequence of this failure to maintain military supremacy is the central lesson to be learned from Vietnam, according to Rostow:

> This is the true moral of Vietnam, above and beyond a good many others about the failure to press for military victory. The deterioration of our nuclear advantage led to the erosion of our position, and profoundly affected the final stages of the conflict. [9]

The only thing we learn from history is that we don't learn anything from history, a sage once quipped. The CPD's program is nothing less than a return to the halcyon yesteryear of nuclear superiority when the United States could routinely threaten first-use of nuclear weapons when CIA-orchestrated coups and other sundry forms of counterrevolutionary terrorism in the imperial arsenal had failed. As Daniel Ellsberg has made plain, this was and still remains the *sine qua non* of the national security code.[10] The adamant refusal by Reagan's first Secretary of State, Alexander Haig, to renounce "first-use" only served to confirm its continuing central role in the calculus of the present regime. [11]

The road back to the lost Eden of military predominance in the contemporary era has already set off a quantum leap in technology and spending, not unlike the arms race that followed NSC-68 — with a notable exception. While the motive for development of nuclear weapons may remain unchanged, the unleashing of today's crop whether by intent or miscalculation, foredooms the planet to a specter of destruction unimaginable at the time of NSC-68. Men like Nitze and Rostow, serve to remind one of Albert Einstein's melancholic observation that nuclear weapons have changed everything but the way we think. To break the tightening death grip of this ultimate contradiction of our existence, we must consider what is at stake that is possibly worth the risk of human extinction.

* * *

Having emerged as the pre-eminent power of the postwar world, the United States inherited the financial, economic, and military-political leadership of the capitalist world system. Far from the shambling and munificent Uncle Sam of folklore who accepted global responsibility only with great reluctance, America's imperial role was the culmination of a restless expansion that swept across a continent, fanned throughout the hemisphere, and spread over the Pacific, pausing finally to catch its breath only after circling the globe. As William Appleman Williams, among others, has persuasively shown, the aggressive huckstering of U.S. commercial, political, and cultural interests etched empire into the national consciousness as a deeply engrained "way of life." [12]

There was an important difference after 1945 however. As global banker and policeman, state policy was forced to look beyond the provincial interests of "open door" expansionism to the overall equilibrium and stability of a transnational system of privilege, a *Pax Americana*. The task of devising and presiding over such an imperial framework was entrusted to a foreign policy/national security establishment (hereinafter Establishment) made up of elites whose background and experience prepared them well for the ecumenical outlook needed to bridge the worlds of finance and power and integrate them into the new *Weltanschauung* of containment.

Communism was the object of containment to be sure, but there was much more as well. Under the guise of combatting the spread of an antidemocratic ideology, the United States proceeded to impose its Amercentric notion of world order on other nations and peoples struggling to achieve their own freedom from want and repression. As this imperial undertaking met resistance, containment became increasingly dependent on military force, a strategy — codified in NSC-68 — which I will refer to as Containment Militarism. Two things about this doctrine, often misinterpreted, must be stressed at the outset: first, it is a product not of strength, but weakness; second, it was founded in controversy and remains the subject of bitter debate. This contradicts conventional wisdom which depicts containment as omnipotent abroad and universally celebrated at home.

Containment was built upon the indissoluble projection of economic, political, and military power. In the postwar period, the Marshall Plan symbolized its economic pillar, the universalistic language of the Truman Doctrine constituted the political buttress, and the nuclear annihilation of Hiroshima and Nagasaki served as a reminder of the military mainstay that anchored the new world order of containment. As the century reached midpoint however, each of the elements of *Pax Americana* had fallen into a state of disrepair.

The most dramatic blow to containment was struck at the U.S.

nuclear monopoly when the Soviet Union exploded an atom bomb of its own in August 1949, serving notice that atomic diplomacy was destined for a shortened career unless the nuclear ante was raised to still higher levels of destruction. Moreover, the "fall of China" coming on the heels of the successful Soviet test, pointed up the vulnerability of interventionist rhetoric when the options were commitment of conventional forces well beyond what political and economic orthodoxy would accept, or falling short of that, reliance on nuclear weapons to stop movements of national liberation. Finally, the near simultaneous events in Russia and China were preceded by a gradual erosion of the economic pillar of containment, the underlying purpose of which was to discourage Western Europe from charting an independent and neutralist course outside the pantheon of East-West struggle. All this in the midst of a recession in the U.S. domestic economy, feared by some as the onset of another Great Depression.

In the mounting climate of crisis that threatened to bring the American Century to an untimely demise not much beyond its infancy, President Truman at Secretary of State Acheson's urging, ordered the policy review designated NSC-68. What emerged from this intense six-week exercise was a blueprint recommending a three-fold increase in military spending on nuclear and conventional forces — a bold program of rearmament that would send a signal to the world that the Truman Administration was ready to pay a steep price to bolster the sagging pillars of containment.

The crisis of empire in the post-Vietnam era has been strikingly similar and even more pronounced. Whereas the Soviets only threatened nuclear superiority in the earlier period, they have now pulled abreast to a position of equality. Moreover, the nuclear virus has spread to five other nations with the prospect of several more not far behind, making the threat of first-use an increasingly dicey proposition. The immorality of such a policy now includes its insanity as well.

The achievement of Soviet parity occurred during the period in which the U.S. sank its resources ever deeper into a losing cause in Vietnam. Here, too, the anticolonial nationalism at work in the Chinese revolution proved an indominable force that continued to shake the foundation of the Amercentric world system. Shattered in Vietnam, the interventionist pillar of containment was sent crumbling to the ground by revolutions in Iran and Nicaragua.

Finally, the roller coaster of stagflation forced disengagement of the U.S. dollar from its pivotal role in the international economic order, exacerbating mounting tensions between the United States and its junior partners of privilege in Japan and Western Europe in the process. As had been the case thirty years before, the new decade began in a mood of crisis that prevailed into the presidential election. The winning candidate in 1980 promised, of course, to restore *Pax Americana* to health and vigor by means of an unprecedented military buildup, harkening back to the remedy prescribed in NSC-68.

* * * * *

The Chinese expression for *crisis* is made up of two characters, one meaning "danger," and the other "opportunity." [13] The CPD's rise to power demonstrates an adroit manipulation of these dual meanings. While the Committee twisted the structural crises of empire into an external *danger* (the Soviet Threat), it was the *opportunity* they saw to shore up its internal scaffolding via a domestic scare campaign that brought the effort into being. Their success has led some observers to remark that we have entered a new era — Cold War II. Indeed a sequel-like reading of the current period receives added support from the discovery of another Committee on the Present Danger (hereinafter CPD-I and CPD-II) with a strikingly similar program in the NSC-68 period.

Like its contemporary incarnation, CPD-I was launched ostensibly to counter a Soviet Threat, the alleged danger of which was used as a foil to establish Containment Militarism as official Cold War policy. Where CPD-II reads like a reunion of those who had faithfully executed the doctrine from Korea to Vietnam, the original group was drawn from its first-generation architects. The founders of CPD-I, James Conant, Vannevar Bush, and Tracy Voorhees, figured prominently in NSC-68 and were, like the bulk of the Committee, members in good standing of the Establishment. Set in motion shortly after NSC-68's completion, CPD-I played a critical role over the next few years, disbanding in 1953 satisfied their mission had been accomplished. By that time the military budget had quadrupled and Containment Militarism enjoyed an allegiance within national security circles that would not be seriously challenged until Vietnam. As was true of CPD-II a quarter century after, members of CPD-I assumed key posts in the Eisenhower Administration to implement the militaristic policy they had helped to bring about.

As Containment Militarism came to be applied to Vietnam, however, many of those who had implemented the policy as national security managers, promoted it as members of the foreign policy establishment, and supported it as leaders of the corporate elite, began to question its efficacy as a viable imperial strategy for the late twentieth century. The prevailing assessment of the "correlation of forces" [14] became the subject of bitter debate as did the optimal balance among trade, diplomacy, and military force in the containment formula.

At the center of the controversy was the issue of the long-term effects of militarism on capitalist expansion, as well as the limits of taxation and inflation the public would bear in support of an inter-ventionist foreign policy and a continuation of the nuclear arms buildup. Into this breach stepped the second CPD, reviving the specter of a Soviet menace that necessitated an accelerated military effort and still greater reliance on the threat of military force in containing its alleged global expansion. The appearance and success of such mass appeals directed by similarly constituted ad hoc elite committees raises serious questions about the standard explanations of foreign policy and domestic politics.

Taken together, CPD-I and CPD-II cut a formidable portrait of power, their Establishment credentials setting them quite apart from the myriad lobbies of parochial interests that routinely besiege Washington and badger the public for attention. Moreover, policy elites of such impeccable pedigree ordinarily work behind the scenes, preferring col-legial persuasion within executive councils far from the public eye, to campaigns of mass mobilization. Besides, there is the much-heralded bipartisan machinery whereby the two political parties mediate between elites and masses, shaping a popular consensus between the time policy has been agreed upon within the Establishment and the occasion when it is actually put into practice. Finally, while mass legitimation is critical at this stage, ratification is generally a *pro forma* exercise consecrating plans already well into motion.

The above description of the policy formation process passes muster with both orthodox and radical observers. Where they differ is that the former attributes the public's acquiescence to a democratic value consensus and a representative elite, while the latter argues that such deference can be accounted for through the ideological manipulation of mass opinion by the elite. Given the extraordinary degree of consensus in the interwar years between Korea and Vietnam particularly, orthodox and radical theorists could each make a plausible case for accuracy. Whether the Cold War reflected the will of the people responding to an independently-formed perception of a Soviet Threat, or was a cynical elite drive engineered for global empire, was one of those "prime mover" questions like whether business followed the flag, or the flag followed business. The longer the consensus held the harder it became to separate cause from effect, the leaders from the led, and the validity of one theory from another. In either case, whether one sees elites as servants, or masses as slaves, an elite-orchestrated campaign — and a para-insti-tutional vehicle like the CPD to carry it out — presents a puzzling anomaly to our ordinary thinking about foreign policy and domestic politics.

* * *

These however were not ordinary times. As noted earlier, the epochs bracketing the lives of both CPDs were periods in which *Pax Americana* encountered resistance to its hegemony at several points which, taken together, shook the foundation of the postwar empire. With the increasing intensity of the shocks abroad, cracks began to appear in the edifice of consensus at home. This can be attributed in no small part to the rousing success which marked its creation, a point whose seeming counterintuitive logic requires further elaboration.

Containment's origin is rooted in the Truman Administration's decision in 1947 to hold up a corrupt and oppressive dictatorship in Greece under the pretense of halting communist expansion. In subsequent years, American presidents would carry out similar line-drawing exercises over the entire globe arguing, in the zero-sum logic of containment, that overthrows of status quo governments anywhere represented a danger to the world system everywhere. In this manner, the range of threats became limitless as did counterrevolutionary intervention in the guise of national defense. As Gelb and Betts remark in their study of Vietnam decision-making, "Vietnam was the linear descendent of Greece in 1947." [15]

From the beginning it was recognized that the costs of policing the empire would be staggering and that the public's "isolationism" would have to be replaced by outright mobilization to bear up under the sacrifice. Senator Arthur Vandenberg, a prewar isolationist convert to containment advised Truman at the time of the decision on Greece to "make a personal appearance before Congress and scare hell out of the country." [16] Truman took the Senator's advice to heart and fashioned a Manichean view of a world locked in a titanic struggle between encroaching evil and virtue besieged; on the one side stood the Soviet Union and its "satellites," on the other the United States and its "allies." As containment architect Acheson explained in his memoirs, the "selling" of foreign policy "to the average man on the street" was not an easy task: "Qualification must give way to simplicity, nicety and nuance to bluntness, almost brutality, in carrying home a point." To be perfectly frank, Acheson admitted, the points must be made "clearer than truth." [17]

Unwittingly, in their cleverness, Truman and Acheson "sowed the seeds of their own destruction." While the bogeyman technique effectively served to gain popular support for containment's imperial policies, the alarmist tone and universalistic language soon became a powerful force that threatened to take on a life of its own. The right wing resurgence that Acheson dubbed "the attack of the primitives," a charge laced with heavy irony, served notice that anticommunism was gathering its own momentum and its path was no longer certain. At the same time, the containment doctrine and its Marshall Plan offshoot had not brought about the promised global stability for which they had been touted. Taking stock of the volatile situation, the Republican right saw the opportunity to go to the public with a "remedy" of its own for the "crisis" at hand. [18] The shape of things to come could be ascertained in the ascendancy of isolationist Robert Taft as the GOP frontrunner for 1952, along with the rise to prominence of the demogoguery that bore Joe McCarthy's name — a phenomenon by no means confined to the junior senator from Wisconsin. The Great Debate that shattered the vaunted bipartisan consensus was, as we shall see, a struggle in which political elites engaged in a bitter contest for mass support of competing doctrines, each claiming to be the legitimate response to the threat posed by communism.

CPD-I's purpose, in this context, was one of promoting Containment Militarism as *the* solution to the generalized threat of communism. "Overselling the threat" had two functions: First, there was the obvious one of scaring the public into continued acquiescence so that they would not balk at the costs of the projected military buildup, nor blanch at its interventionist posture. The focus on the Soviet Union as opposed to the diffuse anticommunism of the Right was also calculated to channel popular ideological support toward the primacy of Europe. Second, there was the necessity of cutting off the dissident elite from mobilizing a mass base of its own. The latter function of this dual strategy was the more compelling of the two; the path to the second however led through the first.

The contemporary CPD has operated from remarkably similar principles. Ironically however, the staunchest allies of the CPD in the post-Vietnam period have been the conservative right-wingers of the type who fought against legitimation of Containment Militarism during the Korean War period. The combined impact on the domestic economy of military spending in the trillions, and on domestic politics of Cold War ideology disguised as patriotism, had transformed the reluctant isolationists of the pre-Korean era into ardent imperialists by the time the second CPD launched its campaign after Vietnam.

If adversaries had become allies, the reverse was equally true. In the aftermath of the Tet Offensive in January and February 1968, the precepts of NSC-68 came under growing fire, not just from radical critics of war and militarism, but increasingly from within the heart of the Establishment itself. A mounting conviction began to take hold among an influential segment of this elite that military intervention was no longer cost-effective in an age of revolutionary ferment and rising anticolonialism. Their alternative proposal for the continuing projection of American global dominance called for a reinvigorated system of world trade and the creation of rationalized institutions of financial cooperation in partnership with the expansion of multinational corporate investment. Still Machiavellian in its homage to *realpolitik*, this strategy represented a more managerial — fox-like — approach to empire. Unlike their predecessors in 1950, who dissented from Containment Militarism and were subdued in the NSC-68 review process, this time the Establishment moderates had apparently prevailed judging from their near monopoly over Carter's appointments. The CPD, in contrast, submitted fifty-three names not one of whom was found worthy. The CPD insiders of 1950, working in close conjunction with the Truman Administration had become by the post-Vietnam period, outsiders more at home with congressional right-wingers than with the Trilateral managerialists surrounding Carter.

If the sides in the debate had undergone a notable reversal, the political strategy that inspired CPD-I remained the *raison d'etre* behind CPD-II. Once again a partisan elite effort was launched in the name of bipartisanship and "private citizen" concern to mobilize public opinion in support of a renewed Soviet Threat; this was an end in itself given the costs of the military buildup urged for the 1980s, but also more importantly as in the earlier period, a means to an end of restoring the shattered consensus within the elite. The idea was to create the appearance of a popular resurgent militarism that would thereby serve to discourage Establishment moderates from attempting to construct an alternative foreign policy — in this case the detente-like managerial approach — out of fear that it would trigger a political backlash at home.

The CPD, during the four years of Carter's term, functioned as a virtual Reagan shadow cabinet charging the Administration among other things with "Vietnam syndrome," an affliction deemed responsible for an alleged "failure of nerve" in U.S. leadership manifested, from their point of view, in the "loss of Iran." As a result of this well-organized and even better financed campaign, the policy debate took place within increasingly narrow limits veering sharply to the right. The accelerating momentum of the new mood led finally to Carter's reelection defeat despite the born-again militarism that characterized his Administration's latter years. Drawing once more upon Machiavelli, Reagan's replacement of 'foxes' by 'lions' in top policy posts has served notice that *force* is back in vogue as the bottom line of containment. Once again a Committee on the Present Danger has been instrumental in the critical turn of events and is now back in power, bent on reshaping America and the world in its own imperial image.

* * *

History never quite repeats itself however. It is noteworthy in this regard that, unlike its predecessor, CPD-II has elected to remain active. Rostow's comments on the decision bear repeating:

> Progress has been made, but the struggle to maintain and sustain foreign and defense policy will remain. The resistance to our ideas is tremendous. The natural position of the country is neutrality and isolation. There's a lot of yearning to go back to it. Our policies will always have an opposition.[19]

There are elements of both strength and weakness in the CPD's decision. On the one hand, there is the presumption that by its continuing presence the CPD will be able to control the terrain between domestic politics and foreign policy, a prospect with much to back it up given its track record in the Korean War and post-Vietnam eras. On the other, the latest chapter in the struggle over policy has ended in a sense of vulnerability and uncertainty despite the outward appearance of smashing success. The source of these conflicting interpretations spring from the same dynamic, a conundrum which requires a final word of explanation before setting out to chronicle the two campaigns of these elite "peddlers of crisis."

The quintessence of Containment Militarism's success has been its ability to legitimize the notion that resistance to empire abroad is, *pari passu,* a threat to security at home. This source of strength in the past is today a potential weakness. The interplay of structural forces and resistance movements in the 1980s promise to exact a demanding toll as compared to the halcyon years of cost-free nuclear threats and low-budget intervention. So long as they were out of power, the CPD could attack managerialism, arguing that centrifugal tendencies pulling away from the Amercentric world order in the post-Vietnam era could be overcome by adopting new leadership and old strategies. Once in office however, the CPD-laden Administration was quickly hoisted on its own petard. Carter's dilemma of how to meet the rising economic and political costs of empire in the face of domestic stagflation and global transformation had become their own.

Under the economic circumstances of the 1950s and 1960s the military keynesian marriage of guns and butter became possible, an arrangement that secured a popular political base for the ideological bond between empire and security. In the very different economic climate of the 1980s, Reaganomics has divorced guns from butter, in the process sacrificing security at home to uphold the primacy of empire abroad. In a desperate attempt to protect the profits and power of the hobbled Pax Americana, the American people have been served notice that security in any meaningful sense — from affordable housing to retirement benefits, environmental protection to jobs, public education to health care — must be sacrificed to the Moloch of empire. More and more, security is fast becoming a choice between a militarized national security outfitted with a "nuclear war-fighting" capability and ludicrous scenarios of survival through mass evacuation, and a demilitarized societal security that turns resources now used for global domination to the task of domestic revitalization. Unlike the heyday of the cold war, we no longer enjoy the booming economy nor the nuclear superiority to have it both ways. This is what separates CPD-I and CPD-II, and has kept the latter from basking in retirement.

The long overdue debate on national security has begun to appear on the horizon. With the prospect of accelerated global transformation in the years ahead, and the contours of a new international order nowhere in sight, elite conflict may well become commonplace as the foreign policy establishment searches in vain for the formula that will restore the Amercentric world system shattered in the Vietnam era. How deeply militarism is rooted in America's political culture must rank as the most profound question of our time. Its depths are sure to be plumbed by the CPD and like-minded cold war enthusiasts who have, in the past, so successfully manufactured hysterical fears and turned them to advantage in the higher circles of policy struggle. The litmus test will come when a comparable challenge is mounted to the empire-security linkage at the heart of Containment Militarism.

If the short-lived era of *detente* and the dynamics of the post-Vietnam period are any indication, such an alternative vision cannot be expected from managerial elites within the Establishment since they share the militarists' goal of empire, even as they disagree on the most effective means toward its achievement. Such a challenge will have to come instead from those without a stake either in containment or militarism. In short, it will take a popular movement to seriously combat the present as well as future Committees on the Present Danger. Periods of elite conflict create opportunities for just such an activist challenge since it is in these times that the policy debate must go public in search of mass legitimation. If the bond between empire abroad and security at home is to be broken at such historic moments, then we must understand the process by which they have been bound so tightly together until now.

INTRODUCTION
The Omnipresent Danger

1. "Rostow Starts Digging His Own Hardened Silo," *New York Times*, June 28, 1981, p. E-5.
2. Paul H. Nitze, "Strategy In The Decade Of The 1980s," *Foreign Affairs* 59, (Fall 1980), p. 92.
3. C. Wright Mills, *The Power Elite* (New York: Oxford University Press, 1956), 356.
4. *CBS Evening News*, November 6, 1980.
5. "Group Goes From Exile To Influence," *New York Times*, November 23, 1981, p. A-20.
6. *Ibid*.
7. *Ibid*.
8. Paul H. Nitze, "Is SALT II A Fair Deal For The United States?" (Washington: Committee On The Present Danger, 1979), p. 6.
9. Eugene V. Rostow, "SALT II — A Soft Bargain, A Hard Sell: An Assessment of SALT in Historical Perspective," speech presented at a conference on United States Security and the Soviet Challenge, Hartford, Connecticut, July 25, 1978 (Washington: Committee On The Present Danger, 1978), p. 13.
10. Daniel Ellsberg, "Introduction: Call To Mutiny," in E.P. Thompson and Dan Smith, eds. *Protest And Survive* (New York and London: Monthly Review Press, 1981), iv-vii.
11. In an April 6, 1982 address at Georgetown University's Center For Strategic And International Studies, billed in advance as a major administration statement on U.S. policy, Haig emphasized that 'first-use' of tactical nuclear weapons would remain an option in military planning. The Secretary's statement was designed to head off a call for renunciation of the 'first-use' doctrine from a moderate Establishment faction led by George Kennan, Robert McNamara, William Bundy, and Gerard Smith.
12. William Appleman Williams, *Empire As A Way Of Life* (New York: Oxford University Press, 1980).
13. For this knowledge I am indebted to Johan Galtung, *The True Worlds: A Transnational Perspective* (New York: The Free Press, 1980), 4.
14. This quintessential paradigm of cold war logic states that the outcome of international politics is determined by the perception of power between East and West, measured by a calculus that includes economic, political, psychological, and military factors in its formula.
    Paul Nitze, principal author of NSC-68 and cofounder of the Committee on the Present Danger, attributes the "correlation of forces" notion to Soviet strategic doctrine, a concept that he nonetheless endorses as universally valid in strategic calculation. (Paul Nitze, interview with author, August 24, 1977).
15. Leslie H. Gelb with Richard K. Betts, *The Irony Of Vietnam: The System Worked* (Washington: Brookings, 1979), 79.
16. Eric Goldman, *The Crucial Decade* (New York: Vintage, 1960), 59.
17. Dean Acheson, *Present At The Creation: My Years In The State Department (New York: Norton, 1969), 375.*

18. The conceptual framework is borrowed from Lowi who refined the "oversell" of foreign policy into two techniques which he calls "overselling the threat" and "overselling the remedy." While the oversell of a threat manufactures or exploits crisis, overselling the remedy exaggerates claims for particular formulas to resolve the crisis. See, Theodore Lowi, "Making Democracy Safe For The World", in James M. Rosenau (ed.), *Domestic Sources Of Foreign Policy* (New York: The Free Press, 1967), 320-322.
19. "Group Goes From Exile to Influence," *New York Times*, November 23, 1981, p. A-20.

Chapter 1

NSC-68:
THE MILITARIZATION
OF CONTAINMENT

Without superior aggregate military strength, in being and readily mobilizable, a policy of "containment" — which is in effect a policy of calculated and gradual coercion — is no more than a policy of bluff.

National Security Memorandum #68 [1]

The purpose of NSC-68 was to so bludgeon the mass mind of 'top government' that not only could the President make a decision but that the decision could be carried out.

Dean Acheson, Secretary of State [2]

What I read (NSC-68) scared me so much that the next day I didn't go to the office at all. It seemed to me to establish an altogether convincing case that we had to spend more on defense.

Charles Murphy, presidential adviser [3]

"The Report By The Secretaries Of State and Defense On 'United States Objectives And Programs For National Security,' April 7, 1950," which in the historical lore of the cold war became known as National Security Memorandum No. 68 or NSC-68, was conducted under the auspices of a joint State-Defense Department review of U.S. foreign and

23

military policy. Lasting from mid-February through March 1950, the interdepartmental task force undertook a fundamental reappraisal of containment, calling for such sweeping changes in the doctrine that George Kennan, perhaps its foremost architect, was moved to declare that containment had been transformed by NSC-68 from the original meaning which he had intended into an essentially new approach, i.e., what I call Containment Militarism.

Despite what we now recognize as its radical departure, NSC-68 took special pains to establish its intellectual pedigree and cultivate the appearance of continuity between itself and earlier formulations of containment which date from Kennan's ruminations on U.S.-Soviet relations during the period he served as U.S. *charge d'affaires* in Moscow. From the vantage point of his diplomatic post, Kennan had sent the State Department a somber assessment of Soviet motivations. Known as the Long Telegram, it claimed that the USSR was driven by a messianic amalgam of Bolshevik ideology and Russian nationalism, a message that reached the pages of *Foreign Affairs* magazine the following year as "The Sources Of Soviet Conduct," under the *nom de plume* Mr. X. In the infamous Mr. X article, Kennan argued the case for the policy he coined 'containment.' [4]

Seeming to carry forward in the Kennan orthodoxy, NSC-68 opened with the declaration that ". . . the Soviet Union, unlike previous aspirants to hegemony, is animated by a new fanatic faith, antithetical to our own, and seeks to impose its absolute authority over the rest of the world. Conflict, has, therefore become endemic . . ." [5] But a major qualification to this link with the past was quickly added:

"The growing intensity of the conflict which has been imposed upon us, however, *requires the changes of emphasis and the additions that are apparent*." [6] (emphasis added) The transformation in question was toward a more ambitious interpretation of containment, and "the additions" referred to the plethora of military programs slated for implementation once the defense budget rose three to four times its 1950 level, as advocated in NSC-68.

The transition from a politico-strategic doctrine to full-fledged militarism can be seen in NSC-68's redefinition of the concept of containment:

> As for the policy of "containment," it is one which seeks by all means short of war to 1) block further expansion of Soviet power, 2) expose the falsities of Soviet pretensions, 3) induce a retraction of the Kremlin's control and influence and 4) in general, so foster the seeds of destruction within the Soviet system that the Kremlin is brought at least to the point of

modifying its behavior to conform to generally accepted international standards. [7]

The aggressive tone here seems more compatible with what has come to be known in cold war parlance as the offensive strategy of rollback, rather than the defensive holding action connoted by the term containment. [8] Toward the end of the document, in fact, it is openly admitted that the goal of containment is indeed rollback, generally thought to be a competing school of strategic thinking: "At any rate, it is clear that a substantial and rapid building up of strength in the free world is necessary to support a firm policy intended to check and roll back the Kremlin's drive for world domination." [9] This was no idle threat mentioned merely in passing. A full appreciation of its intent becomes clearer in the following passage which proclaimed that "we should take dynamic steps to reduce the power and influence of the Kremlin inside the Soviet Union and other areas under its control" including "overt psychological warfare" and "operations by covert means in the fields of economic warfare and political and psychological warfare." In justification of their proposed actions, NSC-68's authors relied upon the familiar cold war ploy of mirror-imaging: "In other words, it would be the current Soviet cold war technique used against the Soviet Union." [10]

Moreover, the reader privy to the classified report learned that the fate of the entire world hung in the balance awaiting the U.S. embrace of subversion and terrorism:

> As we ourselves demonstrate power, confidence and a sense of moral and political direction, so those same qualities will be evoked in Western Europe. In such a situation, we may also anticipate a general improvement in the political tone in Latin America, Asia and Africa and the real beginnings of awakening among the Soviet totalitariat.

> In the absence of affirmative decision on our part, the rest of the free world is almost certain to become demoralized. Our friends will become more than a liability to us; they can become a positive increment to Soviet power. [11]

Kennan, and the internationalist perspective he represented, had never endorsed a "zero-sum" view of the world in which all changes in the status quo were tallied up as a gain for one side and a loss for the other. Instead they stressed a limited commitment to the areas of "vital interest" to the United States, namely Western Europe and Japan. [12] Such selective and strategic imperialism was challenged, however, by NSC-68's ideological and universalistic interpretation of containment. This transformation in America's foreign policy (carefully protrayed in NSC-

68 as a natural evolution) would also require a changing emphasis in the means to reach the expanded goals. As NSC-68 explained:

> It was and continues to be cardinal in this policy that we possess superior overall power in ourselves or in dependable combination with other likeminded nations. One of the most important ingredients of power is military strength. In the concept of "containment," the maintenance of a strong military posture is deemed to be essential for two reasons: 1) as an ultimate guarantee of our national security and 2) as an indispensable backdrop to the conduct of the policy of "containment." Without superior aggregate military strength, in being and readily mobilizable, a policy of "containment" — which is in effect a policy of calculated and gradual coercion — is no more than a policy of bluff. [13]

Such thinking represented a substantial departure from "the conduct of containment" embodied in the Marshall Plan's emphasis on economic aid and multilateral trade. In contrast to what would soon be the case, military power played a largely auxiliary reserve role in the years between World War II and Korea. Moderates like Kennan viewed the Soviet challenge primarily in political terms, arguing that the use of the atomic bomb (source of America's military superiority) in other than response to attack on U.S. territory would have been a diplomatic disaster in the ideological competition between Washington and Moscow. Finally, even while the nuclear monopoly guaranteed supremacy in the last instance, the threat implied by its mere possession was not enough to block the Communist victory in China, or the consolidation of Soviet control in Eastern Europe.

Seizing upon the successful atomic test of the Russians, Kennan urged a further distancing between containment and militarism by proposing that the U.S. "should act at once to get rid of our present dependence, in our war plans, on the atomic weapon." [14] The operational policy to which he referred was the "nuclear tripwire" policy in Europe where it was generally understood that the U.S. would use the atomic bomb in the event of a Soviet invasion of Western Europe. Kennan, in contrast, wanted to sever the nuclear option from conventional conflict and retain it solely for purposes of deterrence against an attack in kind, or better yet, as an initial step toward international control and prohibition of nuclear weapons. In hopes of heading off the trillion dollar nuclearized arms race now all too familiar, Kennan argued:

> I still think it vital to our own understanding of what it is we are about that we not fall into the error of initiating, or planning to initiate, the employment of these weapons and concepts, thus

hypnotizing ourselves into the belief that they may ultimately serve some positive national purpose. I doubt our ability to hold the respective weapons in our national arsenal, to fit them into our military and political plans, to agree with our allies on the circumstances of their use, and to entertain the prospect of their continued cultivation by our adversaries, without backs liding repeatedly into this dangerous, and possibly mortal, error. In other words, even if we were to conclude today that 'first use' would not be advantageous, I would not trust the steadfastness of this outlook in a situation where the shadow of uncontrolled mass destruction weapons continues to lie across the peoples of the world. Measured against this alternative, an imperfect system of international control seems to me less dangerous, and more considerate of those things in international life which are still hopeful. [15]

Those who crafted NSC-68, however, were devoid of such vision. Kennan's proposals were given short shrift: "Agreement on the control of atomic energy would result in a relatively greater disarmament of the United States than of the Soviet Union," the document read. Moreover its authors reasoned, in the logic of cold war orthodoxy, "it might be accepted by the Soviet Union as part of a deliberate design to move against Western Europe and other areas of strategic importance with conventional forces and weapons." [16] Extracting concessions from the Russians was uppermost in the minds of NSC-68's planners, even at the risk of causing a worsening of relations between the two superpowers. Binding arms control and foreign policy tightly together in what would later be known as "linkage," NSC-68 read:

If, contrary to our expectations, the Soviet Union should accept agreements promising effective control of atomic energy and conventional armaments, without any other changes in Soviet policies, we would have to consider carefully whether we could accept such agreements . . . In conclusion, negotiation is not a possible separate course of action but rather a means of gaining support for a program of building strength.[17]

Having adopted such a militaristic posture, NSC-68 concluded that "we have no alternative but to increase our atomic capability as rapidly as other considerations make appropriate." [18] In the meantime the paper cautioned against announcing a "no-first strike" pledge on use of nuclear weapons, arguing that it would be bad strategy:

It has been suggested that we announce that we will not use

atomic weapons except in retaliation against the prior use of such weapons by an aggressor. It has been argued that such a declaration would decrease the danger of an atomic attack against the United States and its allies . . . In our present situation of relative unpreparedness in conventional weapons, such a declaration would be interpreted by the U.S.S.R. as an admission of great weakness and by our allies as a clear indication that we intended to abandon them. [19]

To complement the threat of nuclear weapons with conventional forces, NSC-68 reasoned: ". . . it appears to be imperative to increase as rapidly as possible our general air, ground and sea strength and that of our allies to a point where we are militarily not so heavily dependent on atomic weapons." [20] Thus, in sum, the programmatic recommendations of NSC-68 called for a massive military buildup of both nuclear and conventional forces in order to carry out the revised rollback formula of Containment Militarism.

Such a course would involve a considerable increase in military spending over and above what economic orthodoxy at the time would tolerate. NSC-68 recommended the defense budget be increased from the ceiling of about $13 billion then in force to the unheard of level of $35 to $50 billion in order to realize the document's objectives. [21] As a member of the Policy Planning Staff of the State Department, Kennan had made clear in the summer of 1949 just before his resignation, that he thought the military requirements of foreign policy could be adequately met within the $13 billion limit. [22] NSC-68 challenged both the adequacy of this figure as well as the economic rationale that held military spending to that level. If any doubt remained in the minds of those privileged to read through the classified document, its implications were spelled out in the concluding argument which warned: "Budgetary considerations will need to be subordinated to the stark fact that our very independence as a nation may be at stake." [23] After this came a list of numerous programs needed "to frustrate the Kremlin design," all of which would require a "substantial increase in expenditures for military purposes." [24] But the authors wished to make clear that this new military Keynesianism would require only the sacrifice of outmoded ideas about economics, not economic well-being itself. In fact they argued, drawing on the example of World War II, military spending would serve to greatly accelerate economic growth:

From the point of view of the economy as a whole, the program might not result in a real decrease in the standard of living, for the economic effects of the program might be to increase the gross national product by more than the amount being absorbed for additional military and foreign assistance purposes. One of the most significant lessons of our World War II experience was that the American economy, when it operates at a level approaching full efficiency, can provide enormous resources for purposes other than civilian consumption while simultaneously providing a high standard of living. [25]

Daniel Yergin refers to NSC-68 as "the first formal statement of American policy" in the postwar period, ". . . as important as Kennan's Long Telegram and the Truman Doctrine."[26] What marked it as especially important, however, was that it provided the strategic world view that justified the evolution of foreign policy from containment to Containment Militarism. The second version differed from the first in four fundamental ways: First, it's zero-sum calculus greatly increased the purview of "vital interests," a logic which, when accepted, led away from diplomacy and negotiation toward militancy and rollback. Second, as NSC-68 pointed out, the quintessential goal of rollback — the retrogression of Soviet power up to and including collapse of the Soviet government — is nothing more than bluff unless it is backed by the threat of armed force and the appearance of readiness to unleash it. Therefore military strength would have to be greatly increased and diversified to carry out such an aggressive policy. Third, Containment Militarism would necessitate a corresponding increase in military spending, breaking with the economic orthodoxy that had been accepted in containment's earlier version. Finally, while Containment Militarism as outlined in NSC-68 was constructed upon the same ideological foundations that had inspired Kennan's thesis of the Soviet Threat, its reinterpretation as specifically a military threat was the fourth point of departure from the original formulation. It was also the key to the acceptance of the first three points. The legitimacy of the entire NSC-68 program came down to this one question: Did the Soviet Union harbor plans for global conquest by military force or not? This was the central issue of foreign policy debated first in elite circles in the spring of 1950, and then in the wider realm of mass politics by the winter of 1950-51, when the Committee on the Present Danger came into being.

The Soviet Threat

Written like a legal brief, NSC-68 rested its case of Soviet militancy on three axial correlations between: Soviet military capabilities and political intentions, Soviet ideology and behavior, and domestic totalitarianism and international expansionism. Together, the document argued, they worked in harmony toward the realization of "the fundamental design of the Kremlin." What is most unique about NSC-68 is not the desires attributed to the Kremlin leadership, but the notion that they had achieved the capability to launch a plan of global domination by military means. It was no doubt this assertion about Soviet capabilities, and not about bellicose intentions — standard rhetoric by 1950 — that caused Charles Murphy to stay home from the office pouring over his copy of NSC-68 in utter astonishment and dismay (see chapter heading). NSC-68 made the blunt allegation that, "The Soviet Union is developing the military capacity to support its design for world domination." [27] The logic behind this charge was that "the Soviet Union actually possesses armed forces far in excess of those necessary to defend its national territory." [28] In fact, NSC-68 argued, the Soviet Union was so well equipped and in such an "advanced stage of preparation" that it could "immediately . . . undertake and carry out" *simultaneously* an attack that would overrun Western Europe, prevent an allied "Normandy" type counterattack, bomb England, drive toward the Middle East, and still have enough forces remaining for "diversionary attacks in other areas." [29] Such a fantastic scenario of conventional *blitzkrieg* was coupled with the knowingly false claim that the U.S.S.R. had already achieved the capability of delivering an atomic blow to the United States. The U.S.S.R. did not embark upon such a long-range bomber program until the mid-1950's and was not a strategic threat to the United States until at least 1957-58 — a situation then seized upon as a "bomber gap," which turned out to be equally apocryphal.

The first criticism that comes to mind then is the distortion in NSC-68's assessment of Soviet arms. A second is the dubious relationship between capabilities and intentions. Regarding the former, Alan Wolfe writes that NSC-68 "tended to see potential Soviet arms as actual and actual American arms as potential" in order to convey a sense of crisis that would justify a program of militarization even though the United States had "far more military power than anything the Soviets could assemble for some time to come." [30] Paul Y. Hammond's interviews with participants in the NSC-68 review process confirms Wolfe's assessment. Hammond concludes that Nitze devised "the military threat" as a strategy for acceptance of a U.S. arms buildup:

> Anticipating that the military threat would be discounted he (Nitze) wanted to sacrifice a degree of rationality in the analysis of NSC-68 in order to exaggerate the threat, with the hope that the reaction of opinion leaders would be commensurate with the threat — that is to say, would be rational as

measured against the actual threat, though not against the portion of NSC-68 which purported to describe the threat.[31]

The philosophy of Nitze's mentor Acheson, who had persuaded Truman to undertake the review process in the first place, is described in similar terms: "Like Nitze, Acheson was more interested in the polemical values of NSC-68 than in its precise rationality. Evidently he saw it as a device for challenging established policies and premises which he thought needed reexamination." [32] Years after the institutionalization of Containment Militarism in American foreign policy, Acheson confirmed this thesis with the infamous words that preface this chapter: "The purpose of NSC-68 was to so bludgeon the mass mind of 'top government' that not only could the President make a decision but that the decision could be carried out." [33]

Kennan, whom Nitze had replaced as Director of Policy Planning, could not have agreed more with Acheson's choice of metaphor. He and Charles Bohlen, the two senior Russian experts in the State Department, reportedly were flabbergasted by NSC-68's call to arms based on an imminent Soviet military threat. Not only were capabilities exaggerated, Kennan argued, but the very equation of capabilities with intentions was a crude oversimplification for predicting Soviet actions. [34] Charles Bohlen, the other senior Russian expert in the State Department, agreed. When the State-Defense study group prepared a preliminary draft listing world domination as the primary objective of Soviet policy, Bohlen challenged the assertion. Arguing from a more conciliatory perspective, he reasoned that the Kremlin had no such grand design at all, indeed could not afford to think in such grandiose terms without dangerously overextending the capabilities it did possess, and thus threatening the stability it had already achieved over areas under its control.[35] Even NSC-68 begrudgingly conceded the point about "Russian caution" in foreign policy:

> Its strategy has been one of attempting to undermine the complex of forces, in this country and in the rest of the free world, on which our power is based. In this it has both adhered to doctrine and followed the sound principle of seeking maximum results with minimum risks and commitments. The present application of this strategy is a new form of expression for *traditional Russian caution*. [36] (emphasis added)

However, the authors then proceeded to tack on the caveat that "there is no justification in Soviet theory or practice for predicting that, should the Kremlin become convinced that it could cause our downfall by one conclusive blow, it would not seek that solution . . . The Kremlin uses

Soviet military power to back up and serve the Kremlin design. It does not hesitate to use military force aggressively if that course is expedient in the achievement of its design." [37]

Kennan and Bohlen argued that, on the contrary, there was very good reason to believe that the Soviet Union was not contemplating any such aggressive action. While Soviet leaders might harbor fantasies of hegemony, the two senior Russian hands pointed out they did not possess the capability for pursuing such a course, nor did the evidence indicate intentions to engage in such an undertaking, certainly not by military means. The prime Soviet threat, Kennan maintained, remained a political, economic, and diplomatic challenge to the West. It followed then that the U.S. response should be directed toward these areas and not toward a military resolution. If one could speak of a military threat at all, Kennan argued in the National Security Council deliberations, it was only of limited military challenges in disputed areas which would require a level of conventional forces that could be readily accommodated to existing budgetary constraints. [38]

The relatively sanguine view of the Soviet Union may seem strange coming from Kennan, given his pioneering role in Cold War demonology. By 1950, however, he had become a critic rather than a promulgator of containment. [39] This was due in no small part to the manipulation of his original formulation, an interpretation that was fast becoming the ideological justification for the evolution of containment from a "balanced" doctrine to one that relied almost exclusively on the threat of armed force. In his memoirs, Kennan expresses his regret that the formula introduced in the Long Telegram and made public in the Mr. X article, had not been more emphatic in its rejection of militarism. Its most serious defect in Kennan's retrospective judgment was:

> ... the failure to make clear that what I was talking about when I mentioned the containment of Soviet power was not the containment by military means of a military threat, but the political containment of a political threat. [40]

Thus, by 1950, Kennan rightly feared that continuing support of containment logic as it was freely translated in NSC-68 would result in the militarization of American foreign policy. His concern was well-founded. NSC-68's line of argumentation not only deduced intentions from capabilities, but also made the case that the buildup of capabilities was the inexorable product of intentions as evidenced in the following claim: "The capabilities of the Soviet world are being exploited to the full because the Kremlin is inescapably militant." [41] Intentions and capabilities rebounded off one another in escalatory fashion, i.e., expanded military capabilities whetted the Kremlin appetite for world hegemony, a motivation which in turn pushed the arms buildup to ever-higher levels to see "the design" through. If this model of interacting capabilities and intentions is taken seriously, NSC-68's clarion call to arms does take on a certain rationality, indeed becomes a moderate option under the circumstances — as opposed to "preventive war." That is exactly what its authors argued in the document's conclusion.

But what evidence was there that the Soviet Union was in fact "inescapably militant?" This promised to be a difficult argument given the fact that at the time NSC-68 was undertaken, the Soviet Union had organized the first of several international peace conferences, one measure of which called for a ban of nuclear weapons. [42] The architects of Containment Militarism were even forced to admit in the text of NSC-68 that "at the military level the Kremlin has thus far been careful not to commit a technical breach of the peace."[43] Nevertheless, the final product summarily dismissed Soviet behavior that would have contradicted its worst-case analysis, preferring instead to ground its apocalyptic interpretation of Soviet goals in ideology and domestic practices. Accordingly, the answer to the Soviet Union's "inescapable militancy" read as follows:

> It is inescapably militant because it possesses and is possessed
> by a world-wide revolutionary movement, because it is the
> inheritor of Russian imperialism and because it is a totali-
> tarian dictatorship. [44]

The NSC-68 argument, in effect, was that "the Kremlin's fundamental design of world demination" is an ineluctable product of the interacting forces of Russian nationalism, Soviet totalitarianism, and international communism. Rather than view these forces in terms of their many actual and potential contradictions, NSC-68 assumed a harmony of purpose "animated by a new fanatic faith" which "seeks to impose its absolute authority over the rest of the world." [45] How does one know the Soviet Union "seeks to impose its absolute authority" over the entire world? Because of repressive measures carried out within its own borders. As NSC-68 put it, "The Kremlin's design for world domination begins at home." [46] The fallacy lies in the equation of domestic practice with international intent. Overexpansion in foreign policy could, rather than enhance Soviet power, prove its undoing at home. To have admitted this likelihood however, would have undermined NSC-68's carefully crafted contention of monolithic and diabolical purpose.

Finally, NSC-68's treatment of communist ideology as an indicator of future Soviet behavior suffers a similar distortion. As was the case with estimates of Soviet capabilities, Hammond's account again points to Nitze's exaggeration, with Acheson's blessing. His findings are worth quoting at length on this point:

> Nitze had listed Soviet objectives in order of their importance
> to the United States, and in such a way as to emphasize the
> Soviet threat. Apparently, his was largely a rhetorical point.
> Obviously, he recognized that there was more to the motiva-
> tions of the Soviet state than following Communist dogma . . .
> What Nitze did with his original ranking of Soviet objectives,
> it is evident, was to set them in an order which would make that
> portion of the study paper where they appeared carry as much
> of the burden of the argument as he could give it . . . (Nitze)
> adopted and defended a particular order for its persuasive
> impact: If his argument could begin with a convincing state-
> ment which maximized the nature of the Soviet threat, the
> burden of proof of the rest of his case would be reduced. [47]

The foregoing perusal of NSC-68, as a policy review process and as
a document of strategic analysis, presents strong evidence that "the
Soviet Threat" was used to legitimate and implement an aggressive
foreign policy, i.e., Containment Militarism. This then raises two further
questions which we must confront: First, was the Soviet Threat totally
contrived or was it exaggerated either in degree or kind? Second, whether
exaggerated or contrived, why was it brought into being by the architects
of NSC-68? My answer to the first is that it was both. While the military
threat was indeed contrived, a real Soviet threat — of a political nature —
did exist. It was exaggerated. The reason for this hyperbole was fear that
Western European nations would adopt an independent neutralist course
which would greatly diminish American imperial power, both economic
and political, first in that vital region and then in other parts of the
world.

To combat such a domino effect of non-alignment and self-determination in international politics would necessitate a vastly increased
commitment in aid by the United States. For a number of reasons —
strategic as well as economic — rearmament became the most attractive
means of funneling aid to Western Europe, establishing a pattern that
would soon become worldwide. Not the least of these reasons was the
domestic political climate of the United States, which was extremely
hostile to continuing economic aid to Europe under the provisions of the
Marshall Plan. Thus as we will see, Containment Militarism was designed to contain American allies from within, rather than to contain
Soviet aggression from without. Or, as NSC-68 explained it: "Even if
there were no Soviet Union we would face the great problem . . . (that)
the absence of order among nations is becoming less and less tolerable."[48]

The Containment of Neutralism

The near simultaneous and sudden events in the Soviet Union and China in the fall of 1949, which served as dramatic challenges to American power in the post-war world, were preceded by the gradual erosion of what was from the internationalist view the principal pillar of containment: the economic stability and prosperity of Western Europe. Popularly known as the Marshall Plan, the European Recovery Program initiated in 1948 was designed to integrate the American and European economies, and concomitantly to bring about greater political cooperation and closer military ties across the Atlantic. While European recovery had achieved a certain level of economic growth, integration among European nations and between Europe and the United States — either in economic or political terms — was lagging far behind. Moreover, an already stingy Congress was showing even greater reluctance to commit further aid to Europe's reconstruction. To make matters worse, the military alliance of NATO was largely a paper organization, scarcely ready to defend Western Europe in case of attack by the Soviet Union, no matter how improbable that possibility might be.

The nub of the European problem was an imbalance in trade between the United States and Europe known as the dollar gap. A principal goal of the Marshall Plan was to alleviate the European trade deficit and corresponding U.S. trade surplus that made it impossible for European nations to earn enough dollars to purchase American goods. Along with the massive influx of dollars into Europe under the Marshall Plan, the United States also sought to eliminate tariffs, import quotas, and restrictive bilateral trade agreements that stood in the way of a free trading international economy. But still the dollar gap persisted. The magnitude of the problem can be grasped by considering the fact that in 1948 U.S. exports amounted to $13.4 billion, primarily to Europe. In contrast, Europe would have available from all sources only $2 billion to purchase goods from the United States once the Marshall Plan came to a halt as scheduled in 1952. [49] The gravity with which the situation was viewed in Washington can be gleaned from a memorandum Secretary of State Acheson penned to the President urging quick action to avert what he and his advisers perceived as an impending economic crisis. Acheson's detailed memo read in part:

> It is expected that unless vigorous steps are taken, the reduction and eventual termination of extraordinary foreign assistance in accordance with present plans will create economic problems at home and abroad of increasing severity . . . as ERP is reduced, and after its termination in 1952, how can

Europe and other areas of the world obtain the dollars
necessary to pay for a high level of United States exports,
which is essential both to their own basic needs and to the
well-being of the United States economy? This is the problem
of the "dollar gap" in world trade . . . It is of such importance . .
. that I believe the whole machinery of government must be
brought into play if we are to achieve success. [50]

Throughout the fall and into the winter of 1949, as the world
shattering events in Russia and China were setting in, the dollar gap crisis
worsened. High-level staff reports to key decision-makers in Washington
warned that, "Any substantial drop in our exports will seriously affect
our domestic market, forcing a sharp contraction in production and
domestic consumption." [51] But what to do about it? Continuing aid in the
form of economic grants simply was no longer tenable to a Congress that
had already slashed the four-year appropriation for the Marshall Plan
from $29 billion to $13 billion. At the same time, increased imports were
out of the question in a recession. Demonstrating its increasingly trucu-
lent mood, Congress had on the matter of imports inserted a "peril point"
clause in the Reciprocal Trade Agreements Act which prevented tariff
reductions on any product as soon as an American industry felt the pinch
of foreign competition. [52] Such actions of course only served to exacerbate the dollar gap.

The severity of the trade imbalance by the spring of 1950 is
demonstrated by the fact that the dollar gap dilemma is given greater
attention than any other issue in NSC-68's listing of unfavorable international trends. [53] Moreover, following Acheson's lead, NSC-68 fore-
casted serious economic consequences on both sides of the Atlantic
unless the dollar gap was remedied: "There are grounds for predicting
that the United States and other free nations will within a period of a few
years at most experience a decline in economic activity of serious
proportions unless more positive governmental programs are developed
than are now available." [54] But catastrophe would not be confined to the
economic realm. Failure to resolve the dollar gap would have grave
consequences on the international balance of political power as well. At
one point, for instance, NSC-68 argues the case for aid to Britain on the
basis that:

. . . a strengthening of the British position is needed if the
stability of the Commonwealth is not to be impaired and if it is
to be a focus of resistance to Communist expansion in South
and South-East Asia. Improvement of the British position is
also vital in building up the defensive capabilities of Western
Europe. [55]

But of even more serious nature would be the challenge to U.S. leadership of the Western alliance if it did not demonstrate the resolve to confront the dollar gap problem: "This pressure (away from American hegemony) might come from our present allies, who will tend to seek other 'solutions' unless they have confidence in our determination to accelerate our efforts to build a successfully functioning political and economic system in the free world." [56]

The "other solutions" that the authors of NSC-68 feared fall under the general rubric of neutralism, an orientation categorically rejected in NSC-68 as unacceptable in the zero-sum world of cold war politics. It is imperative, the document warned, that "our allies do not as a result of a sense of frustration or of Soviet intimidation drift into a course of neutrality eventually leading to Soviet domination . . . . The idea that Germany or Japan or other important areas can exist as islands of neutrality in a divided world is unreal, given the Kremlin design for world domination." [57] Since there is no middle ground in the Manichean struggle between capitalist expansion and communist closure, it is but a short step to erasing the distinctions between political competition and military threats. In this regard, NSC-68 argued: "Soviet domination of the potential power of Eurasia, whether achieved by armed aggression or by political and subversive means, would be strategically and politically unacceptable to the United States." [58]

Unlike the Soviet military threat, which was greatly exaggerated, the threat of an independent Europe was a very real possibility in 1950. Throughout Western Europe, neutralist sentiment influenced the parties of both the Left and the Right. Despite the differences between the Left's rhetoric of peace and economic justice and the Right's call for national grandeur and power, both political tendencies challenged the containment ideal of governments throughout the world linked through military alliances and economic trade with the United States. The foundation of support for containment in Western Europe came from "third force" political parties, i.e., moderate socialists, Christian Democrats, and liberals, as opposed to the Communists, left social democrats, and the far Right. However, coalition governments formed from these parties were quite unstable, since they had to pursue economic recovery through policies favorable to large corporations, while maintaining popular support through social spending and increases in consumption. [59]

Whether a policy of neutralist non-alignment would have accrued to the U.S.S.R. is only conjecture and remains today a key issue in the debate over the future of the Atlantic Alliance. On the one side are those who maintain that the risk of an independent course in Western Europe would weaken the hold of the Soviet Union over Eastern Europe, while others argue in the zero-sum fashion of Containment Militarism that such an alternative in Europe would quickly become a subservient "satellite" in the Soviet "orbit". Whichever interpretation is correct, both Soviet leaders and American policymakers *acted as if* the neutralist course would enhance Soviet influence while diminishing the power of the United States to the same degree. During the years prior to NSC-68, the Soviet Union had actively campaigned for a neutralist Europe by making diplomatic relations with the Soviet Union seem as attractive as possible, a policy which if successful would inhibit the economic interdependence of Western Europe with the United States and clear the way for closer economic ties with the Soviet Union. [60]

The key to Europe's future direction lay in the course that Germany would follow. As NSC-68 argued, "If this (neutralism) were to happen in Germany the effect upon Western Europe and eventually upon us might be catastrophic." [61] The leaders of the Kremlin apparently agreed with NSC-68's assessment. The U.S.S.R. attempted to generate support for a neutralist Germany by pressing diplomatically for fulfillment of the three major aspirations of the German people: peace, a unified Germany, and the revival of German political power. [62]

Even after the Russian explosion of the atom bomb, American policymakers themselves saw the Soviet Threat in *political* and not *military* terms. As Nitze argued at the end of 1949, "Nothing about the Soviets' moves indicates that Moscow is preparing to launch in the near future an all-out military attack on the West." Instead, he predicted, the Soviets would consolidate their gains, take precautions against foreign and internal dangers, and exert power in situations where the U.S. and its allies were weak, i.e., where a neutralist course might be considered. Moreover, the kind of power that the U.S.S.R. would likely exert, according to Nitze's calculations, was political: "The U.S.S.R. considers this a favorable and necessary moment for increased political pressure, and, when feasible, taking aggressive political action against all or most soft spots in its periphery." [63] Why then was the confrontation posed as a military one in NSC-68?

The Logic of Containment Militarism

NSC-68 plainly stated that European non-alignment, as well as Soviet influence in Europe even by political means were unacceptable to the fundamental interests of the United States. The different audiences needed to validate this world view if it were to prevail in the conduct of international politics were three: the Russians, the Europeans, and the Americans. Containment Militarism was the one strategy that promised to elicit the desired response from each. For the Russians, the vast military buildup would serve as a signal that the U.S. intended to back its foreign policy objectives with military force and unless the U.S.S.R. wanted war should beat a diplomatic retreat to its own borders. To the Europeans, the increasing aid that would come their way as a result of a program of rearmament would close the dollar gap and at the same time discourage the neutralist alternative. For the Americans, a program of militarization at home and military aid to Europe would be sold on the basis of blocking Soviet expansionism and thus averting a certain military attack on the United States itself. To get these messages across and have them accepted by each of the constituent actors in the situation, however, would require radical changes in the substance of containment policy as well as in the traditional manner in which elites formulated foreign policy and saw to its acceptance in domestic politics.

Turning first to the Russian signal, such a strategy required an adjustment in the "correlation of forces" that buttressed the containment doctrine, a shift from a primary reliance on economic measures and diplomatic initiatives to bald military force. While U.S. policy had been evolving from diplomacy to militancy since Kennan's telegram from Moscow and was well on its way to consummation by the time of NATO's formation in 1949, NSC-68 set down in writing in a high-level policy paper what many in the foreign policy establishment had been moving toward for some time. The Council on Foreign Relations, bellwether of elite opinion, for instance argued:

> The danger was that the Soviet Union, being presumably under no compulsion to beat a strategic retreat, would so exploit its opportunity to play upon the hopes and fears of the free world as to aggravate present disunities and perhaps emerge with new tangible advantages. [64]

In other words, if self-determination should become the fashion in Europe the Russians would be tempted to turn U.S. reverses into Soviet gains unless the U.S. backed up its foreign policy claims with the threat of military attack. NSC-68 extended the argument as follows:

> The frustration of the Kremlin design requires the free world to develop a successfully functioning political and economic system and a vigorous political offensive against the Soviet Union. These, in turn, require an adequate military shield under which they can develop. It is necessary to have the military power to deter, if possible, Soviet expansion, and to defeat, if necessary, aggressive Soviet or Soviet-directed actions of a limited or total character. [65]

The creation of an integrated U.S.-European military force under NATO was meant to convey to the Russians, U.S. intent to achieve its political goals through military means. However, it was widely felt among policymakers that the implicit threat in this message rang hollow without a massive increase in combat capabilities. One year before NSC-68, and six months prior to the Russian atom bomb test that served as the ostensible pretext for its writing, an American military mission with State Department representation in the person of Paul Nitze concluded that the threat of military force to be credible would require an expenditure of $30 billion to $40 billion a year. This sum was well beyond the economic capabilities of the Europeans, as it was outside the realm of political response by the United States. [66] By the summer of 1949, the State Department's Policy Planning Staff had become convinced that budgetary limitations on military spending were seriously impeding foreign policy. [67] Six months before, Acheson had assumed the post of Secretary of State, reportedly with the conviction that the ceiling of $13.5 billion which the Administration was committed to at the time was "pitifully inadequate . . . a mere fraction of what the U.S. could afford." [68] Acheson then brought Nitze into the State Department in a liaison capacity with the Pentagon. After his initial assignment, Hammond writes, Nitze "took back to his work in the Policy Planning Staff of the State Department a deep concern over the budgetary limitations imposed upon American defense policy, and over the relative importance of military and non-military factors in foreign policy." [69]

Subsequently, the Policy Planning Staff launched a study of the relative capabilities of Soviet and American economies to support a large-scale arms buildup. Hammond speculates that Kennan, who was Director of Policy Planning at the time, would never have undertaken such a review on his own initiative, raising the likelihood that it was done at Nitze's urging. Shortly thereafter, Kennan resigned as Director of Policy Planning. Acheson appointed Nitze in his place, a man whom Acheson described as "a joy to work with because of his clear, incisive mind." The writer who quotes Acheson on this point adds, "More importantly, Nitze shared Acheson's view of Soviet military intentions and of the need for a major American rearmament effort in 1950." [70]

In the wake of the Soviet atomic explosion, the Nitze-led Policy Planning Staff went to work in the fall of 1949 on an assessment of the foreign policy implications of the hydrogen bomb and a comprehensive analysis of foreign policy generally. [71] Meanwhile, the Atomic Energy Commission, under the direction of David Lilienthal, had voiced reservations to President Truman about going ahead with the development of the hydrogen bomb for the very reason that its policy implications were yet to be thoroughly comprehended. Truman's response was to appoint Lilienthal, Acheson, and Defense Secretary Louis Johnson, to a special committee to advise him on this issue. [72] In his capacity as a member of this committee, Acheson urged a broad review of foreign and military policy through the National Security Council structure to allay the doubts of those holding Lilienthal's view, but to go forward *simultaneously* with work on the hydrogen bomb. [73] Acheson's point of view carried the day. Truman signed a directive on January 30, 1950, initiating the hydrogen bomb program. Appended to it, Hammond reports, "was a letter drafted in the State Department which directed the Secretaries of State and Defense to make an overall review and reassessment of American foreign and defense policy in the light of the loss of China, the Soviet mastery of atomic energy, and the prospect of the fusion bomb." [74] Thus the review process which had begun some months before and which would soon provide the strategic rationale for a policy of Containment Militarism now had the official sanction of the President.

The Russian atom bomb test and the revolution in China provided an opportunity to alleviate the dollar gap and thus to bolster the faltering economic pillar of containment, a prime necessity if neutralism in Europe was to be averted. If the continued infusion of dollars through economic aid was unrealistic, there was no reason why the trade imbalance could not be remedied by means of military assistance — so the argument went. Accordingly, NSC-68 called for an overall merger of foreign aid, economic and military:

> Progress in this direction (European political stability) will require integrated political, economic and military policies and programs, which are supported by the United States and Western European countries and which will probably require a deeper participation by the United States than has been contemplated. [75]

As was the case with rearmament for purposes of coercion, rearmament to achieve economic goals did not make its initial appearance in NSC-68 either. It had also been making the rounds of high policy circles before 1950. The coordination of economic and military aid had for some time been an interest of Nitze's. [76] It was also a concern of CPD co-founder Tracy Voorhees. As Undersecretary of the Army he had been appointed chairman of a study to determine the Army's responsibilities and capabilities for defense of the United States. Like NSC-68, the Voorhees Report was wide-ranging in its analysis and recommendations, having gone considerably beyond the scope of its mandate. At the conclusion of the study, Voorhees penned a memorandum to Acheson suggesting that both the dollar gap and military rearmament questions could be resolved through the fusion of economic aid with military production and procurement. The document read in part:

The central weakness is that ECA, the one powerful organization we have which holds the principal purse strings, is under
the present law limited in its mission to promoting economic
recovery, not to stimulating military recovery.

Voorhees goes on to suggest that since "the basic necessity for
continuing economic assistance to Europe is to meet the 'dollar deficit',"
it stands to reason that "such inescapable dollar assistance . . . could be so
employed as to effect a corresponding increase in Europe's military
production, as well as to shape and correlate such production into a sound
total defensive plan." Moreover, Voorhees wrote, it would be an economic boon to Europe: "Under the plan herein proposed, increased
military production would also assist in sustaining the Western European
economy by providing a market which it needs." In order to implement
such a program, Voorhees made the further recommendation to Acheson
that "the time has clearly come to merge the United States' organizations
and appropriations for military assistance and for economic aid, under a
modified charter, and to create a single powerful unit to accomplish both
purposes." [77]

Still another study at the time, also undertaken at Acheson's
initiative, reached much the same conclusion after having begun as an
effort to formulate a successor to the Marshall Plan. Headed by
Voorhees' superior, Army Secretary Gordon Gray, this group ostensibly
appointed to investigate the trade imbalance in U.S.-European relations,
was instructed at the beginning of its mission to consider the reorientation
of economic programs to include "the revised and expanded military
plans for the defense of Western Europe." [78] Its conclusion favoring a
consolidation of economic and military programs added further support
to the Acheson-Nitze militarist strategy as it was being codified in NSC-
68.

A month after NSC-68's completion, Acheson unveiled the combined military-economic strategy of Containment Militarism in a meeting
with European leaders in London. The Secretary urged the Europeans to
make a greater effort toward economic and military unity, pledging that
the United States would back up such an effort financially. During these
meetings Acheson alluded to a new American foreign policy, military in
emphasis but aiming at the Marshall Plan's economic goals. [79] Thus just
as the stick of Containment Militarism had been waved at the Russians,
so the carrot of the new policy was presented to the Europeans to
dissuade them from the path of independence.

Before Containment Militarism could be put into practice, however,
it would require acceptance by the third of the three audiences affected by
its strategy — the Americans. It was the latter that would have to reject

the prevailing economic orthodoxy for the new economics of military Keynesianism in order to pay for the enormous increase in the military establishments of the United States and Western Europe. They would also have to believe in the wisdom of maintaining a permanent garrison of American troops abroad, a policy many would be called upon to uphold not only through their tax dollars but by their personal service as well. The difficulty of the task that lay ahead on the domestic front for the architects of Containment Militarism was immediately apparent upon Acheson's return from Europe. A hostile Congress refused the Secretary permission to make his report to a joint session of the full body as he requested. Instead he was forced to address interested members in a meeting room of the Library of Congress. There, before a limited audience, he once again stressed the need to merge economic and military efforts as he urged the assembled Congressmen to grant the billion dollar supplement Truman had requested for the Economic Cooperation Administration (the administrative arm of the Marshall Plan). Acheson ended his plea, which received wide newspaper coverage despite Congress' snub, by stressing the gravity of the situation confronting the United States: "We risk not only all the progress we have made but total failure," [80] he warned. But Congress and the public remained unmoved for all intents and purposes, a foreboding which ran thread-like throughout NSC-68.

NSC-68 referred almost enviously to the Soviet Union's advantages in the Cold War in that it "does not have to be responsive in any important sense to public opinion." [81] In contrast, the authors warned: "Our fundamental purpose is more likely to be defeated from lack of the will to maintain it, than from any mistakes we may make or assault we may undergo because of asserting that will." [82] The productive capabilities of the capitalist economies of the West were portrayed as virtually limitless, restricted only by the constraints of domestic politics:

> The capability of the American economy to support a build-up of economic and military strength at home and to assist a build-up abroad is limited not, as in the case of the Soviet Union, so much by the ability to produce as by the decision on the proper allocation of resources to this and other purposes. Even Western Europe could assign a substantially larger proportion of its resources to defense, if the necessary foundation in public understanding and will could be laid, and if the assistance needed to meet its dollar deficit were provided.[83]

Thus the question became one of how this necessary "public understanding" could be brought about since it was not readily apparent to the citizens of the United States and Western Europe, nor to their representatives in Congress and Parliament, why they should undergo programs of militarization that would greatly transform their respective societies. NSC-68 hinted at a devious strategy to achieve the acceptance of Containment Militarism when it argued for "offensive forces to attack the enemy and keep him off balance" even as the "announcement of policy and . . . the character of the measures adopted" require that "emphasis should be given to the essentially defensive character" in order "to minimize, so far as possible, unfavorable domestic and foreign reactions." [84] Therein lay the underlying need for the Soviet Threat and the defensive-sounding cloak of containment to mask a policy which its creators admitted to themselves was decidedly offensive in purpose. Moreover, if this policy was to be based upon the threat of armed force then it was imperative that the threat emanating from the Soviet Union be couched in a military form. The reason why this had to be so is found in the following discussion of the limits imposed on the conduct of foreign policy in a democratic society:

> The resort to force, internally or externally, is therefore a last resort for a free society. The act is permissable only when one individual or groups of individuals within it threaten the basic rights of other individuals or *when another society seeks to impose its will upon it.*

> The resort to force, to compulsion, to the imposition of its will is therefore a difficult and dangerous act for a free society, which is *warranted only in the face of even greater dangers.* The necessity of *the act must be clear and compelling*; the act *must commend itself to the overwhelming majority* as an inescapable exception to the basic idea of freedom. (emphasis added) [85]

The allegation of a military threat from a nation possessed of an alien ideology and with an atom bomb in its possession, harboring a deep-seated design for global domination besides, served well the need for legitimation. A military buildup of immense proportion and the threatened use of armed violence in foreign policy which, under ordinary circumstances would constitute militarism, was instead presented to the public as a justifiable act of national defense given the extraordinary, i.e., military, nature of the Soviet Threat and its uncompromising expansionism.

If the logic of how to build a consensus behind Containment Militarism was clear, the logistics of how to get the message across was not. If NSC-68 could "bludgeon the mass mind of the elite" as Acheson had so candidly put it, how was the Soviet Threat to be drummed into the mass mind of the public as well as to Congress, which did not have access to the classified study? The record of the meetings of the State-Defense Policy Review Committee during the process of drafting NSC-68 is testimony to the degree of concern over how to transform a secret plan into an accepted policy. Leon Keyserling, chairman of the Council of Economic Advisers, and long-time foreign policy adviser and international banker Robert Lovett, both argued before the Committee that the constraints acting against a $50 billion military budget were not economic but political in nature. [86] The problem, however, as many of the national security consultants called before the Committee foresaw, was that the Truman Administration was in no position to carry out such a campaign of persuasion in the divisive and highly partisan political climate of 1950. Chester Barnard, chairman of the Rockefeller Foundation — and later a member of the CPD — predicted in his testimony before the Policy Review Committee that,

> the government is going to need assistance in getting public support for the national effort which will be called for. This will be a difficult job for the government to handle alone. [87]

Barnard, in his consultant role, went on to recommend the formation of a group of "worthy citizens" who after studying the proposals put forth in NSC-68 "could then say to the people, 'We are thoroughly advised and you can accept what we say'." Nitze, chairing the meeting, asked Barnard for the names of such persons. Barnard suggested General Eisenhower (at the time serving as President of Columbia University), James Conant (President of Harvard), and Robert G. Sproul (President of the University of California), the latter a "sane, prominent churchman" by Barnard's standards. Conant became chairman of the CPD, Sproul served on its executive committee, and Eisenhower would play a prominent role in the CPD's activities from beginning to end. Lovett in his appearance before the Policy Review Committee had cautioned, however, that while such a group of elder statesmen which Barnard had in mind could indeed,

> audit and certify our findings and thereby back up the Administration's statement of the facts. It would probably be better . . . if such a group were not appointed as a commission by the President because it might thereby be tarred with the Administration's brush in the eyes of the people. [88]

As all seemed to agree, convincing the nation of the efficacy of Containment Militarism abroad and military Keynesianism at home as the appropriate response to the alleged Soviet Threat would require a private citizen's lobby outside the Administration. Such a group could then translate NSC-68 into public discourse under the guise of extraordinary bipartisan concern transcending ordinary politics to meet the national crisis. Korea would serve well as the demonstrable crisis, indeed too well as we shall see, while the CPD would press before the public the case for a major buildup of manpower and weaponry, as well as for a vast increase in military aid to Europe — the program of Containment Militarism outlined in NSC-68.

CHAPTER 1

NSC-68

1. U.S. National Security Council, "NSC-68: A Report To The National Security Council, April 14, 1950," *Naval War College Review,* May-June, 1975, p. 68.
2. Dean Acheson, *Present At The Creation: My Years At The State Department* (New York: Norton, 1969), 374.
3. Charles Murphy oral history, pp. 184-87, Truman Oral History Collections, cited in Daniel Yergin, *Shattered Peace: The Origins Of The Cold War And The National Security State* (Boston: Houghton Mifflin, 1978), 403.
4. George Kennan, "The Sources Of Soviet Conduct," *Foreign Affairs,* July, 1947; Moscow Embassy Telegram #511, February 22, 1946, U.S. Department of State, *Foreign Relations:* 1946, 6:696-709.
5. *NSC-68,* p. 53; At another point it was explicitly stated that, "The objectives outlined in NSC-20/4 (November 23, 1948) . . are fully consistent with the objectives stated in this paper, and they remain valid," (*NSC-68, p. 58.*)

    NSC-20/4 was the final product of the review of U.S. policy toward the Soviet Union initiated by then Secretary of Defense Forrestal in the summer of 1948. Drawing on Kennan's original formulation, it remained the definitive statement of U.S. policy toward the Soviet Union until NSC-68. For elaboration, see Thomas H. Etzold and John Lewis Gaddis, eds. *Containment: Documents On American Policy And Strategy, 1945-1950* (New York: Columbia University Press, 1978), 203-211.
6. *NSC-68,* p. 58.
7. *NSC-68,* p. 68.
8. Lo succinctly captures the standard distinction between the two when he writes that rollback "argues that communist regimes must be eliminated through U.S. military conquest or fundamentally altered by military or other means. Rollback differs from the policy of containment, which opposes not communist regimes *per se* but only their expansion." Clarence Y. H. Lo, "The Truman Administration's Military Budgets During The Korean War," Ph.D. dissertation, University of California, Berkeley, 1978, p. 263.
9. *NSC-68,* p. 99.
10. *NSC-68,* p. 100.
11. *NSC-68,* p. 71.
12. John Lewis Gaddis, "The Strategy Of Containment," in *Containment: Documents On American Policy And Strategy, 1945-1950,* p. 27.
13. *NSC-68,* p. 68.
14. Kennan, draft memorandum to Secretary of State, February 17, 1950, U.S. Department of State, *Foreign Relations,* 1950, 1:160-167.
15. Kennan, "International Control of Atomic Energy," U.S. Department of State, *Foreign Relations,* 1950, 1: 37-40.
16. *NSC-68,* p. 80.
17. *NSC-68,* p. 91.

18. *NSC-68*, p. 83.
19. *NSC-68*, p. 84.
20. *NSC-68*, p. 83.
21. Paul Y. Hammond, "NSC-68: Prologue To Rearmament," in Warner R. Schilling, Paul Y. Hammond, and Glen H. Snyder, *Strategy, Politics, And Defense Budgets* (New York: Columbia University Press, 1962), 318-319.
22. *Ibid.*, p. 285.
23. *NSC-68*, p. 100.
24. *Ibid.*
25. *NSC-68*, p. 102.
26. Yergin, p. 401.
27. *NSC-68*, p. 64.
28. *NSC-68*, p. 65.
29. *Ibid.*
30. Alan Wolfe, "National Security And Domestic Politics," (mimeo-graph, 1979), 9-10.
31. Hammond, p. 371.
32. *Ibid.*, p. 372.
33. Acheson, p. 374.
34. Hammond, p. 310.
35. *Ibid.*, p. 309.
36. *NSC-68*, p. 61.
37. *Ibid.*
38. Hammond, pp. 311-312.
39. Yergin, p. 403.
40. George Kennan, *Memoirs 1925-60* (New York: Bantam, 1969), 358.
41. *NSC-68*, p. 61.
42. Lo, p. 166.
43. *NSC-68*, p. 59; Nitze had expressed the same point of view just prior to NSC-68 arguing, "Nothing about the (Soviets') moves indicate that Moscow is preparing to launch in the near future an all-out attack in the West." Minutes of the 171st Meeting of the Policy Planning Staff, December 16, 1949, U.S. Department of State, *Foreign Relations,* 1949, 1: 414.
44. *NSC-68*, pp. 61-62.
45. *NSC-68*, p. 53.
46. *NSC-68*, p. 60.
47. Hammond, p. 309.
48. *NSC-68*, pp. 78-79.
49. Paul Hoffman, *Peace Can Be Won* (Garden City: Doubleday, 1951), 57.
50. Dean Acheson, memo for the President, February 16, 1950, Box 1, Joseph M. Dodge papers, Detroit Public Library, Japan, 1950, cited in Joyce Kolko and Gabriel Kolko, *The Limits Of Power: The World And United States Foreign Policy, 1945-54* (New York: Harper & Row, 1972), 472.
51. Stephen J. Springarn, memo to Clark Clifford, October 3, 1949, Box 17, Stephen J. Springarn Papers, Truman Library, cited in *Ibid.*, p. 470.

52. *Ibid.*, p. 454.
53. *NSC-68*, p. 76.
54. *NSC-68*, p. 77.
55. *NSC-68*, p. 76.
56. *NSC-68*, p. 95.
57. *Ibid.*
58. *NSC-68*, p. 104.
59. Lo, p. 163.
60. Lo, p. 165.
61. *NSC-68*, p. 95.
62. Lo, p. 165.
63. "Study Prepared By The Director Of The Policy Planning Staff (Nitze), February 8, 1950," U.S. Department of State, *Foreign Relations,* 1950, 1: 145-147.
64. Lo, p. 165.
65. *NSC-68*, p. 98.
66. Walter Millis, Harvey C. Mansfield, and Harold Stein, *Arms And The State: Civil-Military Elements In National Policy* (New York: Twentieth Century Fund, 1958), 238.
67. Samuel P. Huntington, *The Common Defense* (New York: Columbia University Press, 1962), 162.
68. Gaddis Smith, *Dean Acheson. The American Secretaries Of State And Their Diplomacy,* vol. 16. Robert H. Ferrell, ed. (New York: Cooper Square Publishers, 1972), 162.
69. Hammond, p. 289.
70. Smith, 184.
71. Hammond, 290.
72. Millis, Mansfield, and Stein, p. 253.
73. *Ibid.*, p. 254.
74. Hammond, p. 292.
75. *NSC-68*, p. 94.
76. Hammond, p. 317.
77. "Memorandum from the Undersecretary of the Army (Tracy Voorhees) to the Secretary of State (Dean Acheson), April 10, 1950, 3: 43.
78. Statement of Problem For Gray Project, n.d., Box 10, Joseph M. Dodge Papers, Detroit Public Library, Budget Bureau, cited in Kolko and Kolko, p. 475.
79. *Ibid.*
80. For numerous sources confirming Acheson's plea, see *Ibid.*
81. *NSC-68*, p. 88.
82. *NSC-68*, p. 81.
83. *NSC-68*, p. 72.
84. *NSC-68*, pp. 98-99.
85. *NSC-68*, p. 58.
86. "Meeting of the State-Defense Policy Review Committee, February 27, 1950," U.S. Department of State, *Foreign Relations,* 1950, 1: 199; see also Hammond, pp. 333-334.
87. "Record of the Meeting of the State-Defense Policy Review Group, March 10, 1950," U.S. Department of State, *Foreign Relations,* 1950, 1: 191.

88. "Record of the Meeting of the State-Defense Policy Review Group, March 16, 1950," U.S. Department of State, *Foreign Relations*, 1950, 1: 200.

Chapter 2

THE POLITICS OF MILITARISM:
Isolationism and Internationalism Reconsidered

A committee should be organized under the President, comprised of respected leaders of American business, professions, education and religion, to sit either constantly or at frequent intervals at the seat of government, to advise with appropriate agencies of government on critical problems of organization, financing, use of man and woman power, and of public opinion, and in assisting the government in all phases of national activity where their experience, knowledge, and effort might prove useful.

Council on Foreign Relations, Letter to President
Truman, December 12, 1950. [1]

We must have a much vaster propaganda machine to tell our story at home and abroad.

Robert Lovett, investment banker and foreign
policy adviser [2]

The popular interpretation of the debate over military rearmament portrays it as having been resolved within elite circles during the NSC-68 review process, and thereafter among the public with the outbreak of the Korean War in June, 1950. Acheson of course lent considerable

51

credence to the first part of this thesis when he wrote in his memoirs of bludgeoning the policy establishment. The Secretary's actions during the critical review process bear out his attempt to shape history in such fashion. When two of containment's principal architects, George Kennan and Charles Bohlen, disagreed with the bellicose tone NSC-68 was taking, the Secretary of State sent them off on foreign assignment. He recalled,

> . . . the way to peace and action required the separation of the chief contestants for a cooling-off period. Accordingly, one stayed in Washington, one went to South America, and the third to Europe. [3]

Kennan was sent to Latin America on a six-week fact-finding mission which coincided with the time period needed to complete NSC-68. Bohlen was assigned to the embassy in Paris. Nitze, who replaced Kennan as director of Policy Planning at the State Department, stayed behind in Washington to continue shaping the direction of the policy study in his own image, a perspective which coincided perfectly with Acheson's. [4] Thus were the influential voices of dissent within the national security establishment slated for "diplomatic Siberia" in order to more easily facilitate the exercise in intimidation.

But how successful was the bludgeoning of top government thinking? It is certainly an error, though a persistent one, that consensus had been reached within the Administration by the time NSC-68 was submitted to the President in April, 1950. Truman did not commit himself at this time as is often assumed but instead sent NSC-68 to the National Security Council requesting that they spell out and cost out its programmatic implications. Up until the Korean War, in fact, the Administration wavered between adopting the expanded effort trumpeted by Acheson and the more traditional stance of holding the line on military expenditures, a position advocated by Secretary of Defense Louis Johnson who was furious with the NSC-68 review process and recommendations. [5] So intense had the conflict become that both Army secretary Gordon Gray and undersecretary Tracy Voorhees, firm backers of Containment Militarism, resigned rather than continue working under Johnson. [6]

A staunch fiscal conservative with reputed presidential ambitions of his own, Johnson was brought into the Administration as a watchdog on military spending. Moreover, in opposition to Acheson, his was a voice of skepticism within the Administration as regards Europe's willingness to do its part for rearmament. He was supported in his challenge by a number of conservative, mostly Republican, senators who began to demand extensive European effort as the price of further U.S.

commitment. Truman writes of having been "caught in the middle," between domestic critics demanding proof of European resolve and a Europe unwilling to take the risk and bear the cost of remilitarization until U.S. backing was clearly evident. [7]

The stalemate was broken on September 9, 1950, when at Acheson's urging, Truman disclosed that a substantial number of American troops would be sent to Europe. Three days later, the President announced that higher taxes, restrictions on credit, and wage and price controls might be needed to back the military buildup. Toward the end of this remarkable news conference Truman dropped one more bombshell — that Johnson had resigned as Secretary of Defense. [8] Named to take his place was General George C. Marshall, a veritable archsymbol of Europe-oriented internationalism to the Republican conservatives in Congress. The appointment of Establishment stalwart Robert Lovett as Deputy Secretary of Defense signalled the completion of the Acheson-Nitze takeover of the Truman foreign policy. Thus the "bludgeoning process" within the Administration, begun during the drafting of NSC-68, was finally completed three months after the outbreak of hostilities in Korea and nearly a half year after the document was submitted to the President.

Hammering out a consensus within the Administration quickly proved to be only the first and simplest step however. Contrary to widely-held belief, Congress had already shown that it would not succumb so readily. Samuel P. Huntington's influential national security primer, *The Common Defense*, bears considerable responsibility for this distortion. Referring to the impact of the Korean War on NSC-68, he writes: "The issue (NSC-68's legitimacy) was resolved on June 25 (when North Korea launched its attack on the South)." [9] He is quite emphatic about this, later adding:

> In the winter of 1950-51, Congress approved anything necessary for what seemed to be an imminent general war with the Soviet Union. The *absence of public debate* over the long-term objectives and implications of the arms program speeded the process of rearmament in 1950 and 1951. (emphasis added) [10]

The consensual view enjoys considerable allegiance across the political spectrum. Writing on the cold war from a neo-Marxist perspective, Fred Block is in agreement with Huntington on this point. After discussing the difficulties facing the Truman Administration in getting a rearmament policy past the public and Congress in the spring of 1950, Block concludes: "This dilemma was quickly solved when the outbreak of the Korean War created a political context in which the administration gained a free hand for the pursuit of its rearmament plans." [11]

But, such assessments seriously distort the mood of the time, which was if anything more volatile after the outbreak of the Korean War than before. While it is indeed true that Korea provided an immediate reprieve from having to crank up the "vast propaganda machine" of Lovett's imagination, the breather proved to be shortlived. The wartime atmosphere did make it possible for Truman to go to Congress in July with an emergency request for a $10.6 billion increase in the defense budget, $6 billion of which was destined for Europe. But, at the same time, his plea touched off hearings which lasted over the summer and into the latter part of September before it was finally granted. [12] The logic of a buildup in Europe escaped many observers among both the elite and the public as they watched U.S. troops become increasingly bogged down in Korea. [13]

Far from a panacea, Korea was fast proving to be a double-edged sword. If actual hostilities necessarily softened the stance of the fiscal conservatives in Congress to *some* increases in military spending, they hardly resolved the much larger issue of permanent remilitarization and commitment to Europe called for in NSC-68. Thus while the Korean crisis may have provided the necessary antecedent for the public unveiling of the plans contained in NSC-68, it hardly supplied the sufficient precondition for the acceptance of either their scope or intended direction. In fact, the Europe vs. Asia contours of the impending battle had already begun to surface.

Resurgent Isolationism: Prelude To The Great Debate

If there were doubts about the wisdom of Truman's first request for an increase in military spending in July, they had multiplied by the time of his December requests, which came amidst the flurry of activity that began with the CPD's initial public statement. The momentous scenario unfolded as follows during four dramatic days in the winter of 1950:

December 12 — Harvard President James Conant, former undersecretary of the Army Tracy Voorhees, and atomic scientist Vannevar Bush, co-founders of the CPD, read the manifesto of their Committee and fielded questions from the covey of reporters gathered for the occasion at the Willard Hotel in downtown Washington. The "present danger" according to the CPD spokesmen — "the aggressive designs of the Soviet Union." [14] To counter the Soviet threat, the statement stressed the urgency of European rearmament, the necessity of a greater commitment in aid, troops, and materiel by the United States, and a program of universal military service for American youth at age eighteen — the formula of Containment Militarism. That morning the *New York Times* reported that Secretary of State Acheson would travel to Brussels on the weekend to meet with NATO ministers urging them to speed action on German rearmament and integration of European forces. The *Times* story explained that "official quarters" believed the Soviet government was increasing Communist pressure in Korea in the hope of diverting the United States from the key struggle in Western Europe. [15]

December 13 — The major newspapers carried the story of the formation of the CPD, giving its clarion call to rearm against the Soviet danger lengthy and favorable coverage. The *New York Times* described the establishment-laden Committee as a group of "distinguished private citizens." [16] Meanwhile, President Truman addressed the Congressional leadership on the urgency of additional defense funds. To win backing for his request he warned that the possibility of war with the Soviet Union had never been greater. That same day it was reported, the CPD "met in the Pentagon for an off-the-record briefing" at which they "informally consulted defense officials." [17]

December 14 — President Truman submitted to Congress a fourth supplement to the fiscal 1951 defense budget, designated NSC-68/4 within the Administration. It was immediately followed by a declaration of national emergency.

December 15 — Before a nationwide radio audience Truman declared, "Our homes, our nation, all the things we believe in are in great danger. This danger has been created by the rulers of the Soviet Union." He went on to explain that while actual warfare had erupted in Korea, "Europe and the rest of the world are also in great danger." Continuing in language reminiscent of the CPD's founding statement three days before, Truman argued that in "meeting the present danger" U.S. forces would have to be increased to 3.5 million men (the same figure put forward by the CPD), the production of military equipment would have to be greatly augmented, and allied forces in Europe would have to be integrated and strengthened. [18]

Thus while Truman laid out the Soviet Threat thesis before the political leadership, sought the tools for the implementation of Containment Militarism in the full House and Senate, and publicly declared an extraordinary national crisis in order to create the proper climate for its acceptance, the CPD pushed these same quintessential Cold War themes as a concerned and bipartisan (Conant, Bush, and Voorhees were all three Republicans) group of "distinguished private citizens."

It wasn't the heightened sense of crisis that troubled the doubters. That was real enough. After all, China had entered the Korean conflict only two weeks before and driven American troops to the sea. But like the outbreak of war in June, the Truman Administration used the move by the Chinese as a further opportunity to bring about the rearmament of

Europe, adding three quick supplements to the Defense budget to bring the grand total of military spending in fiscal 1951 to $48.2 billion (up from its original sum of $13.5 billion). On the subject of the additional requests, Hammond writes:

> . . . like the first, but more clearly than it, the second supplement bore a discernible relationship to NSC-68. It was an attempt to schedule for the long pull and to keep the immediate imperatives of Korea properly placed in a larger strategic picture. Of the nearly $17 billion requested, $9 billion would be for major procurement items. Part of the sum would be for materiel expended in Korea, but much of it would be for general rearmament . . . The focus thus remained on a larger purpose for rearmament than the fighting of the Korean War. [19]

This despite the fact that during the second half of 1950, deliveries of war materiel to Europe through the Mutual Defense Assistance Program had doubled irrespective of the pressing demands of Korea.[20] Finally, Hammond notes that the fourth supplement (NSC-68/4), "brought to a conclusion the process of programming and pricing in the Defense Department for NSC-68" as well as providing "the initial guidelines for the fiscal 1952 budget" which Truman was soon to unveil in his State of the Union message in early January. [21] Granted that the Chinese intervention, like the beginning of the war itself, had caused Congress to loosen its hold on the fiscal purse strings; but, it was an entirely different matter to convince them that the major focus of a remilitarization program should be the permanent garrison of American troops in Europe, universal military service, and the continuation of aid to Europe on the massive scale called for in NSC-68.

The 82nd Congress returned from its Christmas recess just in time for General Dwight Eisenhower's controversial departure for Europe. Eisenhower had been named Supreme Allied Commander of Europe some two weeks before (December 20, 1950), after the President was informed in a telegram from Acheson in Brussels that the North Atlantic Council had "completed arrangements for the establishment of an integrated European defense force." [22] The American part of the bargain was to be Eisenhower's leadership and a substantial contingent of U.S. troops. To lend credibility to a policy move of such magnitude and to gain support for it in Congress, Ike was dispatched on a "fact-finding tour" to Europe on January 5, 1951.

The prospect of American troops in Europe and an American commander of an integrated European army did not sit well with many, among them the Republican Party's major aspirant to the presidency

Robert Taft and its elder statesman Herbert Hoover. The day Eisenhower was dispatched to Europe, Hoover warned that it would be "inviting another Korea" to send additional troops or aid across the Atlantic. The nation's only living ex-President urged, instead, a foreign policy based on protecting the Americas in order "to preserve for the world this Western Hemisphere Gibraltar of Western Civilization." He counseled holding the Atlantic and Pacific with air and sea power and waiting for Europe to demonstrate a united will to fight before sending more men and money. "Even without Europe," Hoover contended, "Americans have no reason for hysteria or loss of confidence in our security or our future." [23]

Taft expressed much the same sentiments on the Senate floor. In his address, the senator from Ohio questioned Truman's legal right to commit ground troops to Europe without Congressional approval. Moreover, Taft attacked the very legitimacy of Containment Militarism, saying he did not see any conclusive evidence that "the Russians intend militarily to attack free Europe." Sending troops to Europe would in his estimation, only serve to provoke the Soviets. In a devastating riposte to the Truman-Acheson policies Taft charged,

> One of the greatest present dangers to peace is the conduct of
> the United States Government itself under President Truman,
> and specifically the prospective formation of a European
> Army under the command of an American, General Dwight
> D. Eisenhower. [24]

Finally, Taft argued quite prophetically toward the end of his two and one-half hour discourse that the type of program called for by the Administration would "bring great deficits and inflation, and bring on 'the garrison state'." [25]

These were the same themes that had returned large numbers of conservative Republicans to Congress in the off-year election, narrowing the Democratic majority in the Senate to a scant two votes, 49-47. For the Republican right, Truman's latest policy proposal was seen as only the most recent in a long series of Democratic policy catastrophes dating back to the days of Woodrow Wilson. In the postwar period the Marshall Plan was to foreign policy what the New Deal symbolized domestically. Both were, from the conservative perspective, morally reprehensible and fiscally irresponsible. Moreover, as with the League of Nations and the New Deal, the purveyors of the Marshall Plan were the hated "liberal internationalists" who dominated Democratic administrations as well as the Eastern wing of their own party.

The Republican right wing had gathered additional steam as a result of the Communist victory in China and the Administration's handling of the Korean War. From the right wing perspective, Acheson's infamous White Paper was proof enough that the Administration bore responsibility for "the loss of China" and was generally "soft on communism" in the Far East. The Republicans in fact charged that a strategy of appeasement in Asia, attributed to Acheson, had actually encouraged the North Korean attack on the South. The return of Marshall to the cabinet in September was similarly read as strengthening Acheson's Europe-oriented policies since it was Marshall's mission to China in 1946 that had been crucial in shaping American policy toward Asia.

Still a third current of right wing opposition to Truman's policies had arisen in the early part of 1950 under the leadership of Senator Joseph McCarthy, a vendetta Acheson dubbed "the attack of the primitives." The basis thesis of these stalkers of domestic subversion was that the foreign policy elite had been not the victim of duplicity in events in Asia so much as the willing participant in complicity with the expansion of communism. The magnitude of their anger was apparent on the front page of the *New York Times* the day Truman announced that Acheson would be leaving for Brussels charged with the awesome responsibility of putting together the military plan for the North Atlantic alliance. An accompanying story told of Republican efforts to oust Acheson from his post as Secretary of State in an effort to undermine his leadership with the Europeans. [26]

Indeed according to the press, European leaders were reported to be genuinely alarmed by what they feared was a resurgence of pre-World War II isolationism in the United States. Many on this side of the Atlantic, including the CPD, were concerned as well. Voorhees called a meeting of the Committee on January 6 at the Metropolitan Club in Washington, explaining:

> It has become clear that Mr. Hoover's proposal for a fundamental change in our military policy toward Europe has received wide public acceptance. Mail to Congress is said to be running very heavily in this direction. [27]

The CPD cochairman suggested that under the circumstances perhaps the time was ripe for a major fund-raising effort and an intensive nationwide campaign. In the memorandum he reasoned:

> The thought is that — in addition to effective support of universal military service, which still has a difficult path to travel — the importance of combatting the new isolationist doctrine has created a great and unexpected need for just the kind of non-partisan advice and counsel to the public which this Committee is in an almost unique position to furnish.[28]

In retrospect, this proved to be the blueprint for CPD activity over the next several months. As Conant noted in his memoirs:

Troops for Europe, universal military service and foreign aid were all parts of one package, and all three proposals were highly distasteful to the new isolationism which emerged at the end of 1950. [29]

The substance of the CPD campaign is the subject of the following chapter. It is sufficient to note at this juncture that the combination of the CPD's testimony before the Senate and House on the issue of universal military service, its statements to the press in support of the new Containment Militarism, and its radio broadcasts and pamphleteering to build a popular base for these policies, proved too much for the isolationist right to endure. Once the Committee's activities had begun in earnest a newspaper story about the CPD appeared in the *Washington Times-Herald* headed "$100,000 Sought For Lobbying By Internationalists." [30] The article went on to describe the Committee as "a group of citizens supporting interventionism of the Truman Administration." Moreover, the story charged, the Committee's thirty-three members were "all prominent internationalists" who were on the Committee for the Marshall Plan and "profited handsomely from the spending under the Marshall Plan aid program." The account predicted that "they will also profit from spending under the defense program." [31]

The next week the *Times-Herald* followed with an editorial which referred to the Committee as "a propaganda outfit . . . dedicated to sending U.S. troops to Europe, the drafting of 18 year olds and generally advancing the Truman program." The editorial went on to accuse the Committee's members of having been instrumental in bringing about U.S. involvement in both world wars, the League of Nations, the United Nations, "and the fantastic series of internationalist blunders climaxed in money with the Marshall Plan and in diplomacy with the Russian capture of China." The *Times-Herald's* attack concluded, "The real danger is in letting the CPD have even the slightest influence on U.S. policy." [32]

Representative John T. Wood from Idaho had the article printed in the *Congressional Record* of February 8, 1951. In addition, he provided a few choice remarks of his own accusing the Committee of "whooping it up to draft eighteen year olds, send an army and unlimited supplies to Europe, and thereby hasten the day, so fervently hoped for by Joe Stalin, when we will have spent ourselves into bankruptcy." Wood concluded his diatribe against the Committee saying,

This is the same gang who sold us the Marshall Plan on the promise that it would stop Communism and furnish a market for our surplus production . . . It is time to think and talk and act American; and designate internationalists for what they are — potential traitors to the United States. [33]

The CPD incurred a similar assault in the Senate after it issued a statement to the press simultaneous with a Sunday night broadcast by one of its biggest guns, cotton magnate and former Assistant Secretary of State Will Clayton. The text of the Committee's statement, urging an affirmative vote in the Senate on an upcoming troops-to-Europe measure, was printed in its entirety in the *New York Times* the morning of the Senate vote. In addition, it was inserted into the *Congressional Record* by Senator Herbert Lehman, a prominent internationalist from New York.

Conservative Everett Dirksen could no longer contain himself. Thundering to his colleagues in the Senate, Dirksen charged "now we have a new committee that is selling us a bill of goods — the Committee on the Present Danger." Moreover, he complained, the Committee was a "professional lobby" with a list of members that was "rather imposing." The senator from Illinois went on to note that twelve members of the CPD were also part of the pre-World War II internationalist Committee To Defend America By Aiding The Allies. "So," Dirksen reasoned, "it is the same old business, the same old salesmanship, the same old determination to put America on the road to disaster." [34]

Specifically the CPD stood accused of working in close conjunction with the Truman Administration to bring about a Europe-oriented rearmament program, and more generally, of being firmly entrenched within the liberal internationalist network that had dominated postwar foreign policy. The CPD of course described itself as a nonpartisan group of concerned private citizens without ties either to the Administration or to any one ideological or policy line. The reason for its existence, the Committee maintained, was simply alarm over the Soviet Threat and the conviction that a military buildup was required to combat it.

The remainder of this chapter shows the isolationists to be correct in their allegations. The CPD did work hand in hand with the Administration to legitimate the policy outlined in NSC-68. They also represented a foreign policy establishment moving toward acceptance of a new form of internationalism, namely, from containment to Containment Militarism.

The Construction Of The Vast Propaganda Machine

Despite the urgent tone the CPD's opening statement was meant to convey, its actual founding originated in a very different sort of crisis some four months before. It is worthwhile to review the setting. As noted earlier, by August, 1950, Congress was in the midst of a debate touched off by Truman's first supplemental request for additional military funds after the outbreak of the Korean War. Under particular scrutiny was European aid of any kind, including military support for NATO. Moreover, within the Administration, Acheson's drive for a commitment of troops to Europe to reassure the Europeans of American resolve remained blocked by Secretary of Defense Johnson, who wanted evidence of European will before making any such effort. This was the point, cited earlier, at which Truman referred to having been "caught in the middle," between a Europe seeking signs of American commitment to its defense before embarking on a costly program of remilitarization and those forces within the U.S. who first demanded proof of European determination.

It was a stalemate that had to be quickly resolved, since the North Atlantic Council was scheduled for a critical meeting concerning the future of the alliance in mid-September. The deadline encouraged Acheson to push the President toward a course of action. Truman in turn requested an appropriate plan from a new ad hoc group of the State and Defense Departments which included among its members Paul Nitze and John J. McCloy. It was in the midst of this crisis in U.S.-European relations that R. Ammi Cutter, an old World War II crony of Tracy Voorhees and soon to be founder of the CPD, invited Voorhees and James Conant to dinner at his summer retreat in the mountains of New Hampshire. This inconspicuous occasion, nearly four months before the Committee went public, marked the founding of the Committee on the Present Danger. [35]

Conant had been a consultant on the drafting of NSC-68 the previous spring while Voorhees still remained in active government service as a member of the National Security Council's Ad Hoc Committee in charge of NSC-68's planning. Conant recollects that Voorhees soon launched into an impassioned plea for public action that reminded him "of the cries of alarm in Washington and New York when France fell in 1940." [36] Indeed by the end of the evening Conant felt moved to suggest an approach similar to that of a decade before, the formation of a "citizen's lobby" along the lines of the Committee To Defend America By Aiding The Allies. His memoirs of what happened next read as follows:

> "Get a group of distinguished citizens together," I said, "draw up a program, put it before the public, get people to write Congress and, in general, respond to the gravity of the situation. From what I have just heard, I judge the country is asleep. You should wake it up."
>
> "Would you be one of the leaders in such a committee?"

Voorhees asked.

Conant sums up the significance of the evening saying:

> Without being aware of it, we had just participated in forming
> the Committee on the Present Danger, which was to fulfill a
> useful function until the Korean War was over. [37]

As a member of the NSC group, Voorhees was within the inner
circle of Administration efforts to put NSC-68 into practice. It was this
group upon which he and Nitze jointly served that drafted NSC-68/2,
NSC-68/3, and NSC-68/4 to support Truman's emergency request for
tripling the military budget. A critical and extremely controversial aspect
of NSC-68 was the advocacy of a large standing army and the garrison of
hundreds of thousands of these troops in Europe, policies for which
Acheson now argued with great insistence within presidential councils.
Without such a permanent contingent of U.S. forces, Europeans feared
that their own efforts to rearm might provoke a counter reaction from the
Soviet Union and its allies in Eastern Europe. If such a military buildup
should lead to actual hostilities, Europe would be plunged once again into
a war of devastation. Thus among the foreign policy elite there was the
concern that the Europeans might choose neutralism as a more attractive
alternative than the risk of war with the Soviet Union.

To guard against such an event the shield of American troops
seemed to be the only preventive mechanism available in the face of the
vanishing nuclear monopoly. But if the United States were to commit
forces to Europe in the magnitude called for, it would need a vastly more
efficient and greatly expanded system for funneling men into the military
than the existing Selective Service system could provide. Conant had
been a leading spokesman for just such a revamped and comprehensive
system in recent years. Moreover, as president of Harvard and arguably
the nation's foremost educator at the time, Conant's active support would
be invaluable in overcoming the widespread opposition sure to arise
against a much-expanded system of military service. Given Voorhees'
forceful advocacy at their first encounter, most probably it was with this
obstacle in mind that Voorhees arranged to meet with Conant through
their mutual acquaintance Cutter.

The dilemma for the policy elite was that an expanded system of
military service was, if anything, less popular with Congress and the
public than continuing economic aid via the Marshall Plan. Here they
were confronted with a classical case where the aims of foreign policy as
defined by an elite run up against the constraints of domestic politics
which represent the aspirations of the public. A large standing army in
peacetime and a system of conscription to maintain it had never been

popular in American history. After World War II, military forces were rapidly depleted as a result of the public outcry for demobilization. The Truman Administration had attempted to reverse the situation with a bill for universal military service in 1947. But the measure met defeat in Congress. The following year another such effort became entangled in the struggle over military unification and died in committee. Finally, the Berlin confrontation induced Congress to enact a Selective Service Act along the lines of the original measure of 1940.

Soon after passage of the Act in June, 1948, Conant criticized it as inadequate in his book, *Education In A Divided World*. He argued instead for a more comprehensive system of "universal military service and training." By this he had in mind a scheme whereby every eighteen year-old would be enrolled in a program of training through a national militia system for a period of ten years. [38] As Conant recounts, the founding meeting of the CPD caused him to reactivate his plan:

> When Tracy Voorhees and Ammi Cutter presented their alarming view of the military situation in August, 1950, I had turned to my suggestion of 1948 and modified it to meet the new conditions. Enrollment in the armed forces for service, not enrollment in a national militia for training, seemed to be now required. [39]

Voorhees returned from his summer place in New Hampshire right after Labor Day and went to work to make the Committee a reality. The first step he took was to talk to a number of influentials about the idea for such a group. [40] The response was overwhelmingly favorable. The candid remarks of those with whom he met were also quite revealing, confirming the suspicion that policy elites were more preoccupied with the threat emanating from Europe's "loss of will" than any threat of Soviet attack. Prominent foreign policy adviser Robert Bowie, for instance, baldly stated in his remarks to Voorhees that "the bulk of the people do not want to be liberated." He went on to argue that "American policy must be to unite Europe" and that "the present danger from Russia creates a unique opportunity to bring this about." [41] Thus the Soviet Threat was perceived less as a matter of alarm than as opportunity. The opportunity was to implement the rearmament measures outlined in NSC-68.

The neutralist theme was uppermost in the mind of John J. McCloy, then High Commissioner to Germany, when he went on record as feeling "acutely the need for vigorous action on our part here (formation of the CPD)" for the reason that both Germany and France and others "were taking various kinds of hedging action." Thus McCloy concluded, "What is needed is an immediate increasing of American forces in Europe to show that we intend to fight there." [42]

The point of view expressed by McCloy was also coming to prevail within the Administration over the objection of the recalcitrants, led by Secretary of Defense Johnson. The Nitze-McCloy team submitted their report to President Truman who in early September approved it and promptly announced plans backing German rearmament and integration of NATO forces. This was the point at which Johnson resigned from his Defense post. The consensus within the Administration had been reached just in time. Three days later Acheson presented the completed American proposals to the gathering of European foreign ministers in New York.

This would prove to be only the preliminary bout in the fight for acceptance of NSC-68. Its costs, an estimate of which was under preparation by the Nitze-Voorhees group, were not revealed publicly until December, in the crisis atmosphere of the Chinese intervention in Korea. The battle lines were also clear to the Republican right in Congress whose antagonism toward Truman and his entire Administration was fast approaching heights previously reserved for Acheson and the State Department. By the fall of 1950 then, it had become evident a campaign would have to be carried to wider circles in order to counter the expected resistance to the new direction in containment policy.

While Voorhees tested the waters in official Washington, Conant began to enlist public support for a draconian system of military conscription. The same day that Voorhees talked to Bowie about the necessity of sending U.S. ground troops to Europe, Conant wrote to Henry Wriston, then president of the Association of American Universities, explaining that:

> Since I believe . . . the sooner we have a million combat troops in Europe the better, I am naturally on the side of immediate action to raise the armed forces to 3-5 million men . . . What we need now in my mind is a long-range, sensible scheme for universal military service (not training). If a group of university presidents came forward with such a scheme within the next few months, it might be a matter of great importance. At the very least, they could show the inadequacies of present legislation. [43]

Wriston would soon become an active member of the CPD — as would a host of other university presidents — and the Association of American Universities would prove to be a key wedge in CPD plans, beginning with the sponsorship of a "Citizen's Conference" at the end of September.

From the beginning, university educators played a prominent role both within the CPD itself and in support of CPD proposals in their professional organizations and activities. Nowhere is this better illustrated than in the so-called "Citizen's Conference," sponsored by seven college presidents — among them Wriston — to expound their views on universal military service and its link to an adequate defense posture. General Eisenhower, then president of Columbia University, was slated to give the keynote address. Conant was unable to attend but prepared a statement that was read by the Dean of the Harvard Business School, Donald K. David. In the words of the organizers of the "Citizen's Conference" it was attended by,

> fifty industrialists, heads of many communication services — press, radio, newspapers, and magazines — financiers, educators, heads of farm organizations, life insurance and railroad presidents. [44]

Some of those attending included financier Bernard Baruch, Winthrop Aldrich of the Chase Manhattan Bank, Julius Ochs Adler of the *New York Times* — who would soon become a member of the CPD — Alfred P. Sloan of General Motors, George Whitney of the J.P. Morgan investment firm, and magnates John Hay Whitney, and John D. Rockefeller. Tracy Voorhees was also there. The confidential report of this high-level meeting reveals that it was strictly a briefing for Establishment consumption: "It was agreed that no public record would be made of the views expressed at the conference; hence this memorandum is to be held strictly confidential," wrote Harry Bullis, CPD member and president of General Mills. [45]

What the business and media moguls were treated to was a preview of the CPD's first public statement in December. At this early stage the goal was to disseminate the doctrine of Containment Militarism to the wider circle of "opinion-making elites," a problem that had preoccupied Nitze from the drafting of NSC-68. Eisenhower set the somber tone in the beginning by stating the twin propositions that "the Soviet objective is world domination, and the Russian leaders are willing to use armed force to win." Secondly, Ike contended, "the American people are responsible for this country's present position. The moment the fighting ceased in World War II the cry was to bring Willie home. Now we are reaping the results of that policy." [46] To reverse this trend, he argued, would require additional expenditure for defense and a system of universal military service. Eisenhower's speech was followed by Conant's statement, which again cited the litany of Soviet expansionism and reiterated the need for "the United States to maintain a large force of American combat troops in Europe for at least a decade" to prevent the Russians from realizing their designs. The key to such a policy of containment, Conant emphasized, was to put every able-bodied eighteen year-old in the service of the military. [47] As Conant recognized at the time and stated in later years, "A discussion of a measure affecting the liability of young men for military service may be fundamentally a debate about foreign policy." [48]

To the same degree that the purveyors of the new internationalism extended their ties outward into the larger corporate, media, and academic establishments, they also forged links within the national security bureaucracy. In this regard, Conant writes in his memoirs that the shakeup within the Administration in September was greeted by himself and his colleagues as "good news." With old friends Marshall and Lovett now at the helm of the Defense Department, Voorhees and William L. Marbury — another stalwart establishment insider who served as principal legal assistant to the War Department during World War II — held a meeting with Lovett in early October to discuss the activation of the CPD. Conant writes, "Tracy and I agreed that the Committee could be effective only if it were welcomed (unofficially, but sincerely) by the administration." [49]

Lovett's response was to encourage the fledgling CPD to inform Secretary Marshall of what they had in mind, not surprising considering Lovett's call for a "vast propaganda machine" some six months before. Subsequently a letter to Marshall was prepared, and Conant invited a number of prominent persons to join in the effort. The accompanying letter to prospective CPD members explained that if a favorable reply was received from Marshall, the Committee would then begin its activities sometime between the election and the reconvening of Congress "to arouse public opinion as to the steps which must be taken in this time of crisis." [50]

By the time the letter to Marshall was ready, the nucleus of what was soon to become the CPD had grown to eleven persons, including J. Walter Thompson Advertising Agency president Stanley Resor, former Secretary of War Robert Patterson, and former Assistant Secretary of State Will Clayton. The letter to Marshall began by applauding the President's call to arms in September: "The danger the free world faces is so great that we cannot be satisfied with less than an all-out effort by everyone." The Committee then went on to argue that the "all-out effort" Truman proposed could not be realized without the institutionalization of universal military service. The CPD letter concluded as follows:

> Specifically, we have thought that one way in which such a committee might be of help would be in strengthening the public support for such stern measures as may be necessary. We of course do not wish to involve you in any way whatever relative to this proposal, and write this letter only because we would not wish to proceed if you felt it would not be constructive to do so. [51]

Marshall's reaction to the CPD's letter was positive, as expected. The Secretary wrote a personal note to each of its signatories in which he told them, "Your proposal is an undertaking of great importance." He closed by suggesting that they meet with him in Washington to discuss a possible public statement. [52]

The CPD was quick to respond and the meeting was conducted in Secretary Marshall's office on November 20, 1950. In attendance for the CPD were Voorhees, Bush, Clayton, Patterson, Cutter, Marbury, corporate and national security advisers John Lord O'Brian and Howard C. Peterson, as well as college presidents James Phinney Baxter III, Harold Dodds, and Henry Wriston. While the group received Marshall's blessing the Defense Secretary showed a reluctance to fully embrace the CPD's key proposal of universal military service. In an October meeting shortly after being named to the Defense post, Marshall had complained to Acheson, Nitze, and Averell Harriman about a memorandum being prepared by a "group of prominent educators including James Conant" who advocated adoption of compulsory military service. Marshall expressed doubts about such a measure, arguing that a large standing army would be difficult to maintain because of objections from Congress as well as from the soldiers themselves. [53] Marshall remained unconvinced that the politically volatile universal military service proposal was the only option available on the manpower question, telling the Committee that he would have a definite plan to put forward within two weeks' time.[54] What happened next is a tribute to the unique insider/outsider status of such elite "citizens's lobbies" that afford them the opportunity to both make policy within the state and shape opinion in the larger society.

Immediately after the meeting with Marshall, several CPD members met over lunch with Assistant Secretaries Rosenberg and Leva and General Counsel Larkin to discuss their plans for a manpower bill. Subsequent to this a subcommittee consisting of Bush, O'Brian, Marbury, and Voorhees — all old Pentagon hands — was created to confer with the Department of Defense on the drafting of the Administration's manpower legislation. An October memo written by Voorhees in the early days of the CPD's formation reveals that such coordination with the Administration was a key tactic in the Committee's master plan. Voorhees suggested at this time that integration of the Committee's efforts with the Defense Department would be a way of making the Committee "a live factor and truly effective." He reasoned that once Marshall had approved the letter and general plan they could,

> . . . arrange with Mr. Lovett to have the committee members designated consultants and come to Washington from time to time for briefings . . . this would permit their expenses to Washington to be paid and would make it possible to give

them classified information and place them in a position to give advice which would carry weight. [55]

Accordingly, on December 1, 1950, the CPD subcommittee met with Rosenberg and her staff members Leva, Larkin, and Tyroler. [Tyroler became chairman of CPD-II in November, 1976.] [56] Secretary Rosenberg suggested to the assembled group that the more the Committee urged universal military service, the better it would be for the Defense Department's case. Then she went on to ask whether it would be possible to "have some kind of immediate resolution adopted by a group of educators" supporting universal military service? Voorhees' notes indicate that he replied:

> I said that if she would definitize what she wanted and would telephone the substance of it to my office . . . I would speak with the college presidents who would be attending our committee meeting on Sunday, and who would on Monday be attending the meeting of the Association of American Universities. Mrs. Rosenberg gladly accepted this suggestion. [57]

The president of the Association of American Universities, of course, was Henry Wriston. Other college presidents from the CPD with considerable influence in the organization by virtue of the prestigious institutions they represented were Presidents Dodds (Princeton), Baxter (Williams College), Sproul (University of California, Berkeley), and Conant (Harvard). The measure supporting universal military service was duly passed by the assembled throng of college presidents the following Monday as scheduled, lending substantial weight to the case the CPD was making within the Defense Department and which Defense would soon be making before Congress on behalf of the Administration.

As the CPD leaders prepared to launch publicly "the vast propaganda machine" they had created in the fall of 1950, the Committee's insider role at the Pentagon had become firmly established due to the active intervention of Lovett. The CPD's quasi-official status can be gleaned from their itinerary the day the founding statement was formally released. Before the press conference the Committee held a luncheon at the Metropolitan Club. Afterwards a briefing for Committee members was scheduled at the Pentagon. This apprisal "of the current situation" as the session was billed,

> . . . *is being authorized by the Secretary of Defense to place the Committee in possession of confidential information which it is believed will be of great assistance in its work.* (emphasis added)[58]

In addition to the Committee's favorable reviews in the nation's newspapers and the endorsement of its ideas by the Association of American Universities, its efforts within the Administration were complemented by the Council on Foreign Relations, an organization long-described as synonymous with the foreign policy establishment. On the very day the CPD unveiled its founding statement, Hamilton Fish Armstrong, longtime editor of the Council on Foreign Relations-sponsored journal *Foreign Affairs*, submitted a position paper to the President outlining the Council's latest thinking on foreign and military posture. The cover letter to Truman, signed by a dozen luminaries of the Council including the ubiquitous Henry Wriston, bore a decided resemblance in both form and substance to the CPD statement released to the press. The Council's set of recommendations to the President had grown out of its Study Group On Aid To Europe of which Eisenhower was chairman and Wriston a member. Wriston in fact would appear to be a key figure linking the various facets of the burgeoning Cold War lobby.* As a member of the executive committee of the CPD he had met with Secretary Marshall on November 20, and as president of the Association of American Universities had engineered the endorsement of universal military service in early December. Finally, Wriston had also played a cameo role in September's blue ribbon "Citizen's Conference."

The CFR statement itself was distinguished less by the originality of its ideas than by the repetition of familiar themes. Among them were the imperative need for the rearmament of Europe, accelerated growth of strategic air and naval forces, dispatch of troops to Europe, and universal military service. In the convoluted logic that would become all too common in the cold war era, the Council on Foreign Relations told the President that in "this period of critical danger . . ."

> The only way in which we and our friends can make the Soviets respect our peaceful intent and moral purposes will be by rapidly producing powerful military forces. [59]

But why would the Council on Foreign Relations feel compelled to submit its "recommendations" to Truman when presumably, judging by its actions in September, the Administration was committed to the ambitious goals outlined in the council's position paper? The reason, it would appear, was to let Truman know that in the minefield of domestic politics that lay ahead, the prestigious and *Republican-dominated* Council on Foreign Relations would give its unqualified support to the implementation of the measures outlined in NSC-68. Nevertheless, in

---

*Wriston was not entirely alone in this role. Three other founding members of the CPD were also CFR members, including the Council's executive director, Frank Altschul.

spite of this display of bipartisanship, the Council recognized that its closing of ranks at the top was only the first step in a long struggle to reach a consensus in the conduct of America's imperial policy. To impress upon the public and Congress the importance of the United States mission in the world, they urged the establishment of close collaboration between an ad hoc committee of "respected leaders" and the Administration (expressed in the quotation heading this chapter).

The Committee on the Present Danger and the Internationalist Foreign Policy Network

Right wing charges that the CPD's purpose was interlocked with the efforts of the Truman Administration is borne out by the substantial evidence cited above. The second part of their attack on the Committee's self-described independence and non-partisanship was the claim that its founders and leaders constituted a veritable Who's Who within a foreign policy establishment long-known for its promotion of internationalism. Again, as we will see, the evidence confirms the accuracy of the isolationist allegation.

A perusal of the signatories of the CPD's founding statement pointed to the organization's integral ties to the Establishment. The CPD's profile, judged from family background and Ivy League education, affiliation with exclusive social clubs, and membership in elite foundations, was decidedly upper class. For the most part it was a Republican group identified with the big business Eastern wing of the party. In addition to this corporate capitalist elite however, the CPD also included a prominent scientific-technocratic elite whose ideas were instrumental in the creation and development of the burgeoning national security bureaucracy.

Each of these elite strata — the *corporate* and the *technocratic* — that came together in the formation of the CPD met initially in the early days of World War II, in the summer of 1940 to be exact. On June 19, President Roosevelt appointed Republican Wall Street lawyer and Theodore Roosevelt protege Henry L. Stimson to the post of Secretary of War. Named as his assistant was another Republican corporate lawyer of similar standing, Robert P. Patterson. Both Stimson and Patterson were leading members of the Council on Foreign Relations. A decade later, Patterson would become one of the founders of the CPD. Richard Barnet pinpoints Roosevelt's decision as the origin of the foreign policy establishment. He writes that Stimson was steeped in the world view of Theodore Roosevelt and,

> . . . within six months of FDR's call Stimson had put together
> an impressive staff of like-minded people who also were

imbued with TR's values — struggle, honor, and glory . . . After 1940, the national security managers, working with the military, began to redefine the national interest. [60]

Huntington agrees with Barnet's assessment of their importance but disagrees on their impact, referring to them admiringly as "neo-Hamiltonians" who turned America away from its traditional isolationist tendencies toward world leadership. [61] If Barnet and Huntington differ on the end result of the Establishment's rise to power, each agrees that this exclusive group was critical in the formation of American policy throughout the war and into the post-war period. Stimson's and Patterson's principal assistants in the War Department included John J. McCloy, Robert Lovett, and Harvey Bundy. Like their mentors, each of these men were active members of the Eastern financial and political establishment. McCloy, who served as Stimson's personnel chief, recalled: "Whenever we needed a man we thumbed through the roll of the Council (On Foreign Relations) members and put through a call to New York." [62] Of the twenty-five founding members of the CPD in 1950, a nucleus of seven had gotten the call and served in the office of the Secretary of War. In addition to Patterson, they included Voorhees, Robert Cutler, Edmund S. Greenbaum, William L. Marbury, Howard C. Peterson, and Robert Sherwood.

After the war, Stimson's recruits and their colleagues in Roosevelt's wartime government stayed on as the key architects of postwar national security and foreign policy. Upon Stimson's retirement in 1945, Patterson took over as Secretary of War. Barnet describes the impact of the War Department graduates as follows:

> It was Stimson's and Forrestal's (Secretary of the Navy who would become the first Secretary of Defense) recruits, plus a few others with similar backgrounds, including Dean Acheson, Will Clayton, and Averell Harriman who, after Roosevelt's sudden death, formed the collective picture of the world adopted by the uninformed and ill-prepared Harry Truman.[63]

Summoned from the worlds of corporate law and high finance with little or no experience in government they soon took over the reins of foreign policy from career diplomats in the State Department. Nitze was the archsymbol of those Barnet calls the "new breed." Graduated from Harvard, he joined the prestigious New York investment banking firm of Dillon, Read. After a short stint on Wall Street, he was brought into government by Dillon, Read senior partner Forrestal in 1941, serving in a series of posts in economic mobilization agencies before becoming special consultant to the War Department and Vice Chairman of the

Strategic Bombing Survey from 1944 to 1946. After the war, Nitze moved to the State Department where he specialized in international trade and finance under Will Clayton and was credited with providing much of the impetus behind the Marshall Plan. Following that he became Acheson's Director of Policy Planning in 1950, the post from which he directed the writing of NSC-68.

If Roosevelt's appointment of Stimson and Patterson opened the avenue through which the corporate elite entered the institutions of foreign policy formation, an equally important event occurred that same summer when the technocratic connection to the national security bureaucracy was established. Vannevar Bush and James Conant had together been discussing how scientists could assist in hastening the preparation for entrance into World War II at a meeting of scientists and educators. Shortly thereafter Bush gained access to President Roosevelt through Harry Hopkins, the President's close adviser and confidant, and persuaded Roosevelt to establish a National Defense Research Committee. The National Defense Research Committee was to operate in the executive branch under the chairmanship of Bush, who was at the time serving as president of the Carnegie Institution. Conant writes that aside from the application of scientific technology to weapons development "the committee marked the beginning of a revolution" in another sense. [64] Here Conant was referring to the link between university laboratories and the research and development of weapons which would become a routine feature of the Cold War era.

The National Defense Research Committee was quickly subsumed under a new agency — the Office of Scientific Research and Development, located in the Office for Emergency Management within the Executive. This powerful bureau, which Bush headed from 1941 to 1946, dealt directly with the Joint Chiefs of Staff and the President. When Bush moved to the directorship of the Office of Scientific Research and Development, Conant replaced him at the National Defense Research Committee while at the same time serving as Bush's assistant at Scientific Research and Development. One of their associates James Phinney Baxter III, won a Pulitzer Prize for his tale of the agency's work called *Scientists Against Time*. By 1950 Baxter was president of Smith College and joined Bush and Conant on the membership rolls of the CPD. Another prominent college president who also served in the Office of Scientific Research and Development during the war and later on the executive committee of the CPD was Robert G. Sproul of the University of California, whose name had appeared along with Conant's in the NSC-68 deliberations concerning formation of a "vast propaganda machine" under the direction of influential national opinion leaders.

The primary work of the Office of Scientific Research and

Development was production of the atomic bomb. [65] It was Bush in fact, who in October, 1941, won White House sanction for a full-scale effort to explore the possibilities for an atomic weapons program. [66] When the bomb was dropped on Hiroshima and Nagasaki in August, 1945, the decision to target Japanese cities was recommended to Truman by Secretary of War Stimson based upon the opinion of an Interim Committee under his direction. On this committee of eight civilians charged with responsibility for the monstrous decision were three who would become members of the CPD. They were Assistant Secretary of State Clayton, Bush, and Conant. The Interim Committee recommended unanimously "that the bomb be used against the enemy as soon as it could be done . . . without specific warning and against a target that would clearly show its devastating strength." In fact, according to more than one account, it was Conant who suggested that the only target meeting such criteria was a population center, ideally "a war plant employing a large number of workers closely surrounded by workers' houses." [67]

Once the war had been brought to its abrupt ending, the Interim Committee was again called upon for a judgment of epochal implication: what to do with the atomic bomb? A bitter debate had broken out over the question of whether such knowledge should be placed under international control or maintained exclusively in American hands. Those who argued the former position included many of the scientists who had worked on the successful project. It was their belief that the Russians would be able within a few years to duplicate the U.S. feat, and that international regulation was needed to ward off a nuclear arms race. On the other side were those who argued that the U.S. should maintain tight control over such knowledge and to develop it still further to assure military superiority into the foreseeable future. In the Interim Committee's deliberations, Bush and Conant were instrumental in pushing the Committee to take a stand in favor of national control — a position against the scientists who had labored under their direction during the war. Conant describes his and Bush's role in the following passage:

> One of the tasks urged upon it by Bush and myself was the drafting of legislation to be introduced in Congress immediately after the war ended. Secretary of War Stimson agreed that a draft should be prepared and gave the task to the Undersecretary, Robert P. Patterson. [68]

Patterson in turn brought in two lawyers, Kenneth C. Royall and William L. Marbury, who drafted the position paper. (Marbury, as noted earlier, was also instrumental in the formation of the CPD.) The paper which they put together became the basis of the May-Johnson bill for U.S. control of atomic energy, a position which faithfully reflected the view of Bush and Conant. Robert Oppenheimer in his testimony in favor of May-Johnson said:

> The bill was drafted with the detailed supervision of Dr. Bush and Dr. Conant, with the knowledge and the agreement of the former Secretary of War, Mr. Stimson. I think no man in the country carried a greater weight of responsibility for this project than Mr. Stimson. I think no men in positions of responsibility, who were scientists, took more responsibility or were more courageous or better informed in the general sense than Dr. Bush and Dr. Conant. I think if they liked the philosophy of this bill and urged this bill, it is a very strong argument. I know that many scientists do not agree with me on this, but I am nevertheless convinced myself. [69]

Oppenheimer, reputed father of the atomic bomb, also became a member of the Committee on the Present Danger. The only other witnesses for May-Johnson in hearings before the Senate were General L.R. Groves (director of the Manhattan Project that manufactured the atomic bomb), Patterson, Bush, and Conant. The legislation was blocked, however, before it could reach passage. May-Johnson was soon tainted with the charge of "military control" and subsequently followed by the McMahon Bill which provided for complete governmental monopoly over all plants and fissionable material and for stringent measures of secrecy, but under an all-civilian Atomic Energy Commission. By March, 1946, Truman backed the McMahon legislation, convinced himself, according to his memoirs, that the May-Johnson Bill opened the way to military control. [70] Thus he ordered Secretaries Patterson and Forrestal, who had been strong advocates of the so-called "War Department Bill," to support both the all-civilian commission and government monopoly positions embodied in McMahon.

The Senate adopted the bill in June, 1946, at the request of the Administration, authorizing the creation of the Atomic Energy Commission. Franz Schurmann sums up the outcome of this critical debate as follows:

> The real victors in this controversy were neither the nationalists nor the internationalists but a new breed of political men now called the national security bureaucracy. Atomic energy was not internationalized, nor was its power allowed to remain in the hands of the military. Full control was eventually assumed by the highest levels of the United States government symbolized by the creation of the Atomic Energy Commission (AEC) whose chain of command went directly to the White House. [71]

Moreover, Conant and Bush were still among the powerful despite their setback with May-Johnson. When Truman wanted a committee of civilians to thrash out the American position on atomic energy before the United Nations he appointed Acheson to chair a group which included Bush, Conant, Groves, and McCloy. [72] Finally, when it came time to choose the first chairman of the Atomic Energy Commission, Truman offered the post to Conant. He declined, but did agree to serve on the Atomic Energy Commission's General Advisory Committee, a position he held from January, 1947 to August, 1952, spanning the years he also served as chairman of the CPD.

Thus we find the Committee's leaders integrally linked to the foreign policy/national security establishment, either through its corporate or its technocratic stratum. Fully one-half of the CPD membership in fact had served in the Office of the Secretary of War under Stimson and Patterson, or the Office of Strategic Research and Development under the direction of Bush and Conant. But as early as 1940, in addition to these formal institutional ties, the nucleus of the CPD leadership had also worked together lobbying for the preferred internationalist course in foreign policy just as it would again a decade later.

Turning to the context in which the first such lobby was launched, the summer of 1940 saw the rapid deterioration of the allied position in the war in Europe. By this time the traditional isolationist stance had begun to weaken somewhat but as Millis put the matter, "To lose faith in isolation was one thing; to advocate intervention quite another, and most people looked for a stand in between." [73] However, a significant segment of national leaders favored intervention in no uncertain terms. One such contingent formed a Committee To Defend America By Aiding The Allies, the so-called William Allen White Committee which Dirksen had attacked in the Senate as a forerunner of the CPD. Indeed, among its members were a dozen luminaries who would emerge in the CPD in 1950. Included in this group were Clayton, Patterson, Robert Sherwood (a Roosevelt speechwriter who helped draft the opening statement of the CPD), Julius Ochs Adler of the *New York Times*, Clark Eichelberger (national director of the League of Nations Association), and the ubiquitous Conant. At about the same time another group called the Military Training Camps Association led by Grenville Clark and with much the same membership as the William Allen White Committee, played a major role in stimulating American rearmament and in securing passage of the Selective Service Act from a reluctant Congress. Two of its members were Stimson and Patterson. It was partially due to Clark's advice in fact that Roosevelt appointed Stimson and Patterson to their leadership positions in the War Department. Once the United States entered World War II shortly thereafter, it was Stimson, Patterson, Bush,

Conant, and their colleagues, who developed the policies and implemented the measures that carried the war to its victorious if ignominious
conclusion.

In the transition from world war to cold war, the corporate and
technocratic elites again joined together to win public support for the
latest fashion in internationalist foreign policy, blueprinted in the
European Recovery Program for Western Europe. The hope of this so-
called Marshall Plan was to build a monument to capitalism in Western
Europe that would be impregnable to Soviet penetration from without as
well as neutralist sentiment from within. The ambitious project was
unveiled at Harvard's commencement ceremonies in June, 1947. Conant
introduced Secretary of State Marshall, who outlined the program for
European recovery to the American public for the first time. Joseph
Jones, in his book on the creation of the Marshall Plan, writes of the unity
and unbridled enthusiasm that prevailed in the Truman cabinet at the
time, singling out Forrestal, Patterson, Harriman, Clayton, and Acheson
as particularly forceful advocates. [74]

If the Marshall Plan carried the wholehearted endorsement of the
Establishment it was less popular with the public and Congress. The
European Recovery Program was the centerpiece of a larger design for
the political as well as economic integration of the U.S. and Western
Europe. Not only was this costly in terms of the vast sums of direct aid
needed to build up European economies ripped apart by the ravages of
war, but it would also require a lowering of tariff barriers to provide
markets for European products once these economies had recovered their
productive capacities. The idea was not popular with either domestic
business or labor for obvious reasons. Neither was it particularly palatable to the general public which would receive little tangible benefit for
the investment of its tax dollars, nor to conservative Republicans
traditionally indifferent to the fate of Europe. Finally, such a plan would
require centralization and coordination at the executive level to a degree
that would further erode Congressional power in the foreign policy
arena.

The Marshall Plan was soon saddled with the epithet "internationalist," a code word to rally those who opposed aid to Europe, big
government, and international organization generally. They in turn began
to ply their ideological wares before a public already wary of anything so
costly as the Marshall Plan. In the face of such widespread opposition a
Committee For The Marshall Plan was formed, inspired by an article in
Foreign Affairs by retired Secretary of War Stimson, entitled "The
Challenge To Americans." [75] Subsequently, Stimson served as the
Committee's honorary chairman and Patterson headed its executive
committee and was its active spokesperson. Others on the Committee

who would later become founders of the CPD included the director of the Council On Foreign Relations Frank Altschul, William J. "Wild Bill" Donovan, wartime head of the Office of Strategic Services, and William J. Menninger, the noted psychiatrist who had been a consultant to the War Department during World War II. Also on the executive committee was anticommunist ideologue David Dubinsky, president of the International Ladies' Garment Workers Union, who though not a founder of the CPD became a member in the spring of 1951.

Still another blue-ribbon committee set up in support of the Marshall Plan was the President's Committee on Foreign Aid led by Harriman, who was Secretary of Commerce at the time. On the advisory board of this presidentially-appointed group were future CPD spokesmen Paul Hoffman, president of Studebaker Corporation and first administrative czar of the European Recovery Program, and University of California president Sproul. Both Committees were apparently well-orchestrated from the executive branch, with Lovett and Acheson given considerable credit for what Richard E. Neustadt called "one of the most effective instruments for public information seen since the Second World War." [76] Moreover, Nitze is acknowledged as having "provided much of the intellectual and organizing drive" that made the European Recovery Program a reality. [77] The selling point of the campaign was the urgency of blocking Soviet designs on Western Europe and by so doing frustrating their drive for world domination. Conservatives and isolationists were upset then, when only a few years later new and even more costly programs were proposed for Western Europe, again under the guise of a Soviet Threat, and once again sponsored — as evidenced in the composition of the CPD — by the internationalists of the foreign policy establishment.

Internationalism and Isolationism: A Reinterpretation

In this chapter the CPD has been located at the very center of the foreign policy establishment, an interlocking network whose policy orientation has been popularly termed internationalist or sometimes liberal internationalist. Its detractors were the right wing conservatives who, in the political vernacular of the time, were termed isolationists. Given the CPD's unequivocal promotion of NSC-68 we can trace the ascendance of militarism to those who are characterized as internationalist. Conversely, the antimilitarist stance in 1950 belonged to the conservative isolationists. While these political contours are accurate as broad brush strokes of the period, a richer understanding of the ideological forces that were locked in battle in The Great Debate requires further refinement.

A close reading of NSC-68 in the last chapter showed a foreign policy establishment in transition toward a new form of internationalism. Much of the credit for this transformation goes to Acheson, Nitze, and the small number of key Establishment figures who worked with them in shaping postwar containment policy. Nitze's career is instructive in tracing the doctrine's evolution: As earlier noted, he entered government from Wall Street, specializing at first in international trade and finance. Shortly thereafter, he was among the supporters of the Marshall Plan — which Acheson dubbed "the second instrument" of foreign policy after the failure of multilateralism. [78] Finally, by 1950, Nitze had come to settle — along with Acheson — on "the third instrument", i.e., military force, as the primary means of achieving national objectives in international politics.

While the vision of a Pax Americana constructed upon the foundation of militarism was accepted within the foreign policy establishment — with the notable exception of a few dissidents like George Kennan and Charles Bohlen who were soon drummed out of the club — as well as within presidential councils once Louis Johnson departed from the Administration, it was not so extensively held outside those rarified circles. The wider business community and the wider political community would still have to be persuaded of the wisdom of tripling military expenditures, bankrolling Europe's rearmament, and garrisoning American troops abroad to ensure the success of such an ambitious undertaking. Business leaders could be reached through the ordinary channels of communication that existed with the president, the foreign policy establishment, the corporate elite, and where necessary through extraordinary private briefings and seminars like the "Citizen's Council" of September, 1950.

As had been the case with governmental initiatives dating from the New Deal through the Marshall Plan, business was reluctant to endorse higher levels of government spending. But there was increasing common ground between international business and the foreign policy establishment. What they shared was the belief that Western Europe was the linchpin of a global order favorable to the expansion of profits as well as power. Thus the representatives of corporate capitalism clustered on the Eastern seaboard had little trouble grasping the logic of the new internationalism once it was explained to them by the "best and brightest" from their own ranks who had gone on to become national security managers — men like Acheson, McCloy, Lovett, and Nitze, who assured the corporate elite that the economy could not only accomodate the military Keynesian programs outlined in NSC-68 but could actually benefit from such spending.

Domestic manufacturers and smaller capitalists represented by the fiscally conservative National Association of Manufacturers, would not prove so easy to convince of the merits of huge military budgets. Moreover, with roots in the American heartland, their fervor for conservative politics was the equal of their conservative economic convictions. Containment Militarism was for them not only a policy of economic bankruptcy but was politically bankrupt as well since from their perspective, it was aimed at a profligate Europe that had already absorbed billions of dollars of aid under the Marshall Plan with dubious returns to its American donors. As such they were a natural and potent ally of the Republican right, prompting Leon Keyserling from his post as Chairman of the Council Of Economic Advisers to lament that the obstacles standing in the path of NSC-68's implementation were not economic but political. [79] Keyserling's fears were confirmed with the outbreak of The Great Debate in the winter of 1950-51.

Even though the pitched battle over American foreign policy was fought under the banners of *internationalism* and *isolationism*, these terms do not fully capture the dynamics of The Great Debate. Such polarity is more descriptive of the pre-World War II period than it is of postwar American politics. The terms have their origin in the Wilsonian free trade approach to the restoration of European, and thus international capitalist stability, at the end of World War I. Internationalism became synonymous with multilateralism from that time forward. But we saw how in the post-World War II period internationalism was transformed from the multilateralist hopes of the free traders to the bipolar and zero-sum world view of containment, then finally to the fully-formed Cold War doctrine of Containment Militarism. While this transformation was championed at each turn by the foreign policy establishment traditionally associated with "liberal internationalist" thinking, by 1950 their ideological stance had become rather illiberal and quite nationalistic judging from the line of argumentation advanced in NSC-68. Though it was still worldwide in ambition, containment had abandoned the internationalist dream of minimizing conflicts between national interests and warring ideologies through the power of trade and commerce. The new calculus relied instead on military force which only reinforced the geopolitical interests of nation-states and the influence of ideology in world affairs. Thus by 1948, certainly by 1950, it would seem more appropriate to speak of imperialism rather than internationalism to describe the expansionist ideology of the foreign policy elite.

Isolationism is also a misnomer for those who opposed containment. Just as the internationalist current was in a state of evolution in the period of transition between World War II and the Korean War, so too was the isolationist stance. As the overwhelming passage of Truman's Korean War appropriations showed, Republican conservatives were not averse to foreign involvement *per se*. What they objected to was the thrust of the Administration's policies which routed those funds to European rearmament. In this respect, the Korean War had a double-edged impact on Containment Militarism: On the one hand it provided the crisis by which Truman could break through the constraints of fiscal conservatism that stood in the way of implementing NSC-68. On the other however, the discovery that their affirmative vote on emergency war appropriations had set up a new conduit in which additional aid could be funnelled to Europe infuriated the conservatives in Congress. The Truman-Acheson foreign policy in fact appeared not only devious but almost treasonous given the actual war in progress in Korea. From their perspective, the failure to press for military victory was bad enough, but the fact that this failure occurred in Asia was an indication not of negligence but conspiracy.

The Republican right wing and its business supporters had, since the close of the American frontier in the 1890's, looked to Asia as the land of opportunity, the natural *Lebensraum* for American expansion — economic, political, and cultural — just as the Establishment viewed Europe as the key nexus of global power. It took a Japanese attack on Pearl Harbor to convince the right wing that the United States should become involved in World War II. After the war they opposed the Europe-oriented thrust of containment and what they saw as the other side of that policy — the abandonment of Asia. The Marshall Plan and "the loss of China" came to symbolize the Democratic era to the Republican right, frustrated even more because the Eastern wing of its own party had joined the Democrats in a bipartisan display of consensus.

The conservative right was moving haltingly toward an imperialism of its own, but oriented toward Asia not Europe. This is apparent from the statements issued by the spokesmen of the so-called isolationist current in the opening round of The Great Debate. Both ex-president Herbert Hoover and presidential hopeful Robert Taft called for rearmament, but of Asia not Europe. Hoover argued, "We should give Japan her independence and aid her in arms to defend herself. We should stiffen the defenses of our Pacific frontier in Formosa and the Philippines . . . American eyes should now be opened to these hordes in Asia." [80] Taft too called for basing a Pacific defense on Japan and Formosa (Taiwan) even as he attacked involvement in Europe. The Ohio senator argued for naval and air support to back Chiang Kai-shek's nationalist forces on Formosa, adding that he saw no reason why a state of war with Communist China should not be acknowledged, if only to "untie the hands" of MacArthur in the Far East. [81] Thus as the Truman Administration moved to increase American commitment to Europe in the winter of 1950-51, its opposition on the Republican right countered by embracing a policy of rollback to just that extent in Asia. In so doing, they moved further away from prewar isolationism toward imperialism with a right wing twist, an evolution that would be completed during the MacArthur controversy in the volatile spring of 1951.

Finally then, The Great Debate was no more between internationalism and isolationism than NSC-68 was an argument for a defense-minded containment over an aggressive policy of rollback. The gap between the protagonists was great indeed but the contours of the conflict were quite different than is popularly portrayed. America was already committed to an imperial course. The only question was the form this imperialism would take — economic or military in its principal means of achievement, Europe or Asia as its primary area of domination. Containment Militarism emerged triumphant from this debate not to be seriously challenged again until midway through another war, this one in Vietnam. The next chapter examines the process by which the hegemony of Containment Militarism was established, focussing on the role of the CPD in bringing about its legitimacy.

CHAPTER 2
The Politics Of Militarism

1. Letter to the President of the United States, Harry S. Truman, from the Council On Foreign Relations, December 12, 1950, p. 3, Tab M, Tracy S. Voorhees Papers, Alexander Library, Rutgers University.
2. "Record of the Meeting of the State-Defense Policy Review Group, March 16, 1950," U.S. Department of State, *Foreign Relations*, 1950, 1: 198.
3. Dean Acheson, *Present at the Creation: My Years In The State Department* (New York: Norton, 1969), 272.
4. According to Hammond's extensive account of the NSC-68 deliberations, "His (Nitze's) judgement of the ordering of Soviet objectives was identical with that of Acheson." Paul Y. Hammond, "NSC-68: Prologue To Rearmament," in Warner R. Schilling, Paul Y. Hammond, and Glen H. Snyder, *Strategy, Politics, And Defense Budgets* (New York: Columbia University Press, 1962), 309.
5. *Ibid.*, p. 324.
6. Letter to the President of the United States, Harry S. Truman, February 14, 1950, Voorhees Papers.
7. Harry S. Truman, *Memoirs: Years of Trial And Hope* (Garden City: Doubleday, 1956), II, 252.
8. Samuel P. Huntington, *The Common Defense* (New York: Columbia University Press, 1962), 318; Walter Millis, Harvey C. Mansfield, and Harold Stein, *Arms And The State: Civil-Military Elements In National Policy* (New York: Twentieth Century Fund, 1958), 339.
9. Huntington, p. 53.
10. *Ibid.*, p. 63.
11. Fred L. Block, *The Origins Of International Economic Disorder* (Berkeley: University of California Press, 1977), 108.
12. Hammond, p. 353.
13. Millis stresses that while Korea provided an initial impetus for a general rearmament program it was also true that "the NATO idea, abruptly reinvigorated at the end of June, was again languishing by the end of August." See Millis, Mansfield, and Stein, p. 337.
14. *New York Times*, December 13, 1950, p. 19.
15. *New York Times*, December 12, 1950, p. 1.
16. *New York Times*, December 13, 1950, p. 19.
17. *New York Times*, December 14, 1950, p. 26.
18. *New York Times*, December 16, 1950, p. 4.
19. Hammond, p. 356.
20. *New York Times*, December 31, 1950, p. 1.
21. Hammond, p. 357.
22. *New York Times*, December 20, 1950, p. 1.
23. *New York Times*, December 21, 1950, p. 1.
24. *New York Times*, January 6, 1951, p. 1.
25. *Ibid.*
26. *New York Times*, December 16, 1950, p. 1.

27. Tracy S. Voorhees, Memorandum to the members of the CPD, January 2, 1951, Tab P, Voorhees Papers.
28. *Ibid.*
29. James B. Conant, *My Several Lives* (New York: Harper & Row, 1970), 524.
30. The Committee in fact was seeking $150 thousand. CPD members had started the ball rolling with gifts or underwritings of $40 thousand. Will Clayton had been the most generous, accounting for $10 thousand of this total. (Contributions and Underwritings From Members of Committee, September 1, 1951) As the Finance Committee chaired by Robert Patterson explained: "The balance of the necessary $150 thousand Fund is being sought by appeal to relatively few persons at private meetings now being scheduled for four or five cities throughout the country." (Financial Needs Of The Committee on the Present Danger, February, 1951) Subsequently with the aid of a consulting firm the Committee did manage to raise over $100 thousand. Of the "private meetings," i.e., fund-raising dinners, the one held in Patterson's honor netted the largest total, $14 thousand. (Contributions, September 1, 1951) Tab YY, Voorhees Papers.
31. *Washington Times-Herald,* February 8, 1951.
32. *Washington Times-Herald,* February 13, 1951.
33. *The Congressional Record,* February 8, 1951, p. A668.
34. *The Congressional Record,* April 4, 1951, p. 3271.
35. Conant, pp. 508-509.
36. *Ibid.,* p. 509.
37. *Ibid.*
38. *Ibid.,* p. 521.
39. *Ibid.,* pp. 521-522.
40. *Ibid.,* p. 509.
41. Tracy S. Voorhees, Notes of Talk with Robert Bowie, September 8, 1950, Tab D, Voorhees Papers.
42. Tracy S. Voorhees, Memorandum #2, John J. McCloy, September 11, 1950, Tab D, Voorhees Papers.
43. Conant, p. 522.
44. Confidential Minutes Of The Meeting Of The Citizen's Conference, Harry Bullis, September 28, 1950, Tab L, Voorhees Papers.
45. *Ibid.,* p. 1.
46. *Ibid.,* pp. 1-2.
47. *Ibid.,* p. 2.
48. Conant, p. 335.
49. *Ibid.,* p. 510.
50. Letter to Will Clayton from James B. Conant, October 9, 1950, Tab E, Voorhees Papers.
51. Letter to Secretary of Defense George C. Marshall from the CPD, October 24, 1950, Tab F, Voorhees Papers.
52. Conant, p. 511.
53. "Memorandum Of Conversation, by the Director Of The State Department Policy Planning Staff (Nitze), Meeting, October 9, 1950," U.S. Department of State, *Foreign Relations*, 1950, 3: 364-366.
54. Tracy S. Voorhees, "The Committee on the Present Danger, 1950-1953,"

Voorhees Papers, 1968, p. 16.

55.   Memorandum from Tracy S. Voorhees to the CPD membership, October 11, 1950, p. 3, Tab F, Voorhees Papers.

56.   On the formation of CPD-II, see Chapter 5.

57.   Notes Of Meeting With Defense Department Officials, Tracy S. Voorhees, December 1, 1950, p. 3, Tab F, Voorhees Papers.

58.   Minutes Of Meeting Of Decembr 3, Tracy S. Voorhees, December 5, 1950, p. 4, Tab I, Voorhees Papers.

59.   Letter To The President Of The United States, Harry S. Truman, from The Council On Foreign Relations, December 12, 1950, p. 1, Tab M, Voorhees Papers.

60.   Richard J. Barnet, *Roots Of War: The Men And The Institutions Behind U.S. Foreign Policy* (Baltimore: Penguin, 1971), 53.

61.   Samuel P. Huntington, *The Soldier And The State* (Cambridge: Belknap, 1957), 271-272.

62.   Joseph Kraft, *Profiles In Power* (New American Library, 1966), 67.

63.   Barnet, p. 54.

64.   Conant, p. 236.

65.   *Ibid.,* p. 273.

66.   R.G. Hewlett and O.E. Anderson, Jr., *The New World, 1939-46* (University Park: Pennsylvania State University Press, 1962), 284.

67.   *Ibid.,* pp. 358-360; Barnet, p. 17; Gar Alperowitz, *Atomic Diplomacy: Hiroshima And Potsdam* (New York: Vintage, 1967), 115.

68.   Conant, p. 496.

69.   *Ibid.*

70.   *Ibid.,* pp. 495-496.

71.   Franz Schurmann, *The Logic Of World Power* (New York: Pantheon, 1974), 91.

72.   Conant, p. 491.

73.   Millis, Mansfield, and Stein, p. 36.

74.   Joseph M. Jones, *The Fifteen Weeks* (New York: Harcourt, Brace and World, 1964), 118.

75.   Henry L. Stimson, "The Challenge To Americans," *Foreign Affairs* 26: 5-14, October, 1947.

76.   Richard E. Neustadt, *Presidential Power: The Politics Of Leadership* (New York: Wiley, 1960), 48.

77.   Harry Bayard Price, *The Marshall Plan And Its Meaning* (Ithaca: Cornell University Press, 1955), 42.

78.   Acheson Speech, April 18, 1947, Box 1, Joseph M. Jones Papers, Harry S. Truman Library, cited in Daniel Yergin, *Shattered Peace: The Origins Of The Cold War And The National Security State* (Boston: Houghton Mifflin, 1977), 308.

79.   Memorandum by Hamilton Q. Dearborn of the Council Of Economic Advisers to the Executive Secretary of the National Security Council (James Lay), Approved: Leon H. Keyserling, Chairman, CEA, May 8, 1950, U.S. Department of State, *Foreign Relations,* 1950, 1: 311.

80.   *New York Times,* December 21, 1951, p. 22.

81.   *New York Times,* January 6, 1951, p. 4.

Chapter 3

SHAPING THE COLD WAR CONSENSUS:
Elite Conflict And Mass Legitimation

Dr Conant is engaged in writing his Memoirs . . . One of his purposes, as I understand it, is to use the Committee on the Present Danger as an illustration of a technique of democracy developed in America in time of crisis, which apparently does not exist in other countries.

Tracy S. Voorhees, co-founder,
Committee on the Present Danger, April, 1968 [1]

There is little to suggest that public support for the Cold War was on the wane at the time of the CPD's formation. The preoccupation with internal subversion, exemplified by the trial of Alger Hiss, the sensational charges surrounding the arrest of Julius and Ethel Rosenberg, and the forays by Senator McCarthy into government, had combined with international events to create a crisis atmosphere of considerable intensity. Indeed, in the context of the time, the Committee's campaign appears superfluous at best, incendiary at worst, in its potential to affect the national mood.

The CPD's apparent willingness to court hysteria remains a mystery until we recognize the gravity of elite conflict. *Appointed elites* like Kennan and Bohlen, whose power lay in the State bureaucracy, might be bludgeoned into submission rather quickly once the tide had turned within Establishment circles. But the *elected elites*, whose base of power extended beyond the boundaries of the executive into the party system and the arena of mass politics, would not be so easily subdued. The much-heralded bipartisan consensus backing the policy of containment, fragile from its inception, was thoroughly shattered by the international and domestic shocks of 1949 and 1950. In the restive climate that followed, the Republican right wing became convinced that the time was ripe to go to the public with its own remedies for the crisis at hand, a strategy moreover which if successful could gain them the White House — a prize which had eluded the GOP for nearly two decades.

Opposition from the Republican leadership presented a grave danger to the commitment of men, money, and materiel needed to put NSC-68 into practice. In the absence of bipartisan consensus on Containment Militarism there was no guarantee that the public would make the extraordinary sacrifices to support a 300 to 400 percent increase in military spending, affirm a system of universal military service, and consent to the permanent stationing of troops in Europe. To make matters worse, any attempt to cut off the Republican elite from a popular mass base would prove to be no simple matter in the political climate of 1950. On the contrary, charges by the conservative right wing that the Truman Administration was capitulating to communism in Asia, throwing good money after bad in Europe, and bankrupting the United States in the process fell on a receptive audience after twenty years of deficit spending to alleviate the Great Depression, finance World War II, and establish the postwar Pax Americana. Taxes were already consuming one-third of the national income yet the new international order remained precarious. The British philosopher Bertrand Russell remarked of the period, "Average Americans were oppressed by two fears, fear of Communism and fear of the income tax." [2] The Truman Administration was in the disadvantaged position of having to sell to an increasingly skeptical public the trade-off of one fear for another. The conservative opposition, in contrast, could exploit both arguing that government spending and communism went hand in hand. Thus while the proponents of NSC-68 had presidential authority on their side, the actual power to translate policy into practice was severely hampered by the constraints of domestic politics.

Enter the prestigious, bipartisan, and Republican-dominated CPD in keeping with the advice of Robert Lovett who cautioned during the NSC-68 review that his proposed propaganda machine "not be tarred with the Administration's brush in the eyes of the people." [3] In its more than two years of existence the Committee engaged in four major battles; two involved broad questions of policy legitimation and two concerned the implementation of policy. Conflict over the fundamental purpose and

THE COMMITTEE ON THE PRESENT DANGER
JAMES B. CONANT, Chairman
TRACY S. VOORHEES, Vice-Chairman

*JULIUS OCHS ADLER
New York, N.Y.

*RAYMOND B. ALLEN
President, University of Michigan

*FRANK ALTSCHUL
New York, N.Y.

DILLON ANDERSON
Houston, Texas

*WILLIAM DOUGLAS ARANT
Birmingham, Alabama

*JAMES PHINNEY BAXTER, III
President, Williams College

*LAIRD BELL
Chicago, Ill.

BARRY BINGHAM
Louisville, Kentucky

*HARRY A. BULLIS
Minneapolis, Minn.

*VANNEVAR BUSH
President, Carnegie Institution
of Washington

*WILLIAM L. CLAYTON
Houston, Texas

*ROBERT CUTLER
Boston, Mass.

*R. AMMI CUTTER
Boston, Mass.

MRS. DWIGHT DAVIS
Washington, D.C.

E.L. DeGOLYER
Dallas, Texas

*HAROLD WILLIS DODDS
President, Princeton University

*CHARLES DOLLARD
President, Carnegie Corporation
of New York

*WILLIAM J. DONOVAN
New York, N.Y.

GOLDTHWAITE H. DORR
New York, N.Y.

DAVID DUBINSKY
New York, N.Y.

LEONARD K. FIRESTONE
Los Angeles, Cal.

*TRUMAN K. GIBSON, JR.
Chicago, Ill.

*MISS META GLASS
Charlottesville, Virginia

ARTHUR J. GOLDBERG
Washington, D.C.

SAMUEL GOLDWYN
Los Angeles, Cal.

W.W. GRANT
Denver, Colorado

*EDWARD S. GREENBAUM
New York, N.Y.

PAUL G. HOFFMAN
Pasadena, Cal.

*MONTE H. LEMANN
New Orleans, La.

*WILLIAM L. MARBURY
Baltimore, Md.

STANLEY MARCUS
Dallas, Texas

*DR. WILLIAM C. MENNINGER
Topeka, Kansas

*FREDERICK A. MIDDLEBUSH
President, University of Missouri

JAMES L. MORRILL
President, University of Minnesota

EDWARD R. MURROW
New York, N.Y.

*JOHN LORD O'BRIAN
Washington, D.C.

FLOYD B. ODLUM
Indio, Cal.

J. ROBERT OPPENHEIMER
Princeton, New Jersey

*ROBERT P. PATTERSON
New York, N.Y.

*HOWARD C. PETERSEN
Philadelphia, Pa.

DANIEL A. POLING
Philadelphia, Pa.

*STANLEY RESOR
New York, N.Y.

SAMUEL I. ROSENMAN
New York, N.Y.

*THEODORE W. SCHULTZ
Chicago, Ill.

*ROBERT E. SHERWOOD
New York, N.Y.

EDGAR W. SMITH
Portland, Oregon

*ROBERT G. SPROUL
President, University of California

*ROBERT L. STEARNS
President, University of Colorado

EDMUND A. WALSH, S.J.
Vice-President, Georgetown University

W.W. WAYMACK
Des Moines, Iowa

*HENRY M. WRISTON
President, Brown University

J.D. ZELLERBACH
San Francisco, Cal.

*Member of the Executive Committee

direction of America's foreign policy dominated The Great Debate of 1951 — first, troops to Europe which was essentially fought under the banners of internationalism vs. isolationism, and second, the MacArthur controversy couched as an Asia-first vs. Europe-first imbroglio.

It was recognized early that the acceptance of these broad issues of principle would be for naught if the means were not available to put them into practice. Bearing this in mind, the CPD simultaneously lobbied for the measures that would be needed to make NSC-68 strategy a reality, essentially an expanded system of conscription to provide the men and an increased program of foreign aid to provide the money. Finally the question of who would succeed Truman was a matter of concern since if the will to pursue the Cold War according to the NSC-68 blueprint was lacking in the nation's leadership, then neither the architecture nor the machinery much mattered. Accordingly, the CPD's attempt to build a consensus on the fundamental thrust of foreign and military policy and to see that measures were adopted to carry out the policy, were followed by efforts to establish a basis for continuity in executing Containment Militarism once the presidency changed hands in 1952. An account of the CPD's activities in each of these areas is the subject of this chapter.

The Great Debate

The floor of Congress provided the battleground for The Great Debate. The issues around which it revolved were the permanent garrison of United States troops in Europe, its corollary — universal military service, and the continuation of aid to Europe. But just as the debate spilled well beyond the chambers of the Senate and House, so too "troops to Europe," universal military service, and foreign aid came to symbolize much more in the volatile political climate of the time, resulting in a full-scale review of U.S. foreign and military policy.

The year 1951 was critical if the measures outlined in NSC-68 were to be successfully launched. Not only was a troop commitment a matter of urgency to reassure Europe that it would not be abandoned if it embarked on a program of militarization, but the Selective Service Act was scheduled to expire in June and the Marshall Plan by the end of the year. By making these issues his legislative priorities for fiscal year 1952, as expressed in the state of the union message, Truman had firmly committed his Administration to Containment Militarism. [4]

The approval of such measures was contingent upon a demonstrable threat. Spelling out the nature of this threat in his address, Truman charged that "the aggression in Korea is part of the Russian Communist dictatorship to take over the world, step by step." Maneuvering the crisis toward his Administration's policies, he went on to argue that if Western Europe were to fall to Soviet Russia, it would double the Soviet supply of coal and triple the Soviet supply of steel. Thus the Soviets could achieve their objectives, Truman warned, by isolating the United States from Europe. [5] To stave off such a catastrophe, he went on to introduce the quintessential theme of Containment Militarism saying, "We shall need to continue some economic aid to European countries. This aid should now be specifically related to the building of their defenses." [6]

The CPD had made the same points the day before — between Eisenhower's departure for Europe and Truman's state of the union address. The Committee took the propitious occasion to warn the public that Europe is "the next prize Russia seeks" and that this would mean the "absorption of 200,000,000 people, many of them highly industrialized, into the Communist empire against us." Moreover, the CPD asserted, America "had learned belatedly in World Wars I and II, that successful defense of the United States must be made in Europe." [7]

Within an hour of Truman's opening message to the 82nd Congress, Republican conservatives objected to the dispatch of troops to Europe, challenging Truman's legal prerogative for such an action. Senator Kenneth S. Wherry of Nebraska, the Republican floor leader, introduced a resolution in the Senate barring the plan without the expressed consent of the Senate. What Wherry and the generation of Senators who succeeded him were to discover was that foreign policy was fast becoming the exclusive preserve of the national security elite. But in January 1951, this commonplace of the Cold War years was still judged to be a dangerous and unacceptable precedent. Representative Quentin Burdick, a North Dakota Republican, directed a volley at Truman a few days later in support of Wherry's resolution saying:

> The threat of the President to send men to Europe regardless of what Congress thinks, and thereby involve us in war, has about convinced me that the only reason the President wants to draft 18 year old boys is that he intends to use them in Europe regardless of what Congress or any other body thinks.[8]

Given such virulent feeling, it became clear that if NSC-68's measures for the remilitarization of Europe were to be adopted by Congress then, in addition to legislative lobbying, a campaign directed toward the public was essential. A retrospect of where the Committee stood as of May, 1951, explained:

> With the wide appeal of the isolationist philosophy in various forms which took such a hold on the country about January

1st, and with the appointment of General Eisenhower to the command in Europe, it became apparent that education and support of General Eisenhower's mission had to be carried to the public. [9]

This would mean, as an earlier memo had tentatively proposed, "being more explicit with the American people as to the plans for defending Europe." [10] In other words, the Committee's concern was how, and to what extent, to go public with NSC-68. The idea was to squeeze the isolationist diehards between the Administration and a popular groundswell. If successful this strategy would isolate the isolationists from their crucial base of support in mass opinion. Advertising executive Stanley Resor urged that the best means to reach the public was through a nationwide radio broadcast. Subsequently an arrangement was made with NBC for an evening prime time address by Conant once Eisenhower returned from his "fact-finding" mission.

Not surprisingly the General came back proclaiming, "On every side I saw heartening evidence of a regeneration in Europe's spirit." He then proceeded to request that military equipment be immediately sent to Europe, that Congress not place limits on the dispatch of troops to Europe as Wherry had proposed, and finally that no fixed ratio of United States to European troops be established (another obstacle under consideration by the Taft-led Republicans). [11] "Europe's morale, its will to fight, will grow with every accretion to physical strength," the General predicted. His advice to the nation's youth facing the prospects of an expanded system of conscription: "Pursue your schooling until Congress tells you what to do, and then do it with a grin on your face." [12]

The costs alone would make the program difficult to sell to Congress and the public. This was only compounded by the unpopular shift in power toward the executive branch. Only an extraordinary atmosphere of crisis and a credible external threat could justify such a departure from the traditional distrust of centralized power and excessive government spending. Accordingly, in his February 7 address, Conant hammered away at the Soviet Union and its insatiable appetite for expansion as reason enough why the American people should rid themselves of doubt about the course ahead. Citing the litany of Cold War themes Truman had made familiar in his state of the union address, the CPD chairman argued "the United States is in danger. The danger is clearly of a military nature . . . we must take immediate steps to meet the national danger. We urge all citizens to impress upon the Congress and the Administration the imperative need for prompt and adequate action. We have no time to lose." [13] Then the Harvard President took the occasion to pursue his favorite theme — universal military service. As he explained his strategy:

> Continuing to wrap General Eisenhower's mantle around me,
> I asked what we must do at home and gave the General's
> answer: "We have to devise a scheme that we can support if
> necessary over the next twenty years or thirty years, whatever
> may be the time necessary as long as the threat, the announced
> threat of aggression remains in the world." The conclusion
> was the need for a system of universal military service, for
> which I argued at some length. [14]

The exploitation of Eisenhower's reputation was one of the things
that infuriated Everett Dirksen and provoked his attack on the CPD and
the Administration's projected European remilitarization. In registering
his complaint before his colleagues in the Senate, Dirksen said:

> One other reason why I propose to vote against the resolution
> (troops in Europe) is that it becomes something of a smoke-
> screen. We have heard General Eisenhower's name men-
> tioned here a great many times. Why do not those who
> mention his name also mention Truman's name?

Never one to shy away from controversy, the senator from Illinois
added:

> I think it is a shame to make General Eisenhower — a great
> general, with a great record — the instrument and the vehicle
> and the spearhead, when the power for this proposal lodges in
> the Commander-in-Chief. [15]

Shortly after Conant's nationwide radio address the Senate decided
to hold open hearings on the issue of sending troops to Europe under the
joint sponsorship of the Senate Foreign Relations and Armed Services
Committees. The move was led by Taft and Wherry and supported by ex-
President Hoover, who urged Congress to "regain its constitutional
authority." [16] Just before the hearings opened, two of the most prominent
Europe-oriented foreign policy strategists spoke out on the issue. Averell
Harriman, itinerant establishment journeyman serving at the time as
special adviser to the President on foreign policy, attacked what he
termed the "isolationist position," arguing that the Soviet Union was
engaged in a "fanatical mission" that "can only be met by a global
strategy" centered in Washington.[17] Will Clayton complemented
Harriman's attack by taking the positive side of the issue and calling for a
"pooling of all defense resources to build an Atlantic army capable of
resisting Communist aggression in Western Europe." [18]

On the opening day of the hearings, Secretary Marshall testified for the Administration, revealing that the Joint Chiefs recommended, and the President had approved, a policy "which looks to the maintenance by us in Europe of approximately six divisions." [19] If agreed upon by Congress, four more divisions would be sent to supplement the two already there, bringing the number of U.S. troops on duty in Europe to 200,000. In his remarks, Marshall spoke out against any sort of Congressional limitation, indicating that the plan had already been set in motion some five months before. The Joint Chiefs followed Marshall and indeed, as the Secretary had stated, they gave their wholehearted endorsement to the troops-to-Europe measure. [20] While this represented a serious blow to the Republican right's effort to block Truman's Europe-oriented strategy, it certainly did not stop it. Taft's retort to the Joint Chiefs' testimony was, "I do not accept the JCS as experts . . . I suggest that the JCS are absolutely under the control of the Administration."[21]

On February 27, Hoover came to testify before the combined Committees stoking the fires of the increasingly acrimonious debate with his warning that sending "troops to Europe was likely to lead to a hopeless land war with Russia and the massacre of American boys." [22] Hoover's timing couldn't have been better, or more ill-timed from the CPD's perspective. That very day the Senate opened debate on the universal military service bill that would draft 18 year-olds into the service. Hoping to weld the two issues indissolubly together, Wherry proposed that action on the pending manpower bill be delayed until the Senate decided whether to permit the Administration to send troops to Europe. This latest move threatened to bring universal military service to a grinding halt in spite of heavy Administration and CPD lobbying.

The universal military service bill, which the CPD had been instrumental in shaping as Pentagon consultants, was placed under consideration by both the House and Senate in January. Secretary of Defense Marshall and Assistant Secretary Anna Rosenberg introduced the proposed legislation and testified at length in its favor. On January 30, Voorhees went before the Senate Armed Services Committee in support of the Defense proposal. Following Voorhees, other CPD members who testified on various aspects of universal military service included Bush, psychiatrist Menninger, college presidents Dodds and Baxter, and editor Adler of the *New York Times*. Yet despite this onslaught, Conant reported that "Congressional deliberation on universal military service was slow and discouraging." [23] Wherry's proposal paved the way for still further procrastination.

At this point the CPD decided to step up its own offensive by institutionalizing the Conant-style national radio broadcast in the form of a weekly series. The broadcasts would be aired on Sunday evenings

over the Mutual Broadcasting System, which had 550 affiliates throughout the country. The first of these addresses was presented March 4,
1951, by Vannevar Bush. The points he made were lifted right from
NSC-68. The renowned nuclear scientist said that while the atomic bomb
had been a sufficient deterrent in the past, the U.S. could no longer count
on strategic bombing as the only means of "inhibiting Soviet aggression."
Only a combination of ground forces and continued development of
atomic weapons could avert the Russian advance. This in turn called for a
commitment of U.S. troops to Europe to see the proposed remilitarization through. Finally he asserted, universal military service was the
vehicle that would allow the U.S. to fulfill its commitment.

If the purpose of Bush's address was to explain the logic of NSC-68
to the public in order to win support for Administration policy, he also
revealed other heretofore guarded secrets of Containment Militarism as
well. In terms of the doctrine's fundamental purpose, Bush said that the
goal of American policy was to maintain "the military stalemate" which
he then went on to define not in terms of balance or parity between the
United States and the Soviet Union but instead as a situation that was
possible "only by *U.S. superiority*." (emphasis added)[24] Bush's remarks
represented, in effect, the first in a series of addresses by the CPD to
condition the public to the world view of the national security elite and
ultimately to accept the new global order they were in the process of
creating.

The second address in the series was given by former Secretary of
War Robert Patterson, who warned against further delay in implementing
the Administration's proposals. Patterson's effort provides an excellent
illustration of the coordination between the CPD and the Administration.
The *New York Times* had reported a few days earlier that the Administration was exerting strong pressure "in the name of Eisenhower"
for quick approval of troops to Europe.[25] The weight of Patterson's
prestige in fact was only one shot of a high-level volley that included
General Collins of the Joint Chiefs of Staff who warned that vacillation
by the Congress might "paralyze Ike's efforts to build NATO." Finally
Senator Tom Connally, the Administration's chief foreign policy spokesman in the Senate, charged that any further legislative delay would be "at
our mortal peril."[26] Patterson himself attacked "isolationism" and
advocated "full and speedy development of military aid abroad" as "the
surest guarantee against Communism."[27] Moreover, he argued, Containment Militarism was the best way of safeguarding the "manganese the
steel industry needs" as well as blocking the Russian takeover of oil in the
Middle East and uranium in Africa. In conclusion Patterson insisted that
the question of deployment of troops abroad should be left to military
men, i.e., policy is a matter for the executive branch and not the business

of Congress.

The third broadcast of the series was given over to another prestigious member of the CPD, Major General William J. Donovan (ret.), wartime director of the Office of Strategic Services (OSS). Like Bush's ingenuous remarks concerning military superiority, Donovan revealed still another integral aspect of America's fully-formed Cold War doctrine: subversion by means of covert operations. Donovan argued that while the United States continues to build up armaments it must also "develop countermeasures that would prevent the loss of strategic areas." As an example of his proposed strategy, Donovan cited Iran where he said the decision to nationalize the Anglo-Iranian Oil Company was a direct result of "Soviet maneuvers in the economic and political life of that country." Iran would soon become the recipient of Donovan's strategy in the form of the CIA-sponsored coup against the reformist government of Mohammed Mossadeq and his replacement by Shah Mohammed Reza Pahlavi, who ruled with the help of American backing until the dramatic upheaval in 1979. But this was still two years away and the machinery for such a policy was not yet firmly in place. To remedy that deficiency, Donovan called for "all-out employment of the nation's economic, political, and psychological weapons to regain initiative in the Cold War." In fact, he argued, in the peculiar logic of the cold warrior elite, the only way to prevent war was to "put aside our own fears and create fear in the mind of the enemy." If that weren't bizarre enough, what Donovan had in mind was that such efforts should reach inside the Soviet Union:

> Stalin might be deterred by the fear that he cannot determine
> in advance the loyalty of his own people. For no dictator dare
> move if uncertain of his safety at home. Our greatest ally
> therefore can be the Russian people. [28]

Like Bush's willingness to go to the nuclear brink to achieve political goals, the former OSS chief's advocacy of internal subversion within foreign nations was more akin to an aggressive policy of rollback than to the supposedly defensive strategy of containment. And again, like Bush's argument, Donovan's clandestine strategy was also found among the recommendations of NSC-68. In reference to such illegal activities, Lovett, acting in his capacity as consultant to the NSC-68 follow-up group, had argued that "the efforts of a 'Department of Dirty Tricks' should be commensurate with that of all other agencies."

The CPD's weekly radio broadcasts continued for three months. Voorhees writes that these nationwide addresses "had the greatest impact of any part of the CPD's work" and added that "much of this was due to the large press coverage of the radio addresses." [30] In addition to the favorable newspaper attention, the Committee also printed the addresses in pamphlet form for wider distribution. Still other CPD efforts to reach a mass audience with their message included a General Electric-sponsored film "Modern Arms And Free Men," from the book of the same name by Vannevar Bush, and a cartoon-captioned rendition of Containment Militarism entitled, "The Danger Of Hiding Our Heads."[31] The Committee distributed 100,000 copies of this booklet directly while various other organizations reprinted it for still wider dissemination. Voorhees' assessment of this medium was that it very much complemented the impact of the radio series: "It proved to be one of the most effective steps of the CPD in arousing the country to its danger," claimed the CPD vice-chairman. [32]

By the first of April, with the troops to Europe vote ready to go to the floor of the Senate, the CPD issued a statement to the press which called for a renewed spirit of national urgency and unity between the President and Congress on the troops issue. In its widely-disseminated remarks the Committee warned the Senate not to place restrictions on presidential power "which might tend to cast any uncertainty or cloud upon the power of the Commander-in-Chief to take instant action wherever necessary, as emergencies may arise," dismissing the constitutional issue raised by Taft and his colleagues as a "red herring" that could only impede an adequate mutual defense by the United States and Europe. [33]

In the end, as with the Marshall Plan two years before, the objections of the conservatives were surmounted and the Senate voted its approval of troops to Europe on April 4, thus endorsing the latest fashion in Cold War thinking. It was a monumental precedent, committing four divisions of approximately 100,000 men to Europe as well as providing the president with nearly unbridled power in foreign and military affairs. Like so many other decisions of the period, this one would go unchecked until the Vietnam debacle, when finally even some within the foreign policy establishment were forced to condemn the accretion of presidential powers. But in the spring of 1951, concern over executive prerogative was overcome in the face of the crisis in Europe.

Reminiscing on the role of the CPD in The Great Debate, Conant wrote, "I have always cherished the thought that the Committee On The Present Danger by its statements and the broadcasts of several members played an important part in shaping public opinion on this issue." [34] Given the prestigious makeup of its membership and the publicity it gained when it went before Congress and nationwide audiences with its call to arms, the CPD chairman's assessment seems unduly modest in its evaluation of the Committee's impact on the political climate of the time.

But then what of Huntington's thesis on the final outcome of The Great Debate? He argues,

> ... the absence of serious division within the Administration ... forced the critics to define the issue as one of Congress vs. the President . . . No responsible executive official espoused an alternative to the Administration's plan. In the absence of this precondition for public discussion of strategic issues, the Great Debate fizzled. [35]

While conflict among bureaucratic elites within the Administration would certainly have enhanced the case of the conservative Republican challenge to NSC-68, the absence of such debate did not prevent its eruption. Moreover, the manner in which The Great Debate took form — Congress vs. the President — did nothing to lessen its intensity. On the contrary, the issue of growing presidential power was, as we have seen, a very sensitive issue in this period. Finally, while Huntington is quite correct in his claim that *strategic* questions were obscured in public discussion, it does not follow that the conflict was muted as a result. Rather, their rapid escalation into *ideological* issues only served, in the partisan climate of 1950 and 1951, to fuel the fires of the debate rather than causing it to fizzle as Huntington puts it.

It would be more accurate to describe The Great Debate as having been extinguished. The CPD played a critical role — perhaps *the* critical role — in this process. The Committee's efforts severely undercut the popular base of support which the isolationists in Congress desperately needed if they were to mount a successful challenge to the Administration in the field of foreign policy. Thus, just as NSC-68 had bludgeoned the "mass mind" of the national security elite as Acheson so felicitously put it, so the CPD bludgeoned the aspirations of the conservative political elite through its scare campaign to the mass public.

Expressing Establishment opinion on the tide of events, James Reston wrote a laudatory editorial praising the outcome of the Senate vote. The *New York Times* columnist stated that when the Senate ratified the North Atlantic Treaty two years before, it "broke its isolationist tradition." Sending troops to a permanent station in Europe was merely consistent with this earlier commitment. While the effect of The Great Debate had been "bad psychologically" in Reston's opinion, because it suggested that the U.S. might limit its sacrifices and contributions, in the end he argued "the big message to Europe . . . is that the Yanks are coming." [36] While this was indeed a critical victory, giving legitimacy to Containment Militarism as outlined in NSC-68, proposed by the Administration, and publicized by the CPD, celebration was still a bit premature. If "the Yanks" were coming there was still the matter of how to wrench them away from their homes, jobs, and schools, in sufficient numbers to back the expanded containment policy. There was also the matter of how to continue economic aid to Europe once the Marshall Plan was terminated at the end of the year. In other words, if NSC-68 had been accepted in principle, it was still a long way from implementation.

Approval of the measures designed to implement NSC-68 — universal military service and integrated foreign aid — were unexpectedly upstaged by a more immediate problem that threatened the principle itself. Its contours were visible barely two days after the final Senate tally when the *New York Times* reported that the Administration was becoming increasingly irritated with General Douglas MacArthur's public demand that the emphasis of U.S. policy be shifted from Europe to Asia. [37] Soon thereafter MacArthur was relieved of his command, sending shockwaves throughout the nation and touching off a fresh debate over foreign and military policy only a few days after the "troops to Europe" resolution. In the following section we will look at the CPD's role in protecting the fragile legitimacy of the Europe-oriented program of militarization in the midst of the MacArthur controversy, even how the Committee sought to use the maelstrom of events around MacArthur's firing to promote their cause.

The MacArthur Controversy: The CPD Reacts To The Threat To NSC-68

The pursuit of rollback in Asia as advocated by General MacArthur simultaneous with Containment Militarism in Europe — Eisenhower's "great mission" as the CPD referred to it — was an impossibility in the spring of 1951. MacArthur himself emphasized the either/or proposition in an April letter to Representative Joseph W. Martin, the House minority leader from Massachusetts. The General's letter to Martin openly urged the use of the 800,000 strong nationalist Chinese force to open a second front against Communist China, which had entered the war in Korea some five months before. Martin read MacArthur's missive on the floor of the House on April 5, the very day the Senate was approving the Administration's "troops to Europe" package. The statement struck at the heart of the Administration's policy, which after three and one-half months of debate was just gaining acceptance from the upper house. The General argued that the fate of Europe would be decided in the war against communism in Asia. MacArthur charged, "The communist conspirators have elected to make their play for global conquest in Asia — here we fight Europe's war with arms while the diplomats there still fight with words." Finally the letter read, "if the war in the Far East is lost then the fall of Europe is 'inevitable'." [38]

For Truman, MacArthur's letter was the last straw in a situation that had been festering since the General's August pilgrimage to Chiang Kai-shek on the island of Formosa (Taiwan) and his defiant speech the same month to a Veterans of Foreign Wars convention in which he called for U.S. occupation of Formosa and partnership with the Chinese nationalists. It was a confrontation the Administration would have preferred to avoid. Truman's preference in Korea was the quick victory that seemed within grasp in October, before MacArthur's fall offensive that brought the Chinese Communists into the war. This would have gone a long way toward defusing the right wing attacks charging his Administration with appeasement in Asia. [39] There were limits, however, to how far the Administration would go in pursuit of MacArthur's victory strategy. The General's speech before the Veterans of Foreign Wars had been particularly disturbing to the Europeans, who feared that his remarks signalled an imminent shift in policy toward a more aggressive stance in Asia, one moreover about which they had not been consulted and which was likely to be detrimental to their interests. The war after all was a United Nations action, which many members of the body were already reluctant to support. The use of nationalist troops in Korea as MacArthur proposed would have committed the U.N. to de facto support of Chiang Kai-shek's Kuomintang regime at a time when the question of Chinese membership in the international forum was still under debate. Britain had in fact already recognized the Peoples' Republic and backed their membership in the U.N. Thus the adoption of MacArthur's preferred strategy was sure to alienate the allies. [40] Finally, the cost of prosecuting such an effort would upset the Administration's carefully nurtured plans for European remilitarization. Therefore once MacArthur forced the issue into an Asia-first vs. Europe-first battle, Truman had little choice but to relieve him of his command.

The President announced his decision on April 11. The response to MacArthur's dismissal was immediate and predictable. The following day both Taft and Wherry made radio addresses attacking the Administration and impugning Truman's character and integrity. Taft called for "victory over appeasement" in Korea, arguing that the choice "is Acheson vs. MacArthur . . . There can be no unity in this country . . . until Mr. Acheson has been removed by President Truman and an atmosphere of 'sympathy' for communism has been ended in the State Department."[41] On the floor of the Senate itself, Senator William Jenner charged:

> . . . this country today is in the hands of a secret inner coterie
> which is directed by agents of the Soviet Union. We must cut

this whole cancerous conspiracy out of our Government at once. Our only choice is to impeach President Truman and find out who is the secret invisible government which has so cleverly led our country down the road to destruction. [42]

Such stridency was greeted with applause from the public galleries. Senator Richard M. Nixon of California went on to propose — in one of history's ironies — that the Senate censure the President, charging that the firing of MacArthur was tantamount to rank appeasement of world communism. Never to be outdone in the art of demagoguery, Senator McCarthy concluded that Truman was a "son of a bitch" who must have been drunk on "bourbon and benedictine" when he made his fateful decision. He ended his diatribe calling on the American people to fight back, otherwise he warned "red waters may lap at all of our shores."[43]

Meanwhile the House Republican Policy Committee headed by Representative Martin issued a public statement which asked rhetorically, "Has the ground now been laid by the Truman-Acheson-Marshall triumvirate for a super Munich?" [44] Thus very swiftly MacArthur had become the *cause celebre* of right-wingers nursing bruised egos over the decision to send troops to Europe. "Fortress America" was quickly replaced by "Asia-first" as the new rallying cry of conservative Republicans and some Southern Democrats as they completed the transition from isolationism to an imperialism of their own, one that defined America's primary security interests as Asian and not European. If the haughty and proper Acheson was the perfect symbol of all they disdained, MacArthur, the *shogun* of Japan, was an equally fitting image for their own orthodoxy.

The CPD proceeded very cautiously at first, entering the MacArthur fray with much warranted trepidation, aware of the Pandora's Box that might be opened to public inspection in a full-fledged battle over Asia vs. Europe on the heels of the so-called internationalist victory over isolationism. As Robert Cutler counseled his fellow members, some of whom were enthusiastic for an active role like that carried out by the Committee in the first round of The Great Debate:

> To take on a nation-wide basis a strong, sharp position apparently contrary to MacArthur at this time would be to gain nothing but brickbats, mudslinging, and wind from the Wherry-Martin-McCarthy axis. Our effort would be called a "smear" on MacArthur. [45]

Yet the Committee could not ignore the matter either. The *New York Times* reported that MacArthur's triumphant return and address to the joint session of Congress had "divided Washington more profoundly than it has been divided at any time since the start of the Cold War." [46] Judging from its radio addresses during this period of high drama, it appears that the CPD could not make up its mind whether to cast itself in the role of conciliator or combatant. One week the Committee called for "unity at home," the next decried as "plain insanity the point of view that holds that Europe could be abandoned and that the United States should turn the full force of its effort toward fighting Communism in China."[47]

Paul Hoffman was next in line in the weekly radio series after the MacArthur firing. The director of the Ford Foundation and former head of the Economic Cooperation Administration, which administered the Marshall Plan, opened his April 16 address with a rather feckless call for national unity, then went on to push the familiar themes of European remilitarization and universal military service, emphasizing that domestic discord must not detract from national purpose. [48] Despite Hoffman's plea and a similar appeal by the *New York Times* the next day, Senate Republicans demanded a full House-Senate probe of the Administration's foreign and military policies with MacArthur to appear in the role of featured witness.

Having no choice under the circumstances but to face the issue, the CPD devoted its next scheduled broadcast almost entirely to the MacArthur controversy. The format for this program was an interview with General Lucius D. Clay, the former U.S. military governor of Germany, by Julius Ochs Adler, vice president and general manager of the *New York Times* and a reserve general himself. The theme of the interview was "unity at home" to back the Administration's policies abroad. Clay expressed his hope that the controversy surrounding MacArthur had not endangered the "European defense program." Moreover, he added his certainty that MacArthur would urge "that our preparations, to be strong in Europe, must proceed apace." [49]

The following week the Committee took the offensive, abandoning its tone of reconciliation. Robert Sherwood, former speech writer for Roosevelt and one of the authors of the CPD's opening statement, did the honors. Speaking from Britain, he reported a great fear among Europeans that once the U.S. was fully involved in Asia, "The Russians would feel free to move into Western Europe." Then he went on to denounce, without mentioning any names, as "plain insanity" the Asia-first position. [50]

A flurry of private correspondence between various CPD members during this period confirms the sense of confusion about what role the Committee should adopt in the MacArthur crisis. Where it had previously devoted wholehearted attention to turning on the spigot of public sentiment, some members now felt that the Committee and its Eurocentric views were in danger of being engulfed by the level of public arousal at the firing of MacArthur. After the exchange Voorhees put together the beginnings of a CPD strategy in an internal document headed, *Areas of Agreement In The MacArthur Controversy.* In the lengthy memorandum Voorhees stressed the positive effect of the MacArthur situation. He argued that,

> . . . almost unnoted is the impact of General MacArthur's return and his address to Congress as an effective antidote to the spirit of complacency about our nation's danger.

What some members chose to define as fickle behavior, Voorhees saw as a profound change in public consciousness for the better:

> As we scan today's headlines, it is easy to forget: 1) That for several months the country was split by new proposals of varying degrees of isolationism; 2) That after the December defeat in Korea and appalling growth of the casualty lists, the Hoover/Kennedy proposals to end any wholehearted support of Europe with our ground forces, as part of a joint army, had tremendous appeal throughout the country. [51]

At this point Voorhees began to outline the CPD strategy that would come to prevail in the ensuing weeks of the MacArthur crisis. Its essential features were: to distance MacArthur from his isolationist supporters in Congress, to defuse the ideological conflict in the Europe-first vs. Asia-first issue by redefining it as a debate over military strategy and not foreign policy, and to conjure up a general commonality of principle between the Administration and MacArthur. As evidence for the potential of such a strategy, Voorhees quoted from MacArthur's statement to Congress to demonstrate how one could make an argument for a congruence of viewpoint between the antagonists, saying: "No clearer call has been sounded against appeasement and isolationist thinking in all their forms than General MacArthur's statement." Thus it was Voorhees' upbeat opinion that,

> . . . with General MacArthur's popular appeal and the Republican support he enjoys, this may well be the final burial of the new isolationism which only yesterday threatened to tear our country's foreign policy apart, and weakened the faith of our allies in us.

From there the CPD's vice-chairman concluded:

> It is time for all of us, as far as possible, *to close the ranks*, recover our balance and restore some sense of unity. To this

end, the major points on which agreement now exists need attention. [52]

In other words, while the MacArthur forces were attempting to open up foreign and military policy to the broadest public and ideological scrutiny, the Committee was by this time trying to restrict the debate to the smallest circles possible, where Containment Militarism enjoyed clear hegemony.

There is no indication either from the CPD's internal correspondence or its public utterances that it opposed MacArthur's proposals in Asia on principle. What deeply concerned them was that rollback in Asia not interfere with the remilitarization of Europe. As Will Clayton wrote to his fellow Committee members:

> Our action in the Far East must be consistent with our established policy of an alliance with Europe under the North Atlantic Treaty. We should examine with the utmost care, and before adopting proceed with the greatest caution, any proposal which would involve serious risk of provoking the outbreak of World War III, or would give priority to other areas over Western Europe.

Thus while the CPD acted as conciliator and stressed national unity around the general principle of global containment, it also descended into the fray to lobby for the primacy of Europe over Asia within the overall imperial framework.

Once again, as was the case in the troops to Europe controversy, the CPD's strategy appeared to be intertwined with that of other institutions representative of Establishment opinion. The *New York Times'* editorials during this period, for instance, were identical in tone to the views of the CPD and were expressed in practically the same language. [It would be reasonable to conclude that this was more than coincidence since Julius Ochs Adler, whose name appeared on the masthead of the *Times* as vice-president and general manager, played a major leadership role on the CPD executive committee.] The *Times* editorial of May 9, for instance, was called "The Area Of Agreement," parroting Voorhees' April 26 memorandum under the same heading. Its content likewise reiterated the strategy outlined in the Voorhees memo. The *Times* argued that the agreements between MacArthur and the Administration "on the whole global struggle against Communist imperialism . . . are much more fundamental than are the agreements between General MacArthur and many of his ardent supporters." [54] An earlier editorial had referred to these supporters as "extreme Republicans who would 'scuttle' Europe by withholding troops and retreating to the Western Hemisphere and a few outlying bases." [55]

Turning MacArthur's testimony against his backers and even against the General himself, the *Times* maintained that certain points made by MacArthur were evidence for his support of the European thrust of Administration policy. The quotation taken from MacArthur, liberally interpreted to make the Establishment's point, was to the effect that "the issues are global and so interlocked that to consider the problems of one sector oblivious to those of another is but to court disaster for the whole." From this the *Times* concluded, "Like the Administration and the vast majority of Americans" and in sharp contrast to "many of his professed followers" MacArthur recognized that the global struggle against "Soviet imperialism" had two fronts, one in Asia and the other in Europe. Again following the CPD's lead, when the *Times* was forced to acknowledge the great chasm separating the Administration and MacArthur on the question of which continent should receive primary attention, it treated the disagreement as a matter of technical strategy and not political policy. Referring to the rift between Truman and MacArthur, the *Times* argued that the differences between the two "are now reduced in the main to differences regarding the means of giving effect to the principles on which there is agreement." [56] Furthermore, the public was reassured that "the issue is not one of appeasement" as was being charged by MacArthur and his supporters, "but of choosing the ground on which we wish to fight." [57] The *Times* then casually added that choosing the Asia-first course could lead to the destruction of the United Nations and the North Atlantic Alliance, leaving the U. S. to fight a war against communism alone.

This two-tier strategy of emphasizing a general unity around Containment Militarism and then asserting in no uncertain terms the primacy of Europe was adopted for the next three Sunday night broadcasts by the CPD. The addresses were timed to coincide with the Administration's defense of its foreign policy before the two combined Congressional committees investigating MacArthur's allegations. On May 14, Voorhees shared billing with General Clark Eichelberger who formerly served as second in command and leader of all ground forces under MacArthur. Eichelberger's testimony to the nationwide radio audience was a real boon to the CPD and the Administration's position. He stated that strong action taken by Truman in Korea had "slowed down the Russian timetable" but that the danger remained great. In this connection, however, he shifted his focus of concern from Asia to Europe, stressing the importance of General Eisenhower's role as commander of NATO armies in Europe. Eichelberger went so far as to assert:

Never even on the days of the landing in Normandy, has so

much of the future of the world been wrapped up in success of the mission of one man. I wish America really knew this. [58]

But on May 20, the CPD managed to pull off its biggest coup in separating MacArthur from the right and defusing the Europe vs. Asia conflict. Two rabid right-wingers and supporters of MacArthur were snared for this broadcast. They were the Reverend Daniel J. Poling, who had made a statement backing MacArthur at the time of his firing, and the Reverend Edmund A. Walsh, the Georgetown Jesuit who started Joe McCarthy on his infamous career by suggesting that "communism" was the scourge of the modern age at a time when McCarthy was in search of a hot re-election issue. Once the two clergymen delivered their message that "Communism was out to capture the very souls of men," Poling got to the point the CPD was most eager for him to make. He said he had talked at length with MacArthur and the General had stressed that "his program of strategy in the Far East must not be confused as meaning the neglect of support for Ike in Europe." [59]

That such a mood of reconciliation was the farthest thing from MacArthur's mind is vividly revealed in the minutes of a private interview with the General conducted by the CPD's Adler in MacArthur's hotel suite a few days later. The meeting between MacArthur and Adler represented a strategy on the part of the Committee not only to neutralize MacArthur but to enlist him in their own efforts. The CPD strategy was to cut the right wing base from under MacArthur and mangle his statements in such a way as to make it appear that he supported the Truman Administration's European thrust as part of a policy in global containment. Perhaps, they reasoned, the civil-military crisis engendered by the dispute could also be used to bolster their pet project of universal military service which was fast being stripped of its substance in the legislative process. A Republican-led drive to kill universal military service had already forced concessions in both the House and Senate. The Administration's position, moreover, had atrophied to little more than an extension of Selective Service complete with college deferments in spite of the CPD's steady harangues against the erosion of universal military service in its weekly radio broadcasts. If only they could get MacArthur to publicly endorse universal military service the mounting opposition to the bill would be seriously undermined. The task of enlisting MacArthur's support fell to Adler, who met privately with the General on May 23, 1951.

In a lengthy memorandum to his fellow Committee members, he reported that the subject of universal military service was clearly not uppermost in MacArthur's mind, convincing Adler that his mission was doomed:

It was difficult to hold him to a discussion of UMST (universal military service and training) and I found it necessary to guide the conversation back to it on at least three different occasions. Actually not more than ten minutes of our conversation was devoted to it. At the end he promised to consider making a statement in some form, but I came away with the feeling that he probably would not. [60]

What MacArthur did want to discuss was his enmity for Truman and the Administration's European strategy. In contrast to the public face of reconciliation that the Committee and the *Times* hoped to promote, Adler wrote to his colleagues confessing to the seriousness of the rift between MacArthur and the Administration. During the course of the meeting MacArthur made it clear that he had no intention of endorsing one indivisible global policy of containment as perpetrated by Truman's backers. Adler was taken aback by the General's truculence in this matter, reporting that MacArthur twice during the interview "emphasized that our front line was not the Elbe but the Yalu River." At one point Adler surmises, "Apparently there is bad blood, or at least great jealousy, between him and General Ike — at least on MacArthur's part." [61]

As was true of the constitutional clash between Truman and Congress in the troops to Europe battle, and of the civil-military conflict over the MacArthur issue, "bad blood " between the generals was only another manifestation of the profound policy differences that went to the very marrow of American foreign and military policy in the spring of 1951. The role of the CPD throughout was to support the militarized doctrine of containment outlined in NSC-68, although its methods were altered to match the changing circumstances. In the troops to Europe debate, for instance, the CPD goal was to build a policy consensus for the remilitarization of Europe by attacking and isolating the isolationist opposition in Congress. In the MacArthur controversy the strategy was to keep the shaky consensus from eroding by invoking the precedent of the recent Senate vote to legitimize its call for national unity. Again, as in the troops to Europe battle, the underlying strategy of the CPD through its nationwide radio broadcasts was to cut the potential mass base out from under the right wing conservatives in Congress. This was to be accomplished by minimizing the quarrel between MacArthur and Truman in order to prevent the Right from turning MacArthur's dismissal into a new-found cause around which they could recoup their energies.

The MacArthur issue — Europe vs. Asia — however, could not be resolved in the decisive fashion of a Senate vote as had the troops to Europe — internationalism vs. isolationism — controversy. The Europe vs. Asia question reached a peak in May and June, but was blunted without really being decided when peace talks opened at Panmunjon in the summer of 1951. The truce negotiations themselves proved to be a long drawn-out affair in which the fundamental dispute in the two policy orientations simmered just below the boiling point. The conflict only took new form when the Eastern Establishment wing of the party managed to beat back the attempt by the Right to have the Republican Party adopt either MacArthur or Taft as its candidate in the presidential election of 1952.

Eisenhower's victory proved to be the denouement of rightwing opposition to containment and the triumph of NSC-68 as America's official Cold War doctrine, even as it left unresolved questions of its application in Europe and Asia. A former CPD staff member recalled in this regard that one of the central purposes of the Committee was to get Eisenhower elected president. [62] But this is jumping ahead in the story. Before the CPD could phase out of existence, under the assumption its work had been accomplished with the election of Eisenhower, there remained the thorny problem of implementing the principle of militarization outlined in NSC-68 and now legitimated by Congress as an outgrowth of The Great Debate. The twin issues of implementation were about men (universal military service) and money (foreign aid) since without American troops and American dollars the blueprint for Europe was threatened with collapse.

From The Legitimation Of A Principle
To The Implementation Of A Policy

Despite the CPD's intensive lobby for the adoption of universal military service for all men at age eighteen, Congress reported out a manpower bill just before the June expiration date of the Selective Service Act, which essentially extended its provisions for another four years. While the Congressional action endorsed the concept of universal military service, it postponed indefinitely a decision to put the measure into effect. In this respect, Conant noted that "Congress had apparently given its approval to the principle of universal military service, but it had also demonstrated its reluctance to enact such a program." [63] The occasion prompted Assistant Secretary of Defense Rosenberg to send a telegram to Voorhees which read: "Conferees just reported the bill out. Our deepest thanks to you and your committee's wonderful work." [64] Voorhees responded to Rosenberg's telegram expressing the Committee's disappointment with the new manpower bill. As Conant put the matter, "The arguments of worried parents proved more powerful with Congress in 1951 than the reasoned opinions of the educators who supported the program of the CPD." [65] But the Committee was equally miffed that the Administration had acquiesced to the same message and decided against an all-out drive for universal military service in the apparent belief that the uncertainty of the draft was potentially less explosive than the certainty of universal military service. Rosenberg wrote back reassuring the Committee that,

> The recent student deferment plan is, of course, a temporary expedient and should not be considered as a permanent part of this larger picture. It is, in fact, basically contradictory to, and incompatible with, the concept of universal military service. [66]

This was in reply to Voorhees' earlier plaint to Rosenberg that, "I have been repeatedly informed that the President favors real universal military service." In that letter Voorhees also expressed the fear that the selective service system as administered by General Lewis Hershey would "mean mounting opposition on the part of the public to the military authorities because of inequities and uncertainties." [67] Voorhees' prophecy was a generation ahead of its time. It wasn't until the Vietnam war years that General Hershey became a household word as the unpopular draft was vilified and finally discarded in favor of the all-volunteer system.

While the manpower bill was not the *carte blanche* the troops to Europe measure represented, neither did it spell the end of Containment Militarism, notwithstanding Conant's requiem summation. At worst it would require making do with the unwieldy Selective Service System rather than funneling men into the military by the streamlined efficiency of the assembly line as promised by universal military service. A more immediate threat was the possible end of economic aid to Europe as the Marshall Plan drew to a close at the end of the year. Moreover, the stakes in the aid question were increased by the lukewarm response of Congress on the manpower issue. If there was any doubt that the U.S. would back its containment doctrine with men, then money became doubly important as the guarantor of U.S. commitment to Europe. To this end, aid to Europe assumed a central part of the CPD's attention from June, 1951, until the Committee's dissolution after Eisenhower's ascendance to the presidency.

During the period of The Great Debate, the so-called dollar gap had risen to its highest level since 1947. One obvious way of alleviating its impact was to increase exports from European countries into the United States. But as the Korean War dragged on, and despite what it supposedly demonstrated about the intentions of the Soviet Union, Congress became increasingly hostile to any effort designed to aid Europe. Rather than accept European imports Congress reaffirmed the "peril point" clause in the Reciprocal Trade Act, added new quotas for agricultural imports, continued export subsidies, and generally let it be known that it was in a decidedly protectionist mood. Taking the Congressional disposition into account, the Administration dropped all references to "economic cooperation" in favor of "mutual security" when it presented its European aid package to Congress. Allusions to economic aid of any type were couched in terms of "defense support." [68] The rationale for the new nomenclature was that by providing economic assistance in the form of cotton, foodstuffs, coal, and machinery, the United States would free up European resources for defense. The logic, however, failed to impress many in Congress who, under the circumstances of war in Korea and a longstanding hostility toward Europe, thought of the continuation of aid in any form as an extension of the Marshall Plan "giveaway" pure and simple.

It was in this context according to Conant that "the Committee set up what was in effect a new objective along these lines (convincing the public and the Congress of the necessity of an expanded and integrated military and economic program for Europe)." [69] The new objective began with the appointment of a subcommittee to do a full-scale study of the question. Goldwaithe Dorr, a member of the CPD, conducted the study along with W.J. Garvin, an economist hired as a staff member of the Committee. In addition to Dorr and Garvin, the subcommittee consisted of Frank Altschul, Paul Hoffman, Henry Wriston, Theodore Schultz, R. Ammi Cutter, and Voorhees. According to CPD internal memoranda, the parent Committee instructed its economic-military offshoot that it should "consider especially the best way to support General Eisenhower's mission through economic and military aid and through obtaining the appropriations requisite for it." [70] The lengthy paper prepared by Dorr and Garvin was presented to the Committee for its perusal at the end of April. Voorhees appended a message to his fellow members which read:

> If our work is to have maximum usefulness, we should be in a position to come out with a public statement announcing our Committee's position at approximately the time that the President presents the request to Congress (for foreign aid). [71]

Accordingly, on June 18, shortly after the presidential request had been submitted, the Committee issued a news release that it had presented its "non-partisan, objective study" to Congress and to the Administration. Based on its findings, the statement read, the Committee had concluded that "the $8.5 billion dollars proposed by the President for Foreign Aid to resist Soviet aggression should be adopted as quickly as possible." Moreover, it urged that since "military and economic aid are under present conditions essentially the same," both types of aid ought to be administered by one agency. [72] In this regard the CPD position paper argued that the United States could either equip a nation's troops, thus freeing its economic resources, or provide economic aid so that the Europeans themselves could pay for military rearmament.

The legislative battle over what if anything would replace the Marshall Plan began shortly after the CPD's June statement. Both the Senate and House Foreign Affairs Committees opened hearings on the question of foreign aid. By this time the reputation of the CPD had been firmly established in Washington. Its activities that summer in support of the foreign aid appropriation and the reorganization of the foreign aid program attested to the group's growing influence in Congress. After submission of its report to the Administration and Congress, both Voorhees and Hoffman were invited to testify before the House Committee on succeeding days. Speaking as President of the Ford Foundation and as a member of the CPD, Hoffman cited the Committee's study in his remarks and quoted liberally from its substance to support Truman's appropriations request and to make a case for the creation of a single administrative agency. The following day Voorhees appeared before the Committee as vice-chairman of the CPD, reiterating Hoffman's points in his lengthy testimony. Apparently impressed, House Foreign Affairs Committee Chairman James P. Richards requested that the CPD draft a bill for the House embodying the recommendations made in testimony to the Committee. The CPD readily accepted the offer.

When the task was accomplished Voorhees wrote to Richards, "The proposed bill is generally consistent with, and certain provisions are identical with, the proposals introduced yesterday in the Senate by Senators Smith (H. Alexander) and Saltonstall (Leverett)." [73] Indeed, the Senate and House versions should have shown some similarity. At the request of Saltonstall and Smith, both active in defense of the CPD when it was under attack during The Great Debate, the Committee also had taken part in drafting the Senate bill. [74]

Finally on October 10, after drawn-out Congressional hearings and a summer's public debate, the Mutual Security Act of 1951 was adopted. The new legislation abolished the Economic Cooperation Administration that had overseen the Marshall Plan and established in its place the Mutual Security Agency. At the same time, the bill authorized appointment of a Director of Mutual Security who would perform the dual function of coordinating and supervising all foreign aid programs — military and economic — just as the CPD study and NSC-68 had recommended. The final foreign aid appropriation under the new Mutual Security framework amounted to $7.3 billion, down $1.2 billion from Truman's request. Nevertheless, the CPD was quite pleased with the result as Voorhees recounts:

> Considering the inherent reluctance of Congress to provide
> funds for foreign aid, and that the Marshall Plan aid proposed
> had been only at a rate of about $4 billion a year, the final
> appropriation of over $7 billion for foreign aid for the 1952
> fiscal year was a real accomplishment. [75]

In fall 1951, after one year of existence, the CPD took stock of itself
and the nation. Voorhees made a detailed report to his fellow Committee
members, noting that with the exception of universal military service the
measures for which the CPD lobbied had become national policy. The
private document reported that the trend of public and Congressional
thinking during the previous year had developed to a degree beyond the
most optimistic expectations with which the charter members had begun
their efforts. Thus the major issue before the Committee at this point,
after the passage of the Mutual Security legislation, was whether there
was still a function for the Committee to fulfill. Voorhees asked the
membership for its opinion and a spirited exchange followed, culminating
in a meeting to decide the fate of the group's future. One of the major
factors that had to be taken under consideration was the CPD's efficacy
in a presidential election year. The problems involved in continuing under
the shadow of the election were two-fold: First, Congress was highly
unlikely to move on the controversial universal military service issue in
an election year. Second, it would be extremely difficult for the CPD to
continue under the guise of bipartisanship while its members endorsed
and campaigned for one candidate or another.

There was little disagreement within the CPD as to whom should
receive their support for president. Voorhees expressed the prevailing
mood in his reply to William Menninger's letter concerning the Committee's future. Advocating dissolution of the CPD, Voorhees reasoned,

> . . . the biggest thing before our country in my mind is to have
> Ike our next President. The announcement of Taft's candi-
> dacy, although no surprise, makes early work for Ike even
> more important. [76]

Voorhees was anxious to join the Eisenhower campaign but was
finally convinced by Conant, also a strong Eisenhower supporter, that in
Voorhees' words, "I might be more useful to General Eisenhower by
supporting through the Committee the steps necessary for the success of
General Eisenhower's mission in Europe than I could be by working for
his nomination as President." [77] What with the prospects of another tough
fight for the 1952 foreign aid appropriation, a lag in the production of
military items and their delivery to Europe, and universal military service

still only a pipedream, the view in favor of continuing forward also prevailed at the October 24 meeting. In addition to the work that many still saw ahead, some members, following Robert Patterson's lead, argued that the dissolution of the CPD would likely be interpreted as the end of "the present danger" and would "lull the public into a false sense of security." [78] Voorhees summed up the mood of the meeting in an internal paper entitled, "Comment On The Future Of The Committee On The Present Danger":

> Last year the country did not really understand the danger confronting it. Implicit in this was the issue as to whether the U.S. should join vigorously with troops, dollars, and leadership in creating a realistic joint defense of Europe. Today the situation is very different. The country understands the danger and is committed to making a joint defense of Europe. The "present danger" is now really that the carrying out of this program will be inadequate. [79]

If the CPD had in the previous year achieved its aims of legitimating the policy of Containment Militarism and establishing the machinery to put it into practice, there remained the question of national will to carry it out. Because the latter factor was of such an elusive and ephemeral nature, the CPD concluded that there was still a place in national affairs for "a vigorous, dedicated, strong, nonpartisan effort by our Committee in the role of 'vigilantes'." [80] But such vigilance would require the unrelenting zeal and dedication of the Committee's first year of existence, the personal sacrifice of time and energy demanded by membership in such a group, and of course, the raising of more money to sustain the cause and the CPD. Ad hoc lobbies are not known for their ability to perdure over such extended periods of time, at least not in their original form and purpose. Their hope instead is to steer events in the desired direction and then once accomplished, to have the course maintained by statute and executive authority. Accordingly, while the CPD repeated its legislative lobbying of the previous year in the spring of 1952, its eye was on the presidential election in November under the assumption that transition to a sympathetic administration would obviate the need for an enduring presence.

The Transition From Vigilantism To Stewardship

Joining with the rest of the nation, presidential politics dominated the CPD's attention in the summer of 1952. Once Eisenhower secured the Republican nomination, pushing Taft and MacArthur safely out of the picture, the Committee decided on its next move. Under the confident assumption that Ike would emerge victorious, Voorhees wrote to the General on September 29, outlining the Committee's plans. In the letter he related to Eisenhower that Conant had persuaded him he could be of more help "in the things for which you stand" by remaining as vice-chairman of the CPD rather than becoming actively involved in Citizens For Eisenhower. He then went on to inform the Republican nominee that he would be taking the lead for the Committee in establishing a new program having two subcategories of study, organization of mutual security and manpower policy. Voorhees concluded, "I would hope to have such a study in your hands as President-elect sometime in November." [81] Thus the agenda was set in preparation for the changing of the presidential guard and the anticipation of an Eisenhower Administration.

On the manpower front, Conant led a task force of CPD members whose objective was to convince Ike of the absolute necessity of universal military service if the United States was to meet its objectives in the Cold War. In the area of foreign aid and mutual security ". . . responsible officials in charge of this work in Washington had urged . . . a first-hand restudy in Europe by the CPD," according to Voorhees. [82] At the invitation of Special Ambassador Draper and General Gruenther, Voorhees and General Donovan made a visit to Europe in preparation for their mutual security report. Will Clayton was unable to make the trip but joined in putting together the subsequent recommendations. [83]

The two subcommittees came back together December 3, to present their recommendations to the CPD executive committee and to arrange a meeting to present their analyses to President-elect Eisenhower. After making revisions of a minor nature, Conant drafted a letter requesting a meeting with Eisenhower. Ike promptly accepted, and a luncheon meeting was set for December 22. Representing the CPD at the meeting were Conant, Voorhees, and Donovan. Members attending from the Eisenhower team in addition to the President-designate were John Foster Dulles (Secretary of State), Roger Keyes (Deputy Secretary of Defense), Herbert Brownell (Attorney General), and Harold Stassen (Director of the Mutual Security Agency). [84]

In the meeting Conant reviewed the CPD's position on military manpower and Voorhees summarized the Committee's recommendations on mutual security. Eisenhower responded by giving his enthusiastic endorsement to the views presented. Voorhees' recollection of the session was as follows:

> The meeting with the President-elect was the climax and the end of the active work of the CPD. Since the President-elect had stated his belief in substantially all of the important positions which the Committee had taken and urged over a

two-year period, there seemed to us to be little further need for the Committee. [85]

Not only that, but the CPD's principally Republican membership was now being inducted into the Eisenhower Administration to carry out the policies it had helped Democrat Truman bring about. Attrition from the Committee began immediately after the Hotel Commodore meeting when Conant received an offer from Eisenhower to become High Commissioner to Germany, a sensitive post in the key area of military rearmament and economic integration. His acceptance left the CPD without its persistent and energetic chairman. Voorhees followed Conant into the new Republican Administration six months later when he was offered a dual position as Defense Adviser to NATO, and director of Offshore Procurement. The second post proved the more important of the two.

Under Offshore Procurement auspices, the U.S. bought military equipment produced in Europe for NATO forces with U.S. dollars. In this way the program provided contracts for European industry and assured NATO a supply of weaponry for which it would not have to compete with American efforts elsewhere as had been the case with Korea. At the same time it provided a solution to the central dilemma posed in NSC-68 of how to reduce trade imbalance and increase production for rearmament. Finally, under the rubric of defense support, it was able to furnish much-needed dollar aid to Europe without the connotation of "giveaway" or "handout" with which the Marshall Plan program had been saddled. By the summer of 1954, under the leadership of Voorhees, Offshore Procurement had reached $2.3 billion annually and military production was fast becoming a permanent feature of the European economy despite dogged interference from, in Voorhees' words, "Senator McCarthy's attacks and abuse." [86] Thus Offshore Procurement represented one of the integral military Keynesian strategies developed for the implementation of Containment Militarism.

Having accepted important posts in the Eisenhower Administration, Conant and Voorhees were now in a position to put into practice the policies they had long advocated in foreign and military affairs. As chairman and vice-chairman of the CPD they led a whole contingent of other Committee members into the new Republican Administration as well. Among them were Robert Cutler who was appointed Special Assistant For National Security Affairs, a post from which he is credited with increasing the powers of the National Security Council in policy deliberations. Still others served on presidentially-appointed commissions designing the machinery of intervention for the long Cold War ahead. Bush, for instance, was instrumental in drafting a reorganization of the Defense Department that rationalized it along the lines of a giant industrial corporation, a plan that followed very closely the proposals Acheson had advanced before leaving office. [87] With the NSC-68 formula of Containment Militarism apparently firmly established as bipartisan foreign policy and CPD members in positions of great influence within the new Administration, the Committee, in the words of Tracy Voorhees, "naturally finished its active functions." [88]

Legitimating Containment Militarism: A Means And An End

Establishment elites nestled in the executive enjoy considerable autonomy in the formulation of policy. This license is constrained however by the fact that the policy chosen must meet standards of public acceptability if it is to be implemented. Without such legitimation, elite-designed plans may be hobbled by mass apathy or even rendered untenable by active public opposition that effectively blocks the mobilization of resources needed to put them into practice. Thus the campaign to create a mood of impending crisis in the form of the Soviet Threat was very much an *end* in itself during the period of The Great Debate.

At the same time that the CPD campaign was designed to convince the public that their way of life was under imminent attack and that considerable sacrifice would be required on their part to combat this external threat, it was equally designed to dissuade the Republican right wing from the belief that it could activate the growing anticommunist mood to block Containment Militarism and replace containment with its own political formula. In this sense mobilization of the public was a *means* toward restoration of the bipartisan consensus as well as an end. The dynamic of such a strategy requires further elaboration.

If a united elite could not mobilize the public in the political climate of the early fifties as was ordinarily the case, then a mobilized public would have to reunite the elite, reversing the aphorism "He who mobilizes the elite mobilizes the public" to read, "He who mobilizes the public, mobilizes the elite." [89] That is precisely the unique "technique of democracy . . . in time of crisis" (Conant's words heading this chapter) represented by the CPD. It is a technique born of necessity given the inherent tensions which exist between an elite policymaking process and a democratic political system in a period of intense elite conflict.

The technique involved in winning the policy struggle and establishing hegemony for one specific formula or remedy over another, then, was to link it to the generalized myth or crisis in the public mind. [90] This strategy is apparent in the campaign of the CPD in which it was always careful to relate the one to the other — the perduring theme of communism manifesting itself in the form of a Soviet Threat centered in Europe which in turn called for Containment Militarism in response. This in contrast to the Republican right with its more diffuse notion of a "communist threat" whose primary danger lay at home, secondarily in Asia, and lastly in Europe. The fear among the foreign policy establishment was that widespread acceptance of the right wing interpretation of the global crisis would obstruct the implementation of Containment Militarism, which would in turn strike a mortal blow to Pax Americana and its projection of power — political, military, and economic — the key to which was control of Europe.

It is also a technique or strategy that may be employed either to support or reject presidential policy. This distinction will be particularly important as we move from a consideration of the first CPD's activities to that of the present-day CPD in the following chapters. Whereas the original Committee (CPD-I) backed the Administration-formulated policy of Containment Militarism, the contemporary Committee (CPD-II) took the veto form against what they believed to be waning support for Containment Militarism within the foreign policy establishment in the post-Vietnam era.

Chapter 3

Shaping The Cold War Consensus

1.   Tracy S. Voorhees, "The Committee On The Present Danger, 1950-53," Voorhees Papers, 1968, p. 1.

2.   Bertrand Russell, "Looking Backward — To The 1950's," *New York Times Magazine* April 26, 1953, p. 12.

3.   "Record of the Meeting of the State-Defense Policy Review Group, March 16, 1950," U.S. Department of State, *Foreign Relations*, 1950, 1: 198.

4.   *New York Times*, January 9, 1951, p. 1.

5.   *New York Times*, January 9, 1951, p. 12.

6.   *New York Times*, January 9, 1951, p. 9.

7.   *New York Times*, January 8, 1951, p. 1.

8.   *New York Times*, January 9, 1951, p. 1.

9.   Report To Members Of The CPD And Tentative Projection of Activities, May 17, 1951, Tab Y, Voorhees Papers.

10. Memorandum from James Conant to Tracy Voorhees, December 14, 1950, p. 5, Tab I, Voorhees Papers.

11. *New York Times*, February 2, 1951, p. 1.

12. *New York Times*, February 3, 1951, p. 5.

13. *New York Times*, February 8, 1951, p. 10.

14. James B. Conant, *My Several Lives* (New York: Harper & Row, 1970), 516.

15. *The Congressional Record*, April 4, 1951, p. 3271.

16. *New York Times*, February 9, 1951, p. 1.

17. *New York Times*, February 11, 1951, p. 13.

18. *New York Times*, February 22, 1951, p. 9.

19. Walter Millis, Harvey C. Mansfield, and Harold Stein, *Arms And The State: Civil-Military Elements In National Policy* (New York: Twentieth Century Fund, 1958), 349.

20. *New York Times*, February 20, 1951, p. 1.

21. Millis, Mansfield, and Stein, p. 349.

22. *New York Times*, February 28, 1951, p. 1.

23. Conant, p. 526.

24. *New York Times*, March 5, 1951, p. 1.

25. *New York Times*, March 7, 1951, p. 1.

26. *New York Times*, March 8, 1951, p. 1.

27. *New York Times*, March 12, 1951, p. 6.

28. *New York Times*, March 19, 1951, p. 15.

29. "Record of the Meeting of the State-Defense Policy Review Group, March 16, 1950," U.S. Department of State, *Foreign Relations*, 1950, 1: 198.

30. Voorhees, p. 35.

31. *Ibid.*, p. 39.

32. *Ibid.*, p. 42.

33. *New York Times*, April 2, 1951, p. 1.

34. Conant, p. 517.

35. Samuel P. Huntington, *The Common Defense* (New York: Columbia University Press, 1962), 324-325.

36. *New York Times*, April 5, 1951, p. 12.
37. *New York Times*, April 7, 1951, p. 1.
38. *New York Times*, April 6, 1951, p. 1.
39. Clarence Y.H. Lo, "The Truman Administration's Military Budgets During The Korean War," Ph.D. dissertation, University of California, Berkeley, 1978, p. 270.
40. As Schurmann speculates, for the U.N. "to have been dragged into Chiang's campaign to 'counterattack the Mainland' would probably have wrecked the body," see Franz Schurmann, *The Logic Of World Power* (New York: Pantheon, 1974), 238.
41. *New York Times*, April 12, 1953, p. 1.
42. *Ibid.*
43. *Ibid.*
44. *New York Times*, April 13, 1951, p. 5.
45. Letter to Samuel Goldwyn from Robert Cutter, April 25, 1951, Tab Y, Voorhees Papers.
46. *New York Times*, April 20, 1951, p. 1.
47. *New York Times*, April 22, 1951, p. 5; *New York Times*, April 30, 1951, p. 10.
48. *New York Times*, April 17, 1951, p. 6.
49. *New York Times*, April 22, 1951, p. 5.
50. *New York Times*, April 30, 1951, p. 10.
51. Tracy S. Voorhees, "Areas Of Agreement In The MacArthur Controversy," undated, p. 1, Tab Y, Voorhees Papers.
52. *Ibid.*, p. 2.
53. Will Clayton's April 25 memorandum summarized in "Notes As To The Present Status Of The MacArthur Question And What The CPD Might Do About It," Tracy S. Voorhees, May 14, 1951, pp. 3-4, Tab Y, Voorhees Papers.
54. *New York Times*, "The Area Of Agreement," May 9, 1951, p. 32.
55. *New York Times*, April 20, 1951, p. 28.
56. *New York Times*, May 9, 1951, p. 32.
57. *New York Times*, Apirl 29, 1951, p. 28.
58. *New York Times*, May 14, 1951, p. 3.
59. *New York Times*, May 21, 1951, p. 9.
60. Discussion Between General of the Army Douglas MacArthur and Major General Julius Ochs Adler, RE: Universal Military Service and Training Legislation, May 23, 1951, Tab Y, Voorhees Papers.
61. *Ibid.*
62. Fred Warner Neal, interview with author, August 5, 1977.
63. Conant, p. 527.
64. Telegram from Assistant Secretary of Defense Anna Rosenberg to Tracy S. Voorhees, May 28, 1951, Tab Y, Voorhees Papers.
65. Conant, p. 531.
66. Letter from Assistant Secretary of Defense Anna Rosenberg to Tracy S. Voorhees, July 2, 1951, Tab Y, Voorhees Papers.
67. Letter from Tracy S. Voorhees to Assistant Secretary of Defense Anna Rosenberg, June 22, 1951, Tab Y, Voorhees Papers.

68. Harry Bayard Price, *The Marshall Plan And Its Meaning* (Ithaca: Cornell University Press, 1955), p. 162.
69. Conant, p. 517.
70. Minutes of the Meeting of the Executive Committee of the CPD, New York, April 5, 1951, p. 2, Tab Y, Voorhees Papers.
71. Memorandum to the CPD from Tracy S. Voorhees, April 25, 1951, Tab Y, Voorhees Papers.
72. *New York Times,* June 18, 1951, p. 3.
73. Memorandum Accompanying Draft of Foreign Aid Bill, August 3, 1951, Tab FF, Voorhees Papers.
74. Voorhees, 1968, p. 62.
75. *Ibid.,* p. 63.
76. Letter to William C. Menninger from Tracy S. Voorhees, October 18, 1951, Tab KK, Voorhees Papers.
77. Tracy S. Voorhees, Notes of Discussion with Dr. Conant in Cambridge, Massachusetts, December 1, 1951, Tab LL, Voorhees Papers.
78. Notes of Meeting of the CPD, University Club, New York, October 24, 1951, Tab KK, Voorhees Papers.
79. Comment on the Future of the CPD, Tracy S. Voorhees, November 29, 1951, p. 12, Tab LL, Voorhees Papers.
80. *Ibid.*
81. Letter to Dwight D. Eisenhower from Tracy S. Voorhees, September 29, 1952, Tab SS, Voorhees Papers.
82. Voorhees, 1968, p. 88.
83. *Ibid.,* p. 89.
84. *Ibid.,* p. 90.
85. *Ibid.,* pp. 92-93.
86. *Ibid.*
87. Millis, Mansfield, and Stein, p. 387.
88. Tracy S. Voorhees, Notes for Dr. Conant Concerning Mr. Tuttle's Paper, "James B. Conant and Universal Military Training, 1944-1952", p. 13, Tab B, Voorhees Papers.
89. Theodore Lowi, "Making Democracy Safe For The World," in James M. Rosenau, ed. *Domestic Sources Of Foreign Policy* (New York: The Free Press, 1967), 322.
90. *Ibid.,* pp. 320-322.

Chapter 4

NSC-68 TO THE TET OFFENSIVE:
The Long March of
Containment Militarism

*I decided that having put our hand to the plough, we would
not turn back.*
Dean Acheson on Vietnam, Autumn, 1950 [1]

The axial principles of Containment Militarism as developed in
NSC-68 were its zero-sum view of global affairs and its conviction that
military force was the deciding factor in their outcome. Derivatives of the
original doctrine of containment, these ideas nonetheless represented a
significant transformation of the earlier formula. The notion of the Soviet
Union as an expansionist power bent on challenging the United States in
the ideological as well as geopolitical arena formed a continuous theme
from the birth of the containment doctrine in 1947 to the writing of NSC-
68 in 1950. What had changed in the interim was the initial conviction
that such competition should be pursued by economic and diplomatic
means and that the contest could be waged in certain restricted regions of
the world, principally Western Europe. NSC-68 departs from this course
by outlining a strategy of *global containment* by *military means*.

NSC-68 was not so much an abrupt departure as it was the articula-
tion of a growing set of beliefs within the foreign policy elite under the
leadership of Dean Acheson. Nevertheless, outside of this inner sanctum
of the Establishment, economic and political orthodoxy still prevailed
and NSC-68 was greeted as unconscionable heresy. Moreover, as we

119

saw in earlier chapters, these traditionalists were quite close to mass sentiment in 1950, necessitating a campaign of crisis to legitimate Containment Militarism as the touchstone of American foreign policy.

The profound impact this evolution in the containment doctrine would have on the American future was not immediately apparent, however, since the implementation of Containment Militarism occurred in incremental steps spanning numerous Administrations rather than in one leap forward. The more visible the logic of its path became, however, the harder it was to change course — even for presidents. Not until the Vietnam War was its wisdom once again subjected to review, a procedure which threatened to spark another Great Debate over the fundamental purpose and direction of United States policy. As Gelb and Betts, the former a principal author of the *Pentagon Papers*, put it: "Ironically, commitment in Vietnam was to become the child that devoured its parent. Spawned by containment, it discredited containment." [2] In this chapter, I will argue that it was Containment Militarism as distinguished from containment proper that led to Vietnam, and will trace its application from Korea to Vietnam in order to understand the fragmentation of the foreign policy consensus that subsequently gave rise to a new Committee on the Present Danger in the post-Vietnam era.

The Fifties: An Era Of Limits

That the consensus around Containment Militarism should shatter in Southeast Asia is indeed ironic. While NSC-68 paid homage to the global nature of the contest between the United States and its allies and the Soviet Union and "its satellites," the Truman Administration's policies never left any doubt that Europe and not Asia was the clear priority of U.S. commitment. Truman characterized his Administration's posture as follows: "Our entire international position depended upon strengthening Western Europe." [3] Secretary of State Acheson explained this uncompromising Europe-first stance as dictated by limited resources which left them little choice:

> Since our resources are limited, the weight of our effort must be brought to bear in these European countries where the threat of aggression is most immediate, where our aid will be most effective, and where the ability of the economy to stand the financial strain of military expenditure is least. [4]

Acheson reaffirmed the Administration's position in his famous "perimeter" speech of January 12, 1950, later attacked by the right wing as having precipitated the war in Korea. Proclaiming that the United

States would not intervene in China, the Secretary declared that "the vital interests" of the U.S. in Asia were restricted to a chain of Pacific islands running along the Aleutians to Japan and extending to the Philippines. Nonetheless, it was the Truman Administration that first anchored the reputation of the United States to the outcome of events in Vietnam. Just as America would finally disengage from Vietnam because of the impact of its continuing intervention on the stability of Europe and the ability to govern at home, so too its involvement began with these two concerns very much in mind.

Turning first to domestic politics, the Truman Administration had attempted to steer the rising anticommunist sentiment of the Republican right wing to its own advantage in the immediate postwar period without getting locked into a rigid and indiscriminate anticommunism in the conduct of its foreign policy. After the fall of China, however, such discrimination became wishful thinking under pressure from the right wing to oppose all brands of communism wherever they might appear, and not just Soviet expansionism in Europe as Truman would have preferred. Given the acrimonious climate at the time, the Administration felt compelled to take a stand against Ho Chi Minh and support the ill-fated French attempt to control events in Indochina. As the *Pentagon Papers* summary notes:

> After the fall of mainland China to the Chinese Communists, the Truman Administration moved to support Emperor Bao Dai and provide military aid to the French against the Communist-led Vietminh.

> This decision, which was made amid growing concern in the United States over the expansion of Communism in Eastern Europe and Asia, reversed Washington's longstanding reluctance to become involved with French colonialism in Indochina. [5]

Events in Western Europe also dictated America's involvement in Vietnam. European recovery — the vital center of U.S. imperial objectives — was very much contingent upon an economically revitalized France, and a France that politically would accept alliance partnership with a rearmed Germany. If France was to play the pivotal role assigned it, however, it would require American support of its colonial rearguard stand in Indochina. The French were not without supporters within the Administration in their adventure. Dean Rusk, who would later prosecute the war to its fullest as Secretary of State in the Kennedy-Johnson years — and later still become a member of CPD-II — wrote the following memorandum in the spring of 1950 while acting as Deputy

Secretary of State for Far Eastern Affairs:

> The Department of State continues to hold that Southeast
> Asia is in grave danger of Communist domination as a
> consequence of aggression from Communist China and of
> internal subversive activities . . . The Department of State
> believes that within the limitations imposed by existing
> commitments and strategic priorities, the resources of the
> United States should be deployed to reserve Indo-China and
> Southeast Asia from further Communist encroachment. [6]

By May 1950, only a few weeks after the presentation of NSC-68,
Truman acting on Acheson's recommendation, approved a program of
economic and military support for the French reconquest. What started
as an initial $10 million grant had swollen to a $1 billion annual
investment by the time of France's denouement at Dien Bien Phu four
years later.

Finally, the outbreak of war in Korea placed Vietnam even closer to
the center of American foreign policy. The fall of another "domino" in
Asia after China and Korea would do great damage to the Administration's credibility given the monolithic framework they themselves had
created to sell their policies in Europe. Thus, as the *Pentagon Papers*
note, by the summer of 1952 it was the U.S. objective "to prevent the
countries of Southeast Asia from passing into the Communist orbit." [7]
Accordingly, NSC 124/2 added that the Administration should "continue to assure the French that the U.S. regards the French effort in
Indochina as one of great strategic importance in the general international
interest rather than in the purely French interest, and as essential to the
security of the free world." [8]

By the end of Truman's tenure, his Administration was giving the
French as much aid as they wanted and as much advice as they could
tolerate. Together with other forms of aid it received through the Marshall
Plan and the Mutual Defense Assistance Plan, France had become the
single largest recipient of U.S. assistance, reflecting its key role in U.S.
plans. [9] Significantly, however, in keeping with his Administration's
Europe-oriented priorities, U.S. involvement in Southeast Asia remained limited to dollar aid as Truman left office.

The Eisenhower Administration began almost immediately with a
campaign to sell Indochina to the American public. Eisenhower,
Secretary of State John Foster Dulles, and other Administration leaders
spoke of the Indochina situation as the "cork in the bottle," and warned
ominously of a "chain reaction" effect in the wake of a French defeat. [10]
At the height of the Dien Bien Phu siege, Vice President Nixon declared:
"If to avoid further Communist expansion in Asia and Indochina, we

must take the risk now by putting our boys in, I think the Executive has to take the politically unpopular decision and do it." [11] That this was no idle fantasy on Nixon's part is made clear in the *Pentagon Papers* where an American combat presence was under serious consideration at the National Security Council level during the fall of Dien Bien Phu:

> In such a case (French retreat) the United States could either accept the loss of Indochina, or adopt an active policy while France gradually withdrew its troops. Should we accept the latter course, our "most positive" step offering "the greatest assurance of success" would be, NSC estimated, to join with indigenous forces in combatting the Viet Minh until they were reduced "to the status of scattered guerrilla bands." U.S. land, sea, and air forces would be involved. [12]

The major reason such a policy of military intervention was never pursued after the French downfall was the matter of "limited resources" to which Acheson had alluded earlier as the rationale for the Democrats' cautious approach to Southeast Asia. The frugal Republican military posture — termed the New Look— relied on nuclear as opposed to conventional forces. This policy of "massive retaliation" — the brain-child of Secretary Dulles — was designed quite crudely to deliver "more bang for the buck" than could be realized from a buildup of ground forces as advocated in NSC-68. Consequently the Eisenhower Administration did not have the capability for conventional intervention at the time of the French demise.

While nuclear weapons were very seriously contemplated at the time of Dien Bien Phu — with Dulles' active promotion — the idea was abandoned along with that of massive mobilization and the prospect of another Korea. [13] The choice of nuclear attack or protracted ground war, however, did not convince the Eisenhower Administration to abandon Vietnam with the French colonialists. On the contrary, this was the heyday of covert intervention run amok. The CIA was fresh from the overthrow of Mossadeq in Iran and, as Kermit Roosevelt the CIA bureau chief in charge of the operation was later to report, Dulles "was so pleased and sort of licking his chops with the success of this thing he decided that that was the way to deal with any difficult foreign situation." [14] One can only imagine the budget-minded Dulles' glee with a successful coup that cost only $75,000 (used to finance street riots) and left less than a thousand dead — all Iranian. One year later the same frugal thuggery led to the overthrow of the Arbenz government in Guatemala. In Vietnam it led to dirty tricks in the North conducted by the CIA under the direction of Colonel Edward Lansdale between the time of Dien Bien Phu and the signing of the Geneva Accord dividing Vietnam into North and South. [15]

After the Geneva imposition, the United States installed the puppet regime of Ngo Dinh Diem, again with active involvement by the CIA in the decision. Aid to the Diem regime included military and economic support as well as American advisers, this despite dim prospects of success according to a national intelligence estimate of the South's leadership. It advised:

> Although it is possible that the French and Vietnamese even with the firm support of the United States and other powers may be able to establish a strong regime in South Vietnam, we believe that the chances for this development are poor and moreover, that the situation is more likely to continue to deteriorate. . . [16]

The Eisenhower legacy was a mixed one. As Gelb and Betts point out, Ike's refusal to intervene at the time of Dien Bien Phu "kept America out of the war," but by virtue of his Administration's underwriting of the Saigon regime which soon became dependent on Washington for its survival, "he kept America in Vietnam." [17] In the process, the fate of Vietnam came to be seen as ever more central to the destiny of the containment doctrine. As Eisenhower argued before passing on the reins of leadership to John Kennedy: "The loss of South Vietnam would set in motion a crumbling process that could, as it progressed have grave consequences for us and for freedom." [18] Thus had Vietnam become a critical domino in a seamless, zero-sum Cold War.

By elevating the status of Asia to a level of concern equal to that of Europe, the Eisenhower Republicans had in their own way built upon the foundation of Containment Militarism created in the Truman years. The globalism implicit in NSC-68 remained largely symbolic during the Truman period because of the Democrat's decided emphasis on Europe. While Eisenhower had been instrumental in setting up the machinery for the European strategy of Truman and Acheson, as a Republican president he could ill afford to ignore the Asia-oriented predilections of his own powerful right wing. Coupled with the tide of events in Vietnam, the Eisenhower-Dulles team soon granted legitimacy to containment in Asia, in effect globalizing the concept in keeping with the letter if not the intent of NSC-68. Vietnam was no longer a peripheral concern of American policy but a matter of vital interest.

Still this step itself remained symbolic so long as the militaristic aspect of the containment doctrine — armed force and the threat of its use — lacked credibility. Like the Truman Democrats, the Eisenhower Republicans had their own sense of "limited resources" that prevented the full-blown military program advocated in NSC-68. In the case of the

Democrats the limits to militarization were perceived primarily as political barriers, whereas for the Republicans around Eisenhower there ran the deep conviction that there were objective economic limits to military spending beyond which the nation could not go without courting financial collapse. This led them to choose nuclear over conventional programs and to base U.S. military posture on the strategy of massive retaliation, an orientation which proved to be of dubious use as an instrument of policy either in Asia or in Europe.

The Gaither Report: Proclamation Of An End To Limits

While the principles of NSC-68 — globalism and militarism —were endorsed by both Democratic and Republican Administrations in the 1950s, each, because of constraints on the level of resources that could be committed to military purposes, were faced with choices that stood in the way of an all-out implementation of Containment Militarism. Moreover, the manner in which they chose to deal with this dilemma led to serious political problems for their respective administrations. The Truman-Acheson strategy called for the development of militarism to the fullest, advocating a buildup of both nuclear and conventional capabilities, but choosing to restrict the application of global containment to Europe. Thus, it opened itself to charges from the Republican right wing of appeasement to communism in Asia.

The Eisenhower-Dulles doctrine took the opposite course, extending containment to Asia as well as Europe thus making globalism explicit, but choosing to confront the problem of finite limits by restricting the thrust of militarization to strategic forces rather than to the balanced conception of NSC-68 which urged a conventional capability equal to that of the nuclear arsenal. This choice led to charges of rigidity and accusations from prominent members of the Truman-Acheson team that the Eisenhower-Dulles posture was a nonstrategy unable to support U.S. foreign policy goals. Moreover, during Eisenhower's second term, the notion began to grow within the national security establishment that the very idea of finite limits which dictated choice — either in the *range* or in the *means* of Containment Militarism's application — were illusory and should be discarded as outdated in the world of the late 1950s.

Albert Wohlstetter, a strategic theorist of considerable influence, argued that since the Soviet Union had developed nuclear weapons the world had been placed in a "delicate balance of terror", an idea that gained wide acceptance among the policy elite in its critique of massive retaliation. The United States and the Soviet Union, according to this line of argumentation, confronted one another like two giants so weighted down with armor that each was incapable of movement. Such immobility presented no problem if the concern was defense of one's sovereign territory, but became quite problematic if the goal was to utilize military force to achieve foreign policy objectives. In the former circumstance, the U.S. could stand fast secure in the knowledge that no nation would attack its borders facing the certainty of an overwhelming retaliatory response. But if the intent behind military force was to support coercion and intervention then the threat of an all or nothing nuclear strike left much to be desired. To remove U.S. foreign policy from this nuclear straight-jacket, so the argument went, would require a strategy which aimed toward greater *flexibility*. Some sense of what form an alternative posture might assume can be gleaned from a memorandum which Maxwell Taylor, then army chief of staff and now a member of CPD-II, circulated privately within the military establishment as early as October, 1956:

> The National Military Program must be suitable for flexible application to unforeseen situations. It cannot be geared to any single weapons system, strategic concept, or combination of allies. It must be capable of supporting our national policy in all situations. In short, the military policy of the United States should include all reasonable measures to provide general and local war and at the same time contain the potentiality of waging war, large or small, in such a manner as to achieve our national objectives and to bring about a better world upon the unsuccessful conclusion of hostilities. [19]

The gist of Taylor's thesis, as he articulated it in his book of a few years later *The Uncertain Trumpet*, was that given the nuclear standoff "a national military program must make early and adequate provision for responding effectively to local aggression wherever it occurs." [20] This strategy of "flexible response" was subsequently adopted as the basis of the Kennedy Administration's military posture. Taylor also entered the Administration as a military adviser to Kennedy along with the doctrine he had created. But this was not until 1961.

In the interim, support for the Taylor thesis continued to grow within the ranks of the Establishment. It was given a considerable boost by the publication of Henry Kissinger's *Nuclear Weapons and Foreign Policy* in 1957. Kissinger's book was the outgrowth of a Council On Foreign Relations- and Rockefeller-sponsored study over which he served as executive director. As Kissinger described the deliberations of the group, they were, in parallel fashion to Taylor, searching for *flexibility in the use of nuclear weaponry* in a manner short of the massive dosage prescribed in the Dulles doctrine. Nitze, who by this early date had already raised the issue of tactical nuclear weapons for limited theater use, was one of the many Cold War luminaries who sat on the panel. In Kissinger's words:

> One of the most urgent tasks of American military policy is to create a military capability which can redress the balance in limited wars and which can translate our technological advantage into local superiority. [21]

Of equal importance, Kissinger attacked the assumption, sacrosanct in the Eisenhower-Dulles formula, that there was a clear economic barrier which dictated a choice between nuclear and conventional forces. Kissinger wrote: "While there is undoubtedly an upper limit of defense spending beyond which the injury to the economy would outweigh the gain in military strength, it is also the case that this theoretical ceiling has been consistently underestimated." [22] Thus, harkening to NSC-68, the real limitation to a panoply of nuclear and conventional programs came down to the question of national will and the resolve to contain communism wherever and however it might challenge Pax Americana.

A presidentially-appointed commission officially recommended both a nuclear and conventional military buildup to Eisenhower in 1957, the year the Kissinger study was completed. Known as the Gaither Report, the presidential review committee called for a rapid expansion of missile programs and an equally speedy development of mobile forces capable of fighting limited "brushfire" wars. Such a course, the Report warned, would be expensive, but was essential to match the alleged Soviet nuclear buildup and to deter communist subversion around the globe. [23]

In a number of its essential aspects the Gaither Report bore a striking similarity to NSC-68. It should have. President Eisenhower commissioned this latest policy review on the advice of his Special Assistant for National Security Affairs Robert Cutler, a former member of CPD-I who entered the Eisenhower Administration shortly after Conant and Voorhees. Among those selected to serve on the Gaither Committee was James Phinney Baxter III, a former CPD member who had worked for Conant and Bush on the atom bomb project during World War II. In a further note of continuity, Paul Nitze, Robert Lovett, and John J. McCloy were also appointed to the Gaither Panel in an advisory role.

Ostensibly brought together to study a proposal by the Federal Civilian Defense Administration for the construction of a $40 billion blast shelter system, the Gaither Committee soon broadened its mandate to include the whole spectrum of American military policy. [24] As the report was in its final stage of preparation, the Soviet Union announced on October 4, 1957, that it had launched the Sputnik earth satellite. A week later the Gaither Commission reported its findings to the President at a special session of the National Security Council.

The Report presented a frightening picture of Soviet military power. The gist of the argument was that the nuclear stalemate reached a few years before — the "delicate balance of terror" — was fast becoming an imbalance in favor of the Russians. Wohlstetter looms large once again in this shift in thinking. The Committee was influenced on this fundamental question by a classified RAND report prepared under Wohlstetter's direction, in which it was argued that the bombers of the Strategic Air Command, upon which the doctrine of massive retaliation rested, had become vulnerable to a Soviet nuclear attack. [25] Moreover, the Committee warned that by the early 1960s the Soviet Union would have an ICBM capability that could destroy the American retaliatory force. Thus the Report concluded, echoing the Rockefeller-Council on Foreign Relations panel under the stewardship of Kissinger, the entire program of U.S. missile production should be accelerated. At the same time, the Gaither Committee included the concerns of Maxwell Taylor as well, adding as a second recommendation the need for a limited war-fighting capability to meet "local aggression" wherever it might appear.

Upon presentation of their report, the Gaither panel sensed immediately that unlike the Truman presidency in 1950 with NSC-68, this Administration did not share its urgency about the new Soviet Threat. While Truman had clung to the notion of a fixed upper limit on military spending for a time, economic orthodoxy was in due course abandoned. Led by such bedrock conservatives as Dulles and Defense Secretary Charles Wilson, however, economic orthodoxy was entrenched gospel within the Republican Administration. It was not about to be easily dislodged, even by the testimony of such eminent Wall Street spokesmen as Lovett and McCloy. After Eisenhower had expressed his reservations about embarking on such a costly path, Lovett and McCloy assured the inner circle of its wisdom just as they had done for NSC-68 in the Truman years:

> At that dramatic NSC meeting, with some 45 persons crowded into the White House broadcast room, two of the President's most valued friends in the financial world — John J. McCloy and Robert Lovett — pledged to Mr. Eisenhower the complete backing of the American financial community if he would approve the program proposed.

> McCloy and Lovett, both Republicans who held high posts in past Democratic administrations, expressed the conviction that the American public would shoulder the burden and accept the responsibilities of such major increases in the budget. They said also that the American economy was capable of carrying the load. [26]

Still the Administration did not waver from its course. At this juncture the frustrated Gaitherites met to contemplate "the formation of a committee which would seek to convince the American people of the need for greater sacrifices in light of the Soviet threat." [27] In attendance at the dinner meeting held at the Washington home of William Foster were Paul Nitze and Vice President Richard Nixon. In the end, it was decided that the revival of a Committee on the Present Danger was unlikely to be effective in arousing public opinion if it appeared to challenge Eisenhower, given the uncommon deference he was accorded in military matters. An added reason for curtailment of the plan is offered by Morton Halperin in his extensive account of the Gaither proceedings. Halperin suggests that "the leak to the press about the gathering and its purpose made further action by the group more complicated and, in addition, embarrassed the Vice President." [28] Finally, the group agreed its interests would be best served through the public release of its recommendations. Ike, not surprisingly, disagreed with this move as well. Nevertheless, it wasn't long before its contents began, in bits and pieces, to find their way into the public arena.

Aided greatly by leaks of the classified report to the press, the Democrats soon seized upon the issue as their own, first for the Congressional elections of 1958 and then in the presidential contest of 1960. A newly-formed Democratic Advisory Council under the direction of Charles Tyroler, who had worked as an aide to Anna Rosenberg in the Pentagon during the Korean War period and is now director of CPD-II, urged a major military buildup. Its members consisted of the power brokers of the Democratic Party including Truman, Acheson, Harriman, Hubert Humphrey, and Democratic National Committee Chairman Paul Butler. At the same time Lyndon Johnson, Senate majority leader and chairman of the Preparedness Subcommittee of the Armed Services Committee, decided to conduct extensive hearings on U.S. military posture, a forum from which he pressed for full publication of the Gaither Report. Called to testify before the Senate inquiry were the familiar names of Vannevar Bush and James Conant. Still Eisenhower remained steadfast, refusing to release the study and continuing to deny that the U.S. was falling behind the Soviet Union in its military capabilities as alleged by the Democrats.

While the President's words of reassurance to the nation constituted a major obstacle to the militarization desired by the Gaither group, Eisenhower's reaction did not deter its members from speaking out to alert the public to "the imminent dangers" of burgeoning Soviet power. The charges and countercharges that followed culminated in John Kennedy's accusation in his 1960 presidential campaign that there existed a "missile gap" adverse to the United States and that the

Republicans were generally "soft on communism" around the globe. Both themes dovetailed nicely with the clamor to put into practice the military means to achieve the global ends outlined as strategy a decade before in NSC-68.

The Thousand Days And The Institutionalization
Of Containment Militarism

Kennedy's inaugural address in which he pledged that the United States would "pay any price, bear any burden, meet any hardship, support any friend, oppose any foe" was an indication that his campaign charges were more than election year rhetoric. The bellicose tone of the campaign proved a portent of the course he would pursue as President. The Kennedy-McNamara formula followed the main lines of the Gaither Report — an acceleration of missile development, including the Minuteman and Polaris programs, as well as the beefing up of conventional forces for purposes of "flexible response." Although Secretary of Defense McNamara was aware no later than February 1961, that the so-called missile gap did not exist, he recommended adding ten more Polaris submarines to the fleet and doubled the production of the Minuteman ICBM system. The Secretary also ordered one-half of the Strategic Air Command bombers on a quick-reaction general alert. As McNamara explained the buildup:

> In the short term, that is to say, between 1961 and 1962, we have simply taken the steps that were within our capability to increase the megatonnage as rapidly as possible in the alert force. [29]

Conventional forces were also increased with the emphasis placed on highly mobile forces and counterinsurgency. In addition, McNamara laid plans for a ten-division strategic reserve about which one observer commented: "With it, he could handle a Korean-sized engagement and still have several divisions left over for another emergency." [30] Eisenhower's final budget for fiscal 1962, which Kennedy and McNamara inherited, provided $43 billion for military purposes. The Kennedy Administration, by means of three quick supplements to the budget, raised the total to just under $50 billion. The first budget prepared entirely under Kennedy called for $51.6 billion for the military in 1963. [31] Fiscal policy was beginning to catch up with strategic doctrine.

Richard Barnet has written that a president "probably exerts his greatest influence over future policy when he recruits his leading advisers." [32] If that is so, it is no wonder that in his short and tragic time in office Kennedy presided over the establishment of an infrastructure that could for the first time bring to bear the full force of Containment Militarism. The Kennedy Administration included architects of NSC-68 led by Paul Nitze, true believers in its application to Asia like Dean Rusk and Walt Rostow, and strategists and technicians dedicated to designing the military posture to put it into practice like Robert McNamara and Maxwell Taylor. Together they sought to build the machinery, extend the structures, and manage the technology designed for the global containment that had been NSC-68's promise in the early years of the Cold War. Now with the means soon in place and those with the will to implement the policy in power, Containment Militarism could at last be realized. Its testing ground would be Vietnam.

As noted earlier, NSC-68 embodied an implicit globalism which even when it could not be put into practice for reasons of "limited resources" still provided the rationale for maintaining a U.S. presence in Southeast Asia. The Truman-Acheson fear was that an *over* commitment in Indochina could impede the remilitarization of Western Europe. Eisenhower and Dulles worried that such an *over* commitment could wreck the American economy. Neither, however, saw fit to sever the American commitment completely in spite of their reservations. The Truman Administration laid the foundation for that commitment by positing a bipolar, zero-sum world in which Vietnam, under the strains of political pressure and ideological consistency, became a bona fide, if lesser, domino in the conflict between East and West. The Eisenhower years elevated the status of Asia in the Cold War struggle, thus raising the stakes of American involvement in the fate of Vietnam. This was symbolized when the Eisenhower Administration bound U.S. fortunes to the puppet regime of Diem after the French were forced out of Indochina.

Upon assuming office, Kennedy inherited this legacy of escalating commitment. There is little evidence to suggest that the new President brought anything but unflagging zeal to the task. As Senator from Massachusetts, Kennedy had a few years before referred to Diem's regime as "the cornerstone of the Free World in Southeast Asia, the keystone in the arch, the finger in the dike." Vietnam was "a proving ground of democracy in Asia . . . the alternative to Communist dictatorship." Moreover, Kennedy maintained, it was a test of American leadership and responsibility. Invoking the domino theory, he concluded, "The key position of Vietnam in Southeast Asia makes inevitable the involvement of this nation's security in any new outbreak of trouble."[33]

Unfortunately, as was quite clear by the early 1960s, the star the U.S. had hitched its future to in Vietnam — the Diem regime —was proving to be not only corrupt but inept besides. The situation had plunged into a rapid state of deterioration when in the fall of 1961,

Kennedy dispatched Maxwell Taylor and Walt Rostow on the initial leg of what would become an endless parade of fact-finding tours by senior advisers to fathom developments in Southeast Asia first hand. Given the well-known hard-line predelictions of Taylor and Rostow, their report offered no surprises in its recommendation for an expanded military effort to prop up the Diem government. With the knowledge that McNamara was equipping the Army with the capacity to send mobile strike forces into Southeast Asia — a capability lacking at the time of Dien Bien Phu —General Taylor concluded that the deepening crisis in Vietnam could be reversed by the introduction of 8000 American combat troops to bolster the covert operations and technical assistance already underway. The critical point in the Taylor-Rostow report was their recommendation that the "United States should become a *limited partner* in the war" (emphasis added). Then the other shoe dropped with this quickly added caveat:

> If the first contingent is not enough to accomplish the neces-
> sary results, it will be difficult to resist the pressure to re-
> inforce. If the ultimate result sought is the closing of the
> frontiers and the clean-up of the insurgents within SVN (South
> Vietnam) *there is no limit to our possible commitment* (unless
> we attack the source in Hanoi). (emphasis added)[34]

Despite such dire predictions, the Taylor-Rostow mission did not shirk from recommending escalation. Like an eerie preview of the coming quagmire, Taylor stated in his cover letter that an air offensive against North Vietnam might even have to be undertaken at some point in the future. [35]

To his credit, Kennedy did not implement the Taylor-Rostow recommendations whole. At the same time, he did not dismiss them out of hand either. Instead like presidents before and after on the Vietnam question, he chose to split the difference, adding "military advisers" — the Green Beret counterinsurgents — on a gradual but nonetheless steady basis such that the 700 American troops in Vietnam when Kennedy took office had swelled to 11,300 by 1963. [36]

Arthur Schlesinger writes that the effect of the Taylor-Rostow trip, despite the fact that their advice was not received with the same palpable urgency in which it was given, "was to order future thinking about Vietnam in both Saigon and Washington with the unavowed assumption that Vietnam was primarily a military rather than a political problem." [37]

The much publicized division within the Kennedy Administration in the summer of 1963 over what to do with the intractable Diem is a case in point which demonstrates the narrowing of options to solutions that only considered "containing communism" in Vietnam by military means.

According to the insider's account of Roger Hilsman, a highly-placed Administration official at the time, there were two groups of advisers sharply divided over what the U.S. course should be in Vietnam. One group, which put its faith in counterinsurgency methods and the strategic hamlet program, argued for an overthrow of Diem if the "hearts and minds" strategy was to have a chance of success. The second group favored the more traditional use of military force and recommended that the U.S. continue to work with Diem. Hilsman calls the first a "political" approach and the second a "military" one. In a critique of this formulation, however, John C. Donovan astutely points out that these were really "two different *military* approaches to Vietnam: counterinsurgency vs. a military partnership arrangement." [38] Matters had already escalated well beyond a political solution in the minds of the Kennedy cabinet's national security elite.

Johnson's War: The Logic of NSC-68 Applied

If Kennedy bears responsibility for presiding over the institutionalization of Containment Militarism, making its implementation fully possible for the first time, it was during the Johnson years that the machinery was set in motion. From the beginning, Lyndon Johnson's efforts seemed designed with scrupulous continuity in mind. This can be attributed in part, of course, to the tragic manner in which he took over the reins of power. But it was more than that as well. First, like Kennedy, there was little indication from Johnson's past that he did not fully embrace the domino theory at the heart of the containment doctrine. When he visited South Vietnam in 1961 as vice-president, Johnson praised Diem as an "Asian Churchill" and was among the group that pushed for military support of his government in the pre-coup debate of 1963. [39] Second, like his predecessors, he too was haunted by memories of the domestic fallout after Truman's "loss of China," fearing another right wing backlash and charges of appeasement if the U.S. "lost another country to communism" in Asia. Finally Johnson, to a lesser degree than Kennedy, was an unlikely candidate to challenge the momentum building up toward full-scale intervention within national security circles. As inexperienced in foreign affairs as he was savvy in domestic politics, Johnson retained the Kennedy team intact — a group that had a great deal invested in Vietnam by the time it became "Johnson's War" in November, 1963. Four days after Dallas, Johnson signalled his determination to prevail by approving NSAM 273 which, according to Gelb and Betts, "perpetuated the language about assisting the South Vietnamese but for the first time introduced the word 'win' into the U.S. objective." [40]

During 1964, a tumultous year of aftershocks and coutercoups to

Diem's assassination, Administration officials came to a consensus that "American objectives" could only be accomplished if the U.S. effort was increased substantially. The impact of this latest escalation would not be felt in Vietnam, however, until early 1965 because of the 1964 presidential contest in which Johnson was cast as the peace candidate to the Strangelovian Barry Goldwater. In February came the announcement that the President had ordered continuous air strikes against North Vietnam. As one observer of the period put it: "For the President's national security team, 'the war began in February of 1965.' " [41] That month, McGeorge Bundy had gone to Vietnam on the latest fact-finding tour, returning with the assessment that "the situation in Vietnam is deteriorating and without new U.S. action defeat appears inevitable." [42] In response the Administration launched Operation Rolling Thunder, the massive bombing of the North.

It was May 1965, before the decision was taken to send in U.S. ground troops *en masse*, the other half of the Taylor-Rostow formula of 1961. This action followed a report from the CIA that the South Vietnamese government was about to cave in. More than 30,000 American military personnel and special forces units, combined with air raids on North Vietnam, had proven insufficient to stave off defeat of the South's forces. Presidential adviser William Bundy (brother of McGeorge) noted that: "By June it was clear to all the President's senior advisers that we would have to up the level of American troops . . . This is the fork in the road when we crossed into another kind of commitment." [43] The Johnson circle had indeed crossed the Rubicon in Southeast Asia, embarking on a new commitment that would hold hostage not only the future of Vietnam, but America's as well.

At this decisive point in the history of the war, the justifications given by the policy elite for yet another increment in the level of violence in Vietnam threw into sharp relief the operating logic that governed official thinking throughout the Cold War era. In a tone reminiscent of NSC-68, McNamara argued in a memo to the President for an intensified effort to guard against the growth of "*neutralist sentiment* in Saigon" (emphasis added). [44] Accordingly, Johnson cabled Ambassador Henry Cabot Lodge that he was adamantly opposed to "the idea of neutralization wherever it rears its ugly head." He went on to emphasize that there is "nothing more important than to stop neutralist talk wherever we can by whatever means we can." [45] A political solution, i.e., acceptance of neutralism, was at this juncture unthinkable to those schooled in the logic of Containment Militarism. Bundy, for example, reasoned that the outcome of a negotiated settlement between Saigon and Hanoi "would be regarded in Asia, and particularly among friends, as just as humiliating a defeat as any other form." [46] Thus despite the prevailing pessimism within the Administration concerning the viability of the South Vietnamese government, Johnson's inner circle moved relentlessly forward in a scenario of escalating destruction.

The best reason Bundy could muster in an otherwise dismal memo was that such a *Gotterdammerung* policy "would put us in a much stronger position to hold the next line of defense, namely Thailand." [47] Vietnam was characteristically portrayed as a domino in the larger struggle for global hegemony. As a McNamara aide asserted in this turbulent period — an assessment the Defense Secretary initialed his agreement with — the United States' objective in South Vietnam was "not to 'help friend' but to contain China." [48] In the field this logic was translated into a pattern of decisions captured in the now-infamous admission by the American major who after levelling the village of Ben Tre was quoted to the effect that "it became necessary to destroy the town to save it." [49] On the eve of the decision to bomb North Vietnam, Defense Secretary McNamara, far from the heat of battle, expressed the same conviction before the House Armed Services Committee when he exhorted its members that, "The choice is not simply whether to continue our efforts to keep Vietnam free and independent, but rather, whether to continue our struggle to halt Communist expansion in Asia." [50]

George Kennan has expressed the view that containment lost much of its rationale with the death of Stalin and the development of the Sino-Soviet conflict. Be that as it may, the containment world view served as the official justification for the deepening commitment in Vietnam that spanned a generation and several administrations. In his insider's account of decision-making during the fateful years of the Johnson Administration, Townsend Hoopes writes that despite the fact that "by 1965 many of the major elements of the Cold War mosaic had undergone drastic transformation or had ceased to exist . . . the President's advisers were children of the Cold War in the sense that their thinking about world strategy and world politics had been decisively shaped by that phenomenon." [51] Accordingly, the underlying purpose of U.S. commitment was *never once* called into question in the form of an overall policy review but instead, as the Pentagon Papers show, at each critical juncture in the deepening American involvement the debate centered on *how* to contain communism, not *why*. In this regard, Gelb and Betts conclude: "The commitment in principle always determined the scale of the commitment in fact." [52] Acheson set the tone as early as 1950 when he remarked that "having put our hand to the plough, we would not turn back," a poignant illustration of Cold War logic and a fitting epitaph with which to head this chapter.

The beginning of the end for the U.S. in Vietnam — and for Containment Militarism as sacrosanct doctrine — was the decision to carry the war North via bombing raids. When this tactic failed to halt hostilities in South Vietnam, the costly — in both an economic and political sense — introduction of ground troops followed. Perhaps the most persistent advocate of air strikes against North Vietnam was Walt Rostow, who argued as early as February 1964, a year before the bombing began that, "(Ho Chi Minh) has an industrial complex to protect: he is no longer a guerrilla fighter with nothing to lose." The *Pentagon Papers* has Rostow saying for the record that:

> . . . a credible threat to bomb the industry Hanoi had so painstakingly constructed out of the ruins of the French Indochina War would be enough to frighten the country's leaders into ordering the Vietcong to halt their activities in the South.[53]

Rostow's logic is indeed ironic considering he had participated under Nitze's direction in the Strategic Bombing Survey which assessed the effect of allied bombing on German industrial production during World War II. The study showed that bombing can have the unintended result of raising the enemy's morale while marginally reducing its productive capacity. Vietnam would prove a case in point. Nevertheless, faced with the choice of reducing the commitment or escalating the American presence still further in hopes of turning a bad situation around, the Johnson circle made the fateful decision to pursue the latter course.

The decision was fateful in an economic sense because the expenditures for first an air and then a ground war were vastly underestimated. As a result, 1966 witnessed the most rapid price inflation since the Korean War. In response, Johnson proposed a six percent surcharge on personal and corporate taxes to meet the burgeoning costs of the war. The President's proposal received a cool reception from the Congress, however. Wilbur Mills, chairman of the House Ways and Means Committee, insisted on a reduction in domestic social spending as the price of approval for Johnson's tax package. But Johnson was unwilling to submit to cuts in his Great Society programs. While the stalemate was fought out inflation soared, leaving the U.S. with a deficit of $7 billion in its international balance of payments in the last quarter of 1967.[54] Finally, in the aftermath of the Tet Offensive, the instability of the dollar brought tremendous speculation on the international gold exchange. The situation had reached such dire straits by mid-March that the London gold market was closed to check the massive drain. That weekend, treasury secretaries and heads of central banks from seven nations hastily assembled for a secret conclave in Washington to deal with the strain on the international monetary order brought on by efforts to finance U.S.

escalation in Vietnam during the previous two years. [55]

None of this was supposed to happen, of course. NSC-68 and the Gaither Report had insisted that the accelerated spending needed to implement a policy of Containment Militarism could be bought without deleterious economic effects, indeed that it would contribute to a robust growth. Kissinger had assured that we had not begun to explore the upper economic limits of military spending. Emissaries from the financial establishment such as Lovett and McCloy had since 1950 pledged corporate allegiance to military Keynesian formulas. By the spring of 1968, however, the economic logic of Containment Militarism was unravelling rapidly and with it the elite consensus the doctrine had enjoyed up to the time of the Tet Offensive.

The War's political legitimacy was faring as badly as its economic rationale. By 1968, a five-to-three majority of the American public viewed the original decision to go to war as a mistake, although support for the war itself exceeded confidence in the President's handling of it. [56] The most significant political defection occurred within the foreign policy/national security establishment itself. Hoopes portrays the Administration as riddled with doubt about the conduct of the war by the autumn of 1967. [57] Despite 470,000 U.S. troops the combat situation in the South had failed to stabilize. Moreover, intelligence reports indicated that the bombing had not lifted the morale of the South Vietnamese forces any more than it had shaken the confidence of the North. Nor, for that matter, was it successful in stopping the flow of troops and weapons north to south or in moving Hanoi any closer to the conference table. In sum, none of the political objectives that the military strategy was designed to meet were being fulfilled. It was at this juncture that McNamara commissioned the review of decision-making that had brought the United States to the dilemma it faced in the summer of 1967, the first review of its kind since American involvement had begun nearly two decades before. This study would eventually reach the public as the epic *Pentagon Papers*.

Tet: Denouement Of Containment Militarism

If the consensus within the establishment was slowly eroding along with the growing mass mood of disillusionment, it shattered convincingly with the impact of Tet. The simultaneous and coordinated attacks against major population centers and military bases in South Vietnam known as the Tet Offensive, beginning January 31, 1968, and lasting into mid-February, were a dramatic turning point in the war. It meant that after years of fighting, the communist forces were still capable of launching a withering offensive. Not everyone read this the same way however.

The Joint Chiefs Of Staff saw the Tet drive as all the evidence they needed to build a case for another troop increase, since the 510,000 already there had proven inadequate to contain communist advances. General Earle Wheeler returned from Vietnam after consulting with the field commander there, General William Westmoreland, and promptly requested a forty percent increase in the overall combat force level. [58] The implicit strategy behind the troop request was, no doubt, pursuit of a bolder offensive on the ground which in turn would require a still more ambitious bombing campaign against the North to stop the supply of enemy troops and material into the zone of battle.

The civilian dissidents in the Pentagon were by this time convinced that Vietnam had become a bottomless pit into which 206,000 more troops would be swallowed with little or no effect, and which stepped up bombing raids would not be able to penetrate. The opportunity to make their views felt came when Clark Clifford was named to replace McNamara as Secretary of Defense, and Johnson asked Clifford to chair an ad hoc task force to consider the Joint Chiefs Of Staff request. Named to carry out this exercise were Nitze, Paul Warnke, and Phil Goulding from the Defense Department; Rusk, Nicholas Katzenbach, William Bundy, and Philip Habbib from the State Department; General Wheeler representing the Joint Chiefs Of Staff; Richard Helms from the CIA; Treasury Secretary Henry Fowler; and General Taylor and Walt Rostow representing the White House. [59]

From the start Clifford encouraged the Committee to take a broader view, considering the troop request not only in immediate strategic terms, but also in its long-term ramifications for overall policy. The exercise showed the policy elites to be deeply divided into two distinct groups. The inner circle of White House advisers including Rusk, Rostow, Wheeler, and Taylor, joined by Fowler, favored support of the troop request, while the deputies within the Defense Department led by Nitze and Warnke argued that the troop increase would simply be "reinforcing weakness." Instead they urged a policy of gradual de-escalation. Not long into the proceedings, Clifford whose reputation was decidedly hawkish, came around to his deputies' way of thinking. Having done so he was disturbed by the "bunker mentality" of LBJ and the inner circle. Clifford's concern prompted him to propose that the President consult his Senior Advisory Group on Vietnam — the so-called Wise Men — before making a final decision on the troops issue and the next step in the war. The Senior Advisory Group had in November, with Clifford among its members, approved an escalation of the air war and in general supported the Administration's conduct of the war up to this time.

The meeting between the President and his Senior Advisory Group was set for the end of March. By the time it was convened Johnson had suffered a series of severe jolts. Perhaps the greatest shock was the defection of venerable cold warrior Acheson, who reportedly told the President that the Joint Chiefs Of Staff did not know what they were talking about as regards their recommendation of further escalation. As a result of his stern rebuke, Acheson was assigned a governmental staff for purposes of conducting his own independent inquiry. On March 15, having completed the examination, Acheson offered his views to LBJ at a luncheon meeting at the White House. According to Hoopes, Acheson's review had only strengthened his earlier convictions. He admonished the President that:

> . . . he was being led down a garden path by the Joint Chiefs Of Staff, that what Westmoreland was attempting in Vietnam was simply not possible — without the application of totally unlimited resources "and maybe five years." He told the President that his recent speeches were quite unrealistic and believed by no one, either at home or abroad. He added the judgment that the country was no longer supporting the war. [60]

The second shock was the vote of no confidence by the leaders of international finance who conducted their clandestine meeting in Washington shortly after the Acheson session. Any great increase in military spending by the United States in Vietnam, they feared, without cuts in spending for Great Society programs or without an increase in taxes, could quickly lead to renewed speculation, the downfall of the dollar, and a vast international financial crisis. The third shock occurred in the presidential sweepstakes with Eugene McCarthy's surprisingly strong showing in the New Hampshire primary March 12, and Robert Kennedy's announcement of his candicacy on the 16th, the same day the London gold market closed to stem the tide of speculation.

The final blow to Johnson which bound each of these setbacks together was the meeting with the Establishment's "Wise Men," whose devastating opinion of his Administration's handling of the war caused LBJ to remark that "somebody had poisoned the well." [61] The consensus of the group was that some action had to be taken to reduce American involvement in Vietnam and to find a way out of Southeast Asia. Except for a small nucleus of the Senior Advisory Group who supported the Joint Chiefs Of Staff, the majority were convinced that an increase in American forces was untenable. Herbert Schandler, principal chronicler of the two sections of the *Pentagon Papers* that dealt with the Tet period, suggests that the meeting between Johnson and these prestigious figures of the political and corporate establishment marked the denouement of

Containment Militarism in Vietnam:

> Thus the meeting with the Wise Men seemed to have served the purpose that Clifford had anticipated it would. These trusted advisors had now brought home to the president what the newspapers and polls had been telling him for a month. The Tet Offensive had increased the opposition within the country to the war. Further escalation would not be acceptable to a large and influential segment of the American public. It was necessary to call a halt, to change our policy, to restore some balance. [62]

Accordingly on March 31, Johnson in his famous television address announced a halt to the bombings, a willingness to seek a negotiated settlement with Hanoi, and the decision to take himself out of the presidential race.

The road out of Vietnam under Nixon and Kissinger would prove a long and tortuous journey finally ending in the ignominious spectacle of the American ambassador lifted off the roof of the U.S. embassy by helicopter as the National Liberation Front marched into Saigon proclaiming its new name of Ho Chi Minh City. But the decisions of March, 1968, some seven years before this scene, signalled the recognition that Containment Militarism had failed in Southeast Asia. The perturbations of the Nixon-Kissinger years, from rapprochement with China to the invasion of Cambodia, from detente with Russia to the callous Christmas bombings of North Vietnam in 1972, from overtures toward peace in the Paris negotiations to the equipping of South Vietnamese forces with a formidable arsenal under the guise of Vietnamization, were all designed to extricate the U.S. from an acknowledged no-win situation. If the Establishment had reached a consensus on Vietnam in the wake of Tet, the zigzag course adopted by Nixon and Kissinger in succeeding years served as a lightning-rod for drawing out underlying tensions that had remained submerged until the immediate issue of escalation or disengagement was settled.

Once the catharsis of Tet ended, so too did the elite consensus. The dilemma of how to get out which haunted the Nixon Administration led inevitably to "the lessons of Vietnam," a point upon which the architects and technicians who had drafted Containment Militarism and shaped it into policy from Truman to Johnson were in profound disagreement.

Nitze and Warnke, who more than any others persuaded Clifford of the folly of continuing the course of Containment Militarism in Southeast Asia, epitomized the elite consensus transformed into conflict. Nitze was Clifford's Deputy Secretary of Defense while Warnke served as Assistant Secretary of Defense for International Security Affairs, the latter post often called the Pentagon's "little State Department" because of its concern with the linkage between military posture and foreign policy. In an interview, Nitze described the critical conversion of Clifford after Tet, explaining that:

> Once McNamara got driven out and Clark Clifford came in, I devoted myself for at least a month trying to persuade Clark that his hawkish handling of the situation was totally absurd. Then in March he suddenly flipped from being an extreme hawk to being an absolute incontinent cut-and-runner. [63]

Acknowledging the one hundred and eighty degree shift in his thinking, Clifford explained his former hard-line position, saying: "I was a child of the Cold War. I believed that hostilities in Berlin and in Vietnam directly threatened our national security. I accepted all that. I had been raised on it." [64]

"All that" was nothing less than the doctrine of Containment Militarism that had served as the guiding principle of United States policy for a generation. Thus Clifford was not simply declaring the Vietnam War to have been the mistaken application of an otherwise sound doctrine. Instead he was repudiating the very world view that gave meaning to the Cold War confrontation between East and West. Nitze, who had counseled perhaps a forty-five degree turn in Clifford's stance, was understandably shaken by his boss' sudden transformation.

Far from rejecting the doctrine he had founded, Nitze's own reasons for disengagement were the negative pull that Vietnam was exerting on U.S. attention to the strategic balance between the superpowers, as well as on its other global commitments — especially in Europe. In Nitze's words, "One shouldn't take as absolute the objective of denying the subversion of South Vietnam by force. Clearly that was an important objective, but it ought to be looked at in relation to our other objectives and policies as a whole . . . Vietnam was not worth 100 points, but it was worth more than zero points." [65] By the spring of 1968 Nitze concluded, the U.S. had become overcommitted to the point that the costs of containment in Vietnam exceeded its potential gains. To restore some proportion to American policy in Southeast Asia, he favored a reduced-cost approach which entailed a complete halt to bombing on the one hand, coupled with an immediate increase of 50,000 more troops on the other. His rationale was as follows:

> Tet was a disaster for both sides. So I thought the critical question was who could pick themselves up the fastest. Time was of the essence. From Tet to June 30 was the critical period. If the South Vietnamese didn't pick themselves up fast,

then we would be forced to the alternative of disengagement. The range of uncertainty was very great. I thought things could be as bad as Wheeler said, but not necessarily so. I wanted to send those additional troops to deal with uncertainty. I wanted to get them out there before June 30 so they could make a difference; after that it might not matter. [66]

Nitze emphatically rejected a policy of complete withdrawal on the grounds that it would assure a communist victory, the consequence of which would be a change in the "correlation of forces" between the communist world and the West. Expressing dismay with Clifford's broader interpretation of "the lessons of Vietnam," Nitze emphasized:

Goddamn it, I was against our getting in but once in you have to consider how to get out. You just can't pull out arbitrarily without paying for it forever after. I couldn't convince him (Clifford) of this and it became an issue with Clark and me and Paul Warnke who had been one of my ablest and loyalist supporters. He switched to Clifford and from that point on he's been the leader of a point of view that I consider to be totally unwise. [67]

Warnke's critique of the Administration's Vietnam policy which so impressed Clifford and inflamed Nitze went far beyond the reservations voiced by the latter. Warnke came to the conclusion that not only the war, but the policy that led to it were mistaken. Rejecting the zero-sum logic of Containment Militarism, Warnke reasoned:

What happens in Southeast Asia is of only marginal importance to the Soviet Union. Whether Hañoi wins or Saigon manages to hold on indefinitely is not going to have the least impact on Russians in Egypt or Egyptians in Russia or pressure from Berlin or anything else. [68]

The entire Vietnam strategy, Warnke concluded, was based on the erroneous "misconception that Southeast Asia was an arena of superpower confrontation." If he was critical of the *globalism* of Containment Militarism, he also rejected its *militarism*. As regards the latter, he charged:

There is no question of the fact that we can keep on winning the war forever. We always win and we always will, and it won't ever make any difference. Our wins won't make a dent because there is no way in which we can bring about political progress in South Vietnam . . . The more of an American military occupation you engage in the longer you're going to

stay. What Tet exposed was the fact that what we had thought
was political progress was just so thin as to be illusory. [69]

Thus where Nitze made his case to Clifford on the basis of the
misapplication of Containment Militarism, Warnke argued that the
policy orientation was itself the root of the problem: first, the containment
world view was no longer a faithful portrayal of global realities; second,
even if it had been an accurate reflection at one time, Vietnam should not
have become a critical domino in the East-West conflict; and third, the
use or threat of armed force had proven untenable as a means of resolving
issues which were fundamentally political in nature. In the climate of
crisis that enveloped Washington in March, 1968, these profound
differences were minimized by the Senior Advisory Group in order to
present a united front to Johnson so that further disaster in Vietnam might
be averted. But as Godfrey Hodgson speculates, "It was also perhaps the
last occasion on which so many leaders of the American establishment
found themselves united." [70]

The rift between these two currents of thought represented by Nitze
and Warnke had not eased but had widened and grown into open rancor
after the war was finally brought to a halt. When Jimmy Carter nominated Warnke for the twin posts of director of the Arms Control and
Disarmament Agency and head of the SALT delegation almost a decade
after the falling out of the former close friends and colleagues, Nitze
charged before the Senate Foreign Relations Committee that Warnke's
ideas were "asinine" and "screwball." In a letter to John Sparkman,
chairman of the Committee, Nitze explained:

> When, some ten years ago, it became increasingly clear that
> the United States had become strategically and politically
> overcommitted in Vietnam, two schools of thought began to
> emerge as to the proper future direction of our national
> security policy.

Nitze went on to describe these two polar positions as follows:

> In one view, U.S. foreign and defense problems would con-
> tinue, indeed might become more serious as a result of Viet-
> nam, and could well call for even more emphasis and greater
> prudence than had been devoted in the past. In the contrasting
> view, the problems of the past had arisen largely from our own
> errors springing from overemphasis on foreign policy, and
> particularly its defense aspects.

Finally Nitze charged:

> There can be no question that Mr. Paul Warnke . . . has been

one of the most active, vocal and persistent advocates of this (latter) point of view. [71]

Neither is there any doubt that Mr. Paul Nitze — and the contemporary Committee on the Present Danger of which he was a founder — were in the forefront of those promulgating the former perspective. The next chapter will explore the nature of this deep ideological rift which left the foreign policy establishment divided into two warring schools, each with antithetical perceptions of what American imperial policy should be in light of the global realities — about which they also disagreed — confronting the United States in the last quarter of the century.

As we have seen in this chapter, the catalyst for the fragmentation of elite opinion was the application of Containment Militarism to Vietnam. The disaffection of a substantial and influential segment of the elite developed in response to the impact of the war in Asia on the political stability of Europe and America. This is ironic on two counts. First, Containment Militarism had been designed to contain European self-rule and its application in Vietnam evolved with that objective still uppermost in elite thinking. However it was not the fall of a domino in Asia that caused the alliance between Europe and the United States to falter by the late 1960s, but instead the economic and political costs of preventing the fall. Here was a clear case of the adage about the cure being worse than the disease, or more precisely in this instance of the innoculation having effects more serious than the contagion it was designed to prevent.

Second, the application of Containment Militarism had not been undertaken only with European neutralism in mind, but also with American domestic politics very much a consideration. Selling a massive military program slated for Europe under the guise of containing an ideology whose designs were allegedly global in reach, left the Europe-oriented policy team of the Truman Administration open to attack from the Asia-first right wing domiciled in the Republican Party. After the "loss of China," the protracted conflict in Korea, and the sensational recriminations of McCarthyism, Asia could no longer be ignored. Thus the entanglement of European and American politics marked a small Asian nation for its fateful role at the center stage of Cold War history.

Only when a widening of the war in Vietnam threatened to bring on the very situation it was designed to prevent — neutralism in Europe and political recrimination at home — did the majority of the Establishment reach the conclusion that Containment Militarism had been tried and found wanting. The more intriguing question, and the one that shattered the consensus, however, was whether this lesson was narrowly confined to Vietnam or whether it should be more generally, even universally, applied. This was the cause of the irreconciliable polarization between Nitze and Warnke after they had together reeducated Clifford to the folly of the American course in Vietnam. It was also this deepening ideological gulf within the once monolithic elite that called into being a new Committee on the Present Danger for a Great Debate in the post-Vietnam era. This time, however, as we will see, Nitze and the re-incarnated CPD were no longer insiders. Neither did the doctrine of Containment Militarism carry the authority of the presidency as had been the case with NSC-68. Rumblings of change had begun as a result of the Vietnam experience, creating a climate that drove the CPD from its familiar insider role into a thoroughly unfamiliar outsider position. But American politics had also undergone shifts of great consequence from Korea to Vietnam such that the contemporary Committee found that it had inherited a constituency for its cause this time around.

Chapter 4

NSC-68 To The Tet Offensive

1. Dean Acheson, *Present At the Creation: My Years in the State Department* (New York: Norton, 1969), 7.
2. Leslie H. Gelb with Richard K. Betts, *The Irony of Vietnam: The System Worked* (Washington, D.C.: Brookings, 1979), 78.
3. Harry S. Truman, *Memoirs: Years of Trial and Hope, II* (Garden City, New York: Doubleday, 1956), 419.
4. "Statement by Secretary Acheson before the House Foreign Affairs Committee, July 28, 1949," *Department of State Bulletin*, August 8, 1949, 21, p. 191.
5. *The Pentagon Papers: The Defense Department History of U.S. Decision-Making On Vietnam*, New York Times edition (New York: Bantam, 1971), 5.
6. U.S.-Vietnam Relations, Study Prepared by Department of Defense, Committee Print, House Committee On Armed Services, 92nd Congress, 1st Session, *The Pentagon Papers*, 8, p. 288. Cited in John C. Donovan, *The Cold Warriors: A Policy-Making Elite* (Lexington, Massachusetts: D.C. Heath, 1974), 116.
7. *The Pentagon Papers: The Defense Department History of U.S. Decision-Making On Vietnam*, The Senator Gravel edition (Boston: Beacon, 1971), 385-387.
8. *Ibid.*
9. Gelb and Betts, 1979, p. 46.
10. "The President's News Conference of April 7, 1954," *Public Papers of the Presidents; Dwight D. Eisenhower, 1954* (Government Printing Office, 1960), p. 383. Cited in Gelb and Betts, 1979, p. 50.
11. Dwight D. Eisenhower, *Mandate for Change, 1953-1956* (Garden City, New York: Doubleday, 1963), 353.
12. *Pentagon Papers*, (Gravel), 1, p. B-9.
13. Dulles made a secret offer to French Prime Minister Bidault of three tactical nuclear weapons to relieve French troops beseiged at Dienbienphu. *See*, statement by Prime Minister Bidault in the film documentary *Hearts And Minds. See also*, Roscoe Drummond and Gaston Coblentz, *Duel At The Brink* (New York: Doubleday, 1960), pp. 121-22; Richard Nixon, *RN* (New York: Grosset & Dunlap, 1978), pp. 150-55.

    For a compendium with extensive documentation of this and other threats to use nuclear weapons over the course of the Cold War *see* Daniel Ellsberg, "Introduction: Call to Mutiny," in E.P. Thompson and Dan Smith, eds. *Protest And Survive* (New York and London: Monthly Review Press, 1981), pp. v-vi.
14. "How CIA Orchestrated '53 Coup in Iran," Robert Scheer, *L.A. Times*, March 29, 1979. Section 1, p. 1.
15. *Pentagon Papers*, (New York Times), pp. 16-18.
16. *Pentagon Papers*, (Gravel), 10, p. 692.
17. Gelb and Betts, p. 68.
18. "Address at the Gettysburg College Convocation: The Importance of Understanding, April 14, 1959," Public Papers: Eisenhower, 1959, p. 71.

19. *Pentagon Papers*, (Gravel), 11, p. 320.
20. Maxwell Taylor, *The Uncertain Trumpet* (New York: Harper and Brothers, 1959, 186.
21. Henry A. Kissinger, *Nuclear Weapons and Foreign Policy* (Garden City, New York: Doubleday, 1957), 155.
22. *Ibid.*, p. 412.
23. *Deterrence And Survival in the Nuclear Age*, Report To The President by the Security Resources Panel of the Science Advisory Committee, November, 1957.
24. Morton Halperin, "The Gaither Committee and The Policy Process," *World Politics*, 1961, 13: 363.
25. For an extensive account of the inner workings of the Gaither Panel see *Ibid.*
26. Chalmers Roberts, *Washington Post and Times-Herald*, December 20, 1957, reprinted in the Congressional Record, 85th Congress, 2nd session, 1958, p. 858.
27. Halperin, p. 374.
28. *Ibid*, p. 276.
29. William W. Kaufman, *The McNamara Strategy* (New York: Harper and Row, 1964), 54.
30. *Ibid*, p. 79.
31. Donovan, p. 163.
32. Richard J. Barnet, *Roots of War: The Men And The Institutions Behind U.S. Foreign Policy* (Baltimore: Penguin, 1971), 77.
33. *Pentagon Papers* (Gravel), 21, p. 31.
34. *Pentagon Papers* (Gravel), 2, p. 90.
35. Cited in Gelb and Betts, p. 75.
36. *Ibid.* p. 80.
37. Arthur Schlesinger, Jr., "Origins of the Cold War," *Foreign Affairs 46*, pp. 22-52.
38. *Donovan, p. 193.*
39. *Ibid.*, p. 188.
40. Gelb and Betts, p. 187.
41. Eugene Eidenberg, "The Presidency: Americanizing The War In Vietnam," in Alan P. Sindler, ed., *America In The Seventies: Cases In Politics And Public Policy* (Boston: Little, Brown), p. 110.
42. *Ibid.*, p. 111.
43. *Ibid.*, p. 113.
44. *Pentagon Papers* (New York Times), p. 244.
45. *Ibid.*
46. *Ibid.*, p. 341.
47. *Ibid.*
48. *Ibid.*, p. 342.
49. Don Oberdorfer, *Tet!* (Garden City, New York: Doubleday, 1971), 185.
50. Annual Military Posture Statement by Secretary of Defense Robert McNamara to Armed Services Committee, House of Representatives, February 18, 1965, as quoted in *Department of State Foreign Policy Briefs*, March 1, 1965.

51. Townsend Hoopes, *The Limits of Intervention: An Inside Account Of How The Johnson Policy Of Escalation was Reversed* (New York: MacKay, 1969), 9.
52. Gelb and Betts, p. 353.
53. *Pentagon Papers* (New York Times), p. 241.
54. Herbert Y. Schandler, *The Unmaking Of A President: Lyndon Johnson and Vietnam* (Princeton, N.J.: Princeton University Press, 1977), 226-227.
55. *Ibid.*
56. Gelb and Betts, p. 172; Schandler, p. 221.
57. Hoopes, p. 58.
58. For a thorough account of the troop request, *see* Schandler, chapter 6.
59. Donovan, pp. 246-247.
60. Hoopes, p. 205.
61. Schandler, p. 264.
62. *Ibid.*, p. 265.
63. Paul Nitze, interview with author, August 24, 1977.
64. John B. Henry II, "February, 1968," *Foreign Policy*, 1971, 4: 28.
65. *Ibid.*
66. *Ibid.*
67. Nitze, interview with author, August 24, 1977.
68. Henry, p. 28.
69. *Ibid.*, p. 29.
70. Godfrey Hodgson, "The Establishment," *Foreign Policy*, 1973, 10: 24.
71. Letter from Paul H. Nitze to the Honorable John J. Sparkman, Chairman, Committee On Foreign Relations, U.S. Senate, February 7, 1977.

Chapter 5

DETENTE:
The Reawakening Of The Great Debate

I am willing to be just as generous as we possibly can be as long as that's consistent with maintaining clear supremacy.

Jeane Kirkpatrick, United Nations Ambassador
and CPD member, on arms negotiation [1]

The American business community has disgraced itself. No one expected it — except Lenin — that they would be leading the parade.

Norman Podhoretz, editor of *Commentary* and
CPD member, on trade [2]

The communist revolution of 1917 — installed in power the muzhik, the Russian peasant. And the muzhik had been taught by long historical experience that cunning and coercion alone ensured survival . . . Marxism . . . has merely served to reinforce these ingrained convictions. The result is an extreme Social Darwinist outlook on life which today permeates the Russian elite as well as the Russian masses.

Richard Pipes, National Security Council staff
and CPD member, on Russians [3]

By the summer of 1974, a number of key figures in the formation of CPD-II had decided that the nation was virtually catatonic in the wake of Vietnam while its leaders were mesmerized by detente. Eugene Rostow, former under-secretary of state during the Johnson years and unreconstructed hawk on Vietnam, probably had more to do with the creation of the Committee than did any other one individual. Rostow headed the Coalition For A Democratic Majority's (CDM) Foreign Policy Task Force which, that summer, released a position paper critical of detente (CDM was born two years before in the ideological strife that broke out over McGovern's victory as the Democratic Party's nominee in the 1972 election). Many of the key members of CDM followed Rostow into CPD-II. Among them were Richard Pipes, Midge Decter, Norman Podhoretz, Leon Keyserling, Jeane Kirkpatrick, Max Kampelman, Richard Schifter, and John P. Roche, to lend an idea of its participants. In all, thirteen of the eighteen members of CDM's Foreign Policy Task Force found their way onto the membership rolls of the CPD. By 1980, these neoconservative Democrats had come full circle, joining Reagan's entourage first in the presidential campaign and later in the Republican Administration.

The paper that emerged from CDM's efforts, "The Quest For Detente," was an unmitigated attack on the very concept; it questioned the Russians' sincerity in pursuing it and Nixon's exaggerated claims for its achievements. As Rostow argued in a personal letter to Secretary of State Henry Kissinger after the latter's response to the Task Force statement:

> We deny that relaxation of tensions between the two countries had in fact occurred. And we think it is not only wrong, but dangerous to lull western public opinion by proclaiming an end of the Cold War, a substitution for confrontation, and a generation of peace. The key passage in our statement was the assertion that President Nixon claimed too much for his policy.

Rostow admonished Kissinger in their exchange of letters that "Soviet policy never changes." [4]

In what was later to become a mainstay of CPD literature, "The Quest for Detente" argued that for the Soviet Union the policy of detente was little more than Lenin's formula of "peaceful coexistence" where the USSR retains the right "to provide military assistance in wars it regards as just." [5]

Kissinger's response to the CDM Task Force's suggestion of a new

— really continuing — Soviet Threat was equally adamant in its tone. Echoing Kennan a generation earlier he wrote, "We frankly see no evidence of a Soviet 'headlong drive for first-strike capability in both nuclear and conventional arms' that the Task Force position paper has claimed." As the Secretary explained the Nixon-Kissinger approach to the Soviet Union:

> We have sought to rely on a balance of mutual interest rather than on Soviet intentions as expressed by ideological dogma. In dealing with the Soviets, we have, in a sense, appealed to the spirit of Pavlov rather than Hegel. [6]

The exchange between Kissinger and Rostow over detente, a word new to the American vocabulary, revealed itself to be only the latest round of an old debate. Kissinger's assumption that the USSR would behave in a traditional balance-of-power manner, despite its ideological Marxist-Leninism, if handled properly, was the conclusion reached by Kennan and Bohlen in the early years of the Cold War. To a containment enthusiast like Rostow, however, who had proclaimed for a quarter century that the Russians were driven by an insatiable expansionism, the revival of such a notion was heresy.

After the Task Force experience Rostow became convinced of the need for putting together a broadly-based committee to awaken the nation to the Soviet Threat and to return the United States to the expansive global role about which there had been little doubt in the interwar years between Korea and Vietnam. Charls Walker, who had served as deputy treasury secretary in the Nixon Administration and was returned to the White House as an adviser on Reaganomics, said: "Gene (Rostow) and I kicked it around and found that Paul Nitze had been having a similar idea." [7]

Paul Nitze. The insider's insider. By now he had served every president since Truman in either State or Defense or in some special mission in the area of foreign policy and national security. The consummate Establishment figure, he was known for the kind of team play and intense loyalty captured in the following answer to an interview question:

> If you're working for a president, then goddamnit you are working for him, and you maintain discretion even if he doesn't accept your recommendations. [8]

Despite such strong feeling about the subordinate role of advisers and office holders, Nitze resigned in disgust from the SALT delegation in

June, 1974, citing the "depressing reality of Watergate" as an obstacle in the arms talks. [9] Watergate, had in fact, a few months before, cost Nitze an appointment as James Schlesinger's Assistant Secretary of Defense for International Security Affairs. Defense Secretary Schlesinger had intended to bring Nitze into the Pentagon to strengthen his hand against the State Department. Like Schlesinger, Nitze was an open skeptic of detente generally and more specifically of Kissinger's philosophy on nuclear weaponry and his strategy in arms negotiations. Nixon was expected to send Nitze's name to the Senate for confirmation, but Watergate politics intervened leaving Nitze "slowly twisting in the wind" despite the fact that the newspapers had already broken the story of the impending appointment. [10]

In the summer of 1974, Nitze provided the White House with a tersely-worded, one-sentence resignation from his post as senior member of the SALT delegation, soon after letting it be known that he was not about to go quietly. Teaming up with erstwhile detente and Kissinger critic Henry Jackson, Nitze went before the Senate Armed Services Committee on June 20 with the message that Nixon and Kissinger were promoting a "myth of detente." [11] The testimony Nitze gave before the Committee provided Jackson with all the fodder he needed for a new round of attacks on Nixon-Kissinger diplomacy, already undermined by the myriad disclosures of Watergate on the domestic front. Schlesinger, meanwhile, in constant communication with Rostow and Nitze during this period, kept up the pressure against detente from within the Administration.

Following Rostow's lead, Nitze too began to talk to his considerable circle of acquaintances about a high-powered effort to reaffirm the principles of Containment Militarism. About a half dozen men, including Rostow, Nitze, Schlesinger, Walker, former Deputy Secretary of Defense David Packard, and H.H. "Joe" Fowler, Treasury Secretary under Johnson, continued discussing the idea of forming such a group until finally on Thanksgiving Day, 1975, "inspired by a couple of Bloody Mary's before lunch" according to his own account, Rostow sat down and fired off a memo to Walker and Nitze. As Rostow tells it, "I said we'd had preliminary discussions long enough. By God, why don't we just do it?" [12] By this time Schlesinger, the conduit for their viewpoint within the Administration, had just been relieved from his post as Defense Secretary as a result of overzealous efforts to derail detente. This setback no doubt loomed large in Rostow's timing.

In March, 1976, over lunch at the Metropolitan Club in Washington, the group began the process of organizing for the effort ahead. Charles Tyroler II had been invited to attend by Nitze and became director of the Committee. He was a natural for the assignment. During

Eisenhower's second term he haa served as Secretary to the Democratic Advisory Council, the shadow government that promoted the Gaither Report; before that, he was on the staff of Assistant Secretary of Defense Anna Rosenberg during the life of CPD-I. Once again, in the Vietnam era, Tyroler was called to serve as director of yet another important containment-oriented group, the Citizens' Lobby For Peace With Freedom in Vietnam. Founded in October, 1967, it represented in many respects a last-ditch effort to hold together the bipartisan Cold War consensus that threatened to come apart after nearly two decades of invincibility. But their effort was for naught when the consensus shattered convincingly in March, 1968, under the combined weight of international alarm and domestic protest touched off in the wake of the Tet offensive. In addition to Tyroler, seven current members of the CPD were included among the signatories of Peace With Freedom In Vietnam. [13] (James Conant, chairman of CPD-I, was also a member.) Many of the present-day CPD members such as Rostow and Nitze were, of course, in government at this time and so were "ineligible" for formal affiliation with such a private lobbying group.

Tyroler's office became the permanent headquarters of the CPD, as it had been for the Peace With Freedom group, and before that, the Democratic Advisory Committee. During the spring of 1976, two of the Committee's primary tasks were to define themselves as an organization and to devise a strategy to communicate their viewpoint in an election year. That there is much to a name was amply demonstrated in the amount of time and effort that went into the issue at the Committee's early organizational meetings. "We spent endless hours on what the Committee should be called," related Tyroler. "Thirty or forty names were considered." [14] Finally, the one that carried the day was suggested by Rostow who recalled the success of the earlier CPD in alerting the nation to the Soviet Threat in the Korean War era. According to Tyroler, there was a big debate on the name right up to the time the group went public in November, 1976. Some thought it "too alarmist" but finally the group agreed with Max Kampelman, "If there is a present danger — as we all agreed there was — there's no sense in pussyfooting about it." [15]

The other problem was when and how to "go public." Right from the luncheon at the Metropolitan Club, Tyroler reported that "there was a great sense of urgency" to get the Soviet Threat campaign rolling. [16] But the dilemma, as expressed by many CPD members, was how to do this in an election year and remain nonpartisan. After all, while the Committee was dominated by names long associated with Democratic administrations, not a few of its members were Republican. Moreover, it was by no means clear that the Democratic nominee would be sufficiently hardline as to warrant the Committee's support. Therefore, rather than launch an organized lobby in an election year, the strategy became one of using their considerable influence behind the scenes to force candidates to address the Soviet Threat, hedging one's bets as it were, in order to push the entire primary and presidential battle to the right. That this strategy was clearly on Rostow's mind can be seen in a revealing passage of a letter to Schlesinger, who at that point was slated to be vice-chairman of the Committee once it went public with its message. Rostow wrote:

> On another and related subject, I enclose a newspaper clipping about the President's (Ford) recent speech before the American Jewish Committee. I believe the speech must be answered soon, and strongly, in the election debate. I am urging some of the Democrats to speak out on the subject. If you agree, you might pass the enclosed package on to Governor Reagan, perhaps with your own outline of a possible speech. [17]

This intimate glimpse of "bipartisanship" in operation squares well with the Committee's founding statement where it describes its position in the following terms: "Our Committee is wholly independent and non-partisan." But the rest of the sentence reads ". . . with no political axe to grind." [18] On the contrary, the axe the the CPD had to grind was double-edged, meant to be swung from either the Democratic or Republican side as both Gerald Ford and Jimmy Carter were soon to discover.

Committee On The Present Danger
EXECUTIVE COMMITTEE

Chairman, Executive Committee

ROSTOW, EUGENE V. Professor of Law, Yale Law School; former Under Secretary of State for Political Affairs

Chairman, Policy Studies

NITZE, PAUL H. Chairman, Advisory Council, School of Advanced International Studies, John Hopkins University; former Deputy Secretary of Defense

Co-Chairmen

FOWLER, HENRY H. Partner, Goldman, Sachs & Co.; former Secretary of the Treasury

KIRKLAND, LANE. Secretary-Treasurer, AFL-CIO

PACKARD, DAVID. Chairman of the Board, Hewlett-Packard Co.; former Deputy Secretary of Defense.

Treasurer

WALKER, CHARLS E. Charls E. Walker Associates, Inc.; former Deputy Secretary of the Treasury

General Counsel

KAMPELMAN, MAX M. Attorney, Fried, Frank, Harris, Shriver & Kampelman

Executive Committee

ALLEN, RICHARD V. President, Potomac International Corp.; former Deputy Assistant to the President for International Economic Affairs

GULLION, EDMUND A. Dean, Fletcher School of Law and Diplomacy
HAUSER, RITA E. Attorney, Stroock & Stroock & Lavan; former Representative to the Human Rights Commission of the United States
MARSHALL, CHARLES BURTON. School of Advanced International Studies, John Hopkins University; former Member, Policy Planning Staff, Department of State
PIPES, RICHARD E. Professor of History, Harvard University; former Director of the Russian Research Center, Harvard University
ROCHE, JOHN P. Professor, Fletcher School of Law and Diplomacy; Special Consultant to President Johnson
RUSK, DEAN. Professor, School of Law, The University of Georgia; former Secretary of State
WHALEN, RICHARD J. Author and Journalist
ZUMWALT, ELMO R., Jr., Admiral, U.S.N. (Ret.); former Chief of Naval Operations

Director

TYROLER, CHARLES, II. President, Quadri-Science, Inc.; former Director of Manpower Supply, Department of Defense

BOARD OF DIRECTORS

ACHILLES, THEODORE, C. Vice Chairman, Atlantic Council of the U.S.; former Counselor of the Department of State
ALLEN, RICHARD V. President, Potomac International Corp.; former Deputy Assistant to the President for International Economic Affairs
ALLISON, JOHN M. Former Ambassador to Japan, Indonesia, and Czechoslovakia
ANDERSON, EUGENIE. Former Ambassador to Denmark
BARDACH, EUGENE. Associate Professor of Public Policy, University of California
BARNETT, FRANK R. President, National Strategy Information Center, Inc.
BAROODY, JOSEPH D. Public Affairs Consultant
BEAM, JACOB D. Former Ambassador to Poland, Czechoslovakia, and the Soviet Union
BELLOW, SAUL Author (Nobel Prize 1976 in literature)
BENDETSEN, KARL R. Former Under Secretary of the Army
BISHOP, JOSEPH W., JR. Professor of law, Yale Law School
BOZEMAN, ADDA B. Professor of International Relations, Sarah Lawrence College
BRENNAN, DONALD G. Director of National Security Studies, Hudson Institute
BROWNE, VINCENT, J. Professor of Political Science, Howard University

BURGESS, W. RANDOLPH. Former Under Secretary of the Treasury and Ambassador to NATO

CABOT, JOHN M. Former Ambassador to Sudan, Colombia, Brazil and Poland

CAMPBELL, W. GLENN. Director, Hoover Institution on War, Revolution and Peace, Stanford University

CASEY, WILLIAM J. Former Chairman, SEC, Under Secretary of State, and President Export-Import Bank

CHAIKIN, SOL C. President, International Ladies' Garment Workers' Union

CLARK, PETER B. President, The Evening News Association

CLINE, RAY S. Director of Studies, Georgetown University Center for Strategic and International Studies

COHEN, EDWIN S. Former Under Secretary of the Treasury

COLBY, WILLIAM E. Former Director of Central Intelligence Agency

CONNALLY, JOHN B. Former Secretary of the Treasury

CONNELL, WILLIAM. President, Concept Associates, Inc.; Executive Assistant to Vice President Humphrey

CONNOR, JOHN T. President, Allied Chemical Corp.; former Secretary of Commerce

DARDEN, COLGATE W., JR. President Emeritus, University of Virginia

DEAN, ARTHUR H. Former Chairman, U.S. Delegation on Nuclear Test Ban and Disarmament

DILLON, C. DOUGLAS. Former Secretary of the Treasury

DOGOLE, S. HARRISON. Chairman, Globe Security Systems Inc.

DOMINICK, PETER H. Former U.S. Senator

DOWLING, WALTER. Former Ambassador to Germany

DuBROW, EVELYN. Legislative Director, International Ladies' Garment Workers' Union

DuCHESSI, WILLIAM. Executive Vice President, Amalgamated Clothing and Textile Workers' Union

EARLE, VALERIE. Professor of Government, Georgetown University

FARRELL, JAMES T. Author

FELLMAN, DAVID. Vilas Professor of Political Science, University of Wisconsin

FOWLER, HENRY H. Partner, Goldman, Sachs & Co.; former Secretary of the Treasury

FRANKLIN, WILLIAM H. Chairman of the Board (Ret.), Caterpillar Tractor Co.

FRELINGHUYSEN, PETER H.B. Former Member of Congress

FRIEDMAN, MARTIN L. Assistant to President Truman

GINSBURGH, ROBERT H. Major General, USAF (ret.); Editor, Strategic Review

GLAZER, NATHAN. Professor of Education and Sociology, Harvard University

GOODPASTER, ANDREW J. General, U.S. Army (Ret.); former NATO Supreme Allied Commander, Europe

GRACE, J. PETER. President, W.R. Grace & Co.

GRAY, GORDON. Former President, University of South Carolina, and Secretary of the Army

GULLION, EDMUND A. Dean, Fletcher School of Law and Diplomacy
GUNDERSON, BARBARA BATES. Former Civil Service Commissioner
HANDLIN, OSCAR. University Professor, Harvard University
HANNAH, JOHN A. Executive Director, United Nations World Food
    Council; former Chairman, U.S. Commission on Civil Rights and Ad-
    ministrator, Agency for International Development
HARPER, DAVID B. Gateway National Bank of St. Louis
HARRIS, HUNTINGTON. Trustee, The Brookings Institution
HAUSER, RITA E. Attorney, Stroock & Stroock & Lavan; former Represen-
    tative to the Human Rights Commission of the United States
HELLMAN, DONALD C. Professor of Political Science and Asian Studies,
    University of Washington
HERRERA, ALFRED C. Research Associate, Johns Hopkins University,
    Washington Center of Foreign Policy Research
HOROWITZ, RACHELLE. Director, Committee on Political Education,
    American Federation of Teachers
HUREWITZ, J.C. Director, The Middle East Institute, Columbia University
JOHNSON, BELTON K. Chairman, Chaparrosa Agri-Services, Inc.
JOHNSON, CHALMERS. Professor & Chairman, Department of Political
    Science, University of California
JOHNSTON, WHITTLE. Professor of Government and Foreign Affairs,
    University of Virginia
JORDAN, DAVID C. Professor & Chairman, Woodrow Wilson Department
    of Government and Foreign Affairs, University of Virginia
KAMPELMAN, MAX M. Attorney, Fried, Frank, Harris, Shriver &
    Kampelman
KEMP, GEOFFREY. Professor of International Politics, Fletcher School of
    Law and Diplomacy
KEYSERLING, LEON H. President, Conference on Economic Progress;
    Chairman, Council of Economic Advisers under President Truman
KIRKLAND, LANE. Secretary-Treasurer, AFL-CIO
KIRKPATRICK, JEANE. J Professor of Government, Georgetown Uni-
    versity
KOHLER, FOY D. Professor of International Studies, University of Miami
    (Florida); former Ambassador to the Soviet Union
KROGH, PETER. Dean, School of Foreign Service, Georgetown University
LEFEVER, ERNEST W. Professor of International Relations and Director,
    Ethics and Public Policy Program, Georgetown University
LEMNITZER, LYMAN L. General, U.S. Army (ret.);former Chairman, Joint
    Chiefs of Staff, NATO Supreme Allied Commander Europe
LEWIS, HOBART. Chairman, Reader's Digest
LIBBY, W.F. Former AEC Commissioner (Nobel Prize 1960 in Chemistry)
LIEBLER, SARASON D. President, Digital Recording Corp.
LINEN, JAMES A. Director and former President, Time Inc.
LIPSET, SEYMOUR MARTIN. Professor of Political Science and Sociology,
    Stanford University
LORD, MARY P. Former Representative to the Human Rights Commission of
    the United Nations
LOVESTONE, JAY. Consultant to AFL-CIO and ILGWU on International
    Affairs

LUCE, CLARE BOOTHE. Author; former Member of Congress, Ambassador to Italy

LYONS, JOHN H. General President, Ironworkers International Union

MacNAUGHTON, DONALD S. Chairman and Chief Executive Officer, The Prudential Insurance Company of America

MARKS, LEONARD H. Former Director, United States Information Agency

MARSHALL, CHARLES BURTON. School of Advanced International Studies, Johns Hopkins University; former Member, Policy Planning Staff, Department of State

MARTIN, WILLIAM McCHESNEY, JR. Former Chairman, Federal Reserve Board

McCABE, EDWARD A. Counsel to President Eisenhower

McCRACKEN, SAMUEL. Author

McGHEE, GEORGE C. Former Under Secretary of State for Political Affairs, Ambassador to Turkey and Germany

McNAIR, ROBERT E. Former Governor of South Carolina

MILLER, JOHN. President, National Planning Association

MITCHELL, GEORGE C. Executive Director, World Affairs Council of Pittsburgh

MORSE, JOSHUA M. Dean, College of Law, Florida State University

MULLER, STEVEN. President, The Johns Hopkins University

MULLIKEN, ROBERT S. Professor of Chemistry and Physics, University of Chicago (Nobel Prize 1966 in Chemistry)

MYERSON, BESS. Consumer Affairs Consultant, New York City; former Commissioner of Consumer Affairs for the City of New York

NICHOLS, THOMAS S. President, Nichols Co.; former Chairman, Executive Committee, Olin Corp

NITZE, PAUL H. Chairman, Advisory Council, School of Advanced International Studies, Johns Hopkins University; former Deputy Secretary of Defense

O'BRIEN, WILLIAM V. Chairman, Department of Government, Georgetown University

OLMSTED, GEORGE. Chairman and Chief Executive Officer, International Bank, Washington

PACKARD, DAVID. Chairman of the Board, Hewlett-Packard Co.; former Deputy Secretary of Defense

PAYNE, JAMES L. Professor of Political Science, Texas A&M University

PFALTZGRAFF, ROBERT L., JR. Professor, Fletcher School of Law and Diplomacy

PODHORETZ, MIDGE DECTER. Author and Editor

PODHORETZ, NORMAN. Editor, Commentary

RA'ANAN, URI. Professor of International Politics & Chairman of the International Security Studies Program, Fletcher School of Law and Diplomacy

RAMEY, ESTELLE R. Professor, Department of Physiology, Georgetown University School of Medicine

RAMSEY, PAUL. Professor of Religion, Princeton University

RIDGWAY, MATTHEW B. General, U.S. Army (Ret.); former Chief of Staff, U.S. Army

ROCHE, JOHN P. Professor, Fletcher School of Law and Diplomacy; Special Consultant to President Johnson

ROSE, H. CHAPMAN. Former Under Secretary of the Treasury

ROSENBLATT, PETER R. Attorney

ROSTOW, EUGENE V. Professor of Law, Yale Law School; former Under Secretary of State for Political Affairs

ROWE, JAMES H., JR. Administrative Assistant to President Roosevelt

RUSK, DEAN. Professor, School of Law, The University of Georgia; former Secretary of State

RUSTIN, BAYARD. President, A. Philip Randolph Institute

SALTZMAN, CHARLES E. Partner, Goldman, Sachs & Co.; former Under Secretary of State for Administration

SCAIFE, RICHARD M. Publisher, Tribune-Review

SCHIFTER, RICHARD. Attorney, Fried, Frank, Harris, Shriver & Kampelman

SEABURY, PAUL. Professor of Political Science, University of California

SHANKER, ALBERT. President, American Federation of Teachers

SKACEL, MILAN B. President, Chamber of Commerce of Latin America in the U.S.A.

SMITH, FRED. Chairman, Board of Trustees, National Planning Association; former Assistant to the Secretary of the Treasury

SMITH, LLOYD H. President, Paraffine Oil Corporation

SPANG, KENNETH. International Business Adviser, Citibank

STRAUS, RALPH I. Director, Atlantic Council of the United States

SWEATT, HAROLD W. Former Chairman of the Board, Honeywell, Inc.

TANHAM, GEORGE K. Vice President and Trustee, The Rand Corporation

TAYLOR, HOBART, JR. Former Director, Export-Import Bank

TAYLOR, MAXWELL D. General, U.S. Army (Ret.); former Chairman, Joint Chiefs of Staff and Chief of Staff, U.S. Army

TELLER, EDWARD. Professor Emeritus, University of California

TEMPLE, ARTHUR. Chairman of the Board, President and Chief Executive Officer, Temple-Eastex, Inc.

TURNER, J.C. General President, International Union of Operating Engineers

TYROLER, CHARLES, II. President, Quadri-Science, Inc.; former Director of Manpower Supply, Department of Defense

VAN CLEAVE, WILLIAM R. Professor of International Relations, University of Southern California

WALKER, CHARLS E. Charls E. Walker Associates, Inc.; former Deputy Secretary of the Treasury

WARD, MARTIN J. President, Plumbers' and Pipe Fitters' International Union

WARD, ROBERT E. Director, Center for Research in International Studies, Stanford University

WEAVER, PAUL S. President, Lake Erie College

WHALEN, RICHARD J. Author and Journalist

WIGNER, EUGENE P. Theoretical Physicist, Princeton University (Nobel Prize 1963 in Physics)

WILCOX, FRANCIS O. Director General, Atlantic Council of the U.S.;

former Assistant Secretary of State, Chief of Staff, Senate Foreign
Relations Committee
WOLFE, BERTRAM D. Distinguished Professor Emeritus of Russian
History, University of California; Senior Research Fellow, Hoover
Institution on War, Revolution and Peace, Stanford University
ZUMWALT, ELMO R. Admiral, U.S.N (Ret.); former Chief of Naval
Operations

The Strategy of Appeasement

The 1976 election was the first of the post-Vietnam era. For the first
time since 1960, the prosecution of an undeclared war in Southeast Asia
would not dominate the electoral agenda. It was also the first post-
Watergate contest — America's domestic Vietnam. The election was
given still added significance because of its coincidence with a centennial
anniversary coming on the heels of these twin traumas at home and
abroad. It was a time of sobering reflection about the recent past; it was
also a time of urgency about the future. Thus there was more than the
usual attention paid to the presidential nominees and policy platforms
that each party would put forth in this watershed year of national soul-
searching.

Uppermost on the foreign policy agenda for 1976 was the Nixon-
Kissinger policy of detente. As noted in the previous chapter, relaxation
of tensions with communist superpowers Russia and China allowed the
U.S. more latitude in Southeast Asia and was certainly a major — some
would say principal — reason detente was adopted by Nixon and
Kissinger, each of whom prided himself on being a pragmatist and power
realist in international politics. Such *realpolitik* satisfied very few,
however, and became a subject of bitter debate almost from the start.
Conservatives, who supported the renewal of bombing and the Cam-
bodian incursion made possible by detente, nevertheless held a visceral
contempt for negotiated deals with the USSR and People's Republic of
China. Liberals, who applauded the easing of Cold War tensions, were to
the same degree appalled at the cynical application of detente in
reescalating the level of destruction in Southeast Asia.

As American involvement in Vietnam neared its ignominious end,
pent-up resentments on both sides turned into open recriminations, the
policy of detente serving as a lightning-rod for mounting bitterness among
political elites. Conservatives, joined by disgruntled hawks like Nitze,
Rostow, and Schlesinger from within the national security/foreign policy
establishment, buried their differences on Vietnam and began to speak
with one voice urging an end to detente on grounds that the Cold War had

not slackened but intensified. Liberals and Establishment doves like Warnke, on the other hand, attempted to rescue detente from the Metternichian calculation of Kissinger, and in the process transform it into a contemporary version of the old Wilsonian dream of a harmonious world order built upon unfettered trade. This latter interpretation of detente threatened to eclipse not only the militarism of containment, but the geopolitics of Kissinger as well.

In the Great Debate that established the hegemony of Containment Militarism in the Korean War era, the controversy over Soviet military capabilities and political intentions served as a kind of code, masking a hidden agenda about the contours of American policy. The same was true in the post-Vietnam period. The logic of detente, for example, assumed a Soviet Union governed by national interest rather than revolutionary ideology, responding to specific historical opportunities rather than to dreams of world conquest. Looking at it another way, detente represented a realistic appraisal that there were limits to U.S. military capabilities after all, and consequently to NSC-68's political intent to rollback communism. It was this reassessment of ourselves as well as our Cold War adversaries that opened the way to a balance-of-power approach that recognized spheres of influence — the Sonnenfelt Doctrine — provided the impetus for an arms limitation process designed to stop political competition between the two systems short of military confrontation — SALT — and sparked economic relations between East and West through the negotiation of trade agreements.

Similarly, in their adamant denial that the global realities of the post-Vietnam era were appreciably different from a quarter century before, the contemporary CPD membership demonstrated that their own ambitious designs remained unchanged since NSC-68. As staunch defenders of the world view of Containment Militarism, talk of any softening in Soviet intentions was foolhardy according to the CPD. The Committee and the consortium of hardliners with whom they worked had not yet conceded that the Cold War was over. On the contrary, they remained firm in their conviction that East and West were locked in implacable conflict, global in scope, and that military force remained the supreme calculus of political power. When Nitze was asked during the course of an interview how the world differed from the early Cold War years when he drafted NSC-68, he replied that the basic intentions of the Soviet Union — the drive for expansion and global hegemony — remained unchanged. What had changed, however, was the "correlation of forces" which were turning in the Soviets' direction, particularly in the area of military strength. [19] Commenting on Nitze's world view, his fellow CPD founder Eugene Rostow related: "I would say that he feels that the perspective that was put together under Acheson's guidance has remained valid, and it has indeed been confirmed." [20]

Like its forbearer, the contemporary Committee and its ideological allies seem more preoccupied with America and the West than with the Soviet Union and communism. The Soviets' global design is proclaimed with a zeal that allows little room for doubt. What is again uncertain, and calls into being a new CPD, is the resolve of the American people and their leaders to match the alleged Soviet expansionism with an ambitious global design of their own in the contest for world hegemony. As Rostow explains:

> The situation in the world recalls that of the Thirties. The pressure of Soviet policy is increasing steadily, but the perception of the threat in the West has been diminishing. This strange psychological phenomenon is the heart of our foreign policy problem today. [21]

Similarly, *Commentary* editor and CPD/CDM ideologue Norman Podhoretz poses the rhetorical question, "Do we lack the power?" His answer:

> Certainly not if power is measured in the brute terms of economic, technological, and military capacity. By all those standards we are still the most powerful country in the world ... The issue boils down in the end then, to the question of will. Have we lost the will to defend the free world — yes, the free world — against the spread of communism? [22]

Jeane Kirkpatrick, another prominent CPD theorist and current U.S. Ambassador to the United Nations, worries that the dominant culture has become a "culture of appeasement." She explains:

> We are daily surrounded by assertions that force plays no role in the world. Unfortunately it does, in most aspects of society, especially in international relations. Therefore a culture of appeasement which finds reasons not only against the use of force but denies its place in the world is a profoundly mistaken culture — mistaken in the nature of reality. [23]

Much of the problem, CPD members believe, lies in an American penchant for "diplomacy" — as represented by detente — over "strategy" — symbolized by containment. Charles Burton Marshall, executive officer of the CPD and longtime confidant of Nitze, stated the conundrum as follows:

> Strategy is something for the breakdowns. Wars are parentheses in history ... We think about strategy when they occur

then forget about it. There is an enormous longing to get back
to peace; it's part of the American psyche, even among people
in government.

However, the long-time adviser to Democratic presidents exclaimed:
"That's for the birds! *It is a strategic world.* It is a strategically-contested
world. Peace and security must be based upon actions consonant with
that view of the world." [24]

Similarly, Lt. General Daniel Graham, retired Chief of the Defense
Intelligence Agency who would come to play such a prominent role in the
Soviet Threat campaign and is now a Reagan military adviser, laments
that historically "in place of strategy, Americans substituted a naively
idealistic predeliction for a worldwide parliamentary system." The one
bright spot, he argues, has been the formulation of the Containment
doctrine. Commenting on the accomplishments of this period with unabashed enthusiasm, Graham claims:

> The containment strategy was the first and last strategy to be
> devised by the United States or NATO as a whole in the post-
> World War II period. It operated to the great advantage of the
> West until the late 1960's when it was replaced by a concept
> which came to be called 'detente.'

He continues, ". . . ironically, the very perception of success of the
containment policy contributed heavily to its replacement by detente,"
an orientation he disparages as a "non-strategy." [25] Graham's thesis is
that containment so thwarted Soviet expansionism that there came to
develop by the mid-1960s the widespread belief that the Russians also
recognized the futility of their ambitions and had abandoned designs of
world conquest. Thus many moderates reasoned that the Soviet Union
could be dealt with on the basis of their interest in international stability
rather than their ideology of world-wide hegemony. In Graham's and the
CPD's view, however, this is a blatant strategy of appeasement given that
"the Soviet Union has not altered its long-held goal of a world dominated
from a single center . . . Moscow." [26] To believe otherwise is simply a
naive misapplication of the convergence thesis. As the Committee's
second position paper, *What Is The Soviet Union Up To?*, explains:
"This habit of mirror-imaging leads many Americans to ignore, to
rationalize or to underestimate the Soviet challenge." [27]

Containment, in contrast to detente, operates out of a perception of
polarity rather than convergence, what Nitze refers to as the "complementariness of opposing principles." Nitze grounds this notion in the
ancient Greek philosopher Heraclitus' classical definition of beauty and
truth. In response to an interview question, he explained:

> Foreign policy requires strong nerves and a very objective

mind that can look at two sides of lots of different issues. You can never slip into oversimplification with a single fact-driven mindset. You have to follow Heraclitus' definition of truth: truth and beauty are to be found in the tension between opposites. It is difficult for people to keep in mind the complementariness of opposing principles. They finally get tired of it and want something simpler.[28]

While the aesthetic quality of Nitze's world view can be disputed, there is certainly an undeniable truth in the "tension between opposites." Without it, Containment Militarism is devoid of rationale. Its logic holds that if the struggle against communism should cease or even lighten up, Soviet interests will advance and those of the U.S. recede. Conversely, with sustained pressure, Soviet ambitions will be thwarted and American fortunes heightened. Graham unwittingly makes the case in the following passage in which he extols the virtues of containment: "With regard to the fundamental problem of systematic struggle with the communist bloc, the strategy of containment had a positive side as well." He goes on to explain that John Foster Dulles, secretary of state under Eisenhower, need not have talked overtly of rollback in Europe because it is implicit in the very process of containment itself:

> Expansionist drives for empire, especially those based on ideological fervor, either advance or retreat; if advance is checked, retreat ensues. [29]

In other words, in a zero-sum world, the power of nation states as measured by the "correlation of forces" either advances or retreats; equilibrium between adversaries is an illusion. Detente and the specific policies that follow therefrom — arms limitation and trade — represent little more than a strategy of appeasement.

Arms Limitation: Two Views

Nowhere was the claim that detente is merely a ruse harboring Soviet aggression made more frequently or urgently by the CPD and its supporters than on the subject of arms control. The Committee's second position paper explained that "according to Soviet theory, peaceful co-existence is not a concept involving a stable world order, but a strategy that adapts the methods of waging international conflict to the era of nuclear weapons." [30] Graham expanded upon this central theme, claiming that the inability to understand true Soviet motivations is responsible for ill-conceived notions of arms control. He charged, "In the mid-1960's, strange notions were incubated by the general euphoria and self-delusion. Among these were the belief — shared by many military analysts — that the Soviets were settling for a 'minimum deterrent'." [31] If it were true, then it followed that the U.S. would not have to develop further costly nuclear capabilities either. In fact, to do so would be politically destabilizing and economically wasteful. Thus there came into being the doctrine of deterrence predicated upon the recognized ability of either side to launch a devastating second-strike against the other in the event of nuclear attack. The doctrine was known as mutual assured destruction or MAD to its critics, who never ceased to charge that the "mutual" aspect was never taken to heart by the Russians. Instead, they maintained, the Soviet Union had forged ahead in weapons technology while the U.S. committed its resources to the war effort in Vietnam. In this fashion arms limitation, one of the two critical pillars of detente, was dismissed as an illusion. In Charles Burton Marshall's words:

> We have approached the SALT talks as just a new version of the old dream of a non-strategic world. We think SALT is a way out of the complication and that is not what the Soviet Union believes. [32]

What the Soviet Union believes, we learn from Richard Pipes, is that they "could fight and win a nuclear war" if it ever came to that. Pipes, chief Sovietologist in the National Security Council and member of the executive committee of the CPD, was perhaps second only to Nitze in formulating the Committee's strategic views. It is his contention that the American and Soviet nuclear strategies are based on "different conceptions of the role of conflict and its inevitable concomitant, violence, in human relations." [33] Translated into policy, the Soviets conclude that "warfare is an extension of politics," the classical doctrine of the 19th century military strategist Clausewitz — an idea Pipes claims the U.S. has, in the age of nuclear weapons, thoroughly repudiated as evidenced by acceptance of deterrence as official strategic doctrine. The Soviet Union, however, so we are told, never accepted the notion that nuclear weapons altered the Clausewitzian formula. Instead they believe it is possible to engage in a limited nuclear confrontation. Not without losses to be sure, but Pipes has a ready explanation for that contingency as well:

> . . . a country like the Soviet Union which, as Soviet generals proudly boast, suffered in WWII the loss of over 20 million casualties, as well as the destruction of 1,710 towns, and over 70,000 villages and 32,000 industrial establishments to win the war and emerge as a global power, is not to be intimidated by the prospect of destruction. [34]

He adds a rather bizarre twist even to this argument in his claim that it is not just because the Russians are communists that the Soviet Union is bent on world conquest, but also because the communists are Russians. To repeat from the passage heading this chapter:

> The communist revolution of 1917 — installed in power the *muzhik*, the Russian peasant. And the *muzhik* had been taught by long historical experience that cunning and coercion alone ensured survival . . . Marxism . . . has merely served to reinforce these ingrained convictions. The result is an extreme Social Darwinist outlook on life which today permeates the Russian elite as well as the Russian masses. [35]

To avoid the hysteria that accompanied the first Soviet Threat and led to talk of "preventive" nuclear war, Nitze, Pipes, and their coterie of hardline strategists reassure that the Politburo has no actual plan to preside over the carnage of its own population for the chance of political gain. The Russian strategy is aimed not at a winner-take-all apocalypse, we are told, but instead toward the demonstration of such overwhelming military strength that the U.S. would be forced to retreat in a situation of crisis, signalling in the process its withdrawal from a leading role in world affairs. In *What Is The Soviet Union Up To?*, the CPD answers Kissinger's plaint, where the embattled Secretary of State asked, "What in the name of God is strategic superiority? What is the significance of it politically, militarily, operationally at these levels of numbers? What do you do with it?" [36] The CPD response: "Superiority in both strategic and conventional weapons could enable the Soviet Union to apply decisive pressure on the United States in conflict situations." [37] Finally, Nitze reminds us that Clausewitz' view was that "war exists for the benefit of the defender; the aggressor would always prefer to achieve his aims without war." [38]

It is indeed ironic given the case constructed on the basis of fundamental differences between American and Russian culture, principles, and motives in the world, that the only example the CPD could find for such a Clausewitzian tactic was *ourselves*: "The USSR might then compel the U.S. to retreat, much as the USSR itself was forced to retreat in 1962 during the Cuban missile crisis." [39] In other words, for all their "peasant guile and cunning" the strategy the Russians intend to follow calls for doing to us what we did to them — an interesting twist on the convergence thesis.

While some thought the Soviet Union's advances offered an opportunity to proclaim an end to the arms race and to declare the nuclear nightmare to have reached a stalemate of "essential equivalence" beyond which any further escalations were meaningless, the hardliners' argued the case for new and ever more exotic programs in the hopes of returning to the halcyon days of the Cuban missile crisis. The latest strategy proposed to achieve the military superiority needed to carry out the doctrine of Containment Militarism was known as "counterforce." Its sponsor was Secretary of Defense Schlesinger.

In January, 1974, Schlesinger announced that the U.S. would re-target its strategic weapons in order to "provide the President additional nuclear options" in time of crisis. The added flexibility, Schlesinger argued, would give the U.S. the possibility of selective nuclear strikes against enemy military installations and missile sites — counterforce — as distinguished from all-out strikes aimed at maximum damage to population centers — countervalue. Contervalue targeting with its indiscriminate and massive destructive capability was geared toward preventing the use of nuclear weapons; counterforce, premised on the belief that surgical strikes with nuclear weapons were in fact possible, made their use "thinkable." To justify this new and expanded doctrine, Schlesinger reiterated the theme that America's will was being put to the test in the wake of Vietnam: "The burden of responsibility has fallen on the United States," Schlesinger warned in Churchillian terms, "and there is nobody else to pick up the torch if the United States fails to carry it." [40]

"Carrying the torch" promised to be a big burden indeed. Schlesinger argued in his Defense budget request that there should be no perceived asymmetries in levels or capabilities of force — conventional or nuclear. [41] In Fiscal Year 1976, this departure from a strategy of essential equivalence in military strength required a panoply of new nuclear weapons to support counterforce doctrine as well as programs of modernization for the Navy, three additional Army divisions, four tactical Air Force squadrons, enlarged strategic lift capabilities, and maintenance of troop levels overseas. In short, in the first peacetime budget in more than a decade, Schlesinger's request called for an overall beefing up of the war machine.

Once again, like a *deja vu* of NSC-68, we quickly discover that the Soviet Threat which preoccupied the defense secretary was not military but political in nature. In his annual defense report for Fiscal Year 1975, Schlesinger argued that "neither the USSR nor the United States has, or can hope to have, a capability to launch a disarming first strike against the other, since each possesses, and will possess for the foreseeable future, a devastating second-strike capability against the other." This is exactly why critics rejected counterforce, arguing that it contributed nothing to national defense. Schlesinger went on to make the case for counterforce in terms of the importance of maintaining forces judged by the world as superior to those of the USSR. If not, other nations would view this reluctance to modernize as a sign of Soviet ascendancy and tailor their policies accordingly. The consequence, Schlesinger warned, would be an attempt by other nations to accommodate to the USSR, resulting in drastic changes in "political frontiers." [42] Such thinly-veiled references to neutralism and non-alignment, especially as regards Europe, crop up again and again in the current Soviet Threat campaign just as it dominated elite thinking in the early years of the Cold War. In *What Is The Soviet Union Up To?*, for instance, we learn that "they (the Soviets) hope to profit from a growing perception in Western Europe of a decline in United States will and power and a concurrent illusion that the Soviet Threat has ended. This would bring about the fatal weakening of NATO and help ease the United States out of Europe." [43] Unfortunately, the CPD argues, both sides of this dilemma are being fulfilled. On the one hand, Rostow laments:

> . . . a treaty of the United States has proved to be worthless — after a great deal of fighting, it is true, but worthless none-theless. Friends and adversaries alike now wonder — and wonder quite legitimately — what the policy of the U.S. and its allies will be in the face of the rising pressures of Soviet imperial ambition. [44]

Running it back the other way, the Foreign Policy Task Force worries that, "There is considerable feeling particularly in Europe, that the risks are not great (of Soviet aggression against Europe)." [45] Iron-ically, then, the proposed military buildup was proffered not to deter the risk of war but the risk of ending the Cold War. Challenges to the empire from within remained as intolerable in the post-Vietnam era as it had a quarter century before in 1950.

Finally, in the eyes of the hardliners, containment remained a global mission and its outcome, as in an earlier time, rested on the balance of military strength between East and West. In his opening remarks to justify an expanded military program, Schlesinger suggested that the nation should keep in mind that, "When a strong man armed keepeth his palace, his goods are in peace." [46] The proposed change in doctrine and the requested acceleration of spending indicated, however, that neither the goods nor the palace were confined within our national borders but extended forth to cover the entire earth and its bounty. In a straight-forward rendition of *realpolitik*, Schlesinger explained:

> We live in an interdependent world economy, and our foreign economic interests are substantial. The oil embargo of 1973 is only the most recent and pointed reminder that we have a keen and a growing interest in distant lands — their markets and their products.
>
> Our foreign political interests are even more extensive. Even in a period of questioning and self-doubt there remains a

consensus within the country that we have vital interests in Western Europe, the Middle East, the Persian Gulf, and Asia.[47]

If U.S. interests remain global in reach, Schlesinger argued consistently throughout his tenure as defense secretary that there existed an inseparable linkage between the maintenance of America's economic and political position in the world and threat of military force to uphold it. This, of course, represents the *sine qua non* of Containment Militarism which the CPD set out to resurrect in the post-Vietnam period of "questioning and self-doubt," to borrow from Schlesinger. On this point, General Graham emphasized:

> I don't agree that military superiority is not important . . . if you want to make that case, that it doesn't do any good, then one has to make the case that it didn't do us any good at the time of the Cuban missile crisis, and it certainly did us good. And I don't think there are many analysts who would believe that if the Cuban missile crisis should come off today that the end result would be the same, given today's strategic balance.[48]

Nitze is just as certain that military strength and the threat of violence remains the principal currency of international politics. In his view, the Berlin crisis of 1961 and the Cuban missile crisis the following year proved beyond any doubt that strategic nuclear superiority can determine the outcome of U.S.-Soviet showdowns. Nitze wrote regarding Berlin that "our theater position was clearly unfavorable; we relied entirely on our position of strategic nuclear superiority to face down Chairman Khrushchev's ultimatum. In Cuba, the Soviet Union faced a position of both theater inferiority and strategic inferiority; they withdrew the missiles they were deploying." [49]

Thus counterforce was a way back to the good old days of the Cuban missile crisis when the U.S. rather than the USSR could threaten to "fight and win a nuclear war" and through force of arms gain its political objectives. Such a state of affairs may no longer be possible, but that is not yet the conclusion of the CPD and its allies now in the Reagan Administration. As Jeane Kirkpatrick remarked:

> I believe in being strong . . . and the reason I do is because I believe the Soviet Union has been consistently uninhibited in the use of force . . . internally and externally throughout its history.

In contrast, she argues: "We are much more inhibited in our use of force." Finally, in reference to SALT, Kirkpatrick reached the particularly revealing conclusion cited at the beginning of this chapter: "I am willing to be just as generous as we possibly can be as long as that's consistent with *maintaining clear supremacy* (emphasis added)." [50]

Schlesinger did not, of course, introduce counterforce in such terms. Instead he argued that it provided the president a more realistic strategy to "resist coercion." The riposte of the critics, however, was that in the case of the weaponry and targeting doctrine required to carry out a counterforce strategy, the power to coerce by means of a first strike of one's own is indistinguishable from the power to resist by defending against such an effort by an adversary. It was apparent that Schlesinger understood the fine line between the two and intended to exploit its ambiguity to the full extent possible when he warned that the United States would not rule out the possibility of initiating a nuclear exchange under certain circumstances — left unspecified. Advocates of arms control charged that such provocation could be used by Soviet hawks to follow suit with their own counterforce programs which of course would be interpreted by U.S. intelligence as an attempt on their part to acquire a capability to wage limited war. Either way the arms race would be off and soaring to still higher, more dangerous, and wasteful levels of competition for both nations.

Paul Warnke, in an article that appeared in *Foreign Policy*, suggested that the United States and the Soviet Union resembled "two apes on a treadmill" in their quest to gain an advantage in the arms race. [51] Apes On A Treadmill, the title of the piece, was nothing less than an antimilitarism manifesto from within the heart of the foreign policy establishment. In it, Warnke questioned the efficacy of either nuclear or conventional military force in achieving foreign policy objectives. He went on in his much-discussed and highly controversial analysis to attack military spending as wasteful, and finally, to suggest that the United States be the "first off the treadmill" by pursuing a strategy of unilateral initiatives to de-escalate the arms race.

Warnke began by attacking what he called "two fallacies" — shibboleths of the Cold War that go back to NSC-68, although he himself never identified them with that document. The first is "the fiction that protection of our interests implies a global military mission requiring that we maintain the capability to deal with congeries of contingencies throughout the world." [52] Warnke then explained that a distinction must be made between a Soviet military threat on the one hand and political or economic situations unfavorable to U.S. interests on the other. America's military posture should be aimed only at the deterrence of the former, according to Warnke, a qualification dismissed as irrelevant from the seamless, zero-sum perspective of Containment Militarism. The "second fallacy" Warnke defined is the belief that "a failure to maintain a cosmetic military 'superiority' will cause us political disadvantage . . . and the sacrifice of the confidence of our allies." [53] Such thinking, he explained, is simply a formula for endless escalation in military budgets and military interventions. Thus Warnke reaches the conclusion that "our preoccupation with military power as a political tool needs to be faced and overcome." [54]

Turning to the quest for military superiority through nuclear weapons, Warnke argues that since "a fraction of the existing strategic forces on either side is adequate to wreak devastation on the other's society . . . the respective strategic nuclear forces serve only as offsets, not as exploitable resources." This means then that " they are not translatable into sound political currency." [55] As an example, Warnke offered the Mideast oil crisis where the threatened use of military force as advocated by the hardliners would have been not only ineffective but counterproductive in that it might well have driven the Arab states into the protective custody of the Soviet Union.

Not only nuclear weapons, but conventional military capabilities as well, are non-translatable to political ends according to Warnke. Using the Middle East example again, he wrote that conventional forces would have faced an interminable occupation, all the while beset by guerrilla harassment and subversion of the oil fields, if a decision of intervention had been taken. After his experience in Vietnam decision-making, Warnke had become convinced that military interventions were a thing of the past — that the U.S. could not, and should not, pursue any longer, the self-anointed role of global policeman.

Warnke's conclusion was a call for the United States to take the first step away from militarism under the assumption that as regards U.S. actions "the Soviets are far more apt to emulate than to capitulate." In support of his provocative thesis, he explained:

> The "monkey see, monkey do" phenomenon extends beyond the area of strategic arms . . . Even our clandestine operations in foreign countries are rationalized by President Ford on the ground that "Communist nations spend vastly more money than we do for the same kind of purposes."

> It is time I think for us to present a worthier model. The strategic arms competition is a logical place to start . . . We can be first off the treadmill. That's the only victory the arms race has to offer. [56]

Trade: The Calculus of Managerialism

One can readily understand how Nitze came to the conclusion

that his former protege Warnke had adopted a viewpoint that he considered to be "totally unwise." Warnke's views expressed in *Foreign Policy* and elsewhere were an unequivocal attack on the doctrine of Containment Militarism. Perhaps what most disturbed Nitze was that as he put it, "Warnke had become the leader of (that) viewpoint." [57] It was bad enough that Warnke had broken with Cold War orthodoxy; it was even worse that he had an identifiable and influential group of confederates behind him. His was not the voice of the lone dissenter as had been the case of George Kennan or Charles Bohlen in the fifties, nor George Ball and Chester Bowles in the sixties, to name the few mavericks who challenged the wisdom of Containment Militarism from within the the ranks of the Establishment during the Cold War era. Neither was the constituency that championed Warnke's view drawn from the ranks of those convinced that American foreign policy was bankrupt to the core as was the case of another Establishment dissident, Daniel Ellsberg, who had also worked in the Pentagon with Nitze and Warnke. Neither isolated nor banished from power, Warnke symbolized a significant segment of elite opinion after 1968. That is what accounts for Nitze's uncharacteristic personal vendetta against him.

The current Warnke represented might be termed global managerialism, an expanded notion of detente repeated in liturgical fashion in the pages of *Foreign Policy*, itself the product of elite debate over the lessons of Vietnam. The first issue of *Foreign Policy* explained that "in light of Vietnam, the basic purposes of American foreign policy demand re-examination and redefinition" and — in obvious reference to the Council on Foreign Relations' house organ *Foreign Affairs* — "a new magazine, having no institutional memory, can commence this task with a keener awareness that an era in American foreign policy which began in the late 1940's, has ended." [58] A similar sense of epochal transformation demanding a new approach to empire also guided the seminars and position papers of the newly-formed Trilateral Commission, the 1980s Project of the Council On Foreign Relations, the Aspen Institute of Humanistic Studies, the Carnegie Foundation, the Brookings Institution, and almost everywhere else that the foreign policy establishment met to formulate a strategy for the post-Vietnam era.

The global managerial approach challenged both of the twin pillars of the Cold War — containment and militarism — replacing them with two of their own — arms control and trade. First, as regards containment, adherents of the managerial thesis argued that the principal conflict in the world was no longer on an East-West plane, but had shifted to a North-South axis. The cleavage between "the free world" and the Iron Curtain had been superseded by the polarity between developed and underdeveloped nations. Second, given the symbiosis between the industrial and raw materials-producing nations, the power to gain political ends in international affairs no longer rested on the display of unilateral military strength, but instead on the management of a new rationalized international order, the key to which was a somewhat more equitable economic arrangement between North and South. Such a new contract, so the argument went, would better secure access to vital energy resources in the Third World than would any amount of sabre-rattling. As Warnke's choice of illustrations shows, the Mideast oil embargo of 1973 made a major impression on global management strategists.

Vietnam had proven a potent catalyst for this shift in world view. Where Containment Militarism had argued that nationalism in the Third World was a mere illusion fronting for Soviet or Chinese expansionism, Vietnam showed it to be a reality in its own right; where Containment Militarism claimed that military force was the determinant factor of world politics, Vietnam proved that to be an illusion. In a further irony, U.S. intervention in the Vietnamese struggle for independence had been predicated upon an alleged global conflict between East and West, a quagmire from which the U.S. could only finally extricate itself by declaring a truce with the communist superpowers. Moreover, the key to the normalization of relations with Moscow and Peking was trade, further evidence to global management enthusiasts that the Cold War pillars of containment and militarism had not only proven ineffective in international politics but now even stood in the way of the restoration of American economic power.

A continuation of the arms race through strategies like Schlesinger's counterforce jeopardized the opportunity to construct the institutional arrangements that could turn the promise of detente into the reality of world order envisaged by Warnke and the moderates of the foreign policy establishment. Clark Clifford, for instance, who since 1968 had become a law partner of Warnke's in the new firm of Clifford, Warnke, Glass, McIlwain and Finny, charged that the Nixon Administration harbored a contradiction so fundamental that it threatened the collapse of detente. The ex-defense secretary warned: "There exists a gap — an undeniable gap — between a foreign policy that purports to deal with a world of detente and a defense policy that is mired in the backward looking attitudes of the cold war." [59] Similarly, the dean of the foreign policy elite, W. Averell Harriman, complained in reference to Schlesinger's actions:

> Tough statements by our Secretary of Defense or others have the same effect in Moscow as tough statements by (Soviet Defense Minister) Grechko have on us here. They pull the rug out from under the more moderate and strengthen the arguments of the militants and other hardliners. [60]

If an influential segment of the establishment was dissatisfied with the Nixon-Kissinger, and later Kissinger-Ford, effort at *reducing military confrontation*, neither were they satisfied with its record in *increasing economic cooperation*, the positive side of the managerial equation. Kissinger himself, rather than his rival Schlesinger, was held directly accountable for this particular failing. C. Fred Bergsten, who served as Kissinger's Assistant For International Economic Affairs, drafted a scathing critique of Kissinger at the request of a national magazine. Although never published, it circulated privately in Washington. A frequent contributor to *Foreign Policy*, Bergsten wrote that "Kissinger's record on economics is dismal." His former aide alleged that "where Kissinger did reluctantly get involved in economic issues, he usually 'bungled' the negotiations." His incompetence was particularly acute, Bergsten charged, in "those major international monetary and trade policy decisions which led directly to the collapse of the postwar economic system in late 1971." [61]

The establishment advisory group that converged on Washington from Wall Street in March, 1969, and the foreign finance ministers who met secretly in Washington during this same fateful period, had warned of the disastrous possibilities for the international economic order if the war were continued. Their worst fears were realized in 1971 when, after two years of the Nixon-Kissinger tactic of escalating and widening the conflict in order to find a way to withdrawal "with honor," its reverberations began to reach the money markets of Western Europe and Japan, threatening the trade alliance around which the imperial system revolved.

The strategy of financing the war through inflation exacerbated an already negative U.S. trade balance, the burden of which was passed along to America's trading partners when the Nixon Administration made the unilateral decision to suspend the convertibility of dollars to gold and to impose a 10 percent surcharge on imports. The U.S. move abruptly ended the 1944 Bretton Woods agreement on which the international monetary system had been founded. It also smacked of protectionism, which if emulated, could lead to economic autarky and a balkanization of the capitalist alliance. Treasury Secretary John Connally, later a member of the CPD, seemed to relish his self-described role as "the bully boy on the manicured fields of international finance," justifying the protectionist measures on the grounds that, "We had a problem and we're sharing it with the world, just like we shared our prosperity." [62]

The nadir of the deteriorating relationship between the U.S. and its allies was reached in the Mideast War and oil embargo of 1973. For Establishment dissidents who had broken with the policy of Containment

Militarism in Vietnam, the Middle East crisis threw into bold relief the lessons learned in Southeast Asia: first, crisis anywhere on the globe did not constitute *ipso facto* a contest between the United States and the Soviet Union; second, the application or threat of military force was detrimental to the resolution of North-South disputes; and finally, costly confrontational tactics only served to drive a dangerous wedge between the U.S. and its allies. The latter point was brought to vivid attention when Kissinger referred to the Europeans as "craven, contemptible, pernicious, and jackal-like" for their unwillingness to endorse the "East-West crisis, military alert" scenario played out by Washington in the Arab-Israeli conflict — this in 1973, which the Administration had earlier proclaimed "the year of Europe." [63] The following spring, after several European nations agreed to meet with Arab states at a summit from which the United States was excluded, Nixon declared:

> The Europeans cannot have it both ways. They cannot have United States participation and cooperation on the security front and then proceed to have confrontation and even hostility on the economic and political front . . . The day of the one-way street is gone . . . We are not going to be faced with a situation where the nine countries of Europe gang up against the United States which is their guarantee of security. [64]

One political observer remarked of this speech that "by stressing the direct link between continuance of the U.S. security role in Europe and concessions in the trade and monetary fields, Nixon's speech marked the high tide of confrontation with our major allies." [65]

With the interlocking transformations in East-West, North-South, and United States-Japanese-Western European relations threatening collapse of Pax Americana and little to take its place but the shuttle diplomacy of a peripatetic Secretary of State, Chase Manhattan Bank chairman David Rockefeller brought together Wall Street investment bankers, multinational corporate directors, and members of the foreign policy establishment identified with its liberal flank to develop a blueprint for a new world order. These elite figures were joined by their counterparts from Japan and Western Europe, hence the organization's christening as the Trilateral Commission. As one observer reported after an early meeting of the Commission, "It was, in short, a remarkable cross-section of the interlocking establishments of the world's leading industrial nations." [66] Only four senators were extended membership in the elite group; one of these was Walter Mondale of Minnesota. One governor, Daniel Evans of Washington, was invited to participate as was one former governor, listed as James E. Carter, Jr. of Georgia. Carter had recently appeared on the cover of *Time's* special issue on the "New

South" and was recommended for Trilateral membership by *Time* editor and Trilateralist Hedley Donovan. [67]

As noted above, *Foreign Policy* began its first issue with the proclamation that "an era in American foreign policy which began in the late 1940's, has ended." The same might be said of David Rockefeller and his Trilateral colleagues' view of the Council on Foreign Relations as an organization. It was bound too closely to the Cold War and Containment Militarism, a policy many of its members still insisted on trying to justify, as evident from the bitter debate within the Council over the lessons of Vietnam. [68] The Trilateral Commission would start anew, incorporating the liberal wing of the Council on Foreign Relations but without the burden of its "institutional memory," to develop the kind of consensus that the Council had furnished for Containment Militarism in the Cold War years. This time, however, the consensus would be built around "the management of interdependence" which a Trilateral position paper identified as "the central problem of world order for the coming years" — as opposed to the containment of communism which had dominated elite thinking for the previous quarter century. [69]

A key Trilateral document, *Towards A Renovated International System*, established three major tasks for the new global system: managing the world economy, satisfying basic human needs, and keeping the peace.[70] The first was concerned primarily with the restoration of the deteriorated relationship with the Trilateral partners, the second addressed the North-South issue, and the last the policy of detente with the Soviet Union.

Turning to the international economic order, the American-Japanese-European composition of the Commission's membership was itself a beginning. From the viewpoint of the Trilateralists, a refurbished world order depended first and foremost on a cooperative and consultative partnership among advanced capitalist nations. Acknowledging the realities of transnational investment that had already integrated the economies of the three regions and left them vulnerable to one another's vicissitudes, the Trilateral position maintained that unilateral actions were inherently destabilizing and no longer tolerable. [71] In response to growing interdependence, they urged that the Trilateral nations not battle one another but present a united front in their dealings with the raw material and energy-producing states of the Third World, as well as with communist countries.

The argument of the document also took special pains to emphasize that the Trilateral relationship should not be a cartel arrangement which would only serve to exacerbate North-South tensions in the manner of the 1973 oil embargo. Instead it called for a stable Trilateral center that would invite selected Third World nations to join in a rationalized world economy that offered them greater promise of gain through dependency than they could hope to achieve through independence. This, of course, would require a more equitable deal for these countries than had been the case in the past, including higher prices for raw materials, lowered tariff barriers on manufactured exports to industrial nations, and relief from mounting debt. The short-run sacrifice of profits, however, would pay dividends to the industrial nations in the long-run as a result of the stability gained from such reforms. In the new world order there would be no losers.

Finally, the Commission thought that peace between the Soviet Union and the United States could best be preserved by promoting trade. America needed markets, energy, and raw materials which Russia could supply; Russia needed technology and wheat which America could provide. The basis was there for a binding commercial relationship in the national interest of both parties. Standing in the way of its consummation was Containment Militarism with its focus on antagonistic ideologies rather than complementary interests. It was a world view which had spurred an arms race that by the 1970s threatened the economies of both the U.S. and the Soviet Union. The solution from the Trilateral viewpoint, therefore, was to accelerate trade while braking arms competition to the same degree. Not only would this exert a healthy effect on the American economy, thus taking pressure off tensions within the Trilateral alliance, but as the Soviet Union became increasingly dependent on Western economic cooperation on a regular and continuing basis, the Russians would — like the Third World — develop a stake in the smooth functioning of the international economic order of capitalism.

As is apparent from the logic of managerialism and the membership of the Trilateral Commission, the quest for global interdependence had grown out of the ascendance of the multinational corporation in the 1960s much as Containment Militarism sprang from the burgeoning national security state of the late 1940s. Trilateralist Marina Von N. Whitman wrote in *Foreign Policy* that, "Together with the Eurodollar market, the multinationals are the primary vehicles of interdependence . . . No other economic agent poses such a conspicuous threat to national economic sovereignty, nor is so effective in promoting international economic integration." [72] The problem as she and others of her persuasion saw it, however, is that while the multinationals are in the vanguard of a new world order based on rational economic calculation, international institutions are governed by the outdated currency of power politics — geopolitical hegemony, confrontational ideology, and military-strategic competition. The challenge became how to create the kind of international environment that would allow the multinational phenomenon to flourish and weave its pattern of interdependence across national borders and political ideologies. Containment Militarism stood in the way of such a new managerial framework, a point not lost on the advocates of interdependence — nor on the Committee on the Present Danger as guardians of Containment Militarism.

The Intra-Elite Struggle Unfolds

If arms control is a sham according to the CPD, trade with the Soviet Union borders on treason. It is little more than the working out of Lenin's alleged prediction that capitalists would compete with one another to sell the rope to Moscow by which they would be hanged. As the CPD saw it, extensions of credit and the transfer of technology to the USSR would only serve to alleviate domestic pressures which in turn would allow Soviet leadership to divert still more resources to the military sector. Lecturing on this theme, Charles Burton Marshall remarked:

> Schumpeter was so correct. You can never rely on businessmen. They operate out of a very narrow frame of reference. Generally speaking the smart ones think about the balance sheet for the year after next. The ordinary ones can't even think that far. [73]

Richard Allen added that "businessmen, not being politically astute," were taken in by the promise of trade:

> U.S. businessmen would go to Moscow and come back supercharged from Vodka parties and the promise of hundreds of millions of orders. They came back and lobbied for MFN's ("most favored nation" trading status) for the Russians. [74]

This notion that the establishment of commercial ties will not only bail the Soviet Union out of its economic woes but compromise American business investors besides, is an oft-repeated chorus among the CPD membership. Rostow's Foreign Policy Task Force made the case early on in its criticism of detente, asserting that "in dealing with the Soviets, private pecuniary gain and the American public interest may not always coincide." [75]

Pipes took this point even further, arguing that the culture of capitalism is actually detrimental to a healthy martial spirit:

> Mistrust of the military professional, combined with a pervasive conviction, *typical of commercial societies*, that human conflicts are at bottom caused by misunderstanding and ought to be resolved by negotiations rather than by force, has worked against serious attention to military strategy by the United States. (emphasis added) [76]

Placing this alleged disjuncture into historical context, Peter Berger wrote in *Commentary*, which had become the intellectual forum for Containment Militarism much as *Foreign Policy* served a similar function for Trilateralism, that until the 1960s:

> . . . the economic elite operated on the notion that the maintenance of American power in the world was in their interest. Vietnam changed all this. Most American intellectuals have since Vietnam come to believe that the exercise of American power is immoral. But what has been less noticed is that Vietnam has changed the mind of a substantial segment of the economic elite as to the economic advantages of world power; it has given rise to the idea that the maintenance of American world power is *unprofitable*. [77]

Berger then went on to ask, "What if Marxism has been wrong all along? What if American world power comes to be seen as an economic disadvantage by the 'ruling circles' of the American economy?" Completing his portrait of "the greening of American foreign policy," Berger concluded: "If the proposition is to diminish American world power, the intellectuals make it seem morally right and the businessmen make it appear realistic." [78]

Commentary editor Podhoretz argued along similar lines that there had emerged since Vietnam a "de facto alliance" between "those who feel the U.S. should do nothing to stop the spread of communism and those who once thought we should but no longer can." [79] The leadership of "those who once thought we should but no longer can" has been provided by the corporate elite according to Podhoretz, who maintained that: "The Russians are not behaving like people who want peace. Most people can see this if they don't have ideological blinders or some special reason to deny it." In response to what kind of "special reason," Podhoretz cited *trade*. "The American business community has disgraced itself. No one expected it — except Lenin — that they would be leading the parade." [80] As an example he pointed to Donald Kendall, president of Pepsico, who was a founder of the American Committee For East-West Accord, a pro-detente group that also included various officials from rival Coca-Cola, as well as El Paso Natural Gas, Control Data Corporation, and the Wall Street firm of Brown Brothers, Harriman, to name a few of the corporate interests represented. The Committee issued a statement calling for "a resolute abandonment of the stale slogans and reflexes of the Cold War; a recognition that this is a new era, with different problems and possibilities; and a determination not to be governed by the compulsions of military competition." [81] Largely drafted by George Kennan, who had become by this time a leading spokesman for detente, the Committee's statement went on to recommend an increase in trade, science, and culture as part of an overall improvement of relations with the Soviet Union.

Podhoretz termed such a perspective "the classic isolationist position based on 'interdependence' which gives you the illusion of an activist foreign policy and the reality of an isolationist foreign policy." [82] Moreover, CPD members hold overwhelmingly to the belief that this point of view — labelled "liberal isolationism" — has captured the national security/foreign policy establishment with which many of them were so long identified. Within the Council on Foreign Relations, the Trilateral Commission, and in the pages of *Foreign Policy* and ever so cautiously in *Foreign Affairs*, there has emerged in Podhoretz' words a "certain atmosphere and set of assumptions that has changed from ten or fifteen years ago. A kind of consensus — better an ethos — from which top appointees are recruited." [83]

When the Carter Administration's cabinet level appointments began to be known, the CPD's worst fears were borne out. Almost without exception the appointees fit into Podhoretz' "de facto coalition" of "liberal isolationists" who had interpreted Vietnam as the requiem for Containment Militarism and since gone on to espouse the new world view of managerialism. There was not an unreconstructed hawk among them unless one counts James Schlesinger, but then he was shunted off to deal with the monumental problem of energy from which he was unlikely to have any of his own left to deal with matters of national security. Zbigniew Brzezinski, of course, had an undaunted reputation as a hardliner, but in recent years his writings had been sprinkled with the global interdependence theme consistent with his position as chair of the Trilateral Commission. Commenting on Brzezinski's directorship of the Commission, Podhoretz noted:

> Zbig has been maneuvering himself toward that stance (global interdependence) for several years. It was a great symbolic moment when he changed his institute at Columbia several years ago from the Research Institute On International Communism to the Research Institute For International Change.[84]

Of the fifty-three names submitted by the CPD, in consort with CDM and the AFL-CIO, for consideration in the field of foreign affairs and national security, not one was tapped for service. Where the hardliners lobbied for the reinstatement of Schlesinger as Defense Secretary, word was out that Carter's transition team wanted archfoe Paul Warnke. Carter compromised by appointing Harold Brown — no dove to be sure —but still a budget-minded administrator who, when he was Secretary of the Air Force, was known as 'Dr. No' for his abrasive proclivity for rejecting the generals' attempts to increase the size of their arsenals. Since his days at the Pentagon, Brown had served on the Trilateral Commission and in contrast to his two predecessors, Donald Rumsfield and Schlesinger, had publicly expressed his skepticism of hardline estimates of the Soviet Union's political intentions as well as military strength to carry out any alleged global designs it might secretly harbor. [85]

Carter's secretary of state would be Cyrus Vance, a member of a study panel, the Rockefeller-funded United Nations Association of the United States, which rebutted the charge that there was a Soviet military threat in the offing. The Association, through its monthly *The Inter-dependent*, instead argued the opposite claiming "the continuing Soviet advocacy of budgetary limitations may augur well for the possibility of attaining an agreement (to limit military spending) if the U.S. is interested." [86] Chaired by Atlantic Richfield President Thornton Bradshaw, United Nations Association then went on to propose in the spirit of Warnke's "Apes On A Treadmill," an immediate moratorium on U.S. and Soviet military spending as well as exploration of mutual reductions if agreements with the USSR appeared promising. Thus the CPD could hardly have been comforted by the appointment of Vance, another member of the Trilateral Commission.

Still other Trilateral figures named to command posts included Secretary of the Treasury Michael Blumenthal, Deputy Secretary of State Warren Christopher, Undersecretary of State for Economic Affairs Richard Cooper, Assistant Secretary of the Treasury for International Affairs C. Fred Bergsten, and of course Warnke, who was nominated for the directorship of the Arms Control and Disarmament Agency as well as chief negotiator to head the SALT delegation. In all, twenty-five Trilater-alists were appointed to top policy making positions. [87]

Given Carter's membership on the Trilateral Commission, as well as that of Vice-President Mondale who played a major role in the selection of the foreign policy staff, the appointments were not a complete surprise, notwithstanding Hamilton Jordan's pledge to resign "if after the inauguration you find Cy Vance as Secretary of State and Zbigniew Brzezinski as head of national security." Even as Jordan made this remark the Democratic Party platform included a section on "The Challenge Of Interdependence," and candidate Carter himself had proclaimed in the third debate that the United States should move from a foreign policy based on "balance of power" to one based on "global cooperation." [88] What was shocking to the hardliners, however, was the extent of the Trilateral coup d'etat.

The situation went from bad to worse when the names appointed to second and third echelon positions in State, Defense, and the National Security Council began to surface. If the cabinet-level posts had been dominated by members of the Trilateral Commission to the exclusion of CPD/CDM/AFL-CIO hardliners, the remainder of the foreign policy team was made up of the decidedly liberal transition team and their friends with nary a hawk in sight.

Anthony Lake, who headed the transition staff responsible for the selection of potential appointees, was given the plum of directing Policy Planning in the State Department, the same position from which Nitze had presided over the drafting of NSC-68. But where Nitze had directed the Strategic Bombing Survey in World War II and gone on to become one of the preeminent Cold Warriors of his generation, Lake's experience with war planning led him to resign from Henry Kissinger's staff in opposition to the invasion of Cambodia in 1970.

Since that time Lake had co-authored several "new international order" articles with Leslie Gelb, who had worked for Warnke in the Pentagon and was himself named director of the Bureau of Politico-Military Affairs in the State Department. Gelb reported that, like many of his colleagues, he had reached the conclusion during the Vietnam period that "fewer and fewer things had to do with the Soviet-American connection." He explained his conversion as follows:

> I had no special wisdom prior to 1967 — the doctrine was in my head, too. My views just changed. It is very hard, looking back at it, to see how Vietnam was important save in terms of that doctrine. I think it is easy to see that its importance was attached solely to our sense that everything happening in the world would impact directly and severely on U.S.-Soviet relations. [89]

Many of the new generation of Carter appointees began their careers as Foreign Service Officers who resigned during the course of the Vietnam War to join the Congressional staffs of such liberal antiwar Democrats as McGovern, Church, Mondale, Kennedy, and Udall. The editor of the New Right journal *Policy Review* suggested that a potent network of like-minded, ex-Foreign Service Officers was established on Capitol Hill during the waning years of the war. Moreover, he charged that the ubiquitous Anthony Lake, while serving on the staff of the National Security Council, was "in close contact with the group of liberal Senate aides who were then in the process of turning our foreign policy around." [90]

What worried the CPD and its larger body of sympathizers about those whom Evans and Novak called the "left-of-center foreign policy network" was stated succinctly in an article in the *New Republic*:

They will proceed to write the memoranda, shade the briefings, bargain with the bureaucrats, manipulate the varying
doubts, prejudices, and ignorance of their superiors, and in the
process quietly shape much of the Carter Administration's
foreign and defense policies. [91]

The long time elite of the foreign policy/national security establishment
—men like Nitze and Rostow who had created and carried out the
policies of Containment Militarism over a period of two decades — were
now on the outside looking in.

Unable to make policy from within did not, however, dissuade them
from the effort to shape it from afar. Nitze and Rostow had been meeting
with the other founders of the CPD in executive committee for marathon
sessions of five and six hours at a stretch since December, 1975. [92]
Finally, with the contours of the incoming administration visible, the
Committee decided that the time had come to go public. After an exhaustive fourteen drafts, the CPD's founding statement *Common Sense And
The Common Danger* made its debut on Veteran's Day, 1976, just three
days after Carter's victorious drive to the presidency. At a time when
Carter was assembling his foreign policy/national security team under
the direction of Vietnam critic and global managerialist Anthony Lake,
the Committee reiterated a familiar Cold War theme lifted right from the
pages of NSC-68: "The principal threat to our nation, to world peace,
and to the cause of human freedom is the Soviet drive for dominance
based upon an unparalleled military buildup." Moreover, the statement
read, "The Soviet Union has not altered its long-held goal of a world
dominated from a single center — Moscow." [93] By going public with their
message, the Committee on the Present Danger had thrown down the
gauntlet to the newly-elected president. The second Great Debate had
begun.

The Establishment: A House Divided

The Establishment that had created and carried out America's Cold
War policies had become a house deeply and bitterly divided over "the
lessons of Vietnam." In a composite sketch of the foreign policy elite,
Gregory Hodgson identified them with what he calls "the three worlds"
of New York, Washington, and Cambridge. [94] Each of these elites that
make up the Establishment — its corporate, governmental, and intellectual components respectively — was instrumental in the formulation
of Containment Militarism as the guiding doctrine of imperial policy, as
well as in the drive for its ratification by Congress and the public in the
Korean War era.

The application of the doctrine to Vietnam convincingly shattered the extraordinary consensus backing Pax Americana. As Podhoretz explained with ill-disguised contempt, "the world of Cambridge," and the "world of New York" had formed a "de facto coalition" consisting of "those who think we should do nothing to stop the spread of communism" and "those who once thought we should but no longer can." His colleague Peter Berger added — "the intellectuals make it seem morally right and businessmen make it appear realistic." But even more disturbing, which Nitze's attacks on Warnke showed, was that the "world of Washington," consisting of those who had followed the well-trodden path from Wall Street brokerage firms and law practices to careers as national security managers — this once monolithic core within the elite — no longer spoke with one voice either. As Nitze explained it to Senate Foreign Relations chairman John Sparkman, two antithetical positions evolved from the Vietnam experience: one led by Warnke that eschewed the use of military force in international politics and his own which maintained the need for its continuing and even growing importance in the post-Vietnam period.

At first, however, several positions emerged along a continuum befitting the splintering process that had taken place in the aftermath of Tet. The manner in which the fragmentation of views coagulated into essentially two polarized camps is important in understanding the events that followed. In one of the more perceptive analyses of the process of fractionalization that took place within the Establishment after Tet, Richard Falk identified four schools of thought. From right to left they were Isolationists, Imperialists, Managers, and Transformers. Starting right of center in Falk's paradigm, his *Imperialists* captures the thinking of Nitze and the CPD. He describes the Imperialist posture as follows:

> Proponents of this position applaud the pre-eminence of the United States, emphasize military prowess . . . and oppose any national move that seems to renounce or reduce America's imperial role. Ultimately imperialists rely upon military force to firm up a disintegrated geopolitical order . . . This position . . . also fails to appreciate the significance of non-military forms of geopolitical power that arise from growing complexity and interdependence. [95]

On the extreme right are the *Isolationists* who consist of "those who seek to restore the tradition of American detachment from geopolitical concerns." This I wish to amend somewhat in keeping with earlier findings. As argued in Chapter Two, isolationism was already in transition toward a militant form of global expansionism in the Korean War period. As such, isolationism has never been a serious force in American politics since that time. Falk himself criticizes the isolationist stance as follows: "The United States is too vulnerable, interpenetrating, and interpenetrated to make a posture of detachment possible." [96] The right wing would, I think, agree. Therefore, I would term their go-it-alone approach in the face of undeniable global integration, a *Unilateralist* rather than an Isolationist outlook. Far from retreating from the world, the right wing since the Korean War era has come to embrace the interventionist position developed by the national security elite and to support the costly efforts to maintain military superiority called for in its doctrines.

Turning to the liberal side of the spectrum in Falk's model, the *Managers* are "those who would entice the dissatisfied to join with the satisfied in a single world system based on explicit procedures and structures for the management of interests." This of course represents the pragmatic approach of the Trilateral Commission. *Transformers*, in contrast, are ". . . those who argue that a new system of world order must be created to avoid a situation of growing planetary danger." While they may "regard it as expedient to join forces with the managers in the short run," Falk argues there exists a fundamental rift between *Managers* and *Transformers* even as each pays homage to increasing global interdependence and the 'need for a "new world order" in keeping with such systemic transformation. [97] In contrast to the *Managers* who seek to harness the energy of change in order to uphold existing structures of privilege, *Transformers* believe the two are incompatible and in the face of this epochal contradiction conclude that the empire system should not be maintained but dismantled. Needless to say, *Transformers* have been branded heretics and swiftly ushered out of the house of power.

What is striking to note is that while the Carter Administration was constituted almost entirely of Trilateral Managers, and despite the fact that the CPD and its confederates had been locked out of government, Carter's policies came increasingly to resemble the converging Imperialist-Unilateralist hardline. Given the makeup of the Administration, there were grounds for predicting major changes in the direction of U.S. foreign policy under Carter. Yet looking back on his tenure in office, one discovers that even the most timid steps toward a posture in line with the global managerial thesis were checkmated time and again by domestic political pressure at the center of which stood the CPD.

How was it then that the hardliners were able to confound any thought of new directions in policy even though an influential segment of business leadership, the foreign policy establishment, and the President and his chosen advisers, called for significant departures from Cold War orthodoxy? In the following chapter, I will argue that the success of the

CPD and its allies can be attributed to their control and synchronized manipulation of *doctrine* and *ideology*, despite the lack of an institutionalized foothold within the state. Conversely, it was the failure of the men around Carter to translate their rhetoric of global interdependence into a doctrine to replace Containment Militarism and a popular ideology that could supplant the Soviet Threat in the minds of the mass public that was their undoing. To borrow from the revised Falk paradigm, the Imperialists and Unilateralists on the conservative side of the spectrum formed a potent coalition in favor of reviving Containment Militarism. Liberal Managers, in contrast, shunned the Transformers in their midst and purged themselves of any semblance of reformist thinking in hopes of placating the hardliners and ending the internecine warfare within the ranks of the Establishment. The price for this conciliatory gesture was merely a return to the patterns that had originally brought on the Cold War — with predictably similar results.

CHAPTER 5

Detente

1. Jeane Kirkpatrick, interview with author, August 31, 1977.
2. Norman Podhoretz, interview with author, August 12, 1977.
3. Richard Pipes, "Why The Soviet Union Thinks It Can Fight And Win A Nuclear War,"*Commentary*, July, 1977, p. 26.
4. Personal correspondence from Eugene V. Rostow to Secretary of State Henry Kissinger, September 4, 1974.
5. Coalition For A Democratic Majority, Foreign Policy Task Force, *The Quest For Detente*, summer, 1974.
6. Personal correspondence from Secretary of State Henry Kissinger to Eugene V. Rostow, August 19, 1974.
7. William Delaney, "Trying to Awaken Us To Russia's 'Present Danger'," *Washington Star*, April 4, 1977, p. 1.
8. Nitze, interview with author, August 24, 1977.
9. "U.S. Negotiator On Arms Quits, Citing The Effects Of Watergate," *New York Times*, June 15, 1974, p. 4.
10. John W. Finney, "Impeachment Politics May Cost Nitze Pentagon Post," *New York Times*, March 22, 1974, p. 24.
11. *New York Times*, August 1, 1974, p. 5.
12. Delaney, *Washington Star*, April 4, 1977, p. 1.
13. The others were Frank R. Barnett, Leo Cherne, Douglas Dillon, Edmund A. Gullion, Oscar Handlin, Paul Seabury, and Eugene Wigner.
14. Charles Tyroler II, interview with author, August 22, 1977.
15. Delaney, *Washington Star*, April 4, 1977, p. 1.
16. Tyroler, interview with author, August 22, 1977; Delaney, *Washington Star*, April 4, 1977, p. 1.
17. Personal correspondence from Eugene V. Rostow to James Schlesinger, May 17, 1976.
18. Committee on the Present Danger, *How The CPD Will Operate — What It Will Do, And What It Will Not Do*, November, 1976.
19. Nitze, interview with author, August 24, 1977.
20. Alan Tonelson, "Nitze's World," *Foreign Policy*, 1979, 35, p. 77.
21. Eugene V. Rostow, Chairman, Foreign Policy Task Force of the Coalition For A Democratic Majority, "Statement on Foreign and Defense Policy to Platform Committee of Democratic National Convention," Washington, D.C., May 19, 1976, p. 8.
22. Norman Podhoretz, "Making the World Safe For Communism," *Commentary*, April, 1976, p. 41.
23. Jeane Kirkpatrick, interview with author, August 31, 1977.
24. Charles Burton Marshall, interview with author, August 25, 1977.
25. Lt. General Daniel O. Graham, *A New Strategy For The West: NATO After Detente* (Washington, D.C.: The Heritage Foundation, 1977), 20-23.
26. CPD, *Common Sense And The Common Danger*, November, 1976.
27. CPD, *What Is the Soviet Union Up To?*, April 4, 1977, p. 4.
28. Paul Nitze, interview with author, August 24, 1977.

29. Graham, p. 30.
30. CPD, *What Is the Soviet Union Up To?*, April 4, 1977, p. 6.
31. Graham, p. 23.
32. Marshall, interview with author, August 25, 1977.
33. Pipes, p. 25.
34. *Ibid.*, p. 29.
35. *Ibid.*, p. 26.
36. Quoted in Paul Nitze, "The Strategic Balance Between Hope And Skepticism," *Foreign Policy*, 1974-75, p. 136.
37. CPD,*What Is the Soviet Union Up To?*, p. 12.
38. Nitze, p. 136.
39. CPD, *What Is the Soviet Union Up To?*, p. 12.
40. James R. Schlesinger, *Annual Defense Department Report FY 1975*, p. 1.
41. James R. Schlesinger, *Annual Defense Department Report FY 1976*, p. 1.
42. "Schlesinger Sees U.S. Heading For Disaster," *U.S. News*, December 22, 1975.
43. CPD, *What Is the Soviet Union Up To?*, p. 8.
44. Eugene Rostow, "What Is Our Defense Program For? American Foreign And Defense Policy After Vietnam," in Francis P. Hoeber and William Schneider (eds.), *Arms, Men And Military Budgets, Issues For Fiscal Year 1978* (New York: Crane, Russak, 1977), xix.
45. Coalition For A Democratic Majority, Foreign Policy Task Force, *For An Adequate Defense*, p. 24.
46. James R. Schlesinger, *Annual Defense Department Report FY 1976*, pp. 1-3.
47. *Ibid.*, pp. 1-4.
48. MacNeil/Lehrer Report, transcript (Public Broadcasting System), January 14, 1977.
49. Paul H. Nitze, "Consequences Of An Agreement" (unpublished position paper), November 1, 1977, p. 11; cited in Alan Tonelson, "Nitze's World," *Foreign Policy*, 1979, 35, pp. 74-91.
50. Kirkpatrick, interview with author, August 31, 1977.
51. *See* Paul Warnke, "Apes On A Treadmill," *Foreign Policy*, 1975, p. 18.
52. *Ibid.*, p. 14.
53. *Ibid.*, p. 15.
54. *Ibid.*, p. 16.
55. *Ibid.*, p. 24.
56. *Ibid.*, p. 29.
57. Nitze, interview with author, August 24, 1977.
58. "Why Foreign Policy?," *Foreign Policy* #1, winter 1970-71, p. 3.
59. Clark Clifford, remarks, October 9, 1973, cited in *The Defense Monitor*, October, 1974, p. 2.
60. W.A. Harriman, remarks, August 14, 1974, cited in *The Defense Monitor*, October, 1974, p. 2.
61. Richard Holbrooke, "Washington Dateline: The New Battle Lines," *Foreign Policy*, 1973-74, 13, p. 183.

62. James Chace, "American Jingoism," *Harper's*, May 1976, p. 43.
63. *Ibid.*
64. *Ibid.*
65. *Ibid.*
66. Robert Christopher, "The World's New Cold War," *Time*, June 16, 1975.
67. W.E. Barnes, "Carter Had Link To Insiders All Along," *San Francisco Chronicle*, December 12, 1976, p. 13.
68. See especially Godfrey Hodgson, "The Establishment," *Foreign Policy*, 1973, 10, pp. 32-35.
69. "An Outline for Remaking World Trade and Finance," *Christian Science Monitor*, February 15, 1977, p. 14.

     The relationship of the Trilateral Commission to *Foreign Policy* parallels in many respects that of the Council On Foreign Relations (CFR) to *Foreign Affairs*. Just as the CFR had in an earlier time served as a forum for hammering out a consensus among America's corporate, governmental, and academic elites, the views of which were espoused in *Foreign Affairs*, so too the Trilateral Commission sought to unify the elites of the Trilateral nations. *Foreign Policy*, in a similar fashion, became the voice of Trilateralism.

     Foreign Policy's managing editor and frequent contributor Richard Holbrooke served on the Trilateral Commission. Editorial board chairman Thomas Hughes, whose writings on the global managerial thesis also appeared regularly in its pages, was also a member. Zbigniew Brzezinski, a Rockefeller protege who was appointed director of the Trilateral Commission, served on the editorial board of *Foreign Policy*, along with fellow Trilateral members Michael Blumenthal and Richard Cooper. Other contributors to *Foreign Policy* whose names graced the membership rolls of the Commission included Richard N. Gardner, Marina Von N. Whitman, and Paul Warnke. Warnke was also listed on the Trilateral executive committee.
70. "An Outline for Remaking World Trade And Finance," *Christian Science Monitor*, February 15, 1977, p. 14.
71. As Trilateralist Richard N. Gardner wrote ". . . the facts of interdependence force nations, in their enlightened self-interest, to abandon unilateral decision-making in favor of multilateral processes," in Richard N. Gardner, "The Hard Road To World Order," *Foreign Affairs*, April 1, 1974, p. 563.
72. Marina Von N. Whitman, "Leadership Without Hegemony: Our Role In The World Economy," *Foreign Policy*, 1975, p. 150.
73. Marshall, interview with author, August 25, 1977.
74. Richard V. Allen, interview with author, August 22, 1977.
75. Coalition For A Democratic Majority, Foreign Policy Task Force, *The Quest For Detente*, summer, 1974.
76. Pipes, p. 22.
77. Peter Berger, "The Greening Of American Foreign Policy," *Commentary*, March 1976, p. 24.
78. *Ibid.*, pp. 25-26.
79. Norman Podhoretz, interview with author, August 12, 1977.
80. *Ibid.*

190   PEDDLERS OF CRISIS

81. "A Plan For U.S.-Soviet Braking Of Arms Race," *San Francisco Chronicle*, November 15, 1976, p. 1.
82. Podhoretz, interview with author, August 12, 1977.
83. *Ibid.*
84. *Ibid.*
85. Dana Adams Schmidt, "New, Less Gloomy, Voice In Pentagon," *Christian Science Monitor*, June 10, 1977, p. 1
86. "A Plan for U.S.-Soviet Braking Of Arms Race," *San Francisco Chronicle*, November 15, 1977, p. 1.
87. Holly Sklar, "Trilateralism: Managing Dependence And Democracy - An Overview," in Holly Sklar, ed., *Trilateralism: The Trilateral Commission And Elite Planning For World Management*, (Boston: South End Press, 1980), 2.
88. Michael Mandelbaum and William Schneider, "The New Internationalisms," *International Security*, winter 1978, p. 95.
89. Leslie H. Gelb, "National Security And New Foreign Policy," *Parameters*, Journal of the United States Army War College, November 8, 1977, p. 10-F.
90. Robert L. Schuettinger, "The New Foreign Policy Network," *Policy Review,* summer 1977, p. 100.
91. "The Junior Varsity," *The New Republic*, February 19, 1977, p. 13.
92. Tyroler, interview with author, August 24, 1977.
93. The Committee on the Present Danger, *Common Sense And The Common Danger*, November 1976.
94. Godfrey Hodgson, "The Establishment," *Foreign Policy*, 1973, pp. 12-13.
95. Richard A. Falk, "Beyond Internationalism," *Foreign Policy*, 1976, 24, p. 84.
96. *Ibid.*
97. *Ibid.*, p. 86.

Chapter 6

BELLWETHER
OF RESURGENT MILITARISM

On Carter's appointments, my views are unprintable.
　　Eugene Rostow, July, 1977 [1]

Every softliner I can think of is now part of the executive branch and the arms control administration.
　　Paul Nitze, August, 1977 [2]

I wouldn't want to say this for publication, but I think there's a point of adversariness between the Committee on the Present Danger and the Administration.
　　Charles Burton Marshall, CPD executive committee, August, 1977 [3]

In the opening sentence of its second position paper, Rostow's Foreign Policy Task Force (CDM) expressed the following conviction: "As they did in the Truman years, liberals and Democrats must again take the lead in rallying Americans to increase our defense capabilities, both nuclear and conventional." [4] But times had changed. A quarter century had elapsed since NSC-68 and the Soviet Threat campaign that sold it to the American public. At that time the major opposition to military Keynesianism at home and the remilitarization of Europe was the conservative wing of the Republican Party led by Robert Taft in the

Senate. A major contender for the presidential nomination in 1952, he threatened to tap the mood of a public which, while certainly not anti-military, was wary of foreign entanglement and higher taxes. Thus a campaign was mounted to sell Containment Militarism to the American people and to isolate the Republican right wing from its base of mass support, a task made easier by the war in Korea but more difficult by the climate of McCarthyism and the drama of MacArthur's dismissal. United behind the original Committee on the Present Danger in this effort were the "liberals and Democrats" to which Rostow alludes, as well as the moderate Republicans and a virtually unanimous foreign policy establishment.

The post-Vietnam CPD found itself in a very different political context. If opposition to Containment Militarism in 1950 came from the Republican right wing, by the mid-1970s they had become its staunchest defenders. Likewise, the liberal wing of the Democratic Party could no longer be counted on for support, having fragmented into Cold War liberals who remained loyal supporters of Containment Militarism, a progressive faction that called for America to "come home" — McGovern's 1972 campaign theme — and concentrate on domestic concerns, and still a third group that embraced global interdependence and joined the trilateralists in their call for renovation of Pax Americana. As noted in preceding chapters, the foreign policy establishment no longer presented a united front, but was itself deeply divided with many, perhaps most, of its key figures eschewing cold war orthodoxy. Finally, the positions of the executive and the public vis-a-vis Containment Militarism had also become the reverse of what they had been in the Korean War era. In 1976, a Democratic president was elected who talked of ending the arms race, promised cuts in the military budget, and spun visions of global harmony. This in contrast to Truman, who once dissuaded from his economic traditionalism, became an enthusiastic devotee of Containment Militarism. The question of mass sentiment, to which we will next turn, was more complicated but seemed to be moving in the CPD's favor.

Public opinion surveys, like the tea leaves and entrails consulted by elites in ancient times in hopes of mastering their fate, are subject to wide interpretation. Toward the end of the Vietnam War for example, opinion surveys showed a markedly diminished enthusiasm for global involvement. This response, which held steady from the late 1960s to the conclusion of the war, produced an outpouring of concern within the Establishment over the growing "isolationist" mood. In the pages of *Foreign Policy* and *Commentary*, neo-liberals and neo-conservatives alike viewed the trend with a mixture of alarm and fascination. Read one way the optimistic advocate of managerialism might conclude that the public's wariness of foreign involvement was primarily a reaction to military intervention, and thus that the person on the street shared his own view of military power as a costly and outmoded burden. Similarly, a proponent of militarism could reason that the popular attitude was anti-detente, anti-United Nations, and anti-Third World — not anti-military at all.

While it was true that towards the end of the war the majority of Americans had wearied of the fighting and favored an end to U.S. involvement in the conflict, some wanted out because of moral outrage, others because of what they perceived as a "no-win" policy. Some wanted to drop bombs as ground troops withdrew, others wanted the troops replaced with reconstruction aid. [5] This same ambiguity was evident in Congress when in October, 1971, the Senate voted down funding for foreign aid programs. Should this have been interpreted as a victory for hawks or doves? Senate liberals said they voted for the measure because military rather than humanistic considerations had come to dominate the allocation of funds; conservatives, because the program failed to gain international support for American policies in return for the billions spent. [6]

Given the polarized climate, both views could find some sustenance from political happenings and opinion surveys. By 1976, however, the CPD had come to believe — and the polls seemed to bear them out — that a discernible shift was underway from "pacifism" to "patriotism" as Podhoretz liked to put it. Renewed enthusiasm for a military buildup was indeed striking: In 1972, only 9 percent of those surveyed took the position that military spending should rise. By 1974, the figure doubled to 17 percent, jumping again in 1976 to 28 percent. The percentage that wanted defense spending reduced dropped from 37 percent in 1972 to 33 percent in 1974, and finally to a low of 20 percent in 1976. Thus a dramatic reversal had apparently occurred in the ratio of hawks to doves — from 9-37 in 1972, to 28-20 by 1976. [7]

The Gallup Poll reported similar findings, concluding that in 1976 "public support for defense spending has increased to the highest point recorded over the last seven years." [8] Their figures indicated that in 1969, 52 percent of the public thought too much was being spent on defense. This in contrast to the interwar years at the height of the Cold War when opposition to military spending uniformly remained below 20 percent. From 1968 to 1973, in contrast, opposition hovered around 50 percent. This figure declined to 44 percent in September, 1974, then dropped eight more points in a little over a year to 36 percent in January, 1976. Conversely, those favoring greater military spending rose from 8 percent in 1969 to 12 percent in 1974, and then almost doubled to 22 percent by January, 1976. It should be noted that together, the advocates of higher defense spending and those who believed it should remain at its present level totalled 54 percent of the public as against the 36 percent who thought that military spending should be cut. [9]

Still another poll conducted over a number of years had asked the public to agree or disagree with the proposition that "the United States should maintain its dominant position as the world's most powerful nation at all costs, even going to the brink of war if necessary." The results of this inquiry bore the same message. In 1972, only 39 percent could agree with such an aggressive posture. In 1974, support rose slightly to 42 percent; but by May, 1976, it garnered 52 percent of mass opinion in its favor. [10]

While the questions the pollsters asked varied somewhat, and their figures differed in places, the trend from poll to poll was clear. America had come a long way from the day when another public opinion seer was moved to ask in the pages of *The Nation* in 1973, "Is This The Year Of The Doves?" [11] By 1976, it seemed inconceivable that only four years before at the Naval War College Admiral Stansfield Turner, who would later become Carter's director of the CIA, could say:

> The American people appear to be desirous of reducing the
> worldwide roles we have been filling for the past twenty-five
> years . . . Thus, it is becoming increasingly difficult to pay for
> all the forces needed to support the strategy of containment of
> Communism that has remained largely unchanged over the
> past quarter century. [12]

Opinion polls likewise revealed that with the increased enthusiasm for military spending there was a simultaneous drop in support for detente, which had only been lukewarm from the beginning among the public. According to NBC surveys in the early 1976 primary states, from 60 percent to 70 percent of the voters believed that the Soviet Union had benefitted more from detente than had the United States. Less than 10 percent believed the U.S. had gotten the better of the bargain. [13] Similarly, a *New York Times*/CBS survey which asked Massachusetts Democrats whether or not they approved of detente found that a majority of 56 to 44 percent said they did not. [14] Reflecting this growing national mood, Gerald Ford dropped detente from his vocabulary during the campaign.

The possibilities inherent in the new mood and the urgency to nurture its continued growth were not lost on those plotting the hardline strategy during the critical 1974-76 period. Norman Podhoretz for instance cited Daniel Patrick Moynihan's antics at the United Nations, for which nearly three-quarters of a representative sampling of the American public had expressed their approval as a reason for optimism:

How exhilarating very large numbers of people in this country find a sheer willingness to proclaim superiority of our political values over the political culture of Marxism and Communism, how sick they are of creeping Finlandization from within the sphere of political discourse, how happy they become when they see the U.S. once again speaking in clear accents as the leader of the "liberty party."

Warming to the contest ahead, he added:

Still, these sentiments have not yet been decisively tested in the national political arena, and until they are so tested, the question — of *whether the new isolationism is as pervasive among the masses of Americans as it is among the elites —* will have to remain moot. (emphasis added) [15]

These remarks, appearing in the April, 1976, *Commentary* under the title "Making The World Safe For Communism," set the stage for the Democratic convention. Rostow went before the Platform Committee of the Democratic Party a month later, beginning his address with the following challenge:

After a period of drift and uncertainty, the American spirit is recovering from the self-inflicted wounds of the last decade. In this regard the lesson of opinion polls and primaries throughout the country is clear: A strong and angry tide of concern about the safety of the nation is running through the country. [16]

Further into the text, Rostow answered Podhoretz' question of a a month before: "On the chief issues of our foreign policy, our people are ahead of our leaders, far more realistic, and far more aware of the true dimensions of the problems we face." [17] Sensing the potential for mobilization, he marvelled later: "Slowly, gradually, and almost without political leadership, American public opinion has come to realize that the Cold War is far from over." [18]

Despite Rostow's upbeat note, there still remained considerable doubt about what the public attitude would bear in the way of foreign and military policy. Even though the direction of the mass mood from the end of the war to the 1976 election was clear, opinion pollsters Watts and Free temper Rostow's exuberance, noting that in terms of depth "these views have not translated themselves into support for a return to the all-out military containment of the Cold War era." [19] Thus as the hardliners gathered to organize another CPD and to plot a new Soviet Threat campaign, the situation appeared hopeful but far from sanguine.

Summing up their sense of the situation, Nitze explained that,

> for the past few years the United States has been going through
> a difficult period with respect to domestic morale, and this
> lower morale has had a direct impact upon the nation's atti-
> tudes toward national security issues. In my view, we reached
> the low point in these indices something over a year ago
> (1974). The progress made to date is not dramatic. But in the
> nation's attitudes towards national security, I see some in-
> creased realism about the limitations of detente. There has
> been an increase in the respect for the military. [20]

The CPD's carefully-crafted founding statement exuded this same
tone of cautious optimism in its assessment of mass sentiment: "We have
faith in the maturity, good sense and fortitude of our people. But public
opinion must be informed before it can reach considered judgments and
make them effective in our democratic system." [21] Here was the rub. As
men whose careers and world views had been shaped in the executive, the
Committee's founders had come to firmly believe that the presidency was
the most effective — and rightful — repository of leadership over foreign
policy and national security affairs. In gearing up for the 1976 Democratic convention the Foreign Policy Task Force (CDM) had pleaded in
this regard, "The will of the people cannot be mobilized unless the
President and the Secretary of State address these issues with words and
deeds adequate to their gravity." [22]

The dilemma for those gathering under the CPD banner was that the
executive branch had failed so completely to provide such leadership in
recent years. If, as Rostow urged, America "must return to the line of
policy initiated by President Truman and Secretary Acheson a generation ago," its legitimation in the post-Vietnam era demanded a fundamentally different strategy from that employed the first time around. [23]
This did not mean giving up on the presidency however. On the contrary,
the critical question was how to get the president out in front leading a
groundswell for Containment Militarism, an ideological coup which
would at the same time isolate the false prophets of detente who
counseled an end to the Cold War.

It was a tall order, one that demanded consummate political skill
and adroit strategy. An inkling of the form the new Soviet Threat
campaign would take can be discerned from the private correspondence
between Rostow and another prominent member of the CPD, Frank
Barnett, who was also director of the National Strategy Information
Center, a lobbying organization dedicated to the preservation of Containment Militarism.

Barnett opened his letter to Rostow telling him that the Center had been granted $1 million to "crank up an all-out effort to meet the current and growing threat from the USSR." He went on to explain that the National Strategy Information Center would be opening a "full-scale Washington office" to engage in the following activities:

1) Interact with policy echelons in the White House and Pentagon (*where we still have friends*);
2) "Tutor" Congressional staffs and brief members;
3) Work with Trade Associations — with an interest in "defense" — which have Washington offices;
4) Generate more public information through friends in the Washington press corps who write about military and foreign affairs.

After explaining the projection of activities listed above — what he called an "interface operation" — Barnett asked Rostow to serve on the Center's board of directors. He added that he would personally be moving to Washington in September [1976] in order to supervise its execution.[24]

Rostow replied to Barnett that he was "honored" to join the Board and expressed his "delight" that the National Strategy Information Center would be opening a Washington office in order "to conduct a campaign of direct and large-scale persuasion to Congress, the Executive Branch, Trade Associations, and the press corps." The letter continued:

On the political and politico-military side, as you know, our new Committee on the Present Danger, of which you will be an active member, is planning a comparable operation. It should be *no problem to coordinate our activities* and indeed *to act jointly* on many issues. (emphasis added) [25]

One can begin to see here the emergence of a two-tier strategy — a pincer operation of sorts designed to squeeze an incoming president between a reassertion of hardline *doctrine* within the national security bureaucracy and from the outside by means of pressure from an interest-backed Cold War *ideology* led by hawkish Congressmen and groups associated with the military-industrial complex and the grassroots right wing. This insider-outsider strategy surfaced immediately after Carter's election, the first in the form of the Team B report and the second in the Warnke confirmation hearings. The CPD provided the vital link between the two, lending expertise to the first and credibility to the second. In the process the Committee quickly became the bellwether of resurgent militarism and the leader of a new Cold War coalition.

The Team B Report: NSC-68 Update

The CPD and its coterie of Cold Warriors were soon given an

opportunity which if carried off successfully would leave a president with little choice but to become the spokesman of their cause. The occasion presented itself as a result of mounting criticism directed at the annual intelligence estimates of the Soviet Union's strength compiled by the CIA. These estimates had over a number of years come under attack both from participants in the process such as Air Force Generals George Keegan and Daniel Graham, as well as from outside critics like Nitze and Richard Pipes; all felt the conclusions of the intelligence establishment showed a pattern of being "soft on the Russians." Graham said in an interview for this book that from his years in the CIA's Office of National Estimates he could only conclude that they were "antimilitary." Moreover, he charged: "There are more liberals per square foot in the CIA than any other part of government." [26]

Finally, in the spring of 1976, with Ronald Reagan making national security an issue in the Republican primaries, President Ford granted permission to CIA Director George Bush to appoint an alternative team from outside the intelligence agencies to appraise the official estimates of Soviet capabilities and intentions. The stakes were high. As one intelligence expert explained, "I have observed increasingly over the years that as intelligence came to play an ever increasing role in important budget, security, and policy decisions an administration could not hope to remain in power for long unless the intelligence community rationalized their hopes." [27] The importance of the annual national intelligence estimates comes from the fact that they provide the guidance for the size and shape of the defense budget, the type of strategic posture the military will assume, as well as the government's overall approach to East-West relations including arms negotiations and trade — the foundation of detente. If the hardline view were to prevail in the estimates and a new Soviet Threat were accepted within national security circles, then policy would be apt to return to the basic contours of Containment Militarism, albeit in an upbeat form in keeping with the modernization that had taken place over time in strategic and conventional forces.

Ford's action followed pressure from the President's Foreign Intelligence Advisory Board which recommended that the estimate of Soviet strength and intent include the view of outsiders. The Board's stance is not surprising. Six of the 16-member Board made the membership list of the CPD when it was released in November. Chairman Leo Cherne let slip the larger purpose he saw in such an endeavor in this passage from an address delivered at the time:

> We are in the midst of a crisis of belief and a crisis of belief can only be resolved by belief. "Will" depends on something most doomsayers have overlooked — crisis, mortal danger, shock, massive understandable challenge. [28]

Cherne labelled as "nonsense" the suggestion that "the project was launched to have any effect on a new administration because there was no expectation among the proponents that there would be 'a new administration'." [29] What Cherne no doubt meant was that "new administration" or not, this Board was determined that whomever became president in November would face a formidable wall of elite opinion united in its warning of a new Soviet Threat.

In June, 1976, Bush put into motion the adversary procedure, appointing a panel of seven outsiders to go over the same classified data as the regular CIA estimators and to develop their own independent judgments of Soviet capabilities and intentions. Pipes was chosen to chair what came to be known as the Team B panel. Nitze was among the seven, as were Foy Kohler and William Van Cleave. All four were members of the CPD. The three remaining outside members making up Team B included Daniel Graham, Thomas Wolfe of the RAND Corporation, and John Vogt, Jr., a retired Air Force General. In addition, Team B included five officials still in government service at the time of the analysis — CIA archcritic Major General George Keegan, Air Force Brigadeer General Jasper A. Welch, Paul D. Wolfowitz of the Arms Control and Disarmament Administration, and Seymour Weiss from the State Department. (Weiss later joined the faculty of the University of Miami's Center for Advanced International Studies, along with Graham and Kohler). When asked why his team was so one-sided, Pipes explained:

> There is no point in another, what you might call, optimistic view. In general there has been a disposition in Washington to underestimate the Soviet drive. The moderately optimistic line has prevailed . . . We have imposed very severe limitations on ourselves. The hope had been that all these steps would lead the Russians to slow down. They haven't. [30]

The charge that the intelligence community led by the CIA was "soft" on the Russians was accepted as a given prior to even looking at the classified data. Herbert "Pete" Scoville, a former CIA deputy director, charged that Team B was "dedicated to proving that the Russians are twenty feet tall." [31] Thus the stage was set. Whereas in the Truman years the battle occurred between the moderates and the militants of the foreign policy establishment, the latest chapter was to take shape in the contest of CIA regulars vs. Team B outsiders. The issues however remained the same ones that had defined the NSC-68 review process a quarter century before.

Once the estimating process had begun, one CIA insider told the *New York Times* of "absolutely bloody" discussions during which the outsiders accused the CIA of dealing in faulty assumptions, faulty analysis, faulty use of intelligence, and faulty exploitation of available intelligence. Team B asserted that the ultimate intention of Soviet strategic aims was to develop forces capable of impeding merchant vessels, denying raw materials to the West, disrupting fuel supplies, defeating the "projection of power from sea to land" by Western forces, and developing strategic forces that would ultimately have a superior first-strike capability. [32] Reminiscent of George Kennan and Charles Bohlen during the NSC-68 review, the intelligence insiders retorted that hard evidence simply did not permit such extrapolations.

Another intelligence officer described the procedure as a "rather unfair set-up" in which the outsiders felt they had a somewhat broader mandate, and used it. [33] The broader mandate was, of course, to reinstate Containment Militarism as the cornerstone of U.S. foreign policy. The restoration of the Soviet Union as implacable foe was as essential to this larger task in the post-Vietnam era as it was in the early days of the Cold War. Finally, as it did in NSC-68, the case rested upon the allegedly timeless "global designs" of the Soviet Union and their intention to realize expansionist goals through military superiority. As Pipes argued in his denial of ideological bias on the B team:

> I don't think the team is distinguished by being 'hard line.'
> They know about weapons, they all know about politics. They
> view Soviet policy in Clausewitzian terms — which is the way
> the Soviets look at it. [34]

As Graham put it, "There's the 'peace through trust guys' and the 'peace through strength guys'."[35] Team B was decidedly of the latter persuasion.

One need look no further than the participants' own statements to discern who had the upper hand in the controversy: "Sometimes we left them speechless," one member of the B team recounted, "we had men of great prestige, some of them with memories going back twenty-five years or more, and they made devastating critiques of the agency estimates."[36] According to an account in the *Washington Post*, "numerous sources on all sides agree that the 'peer pressures' on the insiders were great. Daniel Graham was reported to have said to the CIA group at one point: 'I don't want to tell you guys you're going to lose your jobs if you don't get on board, but that's the way it is.' "[37] What the the Team B panel had on its side were the arguments, as well as the architects, of a doctrine that had governed American foreign policy in the generation of its greatest influence on the world. An official of the CIA summed up the adversary process saying, "It was an absolute disaster for the Agency." [38]

The two teams convened December 2 and 3, before the President's

Foreign Intelligence Advisory Board to present their estimates and criticisms. The *New York Times* reported that the Team B analysts felt they had made a significant impact on the final report of the regulars: "General Keegan was said to believe the insiders shifted 180 degrees as a result of the exchange. He and Professor Pipes were said to be quite pleased with the outcome." [39] High-ranking officials of the CIA referred to the new estimates of Soviet strategic objectives that would be waiting on Carter's desk when he arrived in Washington as the most "somber" in more than a decade. A top level military intelligence officer who had read the estimate commented: "It was more than somber — it was very grim. It flatly states the judgment that the Soviet Union is seeking superiority over the United States forces." [40]

Somehow, as these things tend to happen, the bleak estimates and the Pipes Report — the undiluted Team B analysis — were leaked to the press at the end of December. This may have been precipitated by the nomination of Harold Brown as Secretary of Defense instead of the hardliner's choice, James Schlesinger. After all, Brown had gone on record as skeptical of claims that the Soviet Union was engaged in a massive civil defense program or that a limited nuclear war could be fought without escalating into an all out holocaust. [41] Both opinions challenged the Team B view of the Soviet Union's military plans as well as the strategy of counterforce which they proposed as a response to the Russians' alleged intentions.

One week after public disclosure of the still-classified intelligence estimates Major General Keegan, who had just retired and was on his way to the top post of the U.S. Strategic Institute as well as the editorship of the right wing *Strategic Review*, granted interviews with both the *New York Times* and *Newsweek*. In his remarks, the ex-Team B member escalated the controversy charging that the Soviet Union had already achieved military superiority over the United States and was preparing for war: "I am unaware of a single important category in which the Soviets have not established a significant lead over the United States," he lectured. Furthermore, Keegan alleged:

> ... (this) grave imbalance in favor of Soviet military capability
> had developed out of a failure over the last 15 years to adjust
> American strategic thinking to Soviet strategy, and out of the
> failure of the leadership of the American intelligence com-
> munity to 'perceive the reality' of the Soviet military buildup. [42]

The next few weeks leading up to Carter's inauguration were rife with charges and countercharges that kept the intelligence flap in the headlines right where the hardliners intended it to be. For instance, Keegan's theme was hammered home again at a seminar for news reporters sponsored by the American Security Council in mid-January. The subject of the seminar was military balance and the invited speakers were Team B members Van Cleave and Graham. More than eighty reporters were in attendance including representatives of the Associated Press, United Press International, the *New York Times*, and the *Washington Post*.

Van Cleave stunned the assembled throng when he reiterated Keegan's claims "that overall strategic superiority exists today for the Soviet Union." [43] He backed his charge citing an article by Nitze which appeared concurrently in *Foreign Policy* under the title, "Deterring Our Deterrent." In it Nitze argued that, "Today, after a strategic nuclear counterforce exchange under normal U.S. alert conditions, the Soviet Union would hold superiority in all indices of capability except number of warheads, and even that sole remaining U.S. advantage would be gone within two or three years." [44] Playing the doomsday theme for all it was worth, Van Cleave added: "I think it's getting to the point that if we can make a trade with the Soviet Union of defense establishments, I'd be heartily in favor of it." [45]

Graham complemented Van Cleave's grim presentation, decrying the "lack of U.S. strategy" to meet the Soviet Threat. When he was asked what kind of strategy he would propose, he made it quite clear that it would be nothing less than regaining military superiority. To back his view, he argued that the reason Khrushchev had embraced "mutual deterrence" was "because he couldn't see any way out of the strategic inferiority situation that he was in at the time." The questioner continued: "If parity is not the answer, by extension are you advocating some form of superiority for the United States?" Graham: "The question was, 'Do I advocate superiority for the United States? I say yes." [46] The *raison d'etre* of Team B could not have been stated any more clearly.

Reactions to Team B's alarmist views indicated that "bludgeoning the mass mind of the elite" and restoring the consensus around Containment Militarism within the foreign policy establishment would prove to be more difficult than had been the case in the original drafting of NSC-68. Kissinger in his valedictory address to the Washington press corps on January 10, dismissed public warnings by various Team B members saying, "I do not believe the Soviet Union is achieving military superiority over the United States." In a parting shot to the counterforce enthusiasts, Kissinger added: "Military superiority has no practical significance . . . under circumstances in which both sides have the capability to annihilate one another." Finally, he charged: "Those who are still talking about superiority are not doing the American people a service." [47]

Donald Rumsfeld, in his swan song as Defense Secretary a week later, disagreed. Bolstering the Team B analysis, he argued that while "absolute proof eludes us about the intentions of Soviet leaders . . . no doubt exists about the capabilities of the Soviet armed forces." Furthermore those capabilities, according to Rumsfeld, "indicate a tendency toward war fighting . . . rather than for *the more modish Western models* of deterrence through mutual vulnerability." (emphasis added) [48]

The new administration's response portended a continuation of the battle. After the inauguration, President Carter responded to the Team B charges by saying "we're still by far stronger than they are in most means of measuring strength." [49] Moreover, Brown and Vance, unlike their predecessors at Defense and State, were not at odds with their boss or with one another on this controversial point. Even the Joint Chiefs agreed, refuting General Keegan's publicly aired charges of Soviet superiority before the Defense Appropriations Subcommittee of the Senate. Yet despite the notable absence of hardline ideologues in the new administration, the Cold Warriors had by their domination of the intelligence estimates left behind a legacy that could not easily be ignored. As the *Washington Post* explained:

> The new National Intelligence Estimates, plus the Pipes Report, plus the encouragement given to pessimists or "worst case" theorists on Soviet intentions inside the government, is regarded as a high barrier for the Carter Administration to overcome to carry out its own broader objectives for US-Soviet nuclear arms control. [50]

The account goes on to point out that,

> Even if the Carter Administration disagrees with the new National Intelligence Estimates on Soviet strategy it cannot be readily rewritten. It will appear in two to three volumes that serve as a reference for policy-makers across the top echelon of the government, although they are not bound by it. [51]

There are two key passages in this analysis of the intelligence flap: First, that the "somber" intelligence estimate represents a "high barrier" to the Carter people; and second, the qualification that "they are not bound by it." While Carter may have thought he had resolved the dispute between containment and detente by appointing to the cabinet those from the moderate-to-liberal side of the foreign policy establishment, the fundamental ambiguity in U.S. policy would remain unresolved since the ex-insiders, having lost out in the appointment process, had still managed to write the intelligence guidelines that circumscribe the conduct of foreign policy. On the other hand, however, the hardliners could hardly rest easy with the knowledge that their intelligence estimates would be interpreted and translated into actual policy by persons antagonistic to their views. How Carter would resolve these contradictions was uncertain.

The Anti-Warnke Campaign:
Emergence Of The New Cold War Coalition

Where the intelligence debate over Team B's allegations dominated the month of January, casting an ominous shadow over Carter's inauguration, the hardliners kept their views in the headlines afterward in the effort to deny Paul Warnke a slot in the Administration. If the Team B report was a test of the ex-insiders' ability to ply their beliefs at the level of the state bureaucracy, the Warnke battle was an experiment in another aspect of the Rostow-Barnett pincer operation. It brought pressure to bear from the outside through popular support. Accordingly, the arena of activity shifted from the byzantine politics of national security to the public forum of Congress. In so doing, it also presented the hardliners with an opportunity to tap the potential mass base intimated by the opinion polls, harnessing this popular mood to the Team B affair through the conduit of Congress and grass-root conservative organizations.

The same day that William Proxmire, chairman of the Senate Defense Appropriations Subcommittee, released a report by the Joint Chiefs of Staff critical of Team B's charges, another chapter of the ongoing struggle over America's post-Vietnam policy had begun. The *New York Times* reported that Carter would shortly announce the nomination of Paul Warnke to negotiate an arms agreement with the Soviet Union and to direct the Arms Control and Disarmament Agency (ACDA).[52] When the announcement came a few days later as predicted, the *Christian Science Monitor* said that with the nomination of Warnke, Carter had moved into a "new ideological controversy." [53] A new round in an old controversy would have been more accurate. In essence, it was the same battle over the direction of American foreign and military policy that had been in effect since March, 1968. This was apparent both in the objections to Warnke and in the composition of those leading the protest.

Early criticism of Warnke was fueled by a four-page memorandum accusing him of advocating "unilateral abandonment by the U.S. of every weapons system which is subject to negotiation at SALT." [54] The memo, which remained anonymous for some time, circulated widely throughout Congress when Warnke's name began to be rumored for the ACDA and SALT posts. As it turned out, two staffers of the Coalition For A Democratic Majority drafted the scurrilous attack shortly after the election when, word had it, Warnke was under consideration for Secretary of Defense. One of its authors was Penn Kemble, founder and co-chairman of CDM; the other was Josh Muravchik, son of CDM member and executive director of the Jewish Labor Committee, Emanuel Muravchik, and nephew of the CPD's Midge Decter who in turn is married to Podhoretz. Young Muravchik, after a stint on Moynihan's staff, moved to the editorship of *Political Observer*, the house organ of CDM.

When Warnke's name was withheld from nomination for the top defense post after all, plans to formalize the memo as a CDM release were dropped, only to be quickly revived when it was learned that he would be tapped for the twin arms positions in February. It was not long before it had circulated throughout Capitol Hill, still unidentified either by authorship or affiliation. In the memo, Warnke was accused, among other things, of having been "the principal adviser to George McGovern on National Security issues during the 1972 presidential campaign." [55] As evidence for this transgression, Kemble and Muravchik cited two campaign papers that Warnke cochaired for McGovern which called for cuts in a number of ongoing and projected weapons projects. Moreover, they charged, not only would Warnke cut back the production and development of essential weapons systems — but would do so uni-laterally. In support of their allegation, the CDM staffers quoted liberally from Warnke's "Two Apes On A Treadmill." What Warnke had said very plainly in that article was that the SALT negotiations themselves had served in some instances to accelerate the arms race. To get off this treadmill he offered another possible avenue: "We should . . . try a policy of restraint, while calling for matching restraint from the Soviet Union." [56]

The CDM memo argued that Warnke was wrong on two counts: first, in his belief that the U.S. had been the instigator of the arms race and that the Soviet Union had merely "aped" U.S. behavior; second, in his notion that in the nuclear age, superiority is meaningless, and therefore "unilateral initiatives" would not jeopardize the nation's security. Thus, in the opposition to Warnke, we encounter the same thematic issues: Is the Soviet Union aggressive and expansionist, intent upon achieving superiority, or merely striving for parity following the U.S. lead? Is there even any such thing as military superiority in a nuclear age? Could a perceived quantitative superiority be translated into political advantage, or is it essentially meaningless? The arguments are the same as those encountered in the Team B controversy; the difference in perspective are those of containment and detente, militarism and managerialism, with longstanding roots in NSC-68 and The Great Debate.

In order to legitimize their criticism of Warnke, the anonymous memo writers cited as proven authority the national intelligence estimates which had just been steamrollered through by their own colleagues on the Team B panel:

> The imbalance between his vehement criticism of U.S. policy and relative silence about Soviet activities is rendered all the more remarkable by . . . a situation which has led to a recent report by CIA analysts and independent experts warning that the Soviets may be driving toward all-out nuclear superiority.[57]

The pincer strategy of isolating the arms control viewpoint of figures like Warnke from both the inside (Team B) and outside (public opinion) is evident in a passage where we are informed that "irrespective of whether he is right or wrong" Warnke represents "views which are not shared, for the most part, by a majority of Americans." [58]

Like the authors of the CDM memo, Nitze also utilized the authority of the Team B coup as a rationale for dropping Warnke from consideration as an arms negotiator. Referring to the battle over intelligence estimates, he explained in his letter to Senator Sparkman that:

> In the last year or so, an important battle has arisen over the current state and future trends of the defense situation . . . there is now a wide consensus that the evidence indicates that the situation could become serious at some time in the future, given a continuation of current trends. [59]

It follows then that someone like Warnke, who accepts neither the notion of superiority nor of a "Clausewitzian Russia" intent on its achievement, falls outside the parameters of what Nitze would have liked Sparkman to believe was solid agreement within intelligence circles. The inescapable conclusion — Warnke was unfit for the top SALT post. In this regard, Nitze confided to Sparkman:

> I am concerned that Mr. Warnke, who has spoken with such certainty on matters of military requirements, weapons capabilities, and strategy, may nevertheless not be a qualified student or competent judge of any of these matters. It is claimed that he is a superb negotiator. I am unfamiliar with his successes in this area. I recognize that he has certain abilities as an advocate, but at least with respect to defense matters, these do not include clarity or consistency of logic. I doubt that such advocacy has much chance of success against the strategy and tactics of the highly serious and competent Soviet negotiators. [60]

On the strength of his letter to Chairman Sparkman, Nitze was invited to testify before the Senate committee. Appearing the second day of the confirmation hearings, Nitze mounted a withering attack on Warnke. At one point he called Warnke's views "absolutely asinine" and at another juncture hinted that they were "screwball, arbitrary, and fictitious." [61] A perusal of his lengthy testimony reveals that he called into question Warnke's character, his knowledge of weapons capabilities and general strategies, as well as his credentials to speak on defense requirements. At the same time, Nitze took the opportunity to educate the senators on a wide range of related issues from how the Soviets think — "They look on weakness as weakness and not to be respected" — to a discourse on the concept of "superiority." [62] During the course of his testimony, in response to a question from Senator Charles Percy, Nitze as much as admitted to the larger concerns behind the opposition of Warnke. The senator from Illinois asked the witness if he was concerned that in the SALT negotiations, "the President might also possibly do something that would not be in your definition of the national interest?" Nitze's telling response: "Yes, I do have that view . . . what I am saying is addressed in part to the man but also to the issue." [63]

The most unprincipled attack on Warnke arrived on Sparkman's desk the same day as Nitze's more reasoned if complementary set of arguments against the nomination. In shades of the unorthodox alliance to come, the letter was entered into the Congressional Record by Larry P. McDonald, a member of the John Birch Society and congressman from Georgia. McDonald's letter charged Warnke with responsiblity for release of the *Pentagon Papers*. In his words, "Mr. Warnke has been a spokesman for the extreme proponents of U.S. disarmament and was responsible for setting in motion the chain of events which allowed Daniel Ellsberg to steal the Pentagon papers." [64] As evidence for his alleged complicity, the letter cited the *New York Times* of June 24, 1971, which quoted Warnke as saying that in his view "none of the material published so far could endanger the national security." [65] In a final revival of the weathered tradition of "guilt by association," the letter charged that Warnke was a member of the Board of Advisers of a group which with "its parent body . . . have been in close contact with the World Peace Council, a Moscow directed movement which advocates the disarmament of the West as well as support for terrorist groups." [66] This updated McCarthyism, call it McDonaldism, was directed at the Center For Defense Information, a moderate arms control group headed by Rear Admiral Gene LaRocque (ret.).

After having witnessed these early attacks on Warnke from the likes of such disparate figures as Nitze and McDonald, Anthony Lewis was moved to remark:

There is a peculiar, almost venomous intensity in some of the opposition to Paul Warnke; it is as if the opponents have made him a symbol of something they dislike so much that they want to destroy him . . . it signals a policy disagreement so fundamental that any imaginable arms limitation agreement with the Soviet Union will face powerful resistance. And it signals the *rise of a new militant coalition on national security issues*. (emphasis added) [67]

The new militarism was not long in mobilizing. On the heels of Nitze's testimony to Foreign Relations, and in anticipation of the Armed Services hearings scheduled for a few weeks later, an all-out effort to stop Warnke surfaced. It was led by an ad hoc organization called the Emergency Coalition Against Unilateral Disarmament. The Emergency Coalition symbolized the growing alliance among Cold Warriors like Nitze and Henry Jackson, CDM ideologues like Rostow and Podhoretz, hardline dissenters within the intelligence community like Daniel Graham, and last but certainly not least important, the grassroots right wing or so-called New Right.

It did not seem at all surprising to find the Emergency Coalition working out of 1721 DeSales, the offices of CDM at the time in Washington, nor for that matter to find ubiquitous Team B member Graham as its chairman. But it was a shock to run down the list of its officers and steering committee and discover the new bedfellows of CDM, an organization that Podhoretz proudly proclaimed to be the home of "Cold War liberals." The steering committee of the Emergency Coalition was laden with representatives of the extreme Right including James G. Roberts, Executive Director of the American Conservative Union; Charles R. Black, the former Chairman of the National Conservative Political Action Committee (NCPAC), and then campaign director for the Republican National Committee; and Howard Phillips, National Director of the Conservative Caucus. Conservative Caucus was described by Andrew Kopkind in his investigation of right wing movements as "the key connection" of New Right grassroots organizing efforts for candidates and causes. [68] Another prominent right-winger on the steering committee was Paul Weyrich, Director of the Committee For Survival Of A Free Congress. Weyrich's group is credited with having sent out 600,000 letters urging voters to lobby their senators against Warnke. Weyrich had formerly been with the Heritage Foundation, an influential right wing think tank and publishing house established with money from beer baron Joe Coors. Still other organizations represented by their directors on the steering committee included Young Americans For Freedom, Young Republican National Federation, and the American

Security Council. The last-named organization, a longtime Cold War lobbying group, has been called by one investigator "the soul if not the heart of the military-industrial complex." [69] Its recent activities had included a suit against CBS charging the network with biased reporting on national security matters and the production, along with the AFL-CIO, of a controversial film on the Soviet Threat entitled, "The Price of Peace and Freedom." Finally, Morton Blackwell, the Executive Director of the Emergency Coalition who actually led the anti-Warnke assault on a day-to-day basis, represented perhaps the heart, and probably the soul as well, of the ultraconservative arm of the burgeoning Cold War coalition. Blackwell is contributing editor of *Conservative Digest* as well as editor and assistant publisher of *The Right Report*, both of which are produced from a hub of right wing activity in Falls Church, Virginia. The titular head of the Falls Church complex is one Richard Viguerie.

Viguerie, who first gained notoriety as a fund raiser for George Wallace, describes his own conservatism as the combined influence of "the two Macs — Senator Joseph McCarthy and General Douglas MacArthur." [70] Viguerie's Falls Church center is reportedly the largest political mail operation in the country. By virtue of its computerized access to millions of names and expertise in mobilizing this vast network, the complex was a key institutional link in getting the Right behind the Soviet Threat campaign with the same fervor it had shown for the so-called pro-family — anti-ERA, anti-gay, anti-abortion — movements that had emerged in reaction to the politics of the 1960s.

With the potent alliance of ultraconservatives and Cold War hardliners behind them in the Emergency Coalition Against Unilateral Disarmament, Jackson and Nitze once again teamed up in the Armed Services Committee against Warnke as they had done in the summer of 1974 against the Kissinger-Nixon version of detente. Despite a cameo performance by Nitze before another Senate Committee, Jackson's acrimonious exchanges with Warnke, and the efforts of the Emergency Coalition, Carter was determined after having lost Ted Sorenson as his choice for CIA director, not to cave in on Warnke. In a news conference just before the Senate vote the President charged that opposition to the nomination was "primarily by those who don't want to see substantial reductions in nuclear weapons." [71] After a final four-hour debate the Senate went along with Carter's wishes, confirming Warnke for the arms control post by a margin of 70 to 29, and for the controversial SALT leadership position by 58 to 40. While Carter may have gotten his man, the Cold War coalition claimed the vote as their victory.

Jackson had boasted before the vote was taken that he and his cohorts in the Senate would "weaken Warnke as an international negotiator to the point of uselessness by holding the vote in his favor to 60 or less."[72] What he meant by this was that any treaty that a Warnke-led delegation might reach with the Soviets would still have to be ratified by two-thirds of the Senate. The people who started it all with their anonymous memo claimed that the Senate battle over Warnke "marked an important turning point in the public debate over national defense policy." Moreover, CDM maintained that, despite the apparent paradox, their effort in fact had "strengthened considerably President Carter's hand in his arms control negotiations with the Soviets." [73]

What they meant by this was that now Carter and Warnke would have to take a tough stand in the negotiations to be assured of avoiding an embarrassing fight or even a calamitous defeat in the Senate over ratification of a SALT II agreement. As Elizabeth Drew described the situation, the idea was to "feed Carter's perceptions" and to "affect those decisions before one is presented with them." [74] In that sense the anti-Warnke campaign was the complement of the Team B report. Both actions were designed with the aim of cajoling Carter to lead a campaign against the Soviet Threat — Team B by dominating the official reading of East-West relations, the anti-Warnke effort by exerting the same control over the domestic political mood. The aim of such a pincer strategy was to isolate the spokesmen of managerialism and detente despite their institutional hold on the Administration, thereby cutting them off in the former case from doctrine and in the latter from popular ideology. It was the second strategy that called forth the seemingly unorthodox alliance between ex-establishment insiders and the perennial outsiders of the extreme Right. Such a coalition had been a long time in formation, however, the out-growth of a fundamental realignment of American politics — and with it the transformation of the base of support for Containment Militarism.

The Merger of Clausewitz And Keynes: Ideological Underpinnings Of The New Cold War Coalition

No one would have guessed at the time the original CPD was conducting its campaign that Eugene Rostow and Frank Barnett would be plotting a parallel effort together a quarter century later. Rostow, the New York-born son of Jewish immigrant parents, had risen through academic ranks to become advisor and cabinet member to liberal Demo-cratic presidents. Barnett, founder of the strident National Strategy Information Center, described himself as "by origin a Robert Taft Republican from Peoria, Illinois." [75] It was the conservative Taft wing of the party, of course, that had been most worrisome to the Eastern Establishment-dominated CPD in the Korean War period. When the Cold War consensus crumbled in the Vietnam era, however, it was the pro-New Deal, pro-labor social democrats like Rostow and Norman

Podhoretz who stood together with right wing Republicans like Barnett and John Connally in staunch defense of Containment Militarism even as many of its key architects within the Establishment had concluded that the doctrine had outlived its worth. Neither could anyone have predicted that Nitze, protege of Establishment godfather Dean Acheson, would a generation after NSC-68, find himself in consort with the American Security Council, a group whose existence began in the McCarthyite period with the expressed purpose of hounding Achesonians out of government. To underscore the transformation that had occurred on the American political landscape, Nitze himself had been denied a post in the Eisenhower Administration because of right wing objections to his liberal Establishment pedigree.

In order to understand how such disparate figures coalesced in defense of Containment Militarism after Vietnam, we must turn to the unlikely marriage of Clausewitz and Keynes that produced a domestic Cold War counterpart to the imperial Pax Americana. The success of such an expansionist foreign policy was contingent upon military programs and budgets well beyond the limits of fiscal and political orthodoxy in force up to the Korean War period. However, once it was shown that military spending could act as a macroeconomic stimulant increasing both jobs and profits, a broad constituency arose in support of empire. Where military force came to be accepted as the principal currency of international politics, military spending became a legitimate instrument of domestic policy in its own right, contributing to economic growth and social stability. Thus Keynesian Militarism at home was joined to Containment Militarism abroad, forming a powerful new orthodoxy and a popular coalition to champion the Soviet Threat.

In the generation of global confrontation that followed, New Deal liberals were transformed into Cold War liberals and finally after Vietnam, into neoconservatives. The isolationist right wing of the post-World War II era had evolved into an interventionist right wing by the 1960s, and in response to the social upheaval of that decade, a New Right emerged in the 1970s. Finally, when talk turned to rearranging national priorities in the wake of the Vietnam experience, the entrenched network of interests commonly known as the military-industrial complex had matured into a powerful political force in its own right in the process of meeting the material needs of Containment Militarism. The upshot of all this was that by 1976, the CPD enjoyed the backing of a political-institutional network outside the rarified circles of the White House and the Council on Foreign Relations, as well as the sustenance of popular interests this time around.

The success of Keynesian Militarism in creating a mass political base for Containment Militarism is apparent in the strong input from organized labor in the contemporary CPD. Whereas the first Committee was heavily laden with big business Republicans with a labor Democrat or two included only as an afterthought, the 1976 model featured an entire fleet of labor leaders headed by Lane Kirkland, now president of the AFL-CIO. In addition to Kirkland, who sits on the CPD's executive committee, the list includes Sol Chaikin of the International Ladies' Garment Workers' Union (ILGWU); Evelyn Du Brow, Legislative Director, ILGWU; William DuChessi, Executive Vice President of the Amalgamated Clothing and Textile Workers; Albert Shanker, Head of the American Federation of Teachers (AFT); Rachelle Horowitz, Director, Committee On Political Education AFT; Martin J. Ward, President of the Plumber and Pipefitters' International Union; John H. Lyons, President of the Ironworkers' International Union; J.C. Turner, President of the International Union of Operating Engineers; and professional anticommunist Jay Lovestone, consultant to the AFL and ILGWU on international affairs.

The CPD's close ties with labor are readily apparent in a speech by Barnett, in which he sang the praises of labor before the D.C. League of Republican Women, a group not given to prolabor sentiment. In his address entitled, "Alternatives to Detente," Barnett mounted a scathing attack on American business while applauding labor's hardline foreign policy views:

> Some of our leading businessmen and bankers whose salaries are well over $100,000 per year, flock to Moscow as if they were penurious Polish peasants beseeching the Czar for economic favors.

In contrast, Barnett wished to point out:

> It was George Meany and the American labor movement, not America's businessmen and lawyers, or the Republican White House, who gave Alexander Solzhenitzyn a forum for freedom in this country. [76]

One of the stated goals of Barnett's National Strategy Information Center is "to train young American labor leaders in the critical issues — philosophical, military, and political — that divide the free world from the Communist States." [77] This effort is conducted by means of "educational" seminars in cooperation with Georgetown University, itself a stronghold of Cold War ideology. Georgetown listed seven of its faculty on the CPD membership rolls. The director of Georgetown's International Labor Program, Roy Godson, is both a staff member of the Center and a prominent member of CDM. When the Center moved to Washington from New York to set up what director Barnett described as its $1 million "interface operation," it was Godson who became the Washington representative, working out of CDM until the Center moved into its own facilities a few blocks away.

In addition to its labor ties, CPD-II won the support of neoconservative intellectuals. It is the role of intellectuals not just to join political movements but to use their ideas to give those movements coherent ideological shape. This need became crucial to Cold War Democrats as power began to slip away from them in 1968 with the popularity of Eugene McCarthy and Robert Kennedy. When McGovern received the 1972 presidential nomination, the crisis was clear. Looking back on those events, a staff member of CDM noted that the insurgent forces had "ideas and ideals. The Democratic establishment had neither."[78] These "ideas and ideals" which the Cold War Democrats found so disconcerting and antithetical to their own thinking, seemed to be sweeping wider circles of opinion beyond college campuses, as numerous intellectuals abandoned Cold War shibboleths for the emerging "new politics." Enter the intellectual defenders of the old order. Writers like Ben Wattenberg and Richard Scammon counter-attacked with *The Real Majority*, an ideological tract which attempted to give a new coherence to conservative forces within the Democratic Party. [79]

Ideological cohesion was found in the promotion of growth and continual expansion as the *sine qua non* of the American tradition. Not all went so far as one CDM staffer and ex-Moynihan aide who charged "anti-growth is anti-human;" [80] most preferred the more ideological parlance of Senator Moynihan who suggested that America's decline in birth rate of late represents a decline of America as a civilization. [81] His close friend and fellow social democratic ideologue Podhoretz agreed, maintaining that "certain cultural tendencies such as zero-economic growth and zero-population growth express in the broadest sense a failure of nerve in the culture as a whole," similar in kind to American business' eagerness to trade with the Soviet Union which Podhoretz also ascribed to "failure of nerve." [82]

Those who questioned notions of growth and expansion — whether in international relations, the economy, or the size of the family — were branded elitists. In the backlash climate of the seventies, the neoconservative intellectuals were thus able, in an ironic political twist, to turn the equalitarian ideals growing out of the upheavals of the sixties to their own uses — impugning the efforts of those who would limit the size of the military, the family, or the economy as attacks on both the traditional values and the material security of working people. Thus did these Cold War liberals *cum* neoconservatives advertise themselves as the vanguard of an attack on privilege.

The privilege toward which neoconservatives aimed their attack was not that enjoyed at the highest reaches of wealth and power, but instead toward that which supposedly accrued to a New Class of professionals in government, universities, foundations, and the media. The problem was not simply this intelligentsia's monopoly over knowledge in modern society, but also the alleged adversary content of its message. On this subject Wattenberg comments:

> ... remember the first "Earth Day" in 1970. Young people in California bought a new automobile — and buried it. We laughed. We shouldn't have. The intellectual counterparts of the car-buriers, deeply influenced by that same ecological mentality, are now bureaucrats helping guide the environmental establishment in Washington. [83]

In the moral universe of the neoconservatives, the New Class is imbued with a profound disrespect for traditional culture and authority ranging from the family and religion, to the work ethic and the role of America as leader in a global struggle against communism. Carter's second- and third-echelon appointments at State, Defense, and the National Security Council were taken as a signal of the imminent takeover by the New Class in foreign affairs.

Ironically, American traditionalism was rediscovered in its turn of the century victims — the ethnic working class, lionized by neoconservative writers like Michael Novak, and the labor movement which brought them respectability only after the bloodiest struggle for worker's rights in the industrialized West. [84] Wattenberg writes in this regard:

> ... the labor movement in America is one of the ornaments of our political democracy, a movement essentially pro-capitalist and a movement essentially allied to ideas that are central to business and conservative goals, pro-growth, pro-expansion, deeply suspect of environmental excess and vigorously pro-freedom around the world. [85]

The decline of "the family" at home and of "America" abroad, each because of attacks from within by the privileged graduates of sixties culture was a brilliant ideological coup on the part of the neoconservatives. So was their insistence that the establishment — business, governmental, and academic — had "lost its nerve" and that labor had picked up the gauntlet in defense of Americanism. In so claiming, it opened up the possibility of harnessing the energy of the New Right backlash on domestic concerns and injecting it into the debate on foreign policy while at the same time assuaging the historical antagonism of the right wing toward labor.

Signs had begun to surface in recent years that conservatives, tiring of sectarian purity and ignominious defeat, had also begun to see the possibilities of long-term gains for themselves in such an unseemly alliance. New Right gurus Richard Viguerie and William Rusher, for instance, editorialized in favor of conservative participation in the Democratic Party. The lines of such a strategy were worked out further in a *Conservative Digest* interview with the publicist of Anita Bryant's successful antigay campaign in Florida. The conservatives' goal, as explained in the course of the interview, is to begin with the nucleus of people who are conservative on "the family" and to get them to "go to work together for other issues and other candidates." Specifically tapped for this new conservative coalition are "Democrats, blue-collar workers, and Jewish voters" [86] — Wattenberg's own New Majority.

One attempt to put this strategy into practice took place early in 1978, when prominent New Right kingpins including Viguerie, presidential candidate Philip Crane, Paul Weyrich, and Howard Phillips traveled to labor's turf, Youngstown, Ohio, for a summit with union leaders. The theme of the meeting as reported in the *Washington Post* was "what's good for conservatism is good for labor." [87] The group's common appeal to the labor movement, according to one of the New Right participants, was to "a natural conservative instinct of blue-collar workers who feel overtaxed or — if out of work — deprived of a chance to exercise their deeply ingrained work ethic." [88] Weyrich added that a "turning point" in the meeting came when the New Right spokesmen disassociated themselves from the "Old Guard Republican establishment" and concentrated on "gut issues." Weyrich added, "It nearly blew my mind; I've never heard anyone in the movement talk as harshly about environmental law as these guys did." The group left the labor stronghold encouraged, Phillips concluding on the tactical note that "we have to break down their assumption that conservative equals Republicanism, and Republicanism equals big business." [89]

Editorials by Viguerie and New Right political columnist Patrick Buchanan inveighing against "big business" seemed to demonstrate that Phillips' call was no mere sop to coalition-building. Buchanan, for instance, asked if it was not time for conservatives to "make an agonizing reappraisal of our heretofore almost uncritical support for American business?" [90] Viguerie voiced his strong agreement for such a reassessment, writing: "In recent years . . . the big business community, intent on other goals, has veered from the path we shared." Some of the reasons cited for the falling out, according to Viguerie, were that "big business has subjugated the country's national interests to sales abroad" and "U.S. corporate giants are supporting pornographic publications through their advertising dollars." [91] In the former category, Viguerie placed Ford Motor Company for its decision to build a truck factory in the Soviet

Union and Control Data Corporation for its plan to sell sophisticated computer equipment to the Russians. Thus had the editor of *Conservative Digest* and reputed godfather of the resurgent right wing accused international capitalism of hastening the "decline of traditional values" at home and contributing to "the loss of will abroad" — the twin themes dear to the heart of the neoconservatives as well.

While the New Right demonstrated a changed attitude toward business and labor, Podhoretz offered an olive branch to the New Right from the neoconservative side in a provocative, meanly-argued essay entitled, "The Culture Of Appeasement." The gist of Podhoretz' thesis was that an unhealthy pacifism had pervaded the nation since the Vietnam War, similar to that which characterized England of the 1920s and 1930s. This is a theme quite common in the CPD/CDM literature, one replete with analogies between the United States in the post-Vietnam era and Europe before World War II, punctuated with frequent cries of "Munich!" But Podhoretz took the case one step further, arguing that at bottom the root cause of this erosion of will is homosexuality. In making such an argument, and suggesting that this was similarly the case of England in the earlier period, Podhoretz closes the circle, tying both types of national insecurity — the one manifesting itself as concern over internal breakdown, the other as fear of external attack — together into a small, if not neat, package of demogoguery. Podhoretz concluded his diatribe warning that "the parallels with England in 1937 are here, and this revival of the culture of appeasement ought to be troubling our sleep." [92] This neoconservative overture to Phyllis Schlafly and Anita Bryant brought together, however tenuously, the antigay fight in the domestic arena and the anticommunist battles in foreign policy. In so doing, Podhoretz provided the ideological rationale for a fusion between the mass-based "profamily"forces in vogue on the New Right, and the "Soviet Threat" effort of elite groups led by the Committee on the Present Danger.

An opportunity to extend the New Right's operations from the domestic into the international arena presented itself in the Panama Canal debate during the early months of 1978. Indeed, for ideological purposes the Canal linked the two. Viguerie's direct mail organization dispatched anywhere from seven to nine million letters and was largely responsible for raising three million dollars in a nearly successful attempt to block Senate ratification of the Canal treaties. Though their efforts in this case fell short, two of the leaders who spearheaded the campaign — Crane and Phillips — indicated that they would subsequently point the anti-Canal juggernaut toward the SALT negotiations, unleashing their direct mail and traveling "truth squad" tactics once again in an effort to derail an arms limitation agreement. Aside from gaining new adherents and new financial support, Crane emphasized that "the most important plus was finding that conservative groups can be pulled together to fight a common battle." [93] Like the anti-Warnke campaign, much of the success of the Panama Canal effort was attributed to an ad hoc coordinating committee that served as an umbrella organization linking the various member groups. This same modus operandi would soon be employed in the anti-SALT battle under the auspices of the Coalition For Peace Through Strength.

While Viguerie claimed that the Panama campaign added between 250,000 and 400,000 new names to the conservative cause, Phillips cautioned that "raw numbers alone won't do the job when you're up against something like the American foreign policy establishment. People look to experts for answers, not to a group of outsiders." [94] Thus, the *mariage de convenance* between the *declasse* experts of the CPD in search of a popular base and the *menu peuple* of the New Right in search of authoritative backing, begun during the effort to block Warnke, seemed about to be revived. No more graphic confirmation was needed than Ronald Reagan's trip to Washington in January, 1979, in which his itinerary included in Mary McGrory's words "tete-a-tetes with people who once paled at the mention of his name." [95] Nitze, Rostow, and most of the other executive committee members of the CPD would comfortably fit this category. Nevertheless, whether before or after their dinner together, Reagan was reportedly initiated into the ranks of the Committee on the Present Danger — and on the executive committee at that. [96]

Reconstruction of the Propaganda Machine: The Organizational Infrastructure of the New Cold War Coalition

Neoconservatives can take much of the credit for making possible the unlikely union between the followers of Acheson and the idolizers of Taft and MacArthur who had been at opposite ends in The Great Debate of 1951. One of the centers of ideological bridge-building between Cold War liberals moving right and conservatives edging ever so slightly toward the middle has been the American Enterprise Institute (AEI), a conservative Washington-based think tank, long outclassed by its Democratic counterpart, the Brookings Institution. Founded by William Baroody, Sr., AEI had been rather undistinguished until Baroody began to incorporate the views of disgruntled neoconservative Democrats to spice up the lackluster Republican fare for which it was known. As an assiduous observer of this evolution put it, "One of Baroody's shrewdest moves was jettisoning the right wing's stirring but futile dream of a frontal assault on liberalism." He added, "In this scheme (coalition building)

neoconservatives are the all-important 'missing link.' " Critic Peter
Steinfels continues: "Their sympathy for traditional conservative values
keeps the center of gravity in AEI's policy debates on the right, but they
possess academic respectability and a residue of liberal and Democratic
credentials that have won AEI credibility." [97] Thus we find Irving Kristol
— the Richard Viguerie of neoconservatism and a socialist in his younger
days —sitting on the board of the Republican-dominated AEI. Moreover, the Coalition For A Democratic Majority has practically been
drafted whole into the AEI experiment. Along with Kristol, Michael
Novak and Jeane Kirkpatrick have been resident scholars, while S.M.
Lipset, Richard Scammon, Ben Wattenberg, Peter Berger, and Nathan
Glazer were recruited for various AEI projects. Finally, Lipset and
Wattenberg edit AEI's journal, *Public Opinion*.

To be sure, a rapprochement between traditional conservatives and
ex-liberals turned conservative will not be an easy one. New Right ideologue Kevin P. Phillips took the traditional uncompromising stance for
which the Right is famous in an unflattering portrait of neoconservatism
which he describes as a "half-way house" for disillusioned liberals
without a home. He also refers to them as "Nixiecrats — distressed ex-
liberal Democrats" who in the aftermath of Watergate "found themselves in want of a new banner and rallying point." [98] It is Phillips' firm
conviction that they should be avoided like the plague. As reasons for his
adamant stance toward neoconservatism, he cites as negative charac-
teristics the following factors that would only serve to "turn-off" the
populist-oriented constituency of what he once termed "the emerging
Republican Majority." [99] These flaws include intellectualism — "neoconservatism is long on magazine editors and short on hod carriers"; anti-
populism — "neoconservatism itself is profoundly elitist, and tends to
look down its urbane Eastern nose at the populist politics"; the importance of Israel — "neoconservatism's strong preoccupation with
Israel does suggest a genesis and partial *raison d'etre* not deeply shared
by the country as a whole"; and familiar faces/failure participants —
"Daniel Patrick Moynihan, for example, participated in the failures of
four straight administrations without regard to party." [100] As Phillips sees
it then, neoconservatism is not the radical uprooting of liberal institutions
created in the New Deal-World War II-Korean War era, so much as it is
a concerted effort to conserve this liberal framework and protect it from
enemies without and infidels within. Phillips clearly does not want to see
the New Right involved in a defense of the welfare side of the modern
Warfare-Welfare State given birth in the marriage of Clausewitz and
Keynes. He concludes his acerbic commentary with the unkind parting
shot that far from any new political wave of the future the "great
contribution that neoconservatism can make is *intellectual*, profiling and

spotlighting the passing of the liberal era." [101]

Similarly, from the neoconservative side in a *Commentary* article entitled, "Why The New Right Lost", Jeane Kirkpatrick castigated Phillips' style of thinking for its overestimate of the ideological inclinations of the American public and for what she feels is its unidimensional view of American politics. Kirkpatrick writes: "The New Right theory of politics is not only wrong because it assumes that people who are conservatives on one issue are 'conservatives'; it also errs in assuming that voters are more ideological than they in fact are." [102]

Kirkpatrick's alternative schema divides the political universe into three parts — economic, cultural, and foreign policy. The economic dimension central to the New Deal alignment had been the major focus of political debate in the United States until the 1960s. Political contests revolved around the "marketplace" question of who got what from the American system. Kirkpatrick postulates that, "The 60s changed all that by introducing questions of culture and of foreign policy into the electoral sphere." [103] Most of the misunderstanding about what it is to be a liberal or conservative, she believes, stems from "the attempt to treat this multidimensional political universe as though it all hung together." She goes on to explain in what one might consider a preamble to a neoconservative manifesto:

> ... while it is possible to find persons who take "conservative" positions on every issue (assuming one can decide what a conservative position *is* on every issue), both public-opinion data and electoral behavior make it entirely clear that a great many voters support an active role for government in the economic sphere, oppose challenges to the authority of government, distrust the Soviet Union and support a strong defense posture, or adopt some combination of "liberal" and "conservative" positions. [104]

Finally, Kirkpatrick comes to much the same conclusion about the New Right as Phillips does about neoconservatism — it's not the political wave of the future. She explains why:

> It will fail in its current version because of its hostility to another deeply rooted aspect of contemporary politics — the welfare state, whose benefits no majority in any democratic country has yet foresworn. [105]

The problems of putting together an electoral coalition between neo-conservatism and the New Right was vividly revealed in the 1980 candidacy of John Connally. Connally, archsymbol of the Sun Belt as well as a member of the elite CPD, was embraced by both wings of conservatism as evidenced by his campaign war chest, reputed to have been the largest among presidential candidates. Financial backing for Connally's candidacy came from both the American Jewish Committee —the *Commentary* crowd —and the Viguerie complex. Viguerie, who at the outset had backed Philip Crane, suddenly switched his formidable resources to Connally in the summer of 1979, signalling a shift in support from the New Right generally. The burgeoning alliance did not get past the honeymoon stage, however, before Connally made his "anti-Israel" speech and lost his neoconservative base. The chairperson of the Foreign Affairs Committee of the American Jewish Committee, CPD and CDM executive committees' member Rita Hauser, promptly announced that the forces she represented would be moving their considerable resources out of the Connally camp. [106] Once again, the neoconservatives were left wandering across the political landscape in search of a suitable refuge.

There were then clearly undeniable obstacles to an *electoral* coalition between the New Right and neoconservatives — primarily over the welfare state and labor issues at home, and Israel abroad. At the same time, their potential as an *adversary* coalition could not be discounted. They constituted a formidable political force upholding authority at home and *realpolitik* abroad. Their positions on abortion, gays, feminism, affirmative action, and busing were indistinguishable; as were their stands against SALT, troop withdrawal from Korea, Russians in Cuba, Cubans in Africa, restraint in Iran, and a new world order embodying the concept of global interdependence. As long as they were on the outside as critics they could agree to disagree on economics and still unite against "the erosion of traditional values," subordinating the question of Israel to the larger issue of "the loss of will" abroad. Moreover, each could readily agree that the purveyor of defeatist attitudes was an intelligentsia that, in the case of foreign policy, came to share power in the Carter Administration alongside a beleaguered Establishment that had "lost its nerve." As CDM cochairman Moynihan complained after one year of the Carter Administration, ". . . the high sub-Cabinet policy jobs are peopled heavily with 'militant' liberals who were active in a variety of causes in the 1960s and '70s." [107] Fellow cochair Wattenberg sensed an enormous political stake in the SALT debate in this regard. He wrote:

> There is, in my view, a profound sense in this country that we are a nation that remains "number one," whose sun is ascendant. At the same time, Americans feel that we have been governed for a decade now by men who are afraid to say that, or act upon it, by leaders who are for the most part sitting by impotently while American status around the world di-

minishes. [108]

Indicative of the potential of a working consensus between traditional and neoconservatives were the expanding operations of AEI, described by Steinfels as "the fastest-growing and most vital think tank in the nation's capital." [109] Much of this emphasis was directed toward foreign policy, where AEI and its affiliate, the Center For Strategic And International Studies (CSIS) at Georgetown, set themselves up in competition with such august bodies as the Council On Foreign Relations and the Trilateral Commission. CSIS also established the *Washington Quarterly* as a rival to *Foreign Affairs* and *Foreign Policy*. Writing in the *New Republic* Morton Kondracke speculated that: "If the Trilateral administration should flop, it could be suceeded by one strongly influenced by Georgetown — headed by a mainstream Republican or, perhaps, by a Democrat such as Senator Daniel Patrick Moynihan." [110] Henry Kissinger's decision to domicile himself at CSIS and to become a part of AEI was perhaps indicative of capitulation by the Trilateral Commission itself, given Kissinger's close relationship with David Rockefeller, the Commission's patron.

CSIS's director Ray Cline, a CPD member and former deputy director of the CIA, was a harsh critic of Kissinger during his detente-years, as were many in this Georgetown CPD-CDM stronghold. Since he left government however, Kissinger had been rapidly backpedalling from his former advocacy of more cooperative relations with the Soviet Union. Kondracke concludes that, "With a fine sense of where power is shifting, it is not surprising that Henry Kissinger settled in the Georgetown Center." [111]

Kissinger's metamorphosis has indeed been extraordinary even for one whose reputation had been made on unprincipled broken-field maneuvers. In a rhapsodic joint interview with Moynihan, conducted by Wattenberg in AEI's *Public Opinion*, Kissinger is quoted as saying that a "defeatist consensus" in the "traditional establishment" is apparent in the Administration's approach to SALT — the very same charges that had been levelled at his own efforts by Nitze and company only a few years earlier. [112] A *Time* profile of Nitze was quick to pick this up, noting early in 1979 that ". . . suddenly Nitze finds he is marching at times with old adversaries like former Secretary of State Henry Kissinger." [113] Indeed, a private summit had been arranged between Kissinger and Nitze by AEI the year before, with former President Gerald Ford sitting in. [114] Nitze confided to his *Time* interviewer: "I think it is running our way." [115] Columnist Anthony Lewis of the *New York Times* agreed. Why else, he asked, would Kissinger have been so outspoken against the executive authority that he once cherished? Answering his own inquiry, Lewis concluded that "plainly he is maneuvering for future power. He sees public opinion turning more critical of the Soviets. He sees the Senate leaning toward a link between SALT and higher defense spending. He wants to be on the winning side." [116]

If a Nitze-Kissinger alliance seemed novel, the fact that these masters of bureaucratic intrigue saw their way back to power through the Congress is even more bizarre given both mens' lifelong disdain of Congressional advise and consent in the realm of foreign policy, territory which they unerringly viewed as the *sanctum sanctorum* of the elite Establishment. What caused them to reevaluate their position was the fact that thirty-four senators could either vote down, or hold for ransom, the eventual SALT agreement reached by American and Soviet negotiators. If approved without reservation, an arms treaty would undermine the rationale for Containment Militarism; if rejected, on the other hand, the Carter Administration, as well as future administrations, would have little choice but to increase military spending and return to the expansionist foreign policy the CPD favored. Moreover, from an August, 1977 meeting with Carter, it had become clear to the Committee's leadership that their strategy must be one of outside coercion rather than inside persuasion, if they were to turn American foreign policy back to the preferred destiny outlined for it in NSC-68. This time around however, the relegitimation of Containment Militarism demanded an aggressive Congress and a compromising Administration; an activation of conservatives and the isolation of liberals —the very opposite of the CPD strategy in 1950-53.

The third element of the political triumvirate in support of militarism, joining with the neoconservatives and the New Right behind the elite leadership of the CPD, was the military-industrial complex. Since the tactics of the burgeoning Cold War coalition involved pressuring the Administration through Congress, the military-industrial lobby was a particularly potent ally. Keynesian Militarism had literally created Congressional districts, and military production had become a major industry of many states. This was especially the case in the so-called Sun Belt states where conservative sentiment had always been a strong political force. Given the economic boon military spending had provided this region of the country, Southern Rim Congressmen and their business constituents quickly overcame their aversion to government spending and quickly joined labor in support of the Warfare if not the Welfare side of the modern state. Since the popular base of the New Right is rooted in the Sun Belt and dominates the region's politics, the military-industrial complex served as an *institutional* link between labor and the New Right, in much the same way that neoconservatism provided the *ideological* nexus between the two. Similarly, where neoconservatism provided a bridge between Establishment hawks and Cold War laborites, the military-industrial complex linked the architects of Containment Militarism abroad to the recipients of Keynesian Militarism at home.

The vehicle through which these interconnected currents were set into motion was the Coalition For Peace Through Strength, an ad hoc lobby modeled after the Emergency Coalition Against Unilateral Disarmament. As was the case with the latter, the Coalition For Peace Through Strength originated in the American Security Council, referred to earlier as "the heart if not the soul of the military-industrial complex."[117] The few firms which are acknowledged to be among its supporters, together with those interlocked with the Council through corporate officers who serve on its policy panels, rank among the top defense contractors in the country. Included among them are Honeywell Corporation, General Electric, Lockheed, and McDonnell-Douglas, as well as firms like Motorola who, although not among the giants, depend on military production for their existence. In addition, the leadership and policy committees of the Council include many retired military men of high rank, among them Daniel Graham, and CPD members Lyman Lemnitzer, Andrew J. Goodpaster, and Maxwell Taylor, as well as several Congressmen with a stake in military spending. In an interview for this book, Elbridge Durbrow, vice-chairman of the American Security Council, was asked if the military-industrial characterization bothered him. His reply was emphatic: "Hell no — if our military and industry can't get together how are we going to defend our country?" He added, "The military-industrial complex is a very healthy thing despite the fact it's downgraded in the press." [118]

While the American Security Council grew up with the military-industrial complex during the Cold War era, eventually to become its political arm and public defender, the Council began as an outgrowth of McCarthyism. According to Durbrow, ASC was founded when General Robert Wood, who had retired from the military and taken over as president of Sears, Roebuck "became concerned that we had not won the Korean War and got together some military people and industrialists."[119] They set themselves the task of ferreting out "internal subversion," which when liberally defined was not above holding the Europe-first followers of Acheson as responsible for the Korean outcome. With the financial support of such companies as Sears and Motorola, ASC began to assemble extensive files on individuals, organizations, and publications, suspected of communist leanings. The Council even went so far as attempting to obtain Joe McCarthy's files after his demise in order to pick up where the censured senator had left off. [120]

After this initial foray into red-baiting the Council turned its attention from the internal threat of communism to the "more respectable"

Soviet Threat, not an altogether surprising evolution given its ties to the growing military-industrial complex. As Durbrow explained it, ASC's leadership has made a concerted effort in recent years to avoid the extreme right image of groups like the John Birch Society and the Liberty Lobby that are "still looking for a Communist under every bed," although president and founder John Fisher is quick to add, "They (the John Birch Society) are not the enemy." [121] Neither are old adversaries from the Truman years like Paul Nitze. In this regard, Durbrow reported that he was delighted by the appearance of the CPD on the scene explaining: "They have a very formidable group of people. More so than ours. One reason theirs is so formidable is its diversity and *the fact that they have not always taken that position*." (emphasis added) [122] Given Nitze's critical leadership role in NSC-68, this observation is noteworthy in what it reveals about the changing pattern of American politics rather than what it says about Nitze's thinking. Durbrow characterizes Nitze as "someone who tried to negotiate and got burned, like all the others before him." Likewise, on CPD cofounder Rostow: "He's the same damned way; now he's the most rabid guy in the world — he got burned." [123] As an indication that this new spirit of cooperation was not simply a one-way effort, Durbrow related that a contingent from the CPD's executive committee had visited ASC in order to preview "The Price Of Peace And Freedom," the anti-SALT film that the Council co-sponsored with the AFL-CIO. According to Durbrow, the Committee's leadership was quite pleased with what they saw.

Unlike the CPD, whose members were men of the executive, ASC had a long relationship with Congress, dating from its search for internal subversion when it worked closely with the House Committee on Internal Security — formerly the House Un-American Activities Committee. Once having changed its focus from domestic to international communism, it maintained its foothold in Congress, expanding operations within the legislative body in tandem with the growing influence of the military-industrial complex in Congressional politics.

A portent of the Coalition For Peace Through Strength launched in the summer of 1978, was ASC's Operation Alert which began some eight years before. The methodology of Operation Alert consisted in putting together a series of Congressional votes to create a national security index, from which ratings could be assigned to senators and representatives. As one might expect, the indexing system weighed heavily against liberals, specifically singling out Members Of Congress For Peace Through Law for special criticism — a group that scored an average of "11" on Operation Alert's 100-point scale. [124] Operation Alert charged that, "In practice, this stated concern for 'world peace through world law' has meant a concerted and continuing assault on all elements of American strength, particularly military power." Driving the point home, the ASC-sponsored effort argued:

> It is almost as if there were two different Congresses represented: those who generally support the *concept of Peace Through Strength* and vote in conformity with the wishes of the majority of Americans; and Members of Congress For Peace Through Law who generally support unilateral disarmament and who represent an ideology that is in direct opposition to majority public opinion. (emphasis added) [125]

The year was 1976. A little more than two years later, ASC president John Fisher announced at a flashy news conference that the concept had materialized in the form of the Coalition For Peace Through Strength, an effort to galvanize "the silent majority" in Congress and to apply even greater pressure on those opposed to expansion of military programs and budgets. The timing of the announcement was designed, of course, to put another roadblock in the way of a SALT agreement that depended on ratification by two-thirds of the Senate. The strategy was readily apparent in Fisher's remarks to the assembled press where he announced that the Coalition included 148 members of Congress at odds with Carter's defense policies and in favor of *military superiority* over the Soviet Union. [126] Senator Robert Dole of Kansas, a cochairman of the ASC-organized Coalition, said that the group was alarmed because the Administration was not projecting "an image of strength and firm adherence to consistent principles" abroad. His fellow cochairman, Senator Paul Laxalt of Nevada, reported that he and his colleagues had learned "useful lessons" in recent Congressional foreign policy debates, among them that "there is no substitute for cohesion brought about successfully when like-minded individuals and organizations join together." He added:

> That is what this coalition is all about. We've gathered together some of the most prestigious names and groups in the defense community to build a formidable organization dedicated to the adoption of a national strategy for peace through strength. [127]

Indeed they had. Where Operation Alert served as a forerunner for Peace Through Strength within Congress, the anti-Warnke campaign provided the model for another side of the Coalition, a larger body of organizations and individuals referred to as its "private sector members." The advent of such a network was heralded in the optimism that swept through the budding alliance after the effort to stop Warnke. The upbeat attitude is evident in a letter to "friends and supporters of ASC" in which

President Fisher waxes enthusiastically about having "had the privilege of being a cochairman of the Coalition with Lt. Gen. Daniel O. Graham" and involving ASC in a project in which it "cooperated with many concerned organizations" in the attempt to keep Warnke out of the councils of foreign and military policy. [128]

A perusal of the Coalition's membership, both its Congressional and "private sector" branches, reveals that what ASC had indeed accomplished was to draw together the New Right, neoconservatives, the Cold Warrior elite, and its own military-industrial operation into one formidable coalition. The Congressional core included such spokesmen of the New Right as Jake Garn of Utah and Jesse Helms of North Carolina along with neoconservative hope Jack Kemp of New York. The military-industrial complex was ably represented by longtime ASC members Richard H. Ichord (D-Missouri) and Samuel S. Stratton (R-New York), along with the preponderance of Southern Rim congressmen who dominated the Coalition as representatives of the defense-laden Sun Belt.

The auxiliary arm of the Coalition, which actually carried on its day-to-day lobbying activities and coordinated the efforts of the Congressional branch, was a virtual replay of the Emergency Coalition lineup. Once again, the effort was headed by the ubiquitous Daniel Graham, Team B member and chairman the year before of the Emergency Coalition. Fellow Team B participants George Keegan and William Van Cleave joined Graham as cochairmen. Van Cleave was also a CPD member along with other Coalition members Karl R. Bendetsen (former undersecretary of the Army), General L.L. Lemnitzer (former chairman of the Joint Chiefs of Staff), Clare Booth Luce (former U.S. Ambassador), physicists Edward Teller and Eugene P. Wigner, and last but certainly not the least important of those holding dual membership, Charles Burton Marshall, Nitze's good friend and colleague from the Truman years.

Appearing alongside these disgruntled hawks from the national security establishment were such prominent New Right figures as Philip Crane, Phyllis Schlafly, and Stefan Possony (Director of International Studies, Hoover Institute, Stanford University). Representing the military-industrial complex were Fisher, Durbrow, Admiral Thomas Moorer (former chairman of the Joint Chiefs), and Lt. Gen. Gordon M. Graham (USAF ret.), vice-president of the Washington office of McDonnell-Douglas. Also among the sizeable contingent of retired military men was Major General John K. Singlaub, who had been dismissed from his command because of his outspoken opposition to Carter's announced plans to withdraw American ground forces from Korea. Soon after his retirement, Singlaub joined the staff of ASC. And finally, there was presidential hopeful Ronald Reagan.

Conspicuous by their absence from the Coalition were such neoconservative stalwarts as Jackson and Moynihan. Turning to the list of organizations encompassed by the Peace Through Strength umbrella, however, we find listed among its affiliates the Coalition For A Democratic Majority. In addition, among the list of speakers appearing around the country under the Coalition's auspices was Richard Perle, Senator Jackson's chief aide on military affairs and foreign policy, now in the Reagan Pentagon. As was the case in the Warnke campaign, CDM joined forces with the New Right vanguard represented by the American Conservative Union, the Committee For The Survival Of A Free Congress, Conservative Caucus, and the Young Americans For Freedom. The alliance between the CPD and the New Right was captured well when conservative Utah Senator Jake Garn appeared on "Meet The Press" to denounce the impending agreement between Carter and Brezhnev. Referred to as "SALT point man for the New Right," Garn had shortly before announced the formation of a high-powered Defense Roundtable to advise him on military matters. Accompanying Garn for his nationally-televised onslaught were Nitze and fellow CPD member Elmo Zumwalt, former chief of Naval Operations under Nixon and future chair of the pro-Reagan Americans For An Effective Presidency.[129] As Morton Kondracke had earlier observed, "Underlying the Carter predicament is a significant rightward shift of intellectual and political power on the issue of cooperation with the Soviet Union. It is respectable again to be hardline." [130]

The "new respectability" of Containment Militarism rested on national security expertise and political clout, the former provided by the elite and prestigious CPD, the latter by the interest-group network of the Coalition For Peace Through Strength. As the *Congressional Quarterly* described the relationship between the two: "The Committee (CPD) could be called the brains behind the opposition. While it does not lobby, it kindles the fire of those who do with its detailed analyses of strategic issues." [131] Those who did the actual legwork on Capitol Hill and among the mass public were the organizational affiliates, from the neoconservative CDM to the New Right Conservative Caucus, whose separate fiefdoms were linked together through the Coalition.

In the post-Vietnam era, the CPD needed the network of interest groups and mass organizational expertise provided by the Coalition, and the Coalition needed the elite influence and policy expertise of the CPD, if either was to combat the institutional authority enjoyed by the executive in the arena of foreign policy. While the Committee would have preferred the role of inside confidant to the President, Carter's snub of their services relegated them to the status of outside Cassandras. As the Coalition's eventual chairman Daniel Graham explained in an interview during Carter's first year: "The Administration is filled with a national security/foreign policy cluster which is unapproachable on any point of view other than liberal isolationism . . . the only way to keep the debate alive and get some sensible resolution to it now is through the Congress. It's a matter of Congress turning them around." [132]

The issue *par excellence* that presented the opportunity to challenge the Administration was the impending SALT agreement. While the drive to defeat SALT was presented publicly as a diverse movement of independent experts and grass roots interests with nothing more in common than their mutual alarm over the nation's defenses, the truth was something else. The visible cooperation among the CPD, military-industrial lobbyists, and the New Right was more than matched by the covert financial ties that bound them together. The Committee's tax returns, for example, show that it received $260,000 from Richard Mellon Scaife, an ultra-right multimillionaire who, according to a recent investigation, ". . . has made the formation of public opinion both his business and his avocation." [133] In addition to the CPD of which he serves on the board of directors, other recipients of Scaife's largesse in the foreign policy field included the Heritage Foundation ($3.8 million), the Hoover Institute ($3.5 million), the National Strategy Information Center ($6 million), and the Center For Strategic And International Studies at Georgetown University ($5.3 million), to name only a few of his bigger and better-known favorites. Each, as we shall see, was active in the media *blitzkrieg* against SALT II — conducting countless studies, hosting innumerable seminars, and providing endless briefings —warning of its perils. Together with the CPD, these core Scaife-funded groups would supply the bulk of advisers and appointees to policy making posts in the Reagan Administration. But that would come later. There was still the matter of Jimmy Carter.

The success of the CPD-led coalition's strategy depended upon beating the Administration to the punch in mobilizing, or appearing to mobilize, public opinion as another election year loomed on the horizon. That it was able to accomplish its goal so completely as the decade drew to a close is as much an indication of the collapse of the global managerial position as it was a tribute to the brilliance of the CPD in leading the charge of resurgent militarism. The interaction between these two world views is the subject of the next chapter.

CHAPTER 6
Bellwether of Resurgent Militarism

1. Eugene V. Rostow, letter to author, July 25, 1977.
2. Paul H. Nitze, interview with author, August 24, 1977.
3. Charles Burton Marshall, interview with author, August 25, 1977.
4. Coalition For A Democratic Majority, Foreign Policy Task Force, Statement #2, *For An Adequate Defense*, p. 1.
5. *See* William Schneider, "Public Opinion: The Beginning Of Ideology?," *Foreign Policy*, 1974-75, 17, p. 109; William Watts and Lloyd A. Free, "Nationalism, Not Isolationism," *Foreign Affairs*, 1976, 24, p. 8.
6. Watts and Free, p. 11.
7. George C. Wilson, "U.S. Constituency Favoring Arms Buildup Seen Growing," *Washington Post*, January 2, 1977.
8. The Gallup Poll, January 30-Feburary 2, 1976, *Current Opinion*, Vol. 4, No. 4, April, 1976.
9. *Ibid.; see also* Schneider, p. 108; Bruce M. Russett, "The Revolt of the Masses: Public Opinion On Military Expenditures," in John P. Lovell and Philip S. Kronenberg, (eds.), *New Civil-Military Relations* (New Brunswick, N.J.: Transaction, 1974), pp. 57-88.
10. Walter Slocombe, Lloyd A. Free, Donald R. Lesh, William Watts, "The Pursuit of National Security," *Policy Perspectives* (Potomac Associates), 1977, p. 46.
11. *See* Russett.
12. Stansfield Turner, "The United States At A Strategic Crossroads," U.S. Naval Institute Proceedings (October, 1972), p. 20.
13. Cited in *Political Observer*, March, 1976 (Coalition For A Democratic Majority), p. 1.
14. *Ibid.*
15. Norman Podhoretz, "Making the World Safe For Communism," *Commentary*, April, 1976, p. 41.
16. Eugene Rostow, *Statement On Foreign And Defense Policy*, delivered before the Platform Committee of the Democratic Party National Convention, May 19, 1976.
17. *Ibid.*
18. Eugene V. Rostow, "What Is Our Defense Program For? American Foreign Policy After Vietnam," in Francis P. Hoeber and William Schneider, Jr., (eds.) *Arms, Men and Budgets: Issues For Fiscal Year 1978* (New York: Crane, Russak, 1978), p. xxxiv.
19. Watts and Free, p. 23.
20. Paul Nitze, foreword in Francis P. Hoeber and William Schneider, Jr., (eds.) *Arms, Men and Budgets: Issues For Fiscal Year 1977* (New York: Crane, Russak, 1977), p. xxxv.
21. Committee on the Present Danger, *Common Sense And The Common Danger*, November, 1976, p. 5.
22. CDM, *For An Adequate Defense*, p. 31.
23. *Ibid.*, p. 1.
24. Personal correspondence from Frank Barnett to Eugene V. Rostow, May 24, 1976.

25. Personal correspondence from Eugene V. Rostow to Frank Barnett, June 1, 1976.
26. Lt. General Daniel O. Graham, interview with author, August 28, 1977.
27. "Strategic Balance: Trends And Perceptions," *Washington Report*, April, 1977, p. 4.
28. Leo Cherne, 36th Annual Address Before The Sales' Executives Club, New York, January 9, 1976.
29. Murray Marder, "Carter To Inherit Intense Dispute On Soviet Intentions," *Washington Post*, January 2, 1977.
30. *Ibid.*
31. *Ibid.*
32. David Binder, "New CIA Estimate Finds Soviets Seek Superiority In Arms," *New York Times*, December 26, 1976.
33. *Ibid.*
34. Marder, *Washington Post*, January 2, 1977.
35. Graham, interview with author, August 29, 1977.
36. Binder, *New York Times*, December 26, 1976
37. Marder, *Washington Post*, January 2, 1977.
38. Binder, *New York Times*, December 26, 1976.
39. *Ibid.*
40. *Ibid.*
41. Banning Garrett, "The Coming Battle Over Defense Policy," *International Bulletin*, January 14, 1977; Marder, *Washington Post*, January 2, 1977.
42. *New York Times* account cited in "Somber Views of Soviet Military Goal," *San Francisco Chronicle*, January 4, 1977.
43. "ASC Press Seminar Focuses National Debate," *Washington Report* (American Security Council), February, 1977, p. 6.
44. Paul H. Nitze, "Deterring Our Deterrent," *Foreign Policy*, 1976-77, 25, p. 208.
45. *Washington Report*, February, 1977, p. 7.
46. *Ibid.*, p. 6.
47. "Kissinger Denies Russians Top U.S. in Military Strength," *San Francisco Chronicle*, January 11, 1977.
48. "Rumsfeld Says Russia Could Become Dominant Power," *San Francisco Chronicle*, January 19, 1977.
49. Cited in Garrett, *International Bulletin*, January 14, 1977.
50. Marder, *Washington Post*, January 2, 1977.
51. *Ibid.*
52. *New York Times* account in "Carter's Reported Choice As Arms Negotiator," *San Francisco Chronicle*, January 30, 1977.
53. Daniel Southerland, "Arms Control: 'Dove' Choice By Carter Stirs 'Hawks',"*Christian Science Monitor*, February 3, 1977.
54. Staff of the Coalition For A Democratic Majority, "Anonymous Memorandum, RE: Paul Warnke," p. 1.
55. *Ibid.*
56. *Ibid.*, p. 2.
57. *Ibid.*, p. 4.

58. *Ibid.*
59. Letter from Paul H. Nitze to The Honorable John J. Sparkman, Chairman Committee On Foreign Relations, United States, February 7, 1977.
60. *Ibid.*
61. Warnke Nomination, Hearings Before The Committee On Foreign Relations, United States Senate, 95th Congress, 1st Session, February 8-9, 1977 (U.S. Government Printing Office), Washington, D.C., 1977, p. 143.
62. *Ibid.*, p. 144.
63. *Ibid.*, p. 151.
64. "Congressmen Urge Warnke Rejection," *Congressional Record*, February 8, 1977, p. 3938.
65. *Ibid.*
66. *Ibid.*
67. Anthony Lewis, "The Brooding Hawks," *New York Times*, February 20, 1977.
68. Andrew Kopkind, "America's New Right," *New Times*, September 30, 1977, p. 29.
69. Harold C. Relyea, "The American Security Council," *The Nation*, January 24, 1972, p. 114.
70. Mary McGrory, "The Panama Treaty Foes," *San Francisco Chronicle*, October 1, 1977.
71. "Senate OK's Warnke For Both Arms Posts," *San Francisco Chronicle*, March 10, 1977.
72. "Warnke Foe Hopes To Obtain A Moral Victory," *San Francisco Chronicle*, March 8, 1977.
73. "Warnke Confirmation Battle Heightens U.S. SALT Debate," *Political Observer* (CDM), summer, 1977.
74. Elizabeth Drew, *New Yorker*, April 4, 1977, p. 112.
75. Frank R. Barnett, "Alternatives to Detente," speech before the D.C. League of Republican Women, Washington, D.C., April 5, 1976.
76. *Ibid.*
77. National Strategy Information Center, *Purpose And Policy*, p. 8.
78. Joshua Muravchik, interview with author, September 1, 1977.
79. Ben Wattenberg and Richard Scammon, *The Real Majority* (New York: Coward-McCann, 1970).
80. Muravchik, interview with author, September 1, 1977.
81. Daniel Patrick Moynihan, "The Most Important Decision-Making Process," *Policy Review*, summer, 1977.
82. Norman Podhoretz, interview with author, August 12, 1977.
83. Ben Wattenberg, "SALT Will Be The 'Third Shoe' In The Rightward Move Back to Center," *Washington Post*, December 17, 1978, p. D-5.
84. *See* Michael Novak, *The Rise Of The Unmeltable Ethnics* (New York: Macmillan, 1973).
85. Wattenberg, *Washington Post*, December 17, 1978, p. D-5.
86. Andrew Kopkind, "America's New Right," *New Times*, September 30 1977, p. 28.
87. William Claiborne, "New Right Leaders Reach Out To Unions" *Washington Post*, February 5, 1978, p. 23.

88. *Ibid.*
89. *Ibid.*
90. "Big Business Must Get Back On Track," *Conservative Digest*, July 1977, p. 56.
91. *Ibid.*
92. Norman Podhoretz, "The Culture Of Appeasement," *Harper's*, October, 1977, p. 32.
93. "Canal Treaty Moves On," *San Francisco Examiner and Chronicle*, April 23, 1978, p. A-19.
94. *Ibid.*
95. Mary McGrory, "Off And Running," *San Francisco Chronicle*, January 25, 1979, p. 41.
96. *National Journal*, October 20, 1979, p. 1751.
97. Peter Steinfels, "The Reasonable Right," *Esquire*, February 13, 1979, p. 29.
98. Kevin P. Phillips, "The Hype That Roared," *Politics Today*, May-June, 1979, p. 55.
99. *Ibid.*
100. *Ibid.*
101. *Ibid.*, p. 58.
102. Jeane Kirkpatrick, "Why The New Right Lost," *Commentary*, February, 1977, p. 38.
103. *Ibid.*, p. 37.
104. *Ibid.*, p. 38.
105. *Ibid.*, p. 39.
106. Lee Lescaze, "Proposal On Mideast Costs Connally Two Jewish Campaign Members," *Washington Post*, October 19, 1979.
107. Jerome Watson, "Liberal Carter Aides Faulted For Clash With Centrists," *Chicago Sun-Times*, November 12, 1977, p. 16.
108. Wattenberg, *Washington Post*, December 17, 1978, p. D-5.
109. Steinfels, p. 26.
110. Morton Kondracke, "Home For Hardliners," *The New Republic*, February 4, 1978, p. 21.
111. *Ibid.*, p. 25.
112. "Is There A Crisis Of Spirit In The West?" *Public Opinion*, May-June 1978, p. 27.
113. Hugh Sidey, "The White-Haired Hawk," *Time*, February 26, 1979.
114. Godfrey Sperling, Jr., "Ford's 'Shadow Government'," *Christian Science Monitor*, January 9, 1978.
115. Sidey, *Time*, February 26, 1979.
116. Anthony Lewis, "Kissinger's Turnaround," *San Francisco Chronicle*, September 12, 1979.
117. See Relyea, 1972.
118. Elbridge Durbrow, interview with author, August 31, 1977.
119. *Ibid.*
120. Relyea, p. 114.
121. Richard J. Levine, "Anticommunist Group Lobbies To Keep U.S. A Military Superpower," *Wall Street Journal*, August 1, 1972.
122. Durbrow, interview with author, August 31, 1977.

123. *Ibid.*
124. "1976 National Security Voting Index," *Washington Report*, April, 1976.
125. *Ibid.*
126. Richard Burt, "Pro-Arms Coalition Formed In Congress," *New York Times*, August 9, 1978.
127. *Ibid.*
128. *Washington Report*, March 1977, p. 8.
129. *Newsweek*, April 2, 1979, p. 37.
130. Morton Kondracke, "The Assault On SALT," *The New Republic*, December 17, 1977, p. 19.
131. *The Congressional Quarterly*, June 23, 1979, p. 1217.
132. Graham, interview with author, August 29, 1977.
133. Karen Rothmyer, "Citizen Scaife," *Columbia Journalism Review*, July-August, 1981, p. 41.

Chapter 7

RESHAPING THE COLD WAR CONSENSUS:
Carter's Odyssey From Global Interdependence To Global Confrontation

We must replace balance-of-power with world order politics. It is likely in the near future that issues of war and peace will be more a function of economic and social problems than of the military-security problems which have dominated international relations since World War II.

Presidential candidate Jimmy Carter, June 1976 [1]

An attempt by any outside force to gain control of the Persian Gulf region will be regarded as an assault on the vital interests of the United States of America, and such an assault will be repelled by any means necessary, including military force.

President Jimmy Carter, State of the Union address, January 1980 [2]

In his inaugural address, Jimmy Carter pledged: "We will move this year toward our ultimate goal — the elimination of all nuclear weapons from this earth." [3] Before the United Nations the new president observed that the United States and the Soviet Union had acquired almost five times as many missile warheads as they had had eight years before when arms negotiations began. "Yet we are not five times more secure," he concluded. [4] Two and a half weeks into his term Carter once again struck

235

this bold theme, suggesting that if both sides compromised a bit an early accord could be reached on a new strategic arms limitation agreement. Yet SALT II, the acknowledged linchpin of detente, was not signed by the President and his counterpart Leonid Brezhnev until June, 1979, in the third year of the Carter presidency. Moreover, its chances for ratification by the Senate were doomed as the decade drew to a close, portending of a new round in the escalation of nuclear arms competition in the 1980s — with or without SALT.[5]

By this time, Carter's early optimism had faded into bellicose pronouncements reminiscent of the worst years of the Cold War. On December 12, 1979 — the same day on which it was announced that NATO had agreed to deploy a new generation of nuclear weapons — the President, in a speech before the Business Council, committed the nation to an average real increase in defense spending of 5 percent for the next five years. In 1976, candidate Carter promised to cut defense spending by $5 to $7 billion. To justify military expenditures that would range from $150 to $200 billion per year, Carter made the exact opposite case from his United Nations stand, saying: "In the dangerous and uncertain world of today, the keystone of our national security is still military strength — strength that is clearly recognized by Americans, by our allies and by any potential adversary." [6]

Continuing to sound quintessential themes of Containment Militarism, the President assured that the increase in militarization was needed to counteract a twenty-year military buildup by the Soviet Union and to equip the United States to deal with "the continued turbulence and upheaval" likely in the 1980s. In marked contrast to his Notre Dame speech of 1977, in which he charged that American foreign policy in the post-World War II era had been hobbled by an "inordinate fear of Communism" that "led us to embrace any dictator who joined us in our fear," Carter told the gathering of business leaders that the Vietnam War had shaken but not destroyed the "national consensus . . . around the concept of an active role in America in preserving peace and security for ourselves and for others." [7] To this change of heart, Carter added " . . . we must understand that not every instance of the firm application of power is a potential Vietnam." [8] A few weeks later the President also changed his mind about the folly of embracing dictators, offering a $400 million military aid package to the repressive Zia regime in Pakistan, despite its rush to process weapons grade fissionable material. To quiet Indian fears of a Pakistani nuclear threat, the even-handed Carter resumed shipments of fissionable materials to India.

Finally, Carter announced that the Administration's program to be unveiled in January would require a long-term military commitment on the part of the American people. Among its features would be improvements in U.S. nuclear forces including the production and deployment of the M-X missile in a mobile basing mode, modernization of conventional forces, and the creation of fleets of ships and cargo planes for the rapid deployment of U.S. forces anywhere in the world. An account in the *Washington Post* quoted "one senior official" as saying that this speech revealing plans for the 1980s marked "the end of the Vietnam complex that has so beset American attitudes on defense matters." [9] Indeed, it was as if the Administration's budget had been prepared by the Committee on the Present Danger and the President's speech by the Coalition For Peace Through Strength, so complete was Carter's agreement with the world view and policy recommendations of the hardliners. The one exception was the President's call for Senate approval of SALT II, although his rationale offered nothing of the mood of compromise he had stressed in his first year. Instead he argued that SALT II would prevent the Soviets from "widening any advantage they may achieve in the early 1980s" that might then be used to undermine American leadership and influence in the world. [10]

The crowning point of the President's conversion came in the State of the Union address January 23, 1980, in which he enunciated the new "Carter Doctrine." Fashioned ostensibly in response to the Soviet invasion of Afghanistan in late December — which occurred two weeks *after* Carter's Business Council speech — the Carter Doctrine represented the return to full-fledged Cold War ideology and the relegitimation of Containment Militarism as the foundation of American foreign policy for the 1980s. The new policy orientation bearing Carter's name reasserted the axial principles of Containment Militarism as developed in NSC-68; first, a zero-sum view of international politics in which the entire world is a global balance sheet and all transformations, such as the resurgence of Islam became a debit or a credit to one or the other side in the East-West confrontation, and second, a conviction that military force is the prime determinant of a nation's influence in the international arena. By his declaration, Carter sounded the death knell for the transnational strategy of global management. Any hopes of creating a new world order by means of economic hegemony rather than military force were effectively dashed by the Carter Doctrine.

Comparisons between Truman and Carter have been plentiful under the circumstances. The Administration itself deliberately set out to foster such an appearance, perhaps with hopes of achieving the same electoral outcome reaped by Truman in 1948. In its lead story of January 13 based upon information from high-level Administration sources, the *New York Times* reported that Carter was preparing a major speech to set out a "new American strategic doctrine." The article went on to say that the President himself drew a parallel between the situation he faced and that encountered by Truman in the early period of the Cold War. [11] To emphasize the point, during the week leading up to the State of the Union address, White House aides told journalists to be prepared for a "blockbuster" Carter speech along the lines of the Truman address that had ushered in the Cold War and the doctrine of containment in 1947. [12]

Former Carter Administration official Leslie Gelb points out that while "such historical comparisons are revealing they have their limits."[13] After citing the panoply of military programs unleashed under the Carter Doctrine, for instance, Gelb notes quite correctly that, "There was nothing in the Truman speech . . . to compare to the amazing list of Carter responses to the Russians." [14] What Carter's speech represented in effect was not only a return to the Cold War rhetoric and world view of 1947, *but also* to the tenets outlined in NSC-68 which did not make their public appearance until Truman's State of the Union address of 1951. [15] The more appropriate comparison with the earlier period of the Cold War therefore is 1949-51, the point at which containment proper was being transformed into Containment Militarism.

The Iranian Revolution of 1979, like that in China thirty years before, was aptly described by Don Oberdorfer of the *Washington Post* as "one of those rare international 'hinge events' that change the way people and governments act, therefore altering the course of history." [16] While he wrote these words in reference to the embassy seizure in November, the toppling of the Shah from his Peacock Throne at the beginning of the year had a riveting affect on the 'mass mind of the elite' well before "Iran" had left its indelible imprint on public consciousness.

Business Week was moved to devote a March, 1979 issue to the "decline of U.S. power (and what we can do about it)." A sober- minded piece that spoke candidly, even proudly, of the U.S. imperial role in the creation and maintenance of the post-war empire, it opened with this grave epitaph: "Between the fall of Vietnam and the fall of the Shah, the United States has been buffeted by an unnerving series of shocks that signal an accelerating erosion of power and influence." [17] As had been the case with China, a sitting President was accused of having "let down" a "friend", and having needlessly "lost" another nation that could have been held but for lack of leadership and willingness to rattle the sabre. In Carter's case, the ouster of the nearly half-century rule of the dog-loyal Somozas in Nicaragua that same year only served as added fodder to frustrated interventionists.

It was Iran that jolted the Establishment, managerialists and militarists alike. It was not hard to understand. After all, Iran was second only to Saudi Arabia as a supplier of oil to the West. Unlike the enigmatic Saudis however, a westernized Iran had been "ours" since the CIA overthrow of Mossadeq in 1953. Since then $20 billion of weapons had been poured into Iran as steadily as the oil flowed out, and the U.S. had personally trained the 500,000 man military and secret police force. Yet revolutionary nationalism brought an end to the despotic reign of Reza Pahlevi, and with it the demise of a tenuous rapprochement between warring elite strategies.

The Shah's assigned role as regional policeman for the Persian Gulf was a brand of surrogate empire acceptable to imperialists of both managerial and militarist persuasion. Its appeal to the former was its low profile and cost effectiveness, and from the latter's perspective, it held obvious logistical and tactical advantages. Once the curtain fell on this "middle road", forces gathered quickly on the right in favor of a return to the unilateralist global policeman strategy. As *Business Week* noted with approval, Defense Secretary Brown had proclaimed upon returning from a swing through the Middle East that the region's oil is "clearly part of our vital interests" and that "in protection of those vital interests we'll take any action that's appropriate, including the use of military force." [18] This was the same Brown who one year earlier when the Shah began to falter, said: "We are as yet unsure of the utility of U.S. military power in Persian Gulf contingencies." [19]

The final collapse itself however registered a near-collective change in the elite mind. The same day Brown, on nationwide television, expressed his new-found enthusiasm for intervention, Secretary of Energy Schlesinger, appearing on a rival network, reiterated the same militaristic theme. While this was hardly out of character for Schlesinger, the same refrain was heard from Secretary of State Vance and Senator Frank Church, chairman of the Senate Committee On Foreign Relations. Steeped as they were in the managerial philosophy, with reputations as staunch anti-interventionists besides, each nevertheless affirmed that the American stake in oil supplies was so vital that "it could justify a reversal of America's post-Vietnam reluctance to become involved in foreign military adventures." [20] Thus the consensus for resurgent militarism was renewed and intervention was present long before the Russians rolled into Kabul and well before the embassy seige in Teheran. In a revealing complaint, the former ambassador to Saudi Arabia charged that Persian Gulf nations had not been consulted in the creation of the new doctrine even though by his estimate "it took our government more than a year to draft the 'doctrine'." [21] The Carter Doctrine, like NSC-68 thirty years earlier, appears to have been the culmination of a shift in elite thinking rather than a sudden response to the dramatic events that closed out the old decade and ushered in the new.

Not the least of the parallels between 1980 and 1950 is Afghanistan's similarity to Korea in legitimating a military buildup already planned and in search of a crisis to set it in motion. Just as Korea was grasped as a convenient pretext to implement the military programs outlined in NSC-68, Afghanistan was seized upon as the *crises extraordinaire* for a program of militarization well under way before the Soviet move. One Carter adviser whose hardline viewpoint had been on the ascendance well in advance of the Russian invasion is quoted as saying, "Afghanistan is finally shaking people into shape . . . I think the Soviets have done us a big favor." [22] This recalls the delight of the Truman Administration official who exclaimed in a similar fashion at the outbreak of the Korean War, "We were sweating over it (NSC-68), and then thank God Korea came along." [23]

Finally, as was also true of NSC-68, the Carter Doctrine embraced the extreme view of Soviet intentions — preferring to see Soviet actions in Afghanistan as motivated by a larger design to control Persian Gulf oil, a move that could only be blocked by military force, even the first-use of nuclear weapons if necessary. [24] The losers in the contemporary period, like Kennan and Bohlen in 1950, were those in the Administration who viewed Soviet behavior as cautious and essentially pragmatic and as such, responsive to a combination of diplomatic and economic overtures. Their interpretation of the Russian invasion was, on the one hand, that it occurred because of the heavy investment the USSR had made in the pro-Soviet Afghani regime and, on the other, because of the lack of trade and an arms agreement that could have acted as a constraint if it had not been for the domestic political pressure in the U.S. that blocked such policies. By his pronouncement that the invasion of Afghanistan posed perhaps "the most serious threat to world peace since the Second World War," Carter signalled his Administration's adoption of the containment hardline over the more sanguine interpretation of Soviet actions. [25] Vance's inability to halt the aborted hostage rescue and his subsequent resignation was the *coup de grace* for managerial moderation.

The collapse of the centrist position within the Administration brought to a close the "Great Debate" of the post-Vietnam era. As the Administration entered its final year, an unmistakable pattern of accomodation to Cold War demands emerged as the hallmark of the Carter presidency. Starting with a call for creation of a new world order, Carter finally came around to leading a resurgence of militarism just as Paul Nitze and the CPD had urged from the beginning.

Since the legitimacy of Containment Militarism had been seriously undermined with the Vietnam war, the question looms as to why Carter with his Trilateral team did not simply sweep the doctrine into the dustbin of history and get on with the business of building an international and domestic climate consonant with the managerial vision of empire. One possible answer to this conundrum is the obvious one that Carter and his mentors never had any intention of charting a new course in foreign policy to begin with, a logic consistent with the popular thesis of a monolithic elite. [26] However, as previous chapters have shown, there is simply too much evidence to ignore the profound rift between managerial and militarist strategies within elite circles.

A second explanation of the Carter Administration's evolution from the promise of interdependence to a posture of confrontation is that while the differences between the Administration and its hardline critics were real enough, the managerialists' plans for a new world order had to be abandoned because of Soviet-inspired aggression and a massive military buildup. Even though the Soviets have made significant military improvement over the last decade to reach a point of strategic parity with the U.S., and despite the fact that the worst-case perception of Soviet capabilities and intentions has once again become official dogma, the long history of deliberate distortion for purposes of partisan gain speaks for itself. [27]

A third interpretation, and the one advanced here, is that the momentum of domestic politics was the decisive factor in the Carter Administration's abandonment of detente for an all-out return to a cold war posture. Mobilization of right wing interests and manipulation of public opinion combined to discourage construction of a managerial foreign policy for fear of a political backlash. Unwilling to confront the "present danger" at home, but even less the prospects of a one-term presidency, Carter acted to mollify his critics. As a result, domestic perception of foreign policy came to assume greater importance than the soundness of the policy itself. A recapitulation of the important events of Carter's term will show how the Administration became locked into this impossible position because of its failure to take the initiative and appeal to the public with a counter-ideology of its own. Why it did not must also be considered.

Era Two: One Foreign Policy For Hawks
— Another For Doves

The Administration's initial response to the deep divisions within the ranks of the Establishment was to search for a formula that could accomodate those inclined toward detente as well as satisfy hardline critics whose faith remained in the doctrine of Containment Militarism. Reflecting an eagerness to heal the breach by means of compromise, the Administration by the summer of 1977 had proclaimed the dawn of a new era — one marked by the cooperation of detente and the competition of the Cold War. The determination to *straddle* rather than *resolve* the conflict between these two contradictory policy currents was unveiled in the Administration's initial foray into the international arena — the SALT process — the first phase of which was due to expire in October, 1977, if a new agreement were not reached in the interim. The political fallout that ensued in the wake of the Carter proposal was a portent of the rocky road ahead for a foreign policy whose contradictory fragments when woven together only served to heighten the intensity of the conflict it was designed to reduce. Carter's unwillingness to take a decisive stand early in his Administration at a time when presidential mandate is greatest, strengthened the hand of the CPD in their campaign to push Administration policy into line with their own convictions.

Carter's revised SALT formula, prepared for Soviet consideration by March, 1977, had the earmarks of a bold new direction in arms control. In its calls for weapons reduction, it appeared to be a significant departure from the cautious understandings tentatively agreed to, before the 1976 election intervened to halt negotiations. Unfortunately, however, closer inspection showed the Administration's proposal to have a serious flaw. In its eagerness to placate both sides of the domestic conflict, Soviet interests were overlooked, leaving the Russians feeling that they were being asked to bear the brunt of the Administration's bargain with its critics at home. When the Vance led team unveiled the Carter plan in Moscow the Russians were taken aback, charging that Henry Jackson, hardliner *par excellence* "had so much influence in shaping the U.S. position that he possessed an invisible chair at the talks." [28]

A perusal of the substance of the proposal suggests why the Russians felt upbraided. First, it is well to remember that neither the containment-oriented Cold War coalition nor the detente-oriented advocates of arms control had been happy with the high ceilings allowed on nuclear weapons in the Vladivostok interim agreement. Engineered by Henry Kissinger, Vladivostok sought to institutionalize the status quo in nuclear weaponry much as one might ratify territorial spheres of influence in geopolitical negotiations. Someone in the Carter Administration must have reasoned that both hawks and doves could be united around the idea of scrapping Vladivostok and lowering the threshold of nuclear weapons. Accordingly, the proposal offered the arms control supporters the prospect of a major cut in the development and deployment of nuclear weapons; but, in addition, it called for most of the cutting to come from the Soviet Union's heavy land-based missiles in order to make arms control acceptable to the Cold Warriors. Not surprisingly, Russian sensibilities were ruffled by this abrupt departure from Vladivostok, Foreign Minister Andrei Gromyko calling an unprecedented news conference to denounce the proposal as "unrealistic. . . (and) questionable, if not cheap." [29]

The severity of the Soviet rejection was seized upon by the CPD as an opportunity both to etch the Team B analysis even more deeply into Administration policy and to persuade Carter to become the standard bearer of a Soviet Threat campaign. There was an urgency in gaining Carter's endorsement at this time. As Paul Nitze explained:

> The American public has changed its mind and opted for a stronger defense. It's concerned . . . (But) obviously if the President says there's no problem, and the Secretary of State says there's no problem, and the Joint Chiefs of Staff say there's no problem, then the people may not feel there is one. [30]

Consequently, soon after the Moscow rebuff, with Carter badly embarrassed in his first major policy initiative, the CPD released "What Is The Soviet Union Up To?" The answer and supporting arguments, right out of their earlier statement and the Team B report, emphasized world conquest. Interestingly, at the news conference debut of this latest CPD effort, Nitze praised Carter's leadership and his approach to arms negotiations but added that he "doubted whether Moscow would accept it. . . because it is an equitable deal, and that's what they don't want." [31] Thus the public was treated to the spectacle of containment militarists like Paul Nitze, after having been left completely out of the Administration, backing the mercurial President even as rumblings of dissent against his SALT stand began to be heard among his own appointees.

Similarly, it was the Cold War coalition that applied "human rights" to the Soviets against the liberal wing of the Democratic Party, who thought the term applicable to Latin American dictators. Joining with the liberals were foreign policy professionals and others within the Administration who worried that Carter's "moral strategy" would likely worsen relations and lead to an escalation of arms competition. To counter this growing sentiment, the Coalition For A Democratic Majority released a letter applauding Carter's position on human rights and arms negotiations. The open letter encouraged him to continue the direction he had begun, and thus in effect, to ignore his liberal critics both outside and within his Administration. It ended by painting Carter in favorable hues and urged him to "Hang tough, Mr. President." At the same time it revealed the Pandora's Box Carter had opened for himself:

> You have set off on a long challenging course, but it is the right course. We promise to do all we can to rally the public support that will enable you to pursue it. [32]

And if you should waiver from that course we will do all we can to alert the public of that event, too, the letter might have added, as Carter soon discovered when he dispatched Vance to Geneva in May with the outline of a conciliatory proposal designed to revive the moribund arms talks. But if the Russians were happier with the May outline, the return to the Vladivostok framework only served to confirm the hardliners' suspicions that the President's "toughness" was constructed on a rather shaky ideological edifice. Their doubts were hardly allayed when Carter characterized American foreign policy since World War II as having been dominated by "an inordinate fear of communism which led us to embrace any dictator who joined us in our fear," an obsession moreover said the president, which finally led the United States to the "intellectual and moral poverty" of the war in Vietnam. [33] This occurred at a time when the Administration had opened talks with Cuba, begun negotiations on the future of the Panama Canal, and initiated plans to withdraw troops from Korea.

The Administration's fallback position on SALT could be used to the hardliners' advantage, however — i.e., by portraying the Russians as warmongers who refused to accept peace at any price, which the CPD's response, "Where We Stand On SALT" in fact argued. [34] Released on July 6, 1977, the paper, largely drafted by Nitze, attacked the Soviet Union as expected but also harshly criticized Carter for waffling in his bargaining stance. The President was reportedly very angry with the CPD statement and the broader hardline criticism it engendered. Yet despite the fact that the Committee had characterized Carter's efforts as inexperienced and overeager, the President's only response was to invite its executive officers to a White House meeting to discuss their widening differences with himself, national security chief Brzezinski, and Defense Secretary Brown.

At the same time, in the spirit of dialogue and compromise with domestic critics, the Carter Administration proclaimed a new epoch in international relations — embodying "the competition of the Cold War and the cooperation of the detente period." [35] Dubbed Era Two, this awkward attempt to straddle conflicting currents within the foreign policy establishment was a product of what the *New York Times* described as an "exhaustive five-month interagency study" whose breadth of concern marked it as "the most extensive and ambitious strategic review since one prepared in 1950 for President Truman" (read NSC-68). [36] Unlike NSC-68, however, this study, known as Presidential Review Memorandum #10 (PRM-10), did not provide a catalyst for elite consensus, but instead drove its warring factions even further apart. As Nitze emphasized, "PRM-10 *tried* to be another NSC-68." [37]

PRM-10 was undertaken with the idea of developing a national security strategy that paid homage to the Team B-influenced intelligence estimates while at the same time remaining consistent with the foreign policy goals of Carter's managerial appointees. The exercise only served to further expose the great chasm between the two camps, leaving the Administration in the untoward position of embracing contradictory doctrines and calling the result a foreign policy.

In the apparent hope of ironing out the differences that had divided the A and B teams' assessments of the balance of power between the United States and the Soviet Union, PRM-10 was structured in a similar insider-outsider fashion. This time, however, to avoid the animosity engendered by the Team B operation, they were supposed to work together as one unit rather than engage in a competitive test of wills. Samuel Huntington, an old friend and coauthor with National Security chief Brzezinski was brought down from Harvard to direct the effort. A member of CDM's Foreign Policy Task Force who had made his reputation as an uncompromising Cold Warrior, Huntington seemed an excellent choice as a link between the Administration and the hardliners.

Whether by oversight or design — most probably the latter — Huntington erred on the side of the hawks in choosing the outside review team. According to the *Washington Post*, "several of the people whom Huntington asked to help with the project said privately during its early stages that they hoped to create a document that would scare the Carter Administration into greater respect for the Soviet menace." [38] Thus the outsider's role, as they saw it, was less one of compromise than it was to continue the coercion begun by Team B in order to bring the Carter presidency firmly in line with the doctrine of Containment Militarism — much as the policies of the Truman Administration became inseparable from NSC-68.

An early draft by outsiders that circulated within the national security bureaucracy did in fact take a hardline position. According to the *Washington Post*'s account, however, "this view was sharply disputed within the government." [39] The interbureaucratic struggle that followed was reportedly so intense that PRM-10 was divided into two parts as reflected in its end title, "Comprehensive Net Assessment *and* Military Force Posture Review." Defense Secretary Brown explained PRM-10's dual nature most clearly:

> One part of it, the comprehensive net assessment, looked at the world in general, and the evolving relationship between the United States and the Soviet Union in particular. The second part addressed the capabilities of the current U.S. defense posture under various assumptions and constructed a range of

defense postures for the U.S., along with rough estimates of their costs and what they could accomplish. [40]

The first part concentrating on strategy became the responsibility of Huntington's outsiders; the "defense posture" statement detailing the specifics of the military balance and defense requirements fell under the domain of the Pentagon team led by Lynn Davis, identified by the hard-liners as a member of the "liberal foreign policy network" that had infiltrated the national security bureaucracy with the coming of the Carter Administration. [41] In the end, the Pentagon insiders' modest recommendations bore little relation to the pessimistic worst-case forecast of the outsiders. It was the section by the Defense analysts, characterized as "sanguine" and "optimistic" by the *New York Times*, that came to dominate the overall tone of the study as reported in the press. [42]

On July 6, 1977, the very same day the CPD went public with its displeasure at Carter's new proposal for a SALT agreement, the *Washington Post* broke the story of PRM-10, describing it as the most important "shift in the official outlook here *since* the issuance of somber intelligence estimates just six months before." [43] If accepted, the *Times* added the next day, PRM-10 would ease pressure for an increase in military spending, thus increasing Carter's chances of fulfilling his campaign pledge to balance the federal budget by 1981. [44] At the same time, the *Post* account noted that despite Carter's proclamations about the end of the Cold War, "the document treats the Soviet-American relationship as the overrriding issue of American diplomacy and military strategy, and makes few if any concessions to the vision of a new international order that Carter evoked in his presidential campaign and in rhetoric since January 20." [45] Moreover, an unidentified "senior White House planner" is quoted in the *Times* as saying that PRM-10,

> ... assumed the continuation of present American programs, such as the deployment of multiheaded Trident missiles on submarines or new, highly accurate M-12-A warheads on Minuteman missiles, the development of the cruise missile system and continuing development of a large, land-based mobile missile, known as MX. [46]

As is apparent from the accounts cited above, PRM-10 was giving off not only double but also contradictory messages. Huntington must have looked back on the tranquility of Harvard Square and wondered why, at Brzezinski's beckoning, he had agreed to come to Washington in the first place. Not only was he identified as the principal author of a report that by this time had been saddled with such epithets as "intellectually shoddy" and "inconsistent," but he was also in the unenviable position of having to mold its two contradictory views into some overall conclusion. At this point Huntington apparently huddled with Brzezinski, since the solution to the PRM-10 dilemma clearly bore the latter's mark — a penchant for fusing opposites into trendy slogans, a talent he developed during the breakdown of elite consensus in the early seventies. Accordingly, PRM-10's conclusion was that a new epoch had dawned in U.S.-Soviet relations: "ERA TWO . . . a period that embodies 'both the competition of the Cold War era and the cooperation of the detente period'."[47] Such paste-pot eclecticism, to borrow a phrase from C. Wright Mills, would prove as confusing and volatile as the Janus-faced notion of "human rights" that had gone before it and, like the latter, it would, rather than temper political passions at home, play into the hands of the CPD's escalatory tactics.

Era Two Tilts To The Right

If Carter's overture to the CPD symbolized his eagerness to reach an accord with his critics, even presiding over a hydra-headed foreign policy if need be, the invitation to the White House was read by the Committee as a sign of their strength as outsiders and of Carter's vulnerability to such pressure. The CPD was never actually extended an invitation as an organization. A White House press release said only that a meeting was to take place between the President and "a group of leaders from private industry." [48] But when the CPD's director Charles Tyroler II, began to receive word of the personal invitations to meet with Carter, Defense Secretary Brown, and National Security Adviser Brzezinski, he reported that he thought to himself, "My God, that's our power structure," adding with obvious delight in relating the story, "This is something we hadn't anticipated quite so soon." [49]

The meeting itself, held the afternoon of August 4, 1977, only served to deepen the Committee's growing conviction that their future lay in what was for them the unaccustomed role of outside critic rather than their familiar position in the council of the executive. The meeting apparently began with the President listening attentively and even showing some sympathy for the CPD's contention that the Soviet military buildup presented a grave danger to the U.S. However, the atmosphere quickly grew tense and quite heated when Carter told the group that public sentiment in the U.S. would not support a large defense budget and attendant preparations for intervention. Explaining the anguish this caused the CPD leadership, *Washington Post* columnists Evans and Novak wrote:

> He [Nitze] and others present were dismayed to hear the President echo the dubious judgment of his national security subordinates about what the American people will or will not accept. [50]

Carter's assessment of the public mood rankled the gathered CPD leadership as much as "Where We Stand On SALT" had unglued Carter. "No, no, no," Paul Nitze was overheard murmuring as Carter explained his views. "Paul," the President complained to Nitze, "would you please let me finish?" Evans and Novak report that "that mood of exasperation dominated the one-hour meeting (twice the time scheduled) that left everybody ill at ease." [51]

There are conflicting accounts concerning Carter's purpose in scheduling the summit. One source speculates that the President called the Committee's leadership in to explain that the best the Administration could expect to achieve in SALT II was an agreement along the lines of the one Kissinger had been close to obtaining before he was interrupted by the 1976 election. What Carter wanted from the CPD was their support, or at least their abstention from virulent public criticism of his efforts. Evans and Novak report that over the course of the session Carter's "repeated refrain" was, "I am the President trying to do his best and achieve goals we all agree on; why don't you support me instead of picking on me?" [52] To this end, Carter invited the Committee to establish channels of communication with Brown and Brzezinski to express its judgments of Administration policy rather than to "go public" as it had done with "Where We Stand On SALT." Thus the Committee would seem, after the August meeting, to have been in a strong position to translate its hardline doctrine into policy recommendations assured of a hearing at the highest echelons of policy formulation.

At the same time the CPD's leaders were uneasy about reestablishing close ties to an Administration from which its viewpoint had been excluded. Their wariness was apparent from the conflicting reports of the meeting's outcome. In a *Christian Science Monitor* account, supposedly based on Administration sources, the Committee was said to have made substantial progress in getting its point of view across to the President. One CPD member said of this version, "It didn't come from us. It made it sound like we had a tremendous impact on the President, that we turned the President around." [53] That this was the last thing the Committee wished the public to believe is evident from Evans and Novak's rendition of the August 4 session. Well-known partisans of the Cold Warriors cause, they reported the CPD left worried that Carter was overeager to achieve an arms agreement and wrongly believed the American public was unwilling to spend more for defense.

Why would the CPD shun an image of success for one of disappointment? Because they simply could not afford to come out of the meeting expressing confidence in Carter's leadership without jeopardizing their own source of strength as outside Cassandras. Since proponents of the CPD's unadulterated hardline position were practically nonexistent at the highest level of the Administration's foreign policy and national security network, their only leverage was to invoke the legitimacy of public support for their views. If the CPD leadership gave the impression of being satisfied with what Carter told them, public alarm might decline precipitously and with it, the power of the Committee to hold Carter's policies to the militaristic line of the Team B report. Conversely, an outpouring of public concern about the Soviet Threat would increase the CPD's effectiveness given Carter's reluctance to brave its wrath and challenge its ideological hold in the arena of mass politics. The Committee settled quickly upon the adversary strategy.

Faced with a burgeoning Cold War lobby on his right, Carter promised to increase the defense budget rather than trim it as he had pledged during the campaign. At the same time, he authorized his secretary of defense to make extremely hawkish speeches, such as the September 15, 1977 outpouring to the National Security Industrial Association. Brown began his address by distinguishing between the controversial PRM-10 and "where this Administration is actually headed in the realm of national security policy." [54] The direction the defense secretary had in mind was suggested in the *New York Times* a few weeks before where it was reported that Brown would request full-scale development funds for a new mobile missile system that could "lead to the largest and costliest missile program ever undertaken by the United States." The program in question was the M-X missile, a destabilizing counterforce weapon — capable of a first strike at Soviet missile silos — whose cost estimates ranged anywhere from $60 to $70 billion. As Brown promised the assembled weaponeers in his speech, "We now have, and will retain, our options. We will build and improve our forces as necessary. We will not be outgunned. We will not be bullied. We will not be coerced." [55] It is hard to imagine how James Schlesinger would have worded it any differently if the CPD's choice for Secretary of Defense had been called upon to make the speech instead of the Trilateralist Brown. In a final indication of the extent to which Era Two had tilted backward toward the Cold War, Brown traced the Administration's doctrinal lineage to NSC-68 when he argued the need for maintaining "a defense posture that permits us to respond effectively and simultaneously to a relatively minor as well as to a major military contingency." [56]

A secret order issued by the President in the latter part of August entitled "U.S. National Strategy"(Presidential Directive #18), outlined an expanded conventional program to match the M-X in the nuclear competition. According to the *New York Times*, Carter's national security directive sought "to improve the combat ability of American forces in Europe to absorb an initial shock and calls for light, mobile and flexible forces to meet threats in such areas as the Middle East, the Persian Gulf and East Asia." [57] Concerning the role of these latter forces, the *Washington Post* reported the President's order stressed that "highly mobile Army and Marine divisions must be structured for a quick hit in remote places, with a flare-up in the Persian Gulf one example cited by administration officials." [58] Such a strategy followed the counsel of the CPD's Maxwell Taylor who argued in the pages of *Foreign Affairs* that a force of this sort be quickly created since, "As the leading affluent 'have' power we may expect to have to fight for our national valuables against envious 'have-nots'." [59] The road the Administration seemed to be traveling in fact, bore an uncanny resemblance to the Kennedy years when Taylor's "flexible response" reigned as the official strategic version of Containment Militarism, a policy which, as we saw earlier, led to intervention in Vietnam.

There seemed little doubt that of the two sides of Era Two, confrontation was the ascendant one after Carter's first year in office. In his initial State of the Union message setting the tone for the second year the President revealed a budget that showed a 3 percent real increase in military spending rather than the $5 billion to $7 billion cut he had promised. In a major foreign policy address at Wake Forest College in March, 1978, Carter warned the Soviet Union that the United States would match its military spending and parry Russian thrusts wherever they might occur. The speech had been prepared by the staff of National Security Adviser Brzezinski who had by this time emerged as spokesman of the hardline position within the Administration. Brzezinski told the *Washington Post* three days earlier that the time had arrived for the United States to take a tougher stance toward Moscow to "prove we weren't soft." He added that Carter's recent statements "underline something that I happen to know for a fact — namely that the President is tough . . . and he is not to be pushed around. Neither is the United States." [60] Brzezinski also told the *Post* that he favored dealing roughly with the Soviets from time to time as a matter of strategy. Meeting with Chinese leaders at the Great Wall, the national security chief was widely reported to have joked about whether the United States or China should be the first to go into Africa to oppose the Russians' own clumsy attempts to influence local upheavals in Ethiopia, Somalia, and Eritrea. Moreover, Brzezinski spoke openly of linking a SALT II treaty to Soviet behavior in the Horn of Africa, a point Carter had also stressed at Wake Forest to the chagrin of Secretary of State Vance and his staff. Less than a month later at the commencement ceremonies of the Naval Academy, Carter hurled still another challenge at the Russians, inviting them to choose one of his foreign policies — cooperation or confrontation. The President indicated that the United States was prepared either way the USSR wanted it.[61]

If the intended effect of the tough rhetoric was to increase the Administration's maneuverability in the policy arena, the outcome proved it a failure. Tensions between the U.S. and the USSR escalated throughout the spring of 1978, driving Carter closer still to the hardliners. Rather than beat a retreat from Africa, the Soviets continued their plodding efforts to pick up the account of America's former client Ethiopia and thus recoup their losses after having been summarily dismissed from Somalia. Even including their support of Cuban troops in Angola, however, only the staunchest Cold Warrior could interpret Russian actions as a grand design to conquer Africa and then the world, never mind the question of capabilities for carrying out such a project. A further signal of Soviet intransigence in the face of Carter's threats came with the trials of dissidents Yuri Orlov, Alexander Ginzberg, and Anatoly Scharansky. Finally, as evidence of further deterioration in relations, the Soviet government accused the United States of deliberately blocking a SALT agreement, escalating the arms race, and forming a military alliance with China.

The Administration's hardline was faring little better on the homefront. In the *New York Times* Nitze argued that "tough talk and a threatening verbal posture not backed by the tools to make it stick are not going to accomplish much." Nitze asked rhetorically of Carter: "Has his way with words led him to confuse strength with occasional strong utterances on the necessity of being strong?" He then warned that such an approach "may, in fact, expose us to the humiliation of a rude rebuff... or force us into dangerous actions for which we are psychologically or materially unprepared." [63]

Recognizing the danger of such a discrepancy, one could either tone down the threatening rhetoric or build up the military forces to make the threat credible. The CPD had been lobbying hard for the latter course, charging that, as Rostow put it before the Senate Budget Committee in March: "There is no harmony between the words and the music of the Administration's budget." The chairman of the CPD explained to the senators that "the Executive Committee of the CPD has therefore concluded that the budget proposals of the Administration are inadequate both in conception and in amount." Rostow went on to maintain that unless Congress increased the budget by a substantial amount, " . . . our security position will continue to erode, and our foreign policy to decline in influence." [63] Thus, argued the CPD, the primacy of military force remained the quintessential calculus of international politics just as it had when Containment Militarism was first formulated in 1950.

The other pillar of the doctrine — the zero-sum confrontation — was hammered home as well by the Committee. As Rostow stated the case before the elite Foreign Policy Association, "The centerpiece of the Soviet strategic view of world politics has always been that if Russia could control Western Europe and bring it under its dominion, and the areas upon which Western Europe is dependent in the Middle East and Africa, that it would thereby control the world." [64] Following Rostow in the CPD's panel presentation, Nitze drove the argument home claiming that, ". . . the point of Russia's interest in Africa is to do what the Chinese say, and that is to create positions there which will outflank the Middle East. Why are they interested in the Middle East? Because that will create a position which will outflank Europe and Japan." [65] Once accepting the premise of such elaborate Russian designs, logic dictates the zero-sum paradigm. As Rostow explained to the Senate Budget Committee:

> We are convinced that a definition of the United States national interest confined to the industrialized democracies is insufficient. Beyond the obvious major components of the balance of power — Canada, Western Europe, Japan, and a few other countries — additional areas of the world will be significant to our security, depending upon circumstance and context. *None* can be excluded a priori from the purview of our concern. (emphasis added) [66]

Faced with a stubborn Soviet Union and the mounting Soviet Threat campaign at home, the Carter Administration began to react precisely in the fashion that Nitze had predicted and helped to foster. In May 1978, Carter made ominous threats of covert intervention in Angola, a catastrophe narrowly averted by the Congress which asserted its post-Vietnam prerogative to veto plans for intervention by presidential fiat. [67] In June with his popularity beginning a long descent, Carter opened a NATO meeting in Washington with a call for $60 billion in new military expenditures and a warning that "the Soviet Union and other Warsaw Pact countries pose a military threat to our alliance which far exceeds their legitimate security needs." [68] In a final blow to "cooperation," Carter ordered the National Security Council to review all trade deals with the USSR and to assure that American industry was not "transferring technology" to the Soviets, just as Richard Viguerie had demanded in the pages of *Conservative Digest*. [69] Sperry Rand fell victim to the new regulations and was denied permission to sell the news agency Tass a computer to be used in compiling statistics for the 1980 Olympic Games. Not to be outdone, the Soviets retaliated by exposing a CIA agent whom they had already expelled, arresting an International Harvester tractor salesman on dubious charges of currency violations, and accusing correspondents of the *New York Times* and the *Baltimore Sun* of slander. [70] Clearly, a mood of confrontation was on the upswing, tilting Era Two decidedly to the right.

The favorable turn of events did not dissuade the CPD from continuing to pressure Carter, however. In a flurry of op-ed pieces in the *New York Times*, Podhoretz congratulated Carter for his new-found militancy, chided the President for his past naivete about the ways of the world, charged him with continued impotence in the face of the Soviet Threat, and in a final upbraiding warned that his political future depended upon a purge of managerialists. Podhoretz lectured the President:

> Thus we know from the polls that popular sentiment leans very strongly toward playing an active role in this struggle once again. But we also know from other sources that the opposition to such a role is very strong among certain influential groups, especially within the foreign policy establishment.
>
> If Mr. Carter were a true leader, he would be working toward the resolution of this conflict and the formation of a new consensus. Instead he appears content to go on representing a perfect embodiment of the stalemate in the general climate of opinion.
>
> The problem is that the record low ratings he has been scoring in the polls for his handling of foreign affairs indicate that the American people are not content to go on living in so stagnant and irresolute a state. This means that the Carter Administration may very well fall in 1980 . . . . [71]

Approaching the midpoint of Carter's term, the CPD saw in the worsening relations between the United States and the Soviet Union its best opportunity yet either to kill a SALT agreement, or to hold the negotiations hostage pending a decision to go ahead with a major remilitarization effort. Either way its goal of putting American policy back on the track of Containment Militarism would be accomplished. Seizing the time, the Committee stepped up its efforts to convince the nation of the "present danger," and to convince Carter that he was fated to lead the attack against it if he were serious about a second term in office.

The Assault on SALT

During the campaign to block the confirmation of Paul Warnke it was the CPD, whose leaders were fresh from the Team B controversy, that provided the expertise on policy and doctrine for the Emergency Coalition Against Unilateral Disarmament — the anti-Warnke group. The other faction of the Coalition was made up of the several interest groups with ties to a mass base and popular ideology. Together they proved to be a potent combination which, while not stopping Warnke, certainly served notice to Carter that Senate approval of an arms agreement with the Soviets would be a considerable feat, one by no means with a guaranteed outcome.

After the Emergency Coalition was disbanded the CPD managed to keep the Soviet Threat on the national agenda with a steady barrage of attacks on SALT throughout the first year of the Carter Administration. One of the more dramatic was Nitze's allegation in November that under the terms of the agreement in progress, the Soviets would be able to gain the decisive edge and lock the United States into "a position of inherent inferiority." [72] To support his charges, Nitze made public classified information of the negotiations underway, a tactic which touched off a furor in Washington. [73]

Because of the Committee's prestigious membership, its message of alarm received wide media and editorial coverage as well as Congressional attention. Given the deteriorating climate in the summer of 1978, the CPD decided to step up the tempo of its campaign, building on the momentum it had already achieved. Thereafter, until Carter and Brezhnev signed the much-delayed SALT II agreement in June, 1979, the Committee led a formidable effort to reshape public opinion about SALT and indirectly but forcefully to influence the Administration's own strategy of how to sell SALT to Congress and the public. An indication of their success was the fact that after signing the accord, Carter argued one of the treaty's principal virtues was that it would allow the United States to increase its nuclear arsenal to include such expensive and destabilizing programs as the M-X. No one had been a more forceful advocate for this system than Nitze.

The CPD's position on SALT, repeated as a relentless litany in its policy papers, press releases, and speeches, as well as in the literature of the mass-based Coalition For Peace Through Strength after the summer of 1978, was as follows: First, *the SALT process has not restrained Soviet expansionism nor deterred them from their global design.* As Rostow argued: "The Soviet Union is engaged in a policy of imperial expansion all over the world, despite the supposedly benign influence of SALT I, and its various commitments of cooperation to President Nixon in the name of 'detente.' The Soviet Union is pursuing that course with accelerating momentum."[74] Nitze spun a web of global intrigue worthy of NSC-68 in support of his fellow cofounder's viewpoint:

> For many years the focus of Soviet strategy has been on Western Europe. By achieving dominance over the Middle East, they aim to outflank Europe. They propose to outflank the Middle East by achieving controlling positions in Afghanistan, Iran, and Iraq on one side, South and North Yemen, Eritrea, Ethiopia, and Mozambique on the other, and by achieving the neutrality of Turkey to the north. Concurrently, they are attempting to encircle China by pressure on Pakistan and India, by alliance with Vietnam, and dominance over North Korea. The United States is the only power in a position to frustrate these aims. It is therefore seen as the principal enemy. [75]

The United States in contrast has been hobbled by neo-isolationism and global retreat in the post-Vietnam period. As a CPD policy paper explains: "During those years (after Vietnam) the United States turned away from the foreign policy pursued from Truman right up to the collapse in Vietnam. The new United States foreign policy has been characterized by an unwillingness to compete with the Soviet Union and to hold its drive in check." [76]

Second, *SALT has not not restrained the Soviet drive for military superiority*. The Committee's most comprehensive report, "Is America Becoming Number Two?" responded unequivocally to its title saying, "The early 1980's threaten to be a period of Soviet strategic nuclear superiority in which America's second-strike capacity will become vulnerable to a Soviet pre-emptive attack without further improvements in U.S. weapons." [77] The CPD leadership argued that the U.S. advantage in accuracy, number of warheads, and bombers which prevailed at the time SALT I came into being was fast slipping away even as the Soviets retained their lead in megatonnage, or throw-weight. "The size, sophistication and rate of growth of Soviet military power far exceeds Soviet requirements for defense," the report maintained, concluding that "the Soviet military buildup reflects the offensive nature of the Soviet political and military challenge and the Soviet belief that the use of force remains a viable instrument of foreign policy." [78] Meanwhile, the Committee insisted, the United States had restrained its own military programs out of good faith to the SALT process.

Thus beneath the arcane and technical objections voiced against SALT, the Committee's case in the end rested on the premise that the Soviets were embarked on a course of global conquest and were well on their way to acquiring the military means toward its achievement. By the early to mid-1980s, the Committee warned, the United States would be unable to deter the Soviet Union, leaving the USSR alone to "determine the future course of world politics." [79]

It is worth quoting Nitze at length on the logic of the alleged Soviet strategy:

> It is a copybook principle in strategy that, in actual war, advantage tends to go to the side in a better position to raise the stakes by expanding the scope, duration or destructive intensity of the conflict. By the same token, at junctures of high contention short of war, the side better able to cope with the potential consequences of raising the stakes has the advantage. The other side is the one under greater pressure to scramble for a peaceful way out. *To have the advantage at the utmost level of violence helps at every lesser level*. In the Korean War, the Berlin blockades, and the Cuban missile crisis the United States had the ultimate edge because of our superiority at the strategic nuclear level. That edge has slipped away. (emphasis added) [80]

If it is not yet clear that the CPD's fondest desire is to regain "the ultimate edge" of military superiority, a candid passage by Rostow allays all doubts concerning the *raison d'etre* of the CPD. In this section of his address, reprinted for publication by the Committee, Rostow runs through a series of crises points in the Cold War from which he concludes that "the nuclear weapon was always the decisive factor in the background." [81] He then laments the long-term Soviet military effort that began after the Cuban missile crisis saying:

> The first result of that buildup was evident in Vietnam. In the late sixties and early seventies, our nuclear superiority was no longer so evident as it had been at the time of the Cuban Missile Crisis; indeed, superiority had given way to stalemate. Therefore the *hints* which brought the Korean War to an end could no longer determine the course of events in Indo-China. (emphasis added) [82]

The first order of business before nuclear weapons could again be credibly threatened was to sweep aside the doctrine of deterrence. The problem with deterrence was its acceptance of nuclear equivalence between the U.S. and USSR, thus negating the very notion that military superiority could be achieved by either side through technological improvements in existing weapons systems. The implication was not only that the arms race was wasteful *but also* that it was irrelevant to the balance of global power. As Kissinger had once asked, "What in the name of God is superiority at these levels . . . what can you do with it?" [83] The answer quite simply, according to the proponents of such a course of action, is that it provides the means to realize foreign policy goals in a way that diplomatic or economic approaches cannot. Nitze explained it as follows:

> It is hard to see what factors in the future are apt to disconnect international politics and diplomacy from a consideration of the underlying balance in the real factors of power. The nuclear balance is, of course, only one element in the overall power balance. But in the Soviet view, it is the fulcrum upon which all other levers of influence — military, economic, or political — rest. Can we be confident that there is not at least a measure of validity to that viewpoint? [84]

Nitze of course had staked a career on just such a world view. Thus it became the task of the CPD to press the quintessential themes of Containment Militarism, i.e., the Soviet Union is engaged in a buildup of military capability with the intent of using superior military force for coercive and expansionist purposes, global in scope and insatiable in appetite. If a convincing case could be made that the Russians had no intention of institutionalizing equivalence as agreed upon in SALT, it would lend credence to the hardliners' own desire for a military buildup to include new generations of specialized weapons with high accuracy, greater explosive power, and more warheads — counterforce weapons — which could then be used in the projection of American influence. The difference, of course, similarly explained to the public in the earlier period, was that such an American response would be defensive in nature. Russian hawks were no doubt making the same claims for their side in the Kremlin. Momentum was shifting rapidly, pushing the "two apes on a treadmill" (borrowing Warnke's phrase) to even more dangerous and dizzying heights of arms competition as Carter and Brezhnev prepared to meet in Vienna in June 1979, to sign the long-postponed and much maligned SALT agreement. Far from turning back the ominous tide of the Cold War revival, however, SALT II ratified it.

On May 10, nearly two years after its expiration, Carter announced that the U.S. and USSR had reached an accord on the terms of SALT II. Having shepherded the negotiations around the minefield of linkage, the President was reportedly determined that the agreement would not die in Congress. As one correspondent put it, "Mr. Carter nailed his flag to the mast" when he said of SALT II that "the most important single achievement that could possibly take place for our nation during my lifetime is the

ratification of the SALT Treaty just negotiated with the Soviet Union."
Carter added that rejection of this treaty "... would be a devastating blow
to the United States of America and the Soviet Union; it would be a
massive blow to peace." [85]

The CPD struck back with swift response. Nitze scoffed at the
President's apocalyptic message saying that if the pact were rejected, "I
don't believe the world would come to an end, as the Administration
suggests." [86] This was followed shortly by Nitze's and Zumwalt's afore-
mentioned "Meet The Press" appearance with the New Right's Jake
Garn. Before the nationwide TV audience Zumwalt claimed he had been
kept "very fully informed" on the positions held by the Joint Chiefs of
Staff and that they had "deep reservations" about the impending treaty.
Moreover, he intimated, the Senate would be "shocked at how their views
have been watered down" in the new agreement which had yet to be made
public. [87] Nitze counseled that the U.S. should increase its spending at
least $5 billion a year, hastening to add however that such an increase
would still not make SALT II acceptable to the CPD. [88]

The strategy to be adopted by the White House according to the
press, was to paint those opposed to the treaty as "hardliners who don't
want peace" and thus isolate them from a base of popular support. Said
one top Administration official: "The polls show that a majority of
Americans favor SALT II. We think they'll be behind us in our fight for
ratification and that, at some point, the Senate will get the message." [89]
This reading of public opinion neglected to mention the bad news,
however, namely that the public was equally distrustful of the Soviet
Union in the negotiations. [90] From its own survey, the Committee
concluded that 71 percent of the public who had any opinion at all
opposed SALT II and were not ready to support it without additional
"safeguards" for the United States. [91] Moreover, given the vast number of
respondents who were either misinformed or uninformed about SALT II,
the Committee proposed "an open and searching national debate" on the
question of the treaty's ratification. [92]

The anticipated review of arms limitation never materialized however. Instead the Administration simply capitulated to the demands of the
Cold War coalition in the hopes of gaining their endorsement of SALT II.
One week before the Vienna summit with Brezhnev, for instance, Carter
authorized the Pentagon to go ahead with the M-X system, a negation of
any meaningful arms limitation agreement. The justification for the
mobile M-X had been provided a few weeks earlier by Defense Secretary
Brown who claimed in his commencement address at Annapolis that the
stationary Minuteman force would be vulnerable to a Russian first-strike
in the early 1980s. As Richard Burt of the *New York Times* observed in
his analysis of the speech, with this pronouncement the Administration

had acceded to the Team B view of Soviet intentions. [93]

Following the logic of counterforce that guided Team B, the stationary land-based ICBM's would have to be converted to the underground tracks of the M-X system to protect them from vulnerability. The logic of deterrence in contrast would question the wisdom of maintaining land-based systems at all under the circumstances, arguing that if they were dismantled completely U.S. retaliatory capacity for a devastating second-strike could still be achieved by means of air- or submarine-launched missiles. Given the ambiguous nature of counterforce weapons in which defensive intent is indistinguishable from offensive capability, the M-X was sure to be interpreted by the Russians as a U.S. attempt to regain the overwhelming military superiority it had enjoyed earlier in the nuclear era. Indeed, the President's own arms control impact statement warned of the destabilizing effect that the adoption of the M-X system would have on the nuclear balance, pointing out that the USSR might be tempted to try a surprise attack to overcome the advantage it would give the U.S. [94] As Administration critic Moynihan charged: "Herein resides the final irony of the SALT process. Not only has it failed to prevent the Soviets from developing a first-strike capability; it now leads the United States to do so." [95] Just as containing Soviet expansionism became indistinguishable from rolling back Soviet gains in the zero-sum world view of NSC-68 in 1950, so too the second-strike capability of the counterforce doctrine merged easily into a pre-emptive first-strike potential. Nevertheless, despite such concessions, the Cold War hardliners remained solid in their criticism of Carter. An indication of what lay ahead was provided by Senator Jackson who, a few days after the M-X decision, continued to label SALT II an act of "appeasement."[96] It was clear that if common ground were to be found, it would be the Administration that would do all the compromising.

Shortly after signing SALT II on June 18, 1979, Carter offered another olive branch to the Cold Warriors when he announced the formation of a rapid deployment force available for assignment to the "Persian Gulf, Middle East, Northeast Africa" or wherever else there might be a contingency outside the jurisdiction of NATO. [97] Although known to be under study for some time in the Defense Department, this was the first public confirmation of a final decision to create the new 100,000 man interventionary force. Bounded on the one side by the latest counterforce nuclear weapon and on the other by a conventional force designed for intervention, SALT seemed to convey a clear message to the hawks that the Administration was willing to give up on arms limitation in order to get an arms limitation agreement. A similar overture had been made some months before when hardliner archfoe Paul Warnke was replaced by a military man and former member of the American Security Council,

General George M. Seignious II. The new Arms Control and Disarmament Agency director, in contrast to Warnke's views, was quoted as saying that agreement or not, the "U.S. must continue to modernize its nuclear arsenal." [98] The signal was unequivocal when Secretaries Brown and Vance went before the Senate in the opening session of the ratification hearings maintaining that while the United States and Soviet Union had reached a point of "rough equivalence" the nation must continue to spend more than ever on arms. [99]

In spite of the Administration's mood of compromise, perhaps because of it, the militarist coalition mounted a relentless attack on SALT once they got the opportunity to testify in the Senate hearings. Led by the CPD, whose executive committee members testified on 17 different occasions before the Senate Foreign Relations and Armed Services Committees, it was soon apparent that the price of ratification would be a concerted military buildup requiring Nitze's 5 percent Defense increase above the rate of inflation over the next several years.[100] Time and again the hearings were turned away from the Treaty's alleged shortcomings to the larger accusation of long-term decline in U.S. defense posture. As Rostow explained the strategy to the CPD membership:

> Now that SALT II has been signed by President Carter and Chairman Brezhnev, the critical debate on the adequacy of our defense program, indeed of U.S. foreign policy itself, has already begun to overshadow consideration by the U.S. Senate of the Treaty terms . . . As has been clear for many months, the Committee on the Present Danger is being called on to play a central role in this debate. [101]

The first week of the Senate hearings came to a fiery close when Nitze, pulling out all stops, charged that SALT II "with all its fallacies and implausibilities, can only incapacitate our minds and wills." Appearing with Nitze was General Edward Rowny who had served as his deputy in treaty negotiations before Nitze resigned in protest in 1974. After six years as the representative of the Joint Chiefs in the talks, Rowny followed Nitze's lead after Carter's accord, adding strength to Zumwalt's claims of military dissatisfaction with SALT II. [102]

As the hearings moved into their third week, drama began to build over Henry Kissinger's upcoming testimony before the Senate Foreign Relations Committee. The *Wall Street Journal* had reported that Nitze was actively seeking to persuade Kissinger to oppose SALT II. [103] As chief architect of SALT I, the support of the ex-Secretary of State was considered vital to the accord's ratification. Kissinger, ever the master at holding center stage, kept his position closely guarded to increase the historical aura of the occasion.

When his turn came, Kissinger offered a qualified endorsement of SALT II — the qualifications of which robbed the agreement of substance. He recommended in his testimony three conditions for passage of the treaty, one relatively minor and two of major import. The first was that it be accompanied by amendments clarifying ambiguities in language; second, that the Senate consent to ratification "*only after* the Administration had submitted, and the Congress had authorized and begun appropriating, a supplemental defense budget and a revised five-year defense plan" which would reverse what Kissinger alleged was an accumulating military imbalance in favor of the Soviet Union — the 5 percent formula; third, that the Senate vote every two years on the basis of a report to be submitted to the Administration as to whether the Soviets or their allies are intervening subversively in the Third World and "if the judgment is negative, whether whatever SALT negotiations are taking place should be continued." [104] With the latter caveats, Kissinger not only contradicted his own former convictions, but also violated the canons upon which SALT was established.

The first of these two major conditions — a buildup of strategic forces — represented a sharp departure from Kissinger's celebrated remark questioning the meaning of military superiority in an age of nuclear weapons. When reminded of this in the hearings, Kissinger said that he had uttered the statement at a moment of "fatigue and exasperation" and that he had since come to regret it." [105] But as the late Charles Yost was quick to note at the time, Kissinger had taken a similar position as recently as January, 1977, after he had departed from the demands of public office. At this juncture, Kissinger continued to maintain: "I believe that to achieve a usable superiority in strategic weapons is extremely unlikely and relatively easy to prevent, and the obsession with it distracts me." [106] His professed beliefs had undergone a remarkable transformation since that time, in keeping with the rightward shift of sentiment within the foreign policy establishment.

The second contingency placed on ratification — linkage between Soviet behavior in other areas and cooperation in the limitation of nuclear arms — represented a repudiation of the managerial approach of separating ideological and political opposition from arms competition. Earlier, of course, Kissinger had argued passionately against Henry Jackson's efforts to tie SALT to perceived Soviet policy. By 1979, however, he had bought the hardline that Soviet doctrine had made the two issues inseparable. Thus Kissinger had in effect endorsed the quintessential themes of Containment Militarism in his SALT testimony. One correspondent summed up the hearings before the Senate this way:

> Cumulative testimony on the treaty has had the unexpected result of convincing most of the 15-member committee that the U.S. lags dangerously behind the continued all-out Soviet military buildup . . . in general, Washington believes the approval of the treaty now turns on Congress and the President agreeing to spend billions more on defense; an ironic twist to an agreement intended to improve Soviet-United States detente and reduce military expenditures. [107]

Richard Falk described the mood in the Senate as one of "bipartisan militarism." [108]

Carter Administration officials emerged from the opening round of the SALT II debate admitting to a greater awareness of "public sentiment in favor of increased defense spending." [109] Nevertheless, Administration spokesmen indicated that they still believed it possible "to strike a bargain with the defense-minded senators who are proposing an increase in military spending," adding that "there seems to be a consensus . . . that some increase is needed to match the Soviet Union's relentless military buildup." [110] By the end of the summer, the bargain struck proved to be decidedly Faustian. Rather than temper the rising militaristic sentiment, the Administration attempted to get out in front and take credit for the resurgence of Cold War ideology — a role the CPD had urged on Carter all along.

The new strategy was evident in a speech by Brzezinski in September in which he proudly proclaimed that the Administration had taken a consistently hawkish stand:

> While our critics say they would have been strong for defense if they had remained in office, in fact, defense spending in constant dollars declined in seven of the eight years of the Nixon-Ford Administration. For the past decade, there has been a steady decline in the level of the defense budget in real dollar terms. We began to reverse that trend in the first three budgets of the Carter Administration, and *President Carter is the first President since World War II to succeed in raising defense spending for three straight years in peacetime.* (emphasis added) [111]

Lloyd Cutler, who was brought into the Administration as special counsel to the President with particular responsibility for steering SALT through Congress, took the next predictable step in such a strategy when he placed the onus for America's "declining" national security position on the Congress. Cutler charged that it was Congress that had "starved" the defense budget for over a decade. To buttress his case, the Washington superlawyer argued that Congress had cut presidential recommendations on military programs by $40 billion during the Carter years. One observer said of Cutler's counterattack that, "He thereby throws administration support to the side of the big defense spenders."[112]

For proof in the sincerity of his conversion to the hardline, and to counter the persistent claims by critics that his Administration was "soft," Carter offered a glimpse of the military programs he would request in the 1981 budget. The preview included in addition to the M-X system, a bomber-launched cruise missile, increased spending for NATO forces to include the deployment of the Pershing II missile in Europe, a new supertank and the funding of the rapid deployment force. If there were any doubts about Carter's intention to lead a drive for all-out military superiority of both conventional and strategic forces they were erased in the State of the Union message in which the President reversed his own conviction, as well as the official U.S. position dating from the Nixon Administration, that "sufficiency" or "essential equivalence," i.e., military parity, was America's strategic doctrine. Carter stated instead, referring specifically to military posture: "I am determined that the United States will remain *the strongest* of all nations." [113] While this nuance in language may have escaped the casual listener, for those in the know it was a coded message that counterforce — and the goal of military superiority — had replaced deterrence — and acceptance of strategic parity — as United States policy. With announcement of the Carter Doctrine and a military budget designed to back it up, Jimmy Carter had recommitted the nation to Containment Militarism and Cold War. In the process, the pretense of arms limitation was scrapped, joining the earlier fate of its substance. The elusive SALT II was placed once again in limbo — perhaps this time permanently.

The Managerial Collapse: Elite Conflict And Mass Politics Again

As he prepared for his final year in office, Jimmy Carter had come full circle — from an enthusiast of global interdependence who hoped to develop concrete structures of cooperation that would put detente on a firm and lasting basis, to the leadership of a doctrine of global confrontation that brought with it prospects of Cold War tension for many years to come. The Carter Doctrine unveiled during this period was widely hailed as a sudden and dramatic transformation of the President's views in response to the Russian invasion of Afghanistan. Nothing could be further from the truth. Carter's born-again militarism was simply the crowning reflection of a shift in the elite struggle for power. Despite the fact that the CPD had been locked out of government, Administration policies came increasingly to resemble the wishes of those snubbed in the appointment process.

The CPD, by putting SALT and more generally detente on public trial, had conducted a masterful campaign to relegitimate Containment Militarism. In a retrospect of the Committee's activities in 1979, Rostow included a brochure of newspaper clippings about the CPD's work entitled, "The Third Year As Reflected In The Media." The Chairman noted that the compilation of articles and editorial comment "is by itself sufficient testimony to the effectiveness of our Committee's work and to our ever-growing influence with and acceptance by opinion leaders and the public at large." [114] A State Department official was moved to agree, marveling: "He's (Nitze) done quite a job of getting anti-SALT facts into the hands of editorial writers and commentators. Everywhere I go to speak or meet with an editorial board, somebody has got Nitze's documents and starts asking me questions." [115]

At the CPD's annual meeting Rostow detailed the Committee's accomplishments as follows:

1. During the hearings on SALT II, CPD Executive Committee and Board members have testified, by invitation, on 17 different occasions before the Senate Foreign Relations and Armed Services Committees — more than all other critics of the Treaty put together.

2. Paul Nitze's famous comprehensive papers on SALT II have gone through eleven updatings — about one each month.

3. Our Executive Committee and Board members participated in 479 TV and radio programs, press conferences, debates, public forums, briefing conferences of citizen leaders, and major speeches on SALT and the military balance.

4. We have distributed over 200,000 copies of Committee pamphlets and reports. [116]

According to one account, the CPD had spent $750,000 even before the Treaty was announced. [117] Still, figures fail to tell the complete story of the CPD's influence on the foreign policy debate. Because of the prestige of its membership, the Committee had a catalytic effect on other elite organizations and interest groups who committed resources of their own to the mobilization of public opinion. The Coalition For Peace Through Strength, with its 191 members of Congress who went on record favoring military superiority over the Soviet Union in flagrant violation of the principles of SALT, was perhaps most visible. Its expenditures against SALT in 1979 were expected to top $2.5 million. [118] In addition, many of the Coalition's fifty organizational affiliates carried out independent anti-SALT, promilitarism campaigns using the policy papers of the CPD to support their positions. The American Security Council for one estimated that it would spend, in 1979 alone, $3 million to defeat SALT. The Conservative Caucus reported that it had budgeted $1 million for the SALT campaign. The American Conservative Union which had spent about $1.8 million against a Panama Canal Treaty anticipated spending an equal amount to defeat SALT II. [119]

The Right, which had achieved extraordinary success and considerable notoriety in its "profamily" campaigns (anti-abortion, anti-gay, anti-ERA) through the technique of mass mailing, found the method adept at selling the Soviet Threat as well. The American Security Council targeted 10 million persons for its direct mail operation. The Conservative Caucus expected to reach another 5 million while the American Conservative Union weighed in with a comparatively modest 500,000. Other efforts included a fifty-state, anti-SALT petition drive and speaking tour organized by the Conservative Caucus to supplement the 150-member speakers' bureau set loose under the aegis of the Coalition For Peace Through Strength. In addition, the Conservative Caucus set up a phone bank to urge an estimated 25,000 conservatives to telephone their senators and representatives about America's declining world power and inadequate military posture. Finally, the Coalition For Peace Through Strength, the American Conservative Union, and the American Security Council each produced anti-SALT films which were shown on hundreds of TV stations across the country. [120] Prominently featured in all these efforts were the CPD, its members, their ideas and position papers.

Treaty foes outspent those in favor of SALT on the order of fifteen-to-one. [121] These opponents defended their lavish spending as necessary to offset the built-in advantage enjoyed by the President. The Carter Administration never mounted a comparable drive of its own to tap this alleged potential however, much to the consternation of pro-SALT influentials one of whom was moved to complain that they were "completely ignored by Carter." [122] The widespread feeling of neglect among SALT supporters was captured by another opinion leader who declared that if ratification failed, "I think it will be possible to look back and say it is because the Administration didn't start early enough to counteract Paul Nitze and others." [123]

The question that begs asking is why Carter, with the authority of the presidency on his side, failed to take the initiative in the post-Vietnam foreign policy debate rather than surrender time and again to the cold war coalition's hardline demands? Fresh from an electoral mandate in 1976,

Carter had the best opportunity at that early juncture to resolve the intraelite struggle in favor of managerialism over militarism. As a newly-elected President, he had much good will to count upon among the public. Moreover, many within the elite, particularly those affiliated with the Trilateral-multinational viewpoint, were in favor of a major reevaluation of the relationship between the projection of U.S. influence in the world and the threat of military force. But Carter vacillated. Rather than fulfill his pledge for a fresh course in world affairs by proclaiming a new era of cooperation, he chose instead to seek an accomodation with his critics — the crazy-quilt strategy of Era Two. Leslie Gelb, a high-level Carter appointee, attempted to explain why such a middle-of-the-road course was chosen, despite the fact that there was so little middle ground upon which to stand:

> The general approach of this Administration in the first four months was not to try and mass this disparate, diverse, and sometimes incomprehensible foreign policy universe into a new strategy. There is no Carter Doctrine, or Vance Doctrine, or Brown Doctrine, because of a belief that the environment we are looking at is far too complex to be reduced to a doctrine in the tradition of post-World War II American foreign policy. Indeed, the Carter approach to foreign policy rests on a belief that not only is the world far too complex to be reduced to a doctrine, but that there is something inherently wrong with having a doctrine at all. [124]

Gelb's words, however noble sounding, reveal the fatal flaw of the Carter Administration's approach to foreign policy: Under the guise of flexibility and pragmatism, they left "doctrine" — which lends coherence to policy initiatives — in the hands of their detractors. As a result the cabinet appointees involved in the day-to-day conduct of foreign policy were forced onto the defensive, having to gauge and adjust their efforts to a conceptual framework not of their own making.

There was one way to avoid the surrender of foreign policy initiatives to Cold War doctrines. If Carter were serious about turning America away from its "inordinate fear of communism" he could have constructed a new ideological framework around a doctrine of global interdependence, one that would have placed detente into a larger world order context comprehensible to the public — which it had never been. Since the theme of national security is so obviously important to people, for example, the President could have tried to build a campaign around the notion that an increased arms race, a capacity to intervene, and a foreign policy concerned exclusively with the Soviet Union would bring about not security but its opposite. As an alternative to these manifesta-

tions of Containment Militarism he could have then posed a new definition of national security that did not hinge on Cold War confrontation. As
late as October 1979, the potential for such a mass campaign still existed
despite adverse trends, as evidenced by a Gallup Poll finding that the
public was equally divided on SALT even after the sensationalized
"discovery" of Russian troops in Cuba. [125] Leslie Gelb, who was purged
from the Administration by this time, looked back on the disastrous
outcome of the compromising Era Two strategy he had helped to devise
and counseled that Administration policy must be more than "simply a
patchwork of conflicting views." Moreover, he added in a tone of
urgency, Carter "must take on the right-wing frontally." [126]

Unlike the CPD and the Cold War Democrats who had few qualms
about an alliance with the right wing, Carter and his Trilateral managers
apparently had considerable reservations about enlisting a comparable
progressive base of support to back their moderate position in the
intraelite struggle. The fact that Gelb, who now fervently called for such a
confrontation, was no longer in government was an indication that the
Administration remained loyal to its dogged course of seeking accom-
modation with its hardline critics even as the latter steadfastly refused to
budge from their own ideological moorings. The events of December-
January were the inevitable outcome of the Carter Administration's
consistently greater fear of a leftward direction in policy than the consequences of a shift to the right, affirming Alan Wolfe's observation that
under the circumstances of contemporary politics "the Right becomes
stronger the more the center tries to woo it." [127]

Upon closer scrutiny Carter's apparent error in political judgment
was nothing of the sort. To the contrary, there were deep and compelling
reasons why the President and his Trilateral advisers eschewed the path
of popular mobilization even as its alternative pointed toward revival of
the Cold War. As noted earlier, when the Establishment divided into the
warring camps of militarism and managerialism, the former found that
they and the conservative right had drawn closely together in their convictions. The managerial elite and the progressive left, however, had split
liberalism apart to the same degree during the sixties, a conflict which
peaked but did not end with McGovern's challenge to the Democratic
establishment.

As chief steward of managerial elitism, Carter had little interest in a
mobilization sure to activate progressives who were as opposed to empire
as an end, as they were to militarism as a means. While the managerialists
wished to control the empire with a minimal show of force, the necessary
frontal assault on the Soviet Threat — the official rationale for far-flung
interventions — would have brought to the surface the very question of
empire itself: for what reason if not to defend against Soviet expan-

sionism, for the benefit of whom, at what price? Faced with such a choice, the Trilateral managers around Carter took their chances on reaching a compromise with their elite comrades-in-arms, rather than unleash a process that could well have placed on the agenda not only a review of militarism but the *raison d'etre* of Pax Americana.

In the absence of challenge to the containment world view, managerialism appeared woolly-headed and retreatist by comparison with the more familiar Cold War ideology of its critics. A similar fate had befallen those opposed to the stridency of NSC-68. Either the Soviets posed a threat or they did not. It was a difficult proposition to sell a semi-threat, and a posture that waxed and waned between cooperation and hostility. Hardly the stuff of mass mobilization and patriotic sacrifice. Commenting on the circumspect strategy of the fox-like Trilateralists in this regard, Podhoretz mused:

> Our position makes more sense than the other position. The other position is quite arcane. It doesn't answer to the way most people understand human nature, of individuals or nations. Common sense tells you there must be something to worry about. That is where our reservoir of public support lies.[128]

Moreover, its ideological handicap was more than matched by disadvantages in the arena of interest politics. In the post-World War II period, once it was demonstrated that macroeconomic stimulation could be achieved equally well by military as social spending, a broad constituency arose in support of Keynesian Militarism. In this fashion national security ideology became linked to domestic social security, merging the classic dichotomy of guns and butter. Militarists were thus able to attack the loss of jobs that would come with proposed cutbacks in military spending.

Carter might have countered such fears without resorting to self-defeating protectionist measures by adopting a program of economic conversion from military production to civilian revitalization. The fact that he did not points up the widening gap between international economics and domestic politics. What was a wise move at home would have undermined managerial plans for a global reorganization of the division of labor, shifting older sectors of industrial manufacturing from North to South. In response to the slowdown in economic growth and consequential capital accumulation crisis of the 1970s, as well as the dangerously mounting indebtedness of Third World nations, Trilateral elites sought to accelerate the long-term flow of capital from core to periphery and hasten the penetration of U.S.-based multinational corporations into these regions. [129]

The managerial approach toward a new wave of capitalist expansion depended upon the Administration's ability to cut back public spending. So long as the American economy had remained "demand-constrained," i.e., in need of a Keynesian boost to stimulate aggregate demand, there was an essential harmony in the simultaneous expansion of the burgeoning warfare-welfare state and corporate investment. Midway through the Vietnam War, however, the economy became "supply-constrained," i.e., too many demands placed on too few resources. [130] Under these circumstances, government spending and corporate investment came to increasing conflict over available capital and resources, a dilemma worsened by the slowdown in real growth as the economic crisis deepened. Underlying Carter's predicament was the growing incompatibility of demands generated by capitalism's global expansion, the entrenched interests of the military-industrial complex, and the institutionalized entitlements of the welfare state. Since much of social spending had been mandated by Congress and fell outside the range of discretionary review, military spending was the logical target for budgetary cuts. [131] Not that social programs would be spared. This was clearly not the case, as is apparent from a reading of the Trilateral Commission's controversial study, *The Crisis Of Democracy*.

From the managerial point of view, savings realized from lowered federal deficits were earmarked to further the restructuring of the global division of labor, not to retard it, nor to reindustrialize the American economy. As long as Carter championed managerialism, then, domestic revitalization was not possible. Without it, however, his Administration would not have a leg to stand on if the intraelite struggle went public and mass perception of elite strategy became critical to its outcome.

Faced with the mounting challenge of the militarist coalition, yet unwilling to build a countermovement to offset it, Carter was forced to abandon global interdependence for global confrontation. For a time he attempted to walk the line between a North-South strategy of managerialism and East-West militarism. As Brzezinski explained it, the Administration was trying "to do two things:"

> One: to make the United States historically more relevant to a world of genuinely profound change; and secondly, to improve the United States' position in the geo-strategic balance with the Soviet Union. [132]

This led, however, to a tortuous dual-track foreign policy that saddled the Carter Administration with charges of ineptitude, vacillation, and disingenuous motives both at home and abroad. Carter's overtures toward reform, for instance, appeared tepid and transparent next to Third World demands for a New International Economic Order, or the still more comprehensive Basic Needs approach to development, either of which went well beyond what managerialists of the Trilateral Commission had in mind. [133] At the same time, even these modest efforts —too little and too late in the international arena — were greeted with charges of appeasement by the CPD and the Administration's other right wing detractors. Unwilling — as well as *unable* without abandoning managerialism — to construct an alternative to militarism, Carter succumbed to domestic political pressures, returning the nation to a Cold War footing in the process.

By 1980 Carter's original stated goal of nuclear disarmament, pledge of nonintervention, and promised rollback in military spending were no more. In their place, military spending was on the rise, intervention was once more sanctioned with the announcement of the Carter Doctrine, plans for an interventionist rapid deployment force were set in motion and a program of draft registration was in the works in preparation for longer term forays. Finally, in the heat of the campaign as we will see in the next chapter, the ratchet of the nuclear arms race was advanced still one more notch with Carter's endorsement of counterforce targeting (Presidential Directive #59).

Privately the CPD must have rejoiced at the turn of events, congratulating themselves for having played a critical role in Carter's four-year odyssey. Publicly, however, the Committee remained on the offensive convinced that much work still lay ahead before the President's manifestos would be translated into action.

CHAPTER 7
Reshaping the Cold War Consensus

1. Interview with Leslie Gelb for the *New York Times* in June, 1976; cited in Leslie H. Gelb, "Beyond The Carter Doctrine," *New York Times Magazine*, February 10, 1980, p. 26.
2. Jimmy Carter, The State of the Union, address delivered before a Joint Session of the Congress, January 23, 1980, *Presidential Documents: Administration of Jimmy Carter, 1980,* vol. 16, no. 4: 197.
3. Inaugural Address of President Jimmy Carter, January 20, 1977, *Presidential Documents: Jimmy Carter,* 1977, vol. 13, no. 4: 89.
4. The President's Address to the General Assembly, United Nations, March 17, 1977, *Presidential Documents: Jimmy Carter,* 1977, vol. 13, no. 12: 397.
5. "Why Russia Is Doing It" (Craig R. Whitney, *New York Times*), *San Francisco Chronicle*, January 3, 1980, p. 15.
6. "Carter Seeks A Growing Arms Budget," *San Francisco Chronicle*, December 13, 1979, p. 28.
7. *Ibid.*; The President's Address at Commencement Exercises at the University of Notre Dame, May 22, 1977, *Presidential Documents: Jimmy Carter.* 1977, vol. 13, no. 22: 774.
8. *Ibid.*
9. *Ibid.*
10. *Ibid.*
11. "Carter Doctrine For the 1980s?" *Christian Science Monitor*, January 14, 1980, p. 15.
12. *Ibid.*
13. Gelb, p. 19.
14. *Ibid.*
15. *See* Chapter 3.
16. Cited in Michael T. Klare, "Is Exxon Worth Dying For?", *The Progressive*, July, 1980, p. 22.
17. "The Decline of U.S. Power," *Business Week*, March 12, 1979, p. 36.
18. "The Post-Iran Juggling of Defense Priorities," *Business Week*, March 12, 1979, p. 94.
19. *Washington Post*, January 27, 1978.
20. Quoted material is attributed to the *Washington Post*. Cited in Irene Gendzier, "Keeping Oil Safe For Democracy," *The Nation*, June 9, 1979, p. 694.
21. "Islam's Cold Shoulder To 'The Persian Gulf Doctrine'," *Christian Science Monitor*, February 12, 1980, p. 22.
22. "Washington's 'Realistic' View of Soviet Aims," *Christian Science Monitor*, January 7, 1980, p. 14.
23. Princeton Seminars, October 11, 1953, Papers of Dean Acheson, Truman Library.
24. "Ellsberg Raps Carter On A-Bomb Rattling," *San Francisco Chronicle*, February 23, 1980.

25. Carter, The State of the Union, January 23, 1980, p. 197.
26. See, for example, Earl C. Ravenal, "Foreign Policy Made Difficult: A Comment on Wolfe and Sanders," in Richard R. Fagen, ed. *Capitalism And The State In U.S.-Latin American Relations* (Stanford: University Press, 1979), pp. 82-90.
27. If further reference is desired, see George B. Kistiakowsky, "False Alarm: The Story Behind SALT II," *New York Review of Books* 26 (1979), 4:33-38; E.P. Thompson, "A Letter to America, *The Nation*, January 24, 1981; Alan Wolfe, *The Rise and Fall of the Soviet Threat* (Washington: Institute for Policy Studies, 1980); Fred Kaplan, *Dubious Specter: A Skeptical Look at the Soviet Nuclear Threat* (Washington: Institute for Policy Studies, 1980); as well as Richard J. Barnet, *Real Security: Restoring American Power in a Dangerous Decade* (New York: Simon and Schuster, 1981).
28. David K. Willis, "Why Detente Is Freezing Over This Summer," *Christian Science Monitor*, June 27, 1977.
29. David K. Willis, "Soviet Rebuff Opens New Arms Issue," *Christian Science Monitor*, April 1, 1977.
30. David Binder, "Group Warns On Soviet Expansion," *New York Times*, April 4, 1977.
31. *Ibid.*
32. Coalition For A Democratic Majority, Open letter to President Carter, May 14, 1977.
33. *See* Committee on the Present Danger, *Where We Stand On SALT*, July 6, 1977.
34. CPD, *Where We Stand On Salt*, pp. 12-13.
35. Hedrick Smith, "Carter Study Takes More Hopeful View of Strategy of U.S.," *New York Times*, July 8, 1977, p. A-4.
36. *Ibid.*
37. Paul Nitze, interview with author, August 24, 1977.
38. Robert G. Kaiser, "Memo Sets Stage In Assessing U.S., Soviet Strength," *Washington Post*, July 6, 1977, p. A-14.
39. *Ibid.*
40. "Remarks by the Honorable Harold Brown, Secretary of Defense, at the Thirty-fourth Annual Dinner of the National Security Industrial Association, September 15, 1977," news release, Office of the Assistant Secretary of Defense (Office of Public Affairs), p. 2.
41. Lt. General Daniel Graham, interview with author, August 28, 1977; Kaiser *Washington Post*, July 6, 1977, p. A-14.
42. Smith, *New York Times*, July 8, 1977, p. A-1.
43. Kaiser, *Washington Post*, July 6, 1977, p. A-14.
44. Smith, *New York Times*, July 8, 1977, p. A-1.
45. Kaiser, *Washington Post*, July 6, 1977, p. A-14.
46. Smith, *New York Times*, July 8, 1977, p. A-4.
47. *Ibid.*
48. Rowland Evans and Robert Novak, "A Touchy Carter: Shades of Former Presidents?" *Washington Post*, August 13, 1977, p. 15.
49. Charles Tyroler II, interview with author, August 24, 1977.
50. Evans and Novak, *Washington Post*, August 13, 1977.

51. *Ibid.*
52. *Ibid.*
53. Tyroler, interview with author, August 24, 1977.
54. Brown, NSIA address, September 15, 1977.
55. *Ibid.*
56. *Ibid.*
57. Charles Mohr, "Carter Orders Steps To Increase Ability to Meet War Threats,"*New York Times*, August 26, 1977.
58. George C. Wilson, "New Carter Directive Could Mean Rising, Not Falling, Defense Budgets," *Washington Post*, August 27, 1977.
59. Cited in Michael T. Klare, "Have R.D.F. Will Travel," *The Nation*, March 8, 1980, p. 264.
60. Cited in Banning Garrett, "Detente In Trouble?" *International Bulletin*, March 27, 1978, p. 2.
61. Jimmy Carter, commencement address, U.S. Naval Academy, June 7, 1978, *Presidential Documents: Jimmy Carter*, 1978, p. 1052.
62. *New York Times Magazine*, May 7, 1978, p. 42.
63. "Statement by Eugene V. Rostow, Chairman, Executive Committee, Committee on the Present Danger To Committee On The Budget," United States Senate, March 1, 1978, pp. 2-3.
64. Eugene V. Rostow, "Peace With Freedom: A Discussion By The Committee on the Present Danger," before the Foreign Policy Association, March 14, 1978, p. 28.
65. Paul Nitze, *Ibid.*, p. 29.
66. Eugene V. Rostow, "Statement to the Committee on the Budget, U.S. Senate, March 1," Washington, D.C.: Committee on the Present Danger, 1978, p. 8.
67. *See* Alan Wolfe, "Carter Plays At Hawks And Doves," *The Nation*, June 24, 1978.
68. Andrew Kopkind, "Cold War II," *New Times*, October 30, 1978, p. 39.
69. *Ibid.* See also "Big Business Must Get Back On Track," *Conservative Digest*, July 1, 1977, p. 56.
70. Kopkind, p. 39.
71. Norman Podhoretz, "The Carter Stalemate," *New York Times*, July 9, 1978, IV, p. 17. See also by Podhoretz, "The Red Menace," *New York Times*, May 14, 1978, IV, p. 17; "Countering Soviet Imperialism," *New York Times*, May 31, 1978, p. A-23; "The Cold War Again?" *New York Times*, June 11, 1978, IV, p. 21.
72. "Snag In Arms Talks: Missile Modernizing," *New York Times*, November 2, 1977, p. 7.
73. "Divulging of Secrets In Arms Negotiations Stirs Dispute In U.S.," *New York Times*, November 3, 1977, p. 3.
74. Eugene V. Rostow, "SALT II — A Soft Bargain, A Hard Sell: An Assessment of SALT In Historical Perspective," a speech presented at a conference on United States Security and the Soviet Challenge, Hartford, Connecticut, July 25, 1978: 7.
75. Paul H. Nitze, *Is SALT II A Fair Deal For The United States* (Committee on the Present Danger), May 16, 1978, p. 40.

76. Committee on the Present Danger, *The 1980 Crisis And What We Should Do About It*, January 1980, p. 6.

77. Committee on the Present Danger, *Is America Becoming Number 2? Current Trends In The U.S.-Soviet Military Balance*, October 5, 1978, p. 1.

78. *Ibid.*, p. 46.

79. *Ibid.*, p. 44.

80. Nitze, *Is SALT II A Fair Deal For The United States*, p. 6.

81. Rostow, "A Soft Bargain — A Hard Sell", p. 12.

82. *Ibid.*, p. 13.

83. Quoted in Paul H. Nitze, "The Strategic Balance Between Hope And Skepticism," *Foreign Policy*, 1974-75, p. 136.

84. Paul H. Nitze, "Peace With Freedom: A Discussion by the Committee on the Present Danger," before the Foreign Policy Association, March 14, 1978, p. 14.

85. "Carter Launches SALT Campaign; Hill Critics Reply; US Watches," *Christian Science Monitor*, May 11, 1979, p. 1.

86. "Nitze Urges Senate Alter SALT," *Christian Science Monitor*, May 16, 1979, p. 6.

87. "Zumwalt Says Joint Chiefs Have 'Deep Reservations' on Arms Treaty," *New York Times*, May 21, 1979, p. A-4.

88. "Critic Says Arms Pact May Threaten Safety of American Missiles," *New York Times*, June 1, 1979, p. 6.

89. "Carter's All-Out Push for SALT," *Christian Science Monitor*, May 10, 1979, p. 1.

90. *Christian Science Monitor*, May 11, 1979, p. 8.

91. Committee on the Present Danger, *Public Attitudes On SALT II*, March 15, 1979, p. 9.

92. *Ibid.*, p. 11.

93. Cited in Daniel Patrick Moynihan, "Reflections: The SALT Process," *The New Yorker*, November 19, 1979, p. 104.

94. Cited in Robert C. Aldridge, "The Pentagon Is Gaining," *The Nation*, January 19, 1980, p. 50.

95. Moynihan, p. 152.

96. Joseph C. Harsch, "The MX Missile," *Christian Science Monitor*, June 21, 1979, p. 23.

97. John K. Cooley, "New Contingency Force For US," *Christian Science Monitor*, June 22, 1979, p. 4.

98. Kistiakowsky, "False Alarm," p. 38.

99. Richard L. Strout, "SALT Sellers Try Low-Key Approach To Win Senate Votes," *Christian Science Monitor*, July 11, 1979, p. 6.

100. *Ibid.*; *see also* Richard L. Strout, "Defense Spending: Key To SALT Passage," *Christian Science Monitor*, July 31, 1979, p. 5.; Joseph C. Harsch, "The Price of SALT," *Christian Science Monitor*, July 31, 1979, p. 23.

101. Memorandum from Eugene V. Rostow, Chairman, Executive Committee, to members of the Committee on the Present Danger, August 1, 1979.

102. "Arms Pact Flawed, Critics Tell Senate," *New York Times*, July 7, 1979, p. A-4.

103. *Wall Street Journal*, June 29, 1979, p. 1.
104. Charles W. Yost, "Kissinger vs. Kissinger," *Christian Science Monitor*, August 17, 1979, p. 22.
105. *Ibid.*
106. *Ibid.*
107. Richard L. Strout, "Presidential Politics Peppers SALT Debate," *Christian Science Monitor*, October 25, 1979, p. 3.
108. Quoted in Moynihan, p. 166.
109. Daniel Southerland, "Wary US Public Favors More Defense Spending," *Christian Science Monitor*, August 7, 1979, p. 4.
110. *Ibid.*
111. Moynihan, p. 146.
112. Richard L. Strout, "Placating Anti-SALT Senators," *Christian Science Monitor*, November 29, 1979, p. 3.
113. Carter, The State of the Union, January 23, 1980, p. 197.
114. "Memorandum from Eugene V. Rostow, Chairman, Executive Committee, to Friends and Supporters of the Committee," December 5, 1979.
115. *Wall Street Journal*, June 29, 1979, p. 1.
116. "Memorandum from Eugene V. Rostow, Chairman, Executive Committee, to Friends and Supporters of the Committee," December 5, 1979.
117. "Anti-SALT Lobbyists Outspend Pros 15 to 1," *Christian Science Monitor*, March 23, 1979, p. 1.
118. *Ibid.*
119. *Congressional Quarterly*, June 23, 1979, pp. 1217-1218.
120. Richard Burt, "Money Is Already Starting To Flow From Both Sides In Treaty Debate," *New York Times*, January 23, 1978.
121. "Anti-Salt Lobbyists Outspend Pros 15 to 1," *Christian Science Monitor*, March 23, 1979, p. 1.
122. Fred Warner Neal, "Inertia on SALT," *New York Times*, March 22, 1979, p. A-22.
123. *Wall Street Journal*, June 29, 1979, p. 1.
124. Leslie H. Gelb, "National Security And New Foreign Policy," *Parameters*, Journal of the United States Army War College, November 8, 1977, p. 10-F.
125. "Gallup Poll Finds U.S. Public Evenly Split On Arms Treaty," *San Francisco Chronicle*, October 29, 1979, p. 8. The presence in Cuba of some 2600 Soviet troops became a *cause celebre* in September, at a critical point in the SALT II ratification hearings, despite the fact that it was common knowledge that they had been there for seventeen years. This "new Soviet Threat" was seized upon by hardliners, as all the more reason to scuttle the treaty.
126. Leslie H. Gelb, "The Rightists' Brigade," *New York Times*, September 16, 1979, p. E-19.
127. Alan Wolfe, "Reflections On Trilateralism And The Carter Administration: Changed World Realities vs. Vested Interests," in Holly Sklar, ed. *Trilateralism* (Boston: South End Press, 1980), 548.
128. Norman Podhoretz, interview with author, August 12, 1977.

129. For the Trilateral viewpoint on Third World industrialization, see John Pinder, Takashi Hosomi, and William Diebold, *Industrial Policy And The International Economy* (New York: The Trilateral Commission, 1979).

For further comment, see Immanuel Wallerstein, "Friends As Foes," *Foreign Policy*, Fall, 1980, pp. 119-131; Steven S. Volk, "The International Competitiveness of the U.S. Economy: A Study Of Steel and Electronics," in Fagen, ed. *Capitalism and the State in U.S.-Latin American Relations*, pp. 90-137; Paul Blumberg, *Inequality In An Age Of Decline* (New York: Oxford University Press, 1980), pp. 108-174.

130. For an elaboration of "supply-constraint" and "demand-constraint" see the insightful analysis by Thomas Weisskopf, "The Current Economic Crisis In Historical Perspective," *Socialist Review*, 11: 3, May-June, 1981.

131. *See* Michel J. Crozier, Samuel P. Huntington, and Joji Watanuki, *The Crisis of Democracy: Report On The Governability of Democracies To The Trilateral Commission* (New York: New York University Press, 1975).

132. Richard R. Burt, "Brzezinski On Aggression And How To Cope With It," *New York Times*, March 20, 1980.

133. For discussion of these approaches, see especially Johan Galtung, *The North/South Debate: Technology, Basic Human Needs and the New International Economic Order*, World Order Models Project: Working Paper #12 (New York: Institute For World Order, 1980).

See also Graciela Chichilnisky, "Basic Needs and Global Models: Resources, Trade and Distribution," *Alternatives: A Journal of World Policy*, VI, 3, winter 1980-81; Ward Morehouse, "Separate, Unequal, But More Autonomous: Technology, Equity, and World Order In The Millenial Transition," *Alternatives*, winter 1980-81.

Chapter 8

CONTAINMENT MILITARISM FOR THE 1980s:
Reagan and the CPD Rearm America

In a world which is becoming smaller every day, the United States cannot protect its interests by drawing an arbitrary line around certain areas and ignoring the rest of the world. No region of the world can be excluded in advance from the agenda of our concern. [1]

The Committee on the Present Danger, "The 1980 Crisis and What We Should Do About It," January, 1980

President-elect Ronald Reagan's national security advisers have concluded that "no area of the world is beyond the scope of American interest" and that the United States needs to have "sufficient military standing to cope with any level of violence" around the globe. [2]

New York Times, November 13, 1980 (based on a report from President-elect Ronald Reagan's Foreign Policy and Defense Task Force entitled, "Strategic Guidance").

Just the other day, Al Haig sent a message to Brezhnev: 'Roses are red, violets are blue, stay out of El Salvador and Poland too.' [3]

President Ronald Reagan, explaining his administration's foreign policy, May, 1981

277

Emboldened by the SALT victory, the CPD entered the 1980s confident that Iran and Afghanistan marked the final days of "the Vietnam syndrome." The Committee fanned the volatile mood of the new decade with a January release entitled, "The 1980 Crisis (And What We Should Do About It)." Following in May was its highly-publicized sequel, "Countering the Soviet Threat: U.S. Defense Strategy In The 1980s." In these latest communiques the CPD set out to embellish the hackneyed themes of Containment Militarism with an urgent tone of fresh discovery. In retrospect, the two documents proved to be a remarkable portent of what was to come. As such, they also provided striking testimony to the CPD's influence in shaping the Reagan foreign policy agenda.

Seizing upon Afghanistan, the Committee argued in its January release that the Soviet intervention constituted only the latest flashpoint of an enduring and seamless "world crisis." Overthrow of the brutal dictatorships in Iran and Nicaragua the preceding year moreover, were catalogued as inseparable links in the same "relentless slide to anarchy."[4] Predictably, the Carter Administration was condemned for its alleged restraint in these areas: "The events of 1979 and early 1980 both in the Caribbean and the Persian Gulf make it clear," the Committee charged, "that the Administration's policy is wrong; it must be changed unequivocally and at once." While Carter engaged in a policy of unilateral retreat the CPD inveighed, "The Soviet Union has continued to accelerate its program of worldwide expansion and its rapid military buildup." [5] Blithely dismissing the overwhelming fact of anti-Marxist fundamentalism in Iran, the CPD wrote off the revolution as having been engineered by Moscow claiming: "The violent movements of social and religious protest of the last few years in Iran were actively promoted by the Soviet Union from the beginning." [6] The situation had reached such an ominous stage according to the Committee's calculations that "a Soviet move to seize control of Iran is a distinct possibility." Moreover, in the familiar domino logic of containment, the CPD charged that "control of Iran would open the way to Soviet control of Saudi Arabia and the entire Persian Gulf region." [7]

In similar doctrinaire fashion, the Committee conveniently overlooked the long tradition of indigenous nationalism in Nicaragua so as not to adulterate its thesis of a Soviet grand strategy in Central America, a refrain that would be repeated often in the Reagan Administration before it was discredited in the infamous white paper on El Salvador. In a preview of what was to come, the Committee alleged that,

> in the Caribbean...the Soviet Union has been steadily improving its position. Soviet planes, submarines, and combat

troops are based in Cuba, and military assistance has been given from Cuba to revolutionary movements in Nicaragua, El Salvador, and other countries in the area. A potential is being built up from which the Soviet Union can threaten our Atlantic sea lanes, our communications with Central and South America, and the territory of the United States itself. [8]

To concede otherwise of course, would have blasphemied the iron law of containment which subsumes all movement great and small under the rubric of East-West struggle. The sleight of mind in which centrifugal challenges to empire — "the slide toward anarchy" to invoke the favorite phrase of the January report — become one with a centralizing Soviet totalitarianism has been one of the feats of ideological legerdemain used to defend the Cold War status quo whether from neutralism in Europe, nationalism in Central America, or religious fundamentalism in the Middle East. The importance of discovering all to be Soviet-inspired bears repeating from NSC-68. Uncertain at the time about the requisite public support for its program of remilitarization, Nitze and his pioneering colleagues wrote that even as "offensive forces attack the enemy and keep him off balance...emphasis should be given to the essentially defensive character to minimize, so far as possible, unfavorable domestic and foreign reactions." [9]

The Soviet Threat has served the purpose well for more than thirty years. Myriad interventions and brutal repressions which would otherwise have met with skepticism and resistance have been tolerated, and too often celebrated, as the price of protecting "freedom." Steeped in this tradition, the CPD exhorts in "The 1980 Crisis":

> America is more than a superpower. The idea of the United States is a living part of Western Civilization, with a compelling and altogether special history which belongs to all who cherish human liberty. [10]

Such unabashed chauvanism led easily to the Committee's call for a "prompt and adequate increase in our military strength — strategic, theatre nuclear, and conventional." [11] As the CPD explained, the U.S. must be "able to confront it (the Soviet Union) with an array of unacceptable (military) risks." [12]

Translated into programmatic terms this meant military superiority at the conventional, tactical, and strategic levels of warfare. Among the specific items requested to return to a posture of Containment Militarism, the CPD included on its shopping list the MX, the Trident II submarine, the B-1 bomber, as well as modernization and improvements in the Minuteman system. And this only at the strategic level. For tactical and theatre purposes, the Committee called for ground- sea- and air-launched

Cruise missiles, modernization and deployment of the Pershing system in Europe, and production of the neutron bomb. In addition, the CPD recommended a crash program for the Navy and across-the-boards buildup of conventional forces generally, including reinstitution of the draft to support the revamped global presence. The cost of such a vast remilitarization was not immediately revealed. Not until the May publication of "Countering The Soviet Threat: U.S. Defense Strategy in the 1980's", did the public learn of the price tag for the CPD's recommended course of action. For the next five years the document insisted, military spending would require a staggering increase of $260 billion over that already projected.

Such a global and all-encompassing posture would in turn demand in the Committee's words, discarding of "the outdated strategies of the 1960's," among them deterrence and the "one-and-a-half war strategy." Stressing the urgency for this change of doctrine, the CPD repeated its warning that "no region of the world can be excluded" from American reach and, this being so:

> Our national strategy should be designed to contain Soviet or *proxy aggression* against our interests in the Atlantic and Mediterranean, the Pacific and the Persian Gulf and Indian Ocean — *simultaneously* if necessary — as well as Soviet efforts in the Western hemisphere through the Caribbean basin. [13]

Both themes in this passage would become guideposts of Reagan foreign policy — "proxy aggression" the favorite of the secretary of state, and "simultaneous and protracted war fighting" promoted by the secretary of defense. Other recommendations in this follow-up report would also become familiar as new Reagan directions in defense policy — "expanded civil defense planning and preparations", and arms aid "to endangered friends and allies." [14]

The symmetry between the CPD's wish list and the eventual policies of the Reagan Administration is not very mysterious. Reagan, after all, was himself a member of the Committee. Moreover, as demonstrated in preceding chapters, the CPD's strategic analyses informed and inspired the larger Cold War coalition from which Reagan drew for advice and advisers. Finally, by the time of the May report, the CPD itself — from Democrats to Republicans, executive committee to staffers — were aboard the Reagan juggernaut. While it is true that Nitze and Rostow did not publicly announce their support of Reagan until just before the election, the delay was a tactical choice not a reflection of indecision. To the contrary, the Committee's visceral sense that Carter was beyond rehabilitation was confirmed in a second meeting at the

White House shortly after the announcement of the doctrine that bore his name. What followed was a hydra-headed strategy designed to maximize the CPD's impact on the presidential contest. Carter's response by this time was a foregone conclusion. Containment Militarism would be the victor in November. Voters were left to choose between Carter's reluctance and Reagan's enthusiasm.

The CPD Stamps Its Imprimatur On The Next Administration

Praising the Carter Doctrine for its hardline stance, the CPD nevertheless insisted that the president's budget proposals "did not reflect the urgency of the present crisis nor the magnitude of the United States' commitment which he activated." [15] After all, as NSC-68 had emphasized over a quarter century before, "Without superior aggregate military strength, in being and readily mobilizable, a policy of 'containment' — which is in effect a policy of calculated and gradual coercion — is nothing more than a policy of bluff." [16] In addition to the enormous buildup required to make the doctrine credible, there was the matter of bringing personnel into the Administration who would not flinch at putting it into practice. With these concerns in mind, a second summit was set at the White House between Carter and the estranged hawks of the Democratic party, ably represented by the CPD and its filial ally, the Coalition For A Democratic Majority.

The neoconservative power brokers who trekked to the White House after the announcement of the Carter Doctrine harbored a ray of hope that the President had abandoned his former reservations regarding the use of force, and was about to ask for their forgiveness, and in the election year, for their endorsement. Far from reassurance and reconciliation however, a snag in the reunion developed almost immediately when Carter refused to concede the error of his earlier ways and bristled at the suggestion that he conduct a swift and thorough housecleaning which would, in the words of Daniel Patrick Moynihan, senator from New York and cochairman of the CDM, replace the discredited managerialists with "people whose past judgments comport to the administration's new policies." [17] Moreover, Carter's refusal to embrace the hardline view of Soviet policy was from the CPD-CDM viewpoint, proof positive that he could not be entrusted to lead America out of its self-imposed "Vietnam syndrome." When Carter responded in lukewarm fashion to Norman Podhoretz's impassioned plea for a vigorous human rights offensive against the Soviet bloc, it only served to confirm the group's longstanding image of an insincere Carter. Elliot Abrams, who now serves in the Reagan Administration as Assistant Secretary of State for Human Rights and Humanitarian Affairs left the session in disbelief saying, "Carter was telling us that he was going to continue to pursue the Andy Young foreign policy." Jeane Kirkpatrick conceded that the meeting "did throw cold water on whatever hopes we had that Iran and Afghanistan would have a broad effect on the president's foreign policy orientation." [18] Thus, rather than face another four years of uncertain bully tactics, the CPD's Democrats threw their support to the candidate who shared their conviction that the world had changed little if at all since NSC-68; and furthermore that the decline of American power could be arrested by rediscovery of the elixir of military superiority.

Enthusiasm for Reagan among CPD Republicans was never in doubt. Richard Allen, who would first become Reagan's chief foreign policy adviser and then head of the Office of National Security, worked closely with Reagan from the Committee's beginnings. As a founding member of the CPD, Allen was instrumental in bridging the distance between traditional Republican conservatives and the neoconservative Democrats. When Reagan went to Washington in January, 1979 to raise support for another presidential bid, he joined the ranks of the CPD and was appointed to the executive committee. The only question that remained for the CPD was whether they would be able to capitalize on their bipartisanship and work their influence equally well within the Democratic Party. After the encounter with Carter and an expectedly difficult session with his chief rival Edward Kennedy, the matter was answered.

The migration of stalwart Democrats into the Republican camp was made easier by Reagan's overtures to Committee members. His radio commentaries during the preceding years had been liberally sprinkled with laudatory references to the CPD and effusive praise for the ideas of its leaders. In 1978 for example, Reagan labelled a series of radio broadcasts Rostow I through Rostow VI. Kirkpatrick caught Reagan's attention (via Allen) with her rendition of the differences separating totalitarian from authoritarian practices, a meanly-argued piece destined to become the primer for the Administration's attacks on Carter's human rights policy. As Kirkpatrick tells it, Reagan then wrote her a long, detailed and "very flattering" letter suggesting a meeting to discuss her ideas further. [19] After a series of sessions with Reagan, Kirkpatrick entered the circle of advisers where she distinguished herself as a passionate advocate for military aid to the junta in El Salvador.

In all, during the campaign and transition process, forty-six CPD members served on the Reagan advisory task force. At the core of this group shaping the Reagan foreign and military policy, in addition to Allen and Kirkpatrick, were CPD and Team B members William Van Cleave and Richard Pipes. They in turn were joined by Daniel Graham and Seymour Weiss from the B team. Still other died-in-the-wool hawks in

Reagan's entourage included Lt. General Edward Rowny who had resigned from SALT II negotiations in protest and now spoke openly of engaging the Russians in an arms race under the risky assumption that the Soviet economy would collapse from the strain before that of the U.S. Along with Rostow and Nitze, Rowny would become Reagan's representative in arms negotiations. In their capacity as presidential advisers, the militarists continued to hurl apocalyptic charges of impending vulnerabilities, the difference now being the wider forum for, and greater attention to, their views. Common were headlines which read "Reagan Advisers Hold Somber View of Soviet Intentions" and "Reagan Advisers Urge Military Buildup." The CPD-Team B line, once discredited as "alarmist" and "shrill", was about to become "respectable."

The Committee remained highly visible as a group as well. Their May 1980 report recommending the $260 billion increase was issued under widely-publicized charges that the Carter Administration "is still unwilling to recognize the consequences for the U.S. of the Soviet push for military superiority." [20] At the news conference introducing the CPD's latest effort, Nitze argued somberly that such a sum was "the absolute minimum required to make President Carter's recent warnings to the Soviet Union credible." [21] Shortly after the Republican convention, the Committee was again in the news with a day long briefing held for Reagan at CPD headquarters. According to reports of the gathering, the candidate was told that "the nation must undertake a broad-based military rearmament and proceed with an effort to restore a policy of containment toward the Soviet Union." [22] One account correctly noted that "all these policies Reagan had been advocating on the campaign trail." Indeed, Reagan's stock-in-trade was the charge that Carter had made a "shambles" of defense and was "totally oblivious to the Soviet drive for world domination." In contrast, he promised if elected, to pursue a policy of "peace through strength." [23] Moreover, sounding the favorite theme of the CPD, Reagan took the position that the SALT II treaty should be withdrawn and that the U.S. not abide by its provisions.

Despite Reagan's sterling campaign performance, the CPD still professed to be nonpartisan. Chairman Rostow told reporters that while he was "pleased by both the tone and the substance" of the Republican Party's 1980 platform and Reagan's acceptance speech, the Committee did not take sides. Meanwhile in a move that presented a truer picture of CPD feeling, Admiral Zumwalt, who had crossed swords with Carter in the January meeting over the "readiness" of naval forces, assumed the leadership of Americans For An Effective Presidency, a group of longtime Democrats whose professed goal was to raise "several million dollars" outside the official campaign for the Reagan candidacy. [24]

Rostow's and Nitze's feigning of nonpartisanship was of course a matter of strategy and timing. With the Democratic convention still ahead and establishment credentials dating back to Roosevelt and Truman to call upon, it made little political sense to announce for Reagan before the platform had been hammered out and a final decision reached on the candidate. Besides, rejection of the party's standard bearer just before the election lent an aura of drama to the occasion, i.e., "life-long Democrats unable in good conscience to support a candidate who endangers the nation's security." Accordingly, the two CPD cofounders announced their support for Reagan less than a week before the election.

Carter's reaction to the election-year stampede was to get out in front and take credit for it. His attempted reversal of image struck a hollow note however which only played into critics' charges that, in Reagan's words, Carter stood for "weakness, inconsistency, vacillation, and bluff." [25] Rather than challenge Reagan's call to arms with an alternative to militarism, Carter in familiar fashion adopted a series of measures to make himself appear indistinguishable from the strident opposition. In this regard, he answered to the charge that his Administration was "soft" on defense with the following corrective steps:

... After battling Congress to hold military spending to a 3 percent increase in 1980, he called for a 5 percent increase in 1981;

... After slowing down the pace in development of the MX missile, he sent a handwritten plea to the Democratic National Convention urging full speed ahead on the controversial system;

... After standing firm against pay raises for the military, during the July 4 weekend on board the aircraft carrier Nimitz, he came out in favor of military pay raises;

... After vetoing one military weapons bill because it authorized a nuclear aircraft carrier, with the campaign heating up, he signed the next one — carrier and all;

... In response to Republican attacks at cancellation of the B-1, the Administration confirmed that it was working on a more technologically advanced 'Stealth bomber' capable of evading radar detection.

These "adjustments" paled in significance, however, when compared to Carter's approval of Presidential Directive #59. PD-59 made official the "nuclear war-fighting" strategy endorsed by Reagan and the Republican party at their July convention. Long advocated by the CPD and other hardliners, PD-59 ordered that Soviet military installations, forces and command centers be designated for priority targeting, thus putting an end to the contentious debate over nuclear strategy in favor of the doctrine of counterforce.

With the proliferation of warheads and ever greater accuracy, a perceptible shift toward counterforce targeting had evolved since the 1960s. Nevertheless, deterrence remained official declared policy until PD-59. What PD-59 did in effect was legitimize the notion that nuclear war could be kept limited to selected military targets and conducted over an extended period, much like conventional warfare. Pipes, in his celebrated *Commentary* article — the Team B report edited for public consumption — claimed that the Russians had already adopted such a counterforce strategy. [26] If the U.S. did not follow suit so the argument went, the Soviet Union would be able to launch a limited first-strike which would checkmate an American president, since any retaliatory attack ordered against Soviet cities would be met with a return blow to U.S. population centers. Counterforce targeting was thus touted by its advocates as a defensive measure that would provide the president a "menu of options" short of all-out holocaust. Adoption of such a strategy, proponents claimed, would allow for "flexible response."

The outpouring of criticism that followed the decision insisted that preparation to fight less than a total nuclear war would make nuclear war that much more probable. Moreover, if the temptation were ever taken up many experts warned, a nuclear exchange was unlikely to remain limited for a variety of both human and technological shortcomings. The very strategy would seem to be fatally flawed since, according to plan, the command center needed to exercise the option of surrender before the escalation gets out of control, is itself targeted for destruction. As a Carter Administration official explained it at the time, special emphasis would be placed on threatening "the targets the Soviet leadership values most — its military forces and *its ability to maintain control after a war starts*." (emphasis added) [27] The end result, however, is to heighten the possibility of nuclear war by creating incentive for a preemptive first-strike — known as the "use 'em or lose 'em" syndrome — or at the very least, a sensitive hair-trigger, launch-on-warning system to avoid being caught short in the event of a surprise first-strike. Finally, if all this were not enough, limited nuclear war critics argued persuasively that such a posture would entail much larger and more sophisticated weapons whose production would drain the American economy and turn the nation into a truly garrison state. The case was shortly put to the test by Reagan.

If Carter crossed the Rubicon of nuclear war-fighting haltingly and for reasons of political expediency besides, Reagan entered this *terra incognita* in a mood of cheerful optimism, asserting that a rapid U.S.

arms buildup along such lines would convince the Russians "that we mean business." Questioned as to what he meant by "peace through strength" at one point in the campaign, Reagan answered airily: "I've never seen anyone insult Jack Dempsey." [28] Such comments had in the past made Reagan the butt of jokes concerning his intellectual fitness for the presidency. But this was 1980, the year of the hostages, and subliminally at least, Reagan's pledge to "Rearm America" captured the imagination in Peoria.

By November there was little difference in Carter's born-again militarism and Reagan's longstanding faith in rule by the sword. Voters were left with a contest of images. Carter's shoddy performance during the campaign only confirmed the widespread judgment that he was a man of little principle. Reagan, in contrast, was nothing if not steadfast in his convictions (which soon proved to be as great a handicap in the White House as Carter's penchant for waffling). One need not join Norman Podhoretz in his celebration of the difference between Carter and Reagan, nor even accept its accuracy in fact, to acknowledge that the following passage captures the perception that prevailed the day of the election. Podhoretz observed:

> Most people knew that Carter was wary of American power and inhibited almost to the point of paralysis in the use of it, just as everyone knew that Reagan believed in American power and could be trusted to rebuild it and use it if the need should arise. [29]

Once the election results were in, Rostow reportedly turned to his CPD colleagues and exclaimed that now, "Respectable people cannot dismiss us as cranks, crackpots, and lunatics." [30] The fortunes of Reagan's foreign policy in the years ahead would prove to be as closely tied to the CPD as his candidacy had served as a referendum on the Committee's views. As had been the case with CPD-I and Eisenhower, CPD-II was about to reap the reward of top policy posts in a Reagan Administration. Garnering over thirty high-level positions (fifty if one counts those serving in a part-time capacity), the Committee now had the opportunity to put into practice the policy it had preached since its founding.

Reagan's first news conference as president-elect served to confirm that the CPD would play a powerhouse role in the years ahead. Appearing at his side to introduce the CPD-laden transition team and foreign policy advisory board was Richard Allen, fresh from the taint of his first scandal that sent him on leave until the election results were safely in. Reinstated shortly thereafter, he remained Reagan's chief foreign policy spokesman and afterward national security coordinator until allegations of financial kickbacks drove him from the Administration for good in December, 1981. Before he left however, Allen honeycombed the national security bureaucracy with his friends from the CPD.

COMMITTEE ON THE PRESENT DANGER

Members In The Administration

Ronald Reagan
President of the United States

Kenneth L. Adelman
U.S. Deputy Representative to the United Nations

Richard V. Allen
Assistant to the President for National Security Affairs

Martin Anderson
Assistant to the President for Policy Development

James L. Buckley
Under Secretary of State for Security Assistance, Science and Technology

W. Glenn Campbell
Chairman, Intelligence Oversight Board, and member, President's Foreign Intelligence Advisory Board

William J. Casey
Director of Central Intelligence

John B. Connally
Member, President's Foreign Intelligence Advisory Board

Joseph D. Douglass Jr.
Assistant Director, Arms Control and Disarmament Agency

John S. Foster Jr.
Member, President's Foreign Intelligence Advisory Board

Amoretta M. Hoeber
Deputy Assistant Secretary of the Army for Research and Development

Fred Charles Ikle
Under Secretary of Defense for Policy

Max M. Kampelman
Chairman, U.S. Delegation to Conference on Security and Cooperation in Europe

Geoffrey Kemp
Staff, National Security Council

Jeane J. Kirkpatrick
U.S. Representative to the United Nations

John F. Lehman
Secretary of the Navy

Clare Booth Luce
Member, President's Foreign Intelligence Advisory Board

Paul H. Nitze
Chief Negotiator for Theater Nuclear Forces

Edward F. Noble
Chairman, U.S. Synthetic Fuels Corporation

Michael Novak
U.S. Representative on the Human Rights Commission of the Economic and Social Council of the United Nations

Peter O'Donnell Jr.
Member, President's Foreign
Intelligence Advisory Board

Richard N. Perle
Assistant Secretary of Defense
for International Security Policy

Richard Pipes
Staff, National Security Council

Eugene V. Rostow
Director, Arms Control and
Disarmament Agency

Paul Seabury
Member, President's Foreign
Intelligence Advisory Board

George P. Shultz
Chairman, President's Economic
Policy Advisory Board

R.G. Stilwell
Deputy Under Secretary of
Defense for Policy

Robert Strausz-Hupe
Ambassador to Turkey

Charles Tyroler II
Member, Intelligence Oversight
Board

William R. Van Cleave
Chairman-Designate, General
Advisory Committee, Arms
Control and Disarmament
Agency

Charls E. Walker
Member, President's Economic
Policy Advisory Board

Seymour Weiss
Member, President's Foreign
Intelligence Advisory Board

Edward Bennett Williams
Member, President's Foreign
Intelligence Advisory Board

Source: *New York Times*

If the CPD, by virtue of its members' appointments, could rest assured of having its counsel heard in this administration, Reagan's first public pronouncements as president-elect indicated the degree to which the Committee's pet themes had already won the day. In his remarks, Reagan chose for emphasis two major areas of departure from the Carter foreign policy — arms control and human rights. On the former, he reiterated his campaign pledge to scrap SALT II. While Reagan's stance had come to represent a broad working consensus by this time, it was Nitze, in Podhoretz' words, who "as much as any single individual in this country, may be said to have created it." [31] Finally, sounding Rostow's tireless refrain, Reagan assured that his administration would refuse to consider arms negotiations apart from Soviet behavior in other areas. In other words, Reagan stressed: "I believe in linkage." [32]

On human rights, Reagan paraphrased Kirkpatrick's thesis that right wing governments, and especially those in Latin America, had been treated unfairly in the curbing of military and other forms of aid because of alleged human rights violations. Taking note of her role on Reagan's blue ribbon advisory panel, columnists Evans and Novak speculated in hopeful anticipation "that Kirkpatrick is in an almost unique position to elaborate on this critical aspect of the foreign policy of the incoming

ReaganAdministration." [33]

Remarkably, in this initial news conference, were all the ingredients that would come to make up the Administration's grand strategy once in office. Also of note was the perfect correspondence between Reagan's strategic and ideological concerns and the CPD's functional division of labor: "strategists," Nitze being the principal voice, disparaged arms control as a product of Soviet deception and American retreat; "ideologists," led by Kirkpatrick and Podhoretz, attacked Carter's human rights policy as an exercise in "moral disarmament" matching the "military disarmament" taking place under the guise of arms control. As chairman and CPD spokesman, Rostow's contribution was to lay both on the doorstep of detente, a fall from grace to be halted through the policy of linkage.

From the managerial perspective, detente was not the problem but rather the solution. The problem was a world order in flux. Detente was, in effect, a moderate form of containment neither phobic about global transformation nor myopic about its source. Its goal was to steer and manage the centrifugal forces pulling countries away from the Amercentric postwar order rather than attempt to halt these processes through the threat and/or use of military force. Carter's human rights and early arms control strategies represented refinements of the underlying thrust of detente. As such, they stood in the way of a return to Containment Militarism and would have to be unceremoniously discarded.

"Hitting The Ground Running"

The first six months of a new administration reveal more about its aspirations and intentions than one will ever see again. After this honeymoon period has elapsed, political realities — international and domestic — set in to exact their tribute and temper whatever vision the candidate parlayed into power.

In the case of the Carter managerialists, their early inclination was to put together a strategy of containment capable of managing the transition toward a more pluralistic global system better suited to what Brezezinski spoke of as "the new age of interdependence." They were soon pulled, however, between determined challenges to the American-dominated world system, and a domestic politics dedicated to restoring the old order to its former grandeur. Under the circumstances, the managerial strategy of compromise led to tortuous and self-contradictory policies which when finally forced toward consistency, came down decisively on the side of the status quo. His surrender notwithstanding, the momentum of *ressentiment* engulfed Carter and carried Ronald Reagan and the CPD to power.

Rather than search for a doctrine in keeping with the times as Carter had done, Reagan and the militarists around him made it clear that the world would have to conform to the doctrine. Conflicts between rich and poor, whether of nations or classes, would be recast in East-West terms as part of the fundamental struggle between 'communism' and 'the free world'; North-South formulas and 'human rights' considerations were dismissed as limp-wristed excesses of a leadership that had lost its will. Before the first year was out, the Reagan Administration had produced two ignoble symbols of its determination to beat plowshares back into swords — El Salvador and Cancun.

For the Reagan coterie, reassertion of global containment depended not just on words but on how rapidly a military buildup could be launched and how long it could be sustained. This being the case, there was no place for SALT II, or for any other arms control agreement that the Soviet Union might conceivably find acceptable. The requisite support for re-militarization demanded mobilization of American opinion to a degree that would support the Administration's bold plans to regain military superiority — what Reagan referred to as the "margin of safety." Its limit would be shortly tested in the announcement of a $1.6 trillion buildup accompanied by a policy of studied indifference toward arms control.

The new Administration promised "to hit the ground running, speaking with one voice," and was true to its words. Those observers who tried to console themselves by recalling that it was the anticommunist Richard Nixon who built bridges to Moscow and Peking, were taken aback by the thunderbolts hurled by Reagan and his cabinet appointees during those first weeks in power. Unwilling, perhaps unable, to distinguish the oval office from the campaign trail, Reagan began his tenure charging that "the Soviet Union reserves the right to commit any crime, to lie, to cheat in a persistent campaign to promote global revolution and a one-world communist state." [34] Moreover, in his first news conference as President, Reagan repeated his enthusiasm for linkage, warning that the alleged machinations of which the Soviets stood accused would have repercussions in U.S.-Soviet relations, including especially the arena of arms negotiations. News reports of Reagan's speech noted that it was the strongest anti-Soviet tone taken by an American president upon entering office since Kennedy twenty years before, during the Berlin crisis. A note of comic relief in the otherwise grim resurgence of Cold War posturing occurred when the State Department revoked Soviet Ambassador Anatoly Dobyrin's underground garage privileges which for years had enabled him to enter the State building through a private entrance. Presumably, according to press accounts, the move was designed to "signal the new, sterner attitude." [35]

Even without this diplomatic affront to its longtime ambassador, the Russians were not likely to have missed the message. Early on, in confirmation hearings for the post of secretary of state, General Haig had expressed the opinion that, "there are more important things than peace. . . things we Americans should be willing to fight for." [36] In context, what Haig meant to convey was that the Carter Administration had been overly preoccupied with avoiding conflict to the detriment of the national interest. In his prepared remarks, he spoke of Soviet political and military influence as having succeeded in "perhaps the most complete reversal of global power relationship ever seen in a period of relative peace." [37] Finally, Haig ended his testimony with a plea for linkage.

After his confirmation as secretary of state, on the occasion of his first news conference, Haig again stressed linkage as the centerpiece of the Reagan foreign policy, this time adding the provocative charge that the Soviet Union was "training, funding, and equipping international terrorism." Expounding on this alarming thesis, the new secretary went on to allege in his distinctively peculiar syntax, that the Soviets "today are involved in a conscious policy, in programs if you will, which foster, support and expand this activity which is hemorrhaging in many respects around the world today." Finally, to further establish the tone and direction for the coming months, Haig explained that "international terrorism" would take the place of "human rights" in the Administration's foreign policy.

Behind the terrorism accusation one finds again at work the heavy hand of the CPD. Richard Pipes, by this time touted as the "reigning White House Soviet scholar", had developed the thesis that while the Soviet Union "will not hesitate to use nuclear weapons . . . as part of a global ideology" it "encourages and employs terrorism because terrorism is a handy and relatively cheap weapon in their arsenal to destroy Western societies." Pipes' proof would add a bizarre chapter even to a John Birch Society anthology. He argues:

> The roots of Soviet terrorism, indeed of modern terrorism date back to 1879, when an organization called "The People's Will" was created in a small Russian town, Lipetsk. This small band of political assassins, which, among other things, murdered Czar Alexander II, is the true source of all modern terrorist groups whether they be named the Tupamaros, the Baador-Meinhof group, the Weatherman, Red Brigade or PLO. [39]

Switching roles from "scholar" to policy adviser, Pipes recommended: "We must expose its support of terrorism as widely as possible. . It must be made absolutely clear that these activities will no longer be tolerated." Hardline *Washington Post* columnists Evans and Novak commented admiringly, "What you find in his (Pipes) writings are the scholarly underpinnings for much of what both Reagan and Haig have been saying about the Soviet hand in world terrorism and/or Moscow's master plan for world domination." [40]

Meanwhile, Secretary of Defense Caspar Weinberger sent up Cold War signals of his own that complemented the war cries of Haig, making clear that there would be no counterpoint to militarism in this administration. During confirmation, Weinberger estimated that it would be at least six months before the resumption of arms talks. This despite Reagan's pledge in the waning days of the campaign that he would begin negotiations immediately. Before that occasion Weinberger argued, a military buildup would have to be pressed to close the strategic "gap" between the U.S. and the Soviet Union. Not to be outgunned by his cabinet rival Haig, Weinberger at his first news conference warned that "a strong confident America . . . is willing to fight for its freedom as the best hope for peace."[41] Indicating that he would shortly be revising the Carter budget upward in keeping with the Administration's plans for a buildup both of conventional and nuclear forces, Weinberger added: "I look forward with great enthusiasm and eagerness as we begin to rearm America under the leadership and with the full backing of our new commander-in-chief." [42] In his next public appearance, he intimated that the threat of the vast arsenal itself might not be enough. If "the international political climate continues to deteriorate", Weinberger speculated, "the prospects of our having to employ military force directly or indirectly to safeguard our interests cannot be dismissed." [43] All this *leading up to* Reagan's opening challenge. So consistent, and so vitriolic, were the introductory themes of the president, secretary of state, secretary of defense, and other top officials that one could not help but conclude a garrison state was in the making.

The Administration's initial actions only served to punctuate its rhetoric. To contrast his position to that of the early Carter who began his term with the announcement that U.S. troops would be withdrawn from Korea, Reagan in one of his first decisions pledged that they would remain. At the same time, the Administration agreed to sell South Korea sophisticated F-16 warplanes to seal the relationship. The day following Reagan's South Korea announcement, Weinberger in the course of one news conference, announced that the Administration would consider basing troops in other areas of the world upon request, mentioning Israel as one such possibility; indicated that Reagan would probably reverse Carter's decision to delay production and deployment of the neutron bomb; and expressed his enthusiasm for extending sophisticated radar planes to Saudi Arabia. [44] In a final signal of Administration intent,

General Chun Doo Hwan, President of South Korea, became the first foreign head of state to visit the Reagan White House.

Chun could not have been a more fitting symbol to telegraph the Administration's agenda for the Third World. In his toast to the South Korean president Reagan remarked: "If I have one message to give the Korean people today, it is that we share your commitment to freedom . . . Today we are committed to each other's defense against aggression." [45] The grateful Chun replied: "I'm very happy to find out to my satisfaction that there is a strong, clear and new sense of direction of U.S. policy as leader of the free world." [46] Casting a pall over this ceremony was the fact that Chun's regime had compiled one of the worst records in the world for human rights violations. The record was so gross that the State Department delayed the scheduled release of its annual report on human rights abuses in order to spare Chun embarrassment. South Korea after all, was one of Kirkpatrick's "moderately repressive regimes" that through "quiet diplomacy" could be urged toward "liberalization." As evidence for the proposition, Chun had just commuted the death sentence of major political rival Kim Dae Jung — reducing his punishment to life imprisonment.

Human Rights Takes On A New Look

Emphasis on human rights was especially threatening to containment in that it redefined the principal axis of global conflict in North-South rather than East-West terms. In his controversial Notre Dame speech, Carter had boldly put forward the thesis that the "threat of conflict with the Soviet Union has become less intensive" and the greater threat of peace now came from a world "one-third rich and two-thirds poor." He also let it be known that dictatorial guardians of privilege would no longer be granted the automatic moral authority — followed by military aid — enjoyed under the old East-West paradigm. Instead, in truly managerial fashion, Carter hoped to mediate deep and longstanding conflicts between privilege and poverty, utilizing aid as leverage to prod recalcitrant regimes toward reform before they were swept away by revolution.

As ideologists who understand the power of ideas, Kirkpatrick and Podhoretz could appreciate the dilemma into which the managerialists had painted themselves: What to do when the reform gambit failed to elicit the desired response? At such a point of impasse a president could either continue to press forward at the risk of toppling faithful servants of U.S. interests like the Shah and Somoza, or maintain support despite wanton repression — a politically indefensible position with even the most minimal definition of human rights.

The managerial *leitmotif* that "social change" represented the inexorable working out of "historical forces" with which the United States must "cooperate" was especially galling to Kirkpatrick. With great disdain she questions Brezezinski's claim "that the world is changing under the influence of forces no government can control . . ." She also chides Vance for his confession that "we can no longer stop change than Canute could still the waters." [47] She goes on to cite with equal opprobrium a series of statements from Carter rejecting the use of force in situations like Iran and Nicaragua. Warming to a final riposte, Kirkpatrick asks rhetorically: "What is the function of foreign policy under these conditions?" Mocking the managerialists, she responds:

> It is to understand the processes of change and then, like Marxists, to align ourselves with history, hoping to contribute a bit of stability along the way. [48]

The way out of this quagmire was to turn human rights on its head, or more accurately back on its side, by redefining Third World upheaval once again in East-West terms. In this way, legitimacy would be restored to the upholders of property and defenders of privilege, while popular insurgents would be banished once more from the moral universe — to be labelled "terrorists" and "Soviet proxies". Corporate and geopolitical interests thus would be protected, public opinion would be kept at bay, protest stifled, and all the while, America could feel good about itself again.

Seen in this light, Reagan's campaign reference to the Vietnam war as a "noble cause" that could have ended differently "if only our government had not been afraid to win" would appear as much more than the inadvertent gaffe which it was labelled at the time by most observers. Reagan had, after all, just praised the publication of Podhoretz' *The Present Danger* as "critically important," a work whose ambition was nothing less than to recast recent history and, by so doing, steer popular political culture back to the path of intervention and containment. [49]

The thesis of *The Present Danger*, timed to appear at the height of the presidential election campaign, was that America's reluctance to flex its military muscle stemmed from a misinterpretation of Vietnam. The mistaken version to which Podhoretz referred was the notion that U.S. involvement had been more than an error of judgment — that it had been immoral. The outcome, he charged, was a nation "Vietnamizing its past, present, and future." Accordingly, in the post-Vietnam period "moral disarmament" had accompanied "military disarmament" with the result that "the domestic base on which containment rested was gone." [50] Reflecting on this turn of events, Podhoretz was moved to lament:

The Nixon, Ford, and Carter Administrations robbed the Soviet-American conflict of the moral and political dimension for the sake of which sacrifices could be intelligibly demanded by the government and willingly made by the people. [51]

During the campaign Reagan had promised repeatedly that his mission to "rearm America" included "moral rearmament" as well as "military rearmament", an Aesopian message that human rights was slated for the same fate as arms control. The early announcement of Kirkpatrick for the UN Ambassadorship followed a few weeks later by the nomination of the CPD's Ernest Lefever as assistant secretary of state for human rights and humanitarian affairs signalled Reagan's determination to end human rights in all but name only.

Lefever, like Kirkpatrick, had built a reputation as one of the most persistent critics of human rights policy. In 1978, the founder and director of the conservative Ethics and Public Policy Center wrote a paper entitled, "The Trivialization of Human Rights," an argument for downplaying the concerns he was now nominated to uphold. Testifying before the Senate in 1979, he advocated that "the U.S. should remove from statute books all clauses that establish a human rights standard or condition" for the receipt of military and economic aid. [52] Now nominated to serve as its chief enforcer Lefever was placed in an awkward position, the repercussions of which he attempted to deflect by suggesting that nations' fulfillment of human rights should "not be judged primarily by their internal policies but by their foreign policies." [53] Specifying who should be targeted for such a tribunal, Lefever told the Senate Foreign Relations Committee that, since "the Soviet Union is a massive mischief maker around the world" and "is our sworn adversary," the human rights cudgel should be "a great deal rougher" on the USSR. [54]

While many on the Foreign Relations Committee found Lefever's testimony unsettling, they voted against confirmation for other reasons. (Even so, he remained in the administration as a special consultant to the Secretary of State). What proved mortally damaging to Lefever's nomination was the conflict of interest involving the Nestle Corporation and Lefever's think tank. Nestle's, the major marketer of infant formula in the Third World, had contributed $35,000 to the Ethics and Public Policy Center. Subsequently, after a public campaign was launched against their aggressive promotion of a product whose misuse was linked to infant death, Lefever published an article in *Fortune* magazine attacking Nestle's critics as "Marxists marching under the banner of Christ." [55] He went on to contend that opponents to his nomination were communist inspired.

The campaign led finally to a vote in the United Nations to establish guidelines to control advertising of breast milk substitutes. Lefever acknowledged that while in his acting position as human rights overseer he had discussed the impending vote with Ambassador Kirkpatrick. Kirkpatrick then cast *the sole* vote against establishment of a *voluntary* international code. The rationale given for U.S. opposition was that the measure posed a serious threat to the principle of free trade. The Japanese, who were under pressure at the time to restrict their sale of automobiles in the United States, must have found this new faith in the market grimly amusing. When asked to comment on the vote Kirkpatrick, a self-proclaimed practitioner of "clear-eyed unsentimental analysis," was reported to have merely shrugged and said: "That's too bad." [56]

If this vote did not lay bare the priority of property rights over human rights, Richard Allen removed all doubt on the heels of the Lefever defeat. Responding to what he determined to be confusion over human rights, Allen clarified the shift in its meaning under Reagan. He observed that human rights in the proper sense of the term (are) the rights guaranteed to men under law in any civilized or human society . . . the rights not to be deprived arbitrarily of life, liberty, and property." To further enlighten, Allen lectured:

> The notion of economic and social rights is a dilution and distortion of the original and proper meaning of human rights, and we need to define it as such.

Finally, Allen excused the flagrant violation of even the minimalist Reaganite rights code in Pakistan, South Korea, El Salvador, and other administration favorites, saying:

> Because we believe, or perhaps even because we know that our way of life is best, we may fervently wish that all nations adopt institutions similar to our own. But we are too sensitive to the vast differences in the historical and cultural experience of different societies, and the manifold obstacles many nations face in maintaining even a modest level of political stability, to try to impose our own institutions on them. [57]

Two events in the Administration's first year, one perfunctory and the other seemingly interminable, turned the Administration's harsh anti-human rights rhetoric into hardline containment policy. The first was the conference between rich and poor nations at Cancun, Mexico. Here in a forum called to address the widening gap between economically developed and underdeveloped nations, the Administration disparaged the event as a North-South excess unworthy of serious consideration. In El Salvador, the second case, the U.S. dismissed political rights as well for a rapprochement with authoritarian repression, just as Kirkpatrick recommended.

Turning to Cancun, the World Bank documented in its 1981 annual report that 750 million of the planet's citizens were living in a state of "absolute poverty". The Report went on to predict that the gap between rich and poor would grow still wider in the 1980s. [58] The Third World hardly needed confirmation of the grisly facts. For some time there had been talk of a New International Economic Order that would redress global inequalities through the establishment of less stringent credit terms, better access to markets for industrial products, higher and more stable prices for raw materials, and cheaper oil for the Third World. The Cancun conference was supposed to have been a summit to address these grave matters.

Reagan was on record from the beginning as opposing global negotiations of any kind. So adamant was the Administration in its opposition to anything even remotely global, that funding for such established multilateral programs as the World Bank, the International Monetary Fund, and Export-Import Bank, were being severely slashed even as the World Bank made public its dire predictions. In this regard Reagan's Treasury Secretary Beryl Sprinkel went so far as to claim that there was a "socialist drift" in the Bank bent on redistributing global wealth. [59] In preference to these mainstay institutions of managerialism, Reagan promoted corporate investment and bilateral aid. The reasons were not difficult to comprehend: under the latter type of arrangement leverage could be more directly applied to, and concessions exacted from the recipient.

Warming up to Cancun, Reagan told a gathering of Third World leaders attending the annual meeting of the International Monetary Fund and World Bank that they must rely "on the magic of the marketplace" and reform of their own economies rather than expect aid from the industrial nations. [60] The previous week Secretary of State Haig had delivered much the same refrain at the United Nations, where he counseled Third World leaders that they should "lower their expectations about aid from the 'have' nations and focus more on benefits they can reap by encouraging business investment and development." [61] Reagan struck a similar note in his speech imploring, "Let us put an end to the divisive rhetoric of us versus them, north versus south. Instead, let us decide what all of us, both developed and developing countries, can accomplish together." [62]

The complement to casting aside North-South thinking was to return East-West conflict to center stage. Speaking before the World Affairs Council in Philadelphia on the eve of Cancun, Reagan called on "the world's developing nations to have faith in the free marketplace" and to turn its back on a Soviet system that has "nothing to offer." In what was billed as a major foreign policy address by the White House, Reagan challenged the Russians saying: "We have just one question for them.

Who's feeding whom?" He then ended on his favorite theme, that the answer to development lay not in foreign aid, but instead in free trade.[63]

There was not much left to say by October 22 when the Cancun conference officially opened. The delegates in attendance were talking one direction (North-South), Reagan another (East-West). His speech was a medley of old standards, much to the chagrin of not only Third World leaders but also of such allies as France, West Germany, Japan, and Britain. In reply to Reagan's oft-repeated homily, "Give a hungry man a fish and he'll be hungry again", Nigerian President Ahaji Shehu Shagari replied: "I must hasten to add that man has to be supplied with hooks and nets in order to put into practice his invaluable knowledge of fishing." [64] In an interesting twist on the Kirkpatrick-Allen thesis that American mores are difficult to export, Nigeria's Foreign Minister Ishaya Andu noted that the Third World could hardly emulate the U.S. success with capitalism since the latter had used "cheap labor of black slaves" to get a jump on other nations. [65]

Nevertheless, despite such embarrassing moments, the White House made much of the general conciliatory tone of the conference, supposedly attributable to Reagan's agreement to proceed toward some form of global negotiation. The preconditions laid down for such talks, at a time left unspecified, undermined their meaning however. The qualifying stipulations included: a) that talks take place on a bilateral or regional level, thus doing away with their global dimension; b) that the United States not be bound by any vote on redistribution that might come out of the proceedings; and c) that aid should promote economic growth in a manner closely tied to capitalistic free market economies and not simply transfer wealth from the industrialized to the developing world. One pundit termed it "supply-side imperialism." [66]

Like so many other aspects of Reagan's foreign policy, the strategy revealed at Cancun was found first in the pages of Podhoretz' *Commentary*. In an article with the straightforward title, "Containment For the 80's," neoconservative Walter LaQueur called for a policy of "renewed self-interest" in relations with the Third World, arguing as follows:

> — "needs being equal preference should be given to countries whose attitudes toward the West is friendly rather than hostile";
>
> — "the advantages of bilateral relationships with Third World countries are obvious and, with certain exceptions, they should become the future mode";
>
> — "the worst, the most self-defeating approach, is to deal with the third World in bloc";

— "many countries, not to put it too finely, can safely be left to stew in their own juices. This, for obvious geopolitical reasons, may not be true for Central America. Nor is it true for the Middle East."

— "no progress will be achieved until the U.S. succeeds in regaining respect in these parts, and while this means much more than military power, military power is a necessary minimum."

To justify the renascent policy of Containment Militarism, LaQueur, in a plea similar to Kissinger's plaint that "somewhere, somehow the U.S. must show it can punish an enemy, reward a friend," argued: "The United States has to be recognized as an ally that can be relied upon, a power that cannot be abused with impunity." [67]

As LaQueur, and those in the Administration who followed his calloused advice could not help but be aware, leaving people whose territories had little economic or strategic importance for the U.S. "to stew in their own juices" amounted to a policy of genocide. Aid for international organizations specializing in assistance to the poor, like UNICEF, the World Food Program, and the U.N. Development Program, were cut by $42.2 million — a drop of nearly 20 percent from a meager contribution to begin with. Other international agencies were similarly slashed with the result that aid to Asia and Africa was reduced 33 percent in the first year budget. [69]

These cutbacks in multilateral aid could not be excused in terms of fiscal austerity since overall foreign aid was due for a slight increase under Reagan. Bilateral military assistance for example was slated to rise a whopping 97 percent. [70] The CPD's James Buckley, in his position as undersecretary of state for security assistance, outlined an aggressive arms promotion policy in the Third World. Buckley affirmed that the Administration saw arms transfers as "an important adjunct to our own security . . . facilitating access by American forces to military facilities abroad." Moreover, he charged that the restrictions imposed by Carter — based on considerations of human rights, nuclear proliferation, and unwillingness to be the first to introduce new arms into a region — were part of "an American withdrawal from world responsibilities", itself responsible for Soviet military superiority. Adding insult to injury, Buckley attacked Carter's arms strategy as having "substituted theology for a healthy sense of self-preservation." [71]

As evidence for the new look in Washington, Buckley pointed with pride to one of his first actions after taking office which was to rescind Carter's so-called "leprosy letter" which had instructed U.S. officials abroad not to assist American arms merchants in peddling their wares. A formal White House statement followed to the effect that arms transfers constituted "an essential element of its global defense posture and an indispensable component for its foreign policy." [72] By this time, the Administration had approved major sales of advanced aircraft to Saudi Arabia, Egypt, South Korea, Pakistan and Venezuela. In 1982, sales were expected to exceed $30 billion, surpassing by far previous record years. [73] While Administration officials billed arms transfers as a boon to the economy, assistance grants totalling several billion dollars were made available to those unable to raise the necessary cash. [74] The new rule guiding American foreign policy one senior White House official explained, not mincing words, is "it pays to be a friend of the United States." [75]

According to the authoritative *World Military and Social Expenditures* in its 1981 Annual Report, $550 billion was spent on weapons the previous year, while one-third of the world's people lacked the basic necessities of life. Moreover, the Report stated, fifty-four governments, half of the Third World, are controlled or dominated by military regimes. Finally, over forty of these use their military forces against their own peoples. [76] Among the beneficiaries of the flood of arms to the Third World through sales and gifts were some of the most egregious violators of human rights. The Administration, for instance, approved licenses for over $1 million worth of tear gas and police pistols to the government of South Korea for the expressed purpose of "civilian control." [77] At the same time, Reagan reversed a longstanding policy of opposition to multilateral bank loans to Argentina, Chile, Paraguay, and Uruguay which had been put in place because of their flagrant records of repression. The Administration also repealed prohibitions on military aid to Argentina.

If these actions were not symbol enough, the day after the Argentina decision, food aid to Mozambique was suspended. Earlier the Administration had blocked a $16 million World Bank loan to Nicaragua for a project to prevent flood damage. [78] The reason given for the decision by the U.S. representative at the bank's meeting was that "the current macro-economic environment (in Nicaragua) is not conducive to economic development at this time." Then even wheat flour shipments to Nicaragua were suspended. Meanwhile, El Salvador and Guatemala each received allotments of military aid. This despite an Amnesty International report charging the Guatemalan ruling junta with "conducting a government coordinated campaign of terror" against its people.

Kirkpatrick summed up the new U.S. human rights policy well when, upon returning from a six-nation Latin American tour as UN Ambassador, she reported that the military dictatorships of Uruguay,

Argentina, and Chile could provide valuable advice to Central America on matters of internal security. [79] Two days after her visit to Chile, during which she publicly praised the policies of General Pinochet — as Vice President Bush would similarly laud the Marcos regime in an upcoming junket to the Philippines — and announced intentions to "normalize completely relations with Chile in order to work together in a pleasant way," Chilean officials expelled four prominent politicians. One of them was president of the Chilean Commission on Human Rights, who had tried unsuccessfully to schedule a meeting with Kirkpatrick. [80] By October, the Administration had convinced the Senate to repeal the five-year-old ban on military assistance to the Pinochet regime.

Perhaps most offensive of all was the Administration's fawning overtures to South Africa. President Reagan told Walter Cronkite in March that South Africa was a "friendly nation" and that considering its strategic position, its mineral wealth, and its staunch anticommunism, it deserved better treatment. This was the same period in which Kirkpatrick had met on the sly with five South African intelligence officers, violating official U.S. policy since 1962 of shunning the South African military. At first the meeting was denied. Then Kirkpatrick blithely shrugged it off, claiming she didn't know who they were, and the matter ended. In contrast, when former U.N .Ambassador Andrew Young met with representatives of the Palestine Liberation Organization it touched off a furor that became a *cause celebre* contributing toward his early resignation.

Viewed in the overall context of the tilt of U.S. policy in Africa, such a meeting would seem far from a trivial encounter. More so since these same officers also met with officials of the National Security Council and the Pentagon during the visit. Furthermore, the Administration had applauded South African efforts against "Soviet-backed terrorism" in southern Africa, while refusing to condemn South African incursions into Angola or to back sanctions against South Africa when the subject was raised in the U.N. General Assembly. Kirkpatrick had even watered down a Security Council resolution expressing concern for three black freedom fighters executed by the South African government on the grounds that "rebels who foster violence for political ends should not inspire sympathy." [81] She also tried, although the effort was in vain, to block a resolution demanding sanctions against South Africa for its stonewalling tactics on Namibian independence.

The Administration's affinity for reaction in southern Africa is not only deep-rooted ideologically, but cemented by personal ties as well. The law firm of John Sears, Reagan's close friend and former campaign manager, received in 1980 a reported $500,000 to lobby in behalf of South Africa. [82] Lefever, although denying financial ties, is nevertheless a strong proponent of closer alliance between South Africa and the U.S. Undoubtedly, the most critical link between South Africa and the White House however, was national security adviser Richard Allen.

From his days on Nixon's national security staff, Allen had been a forceful voice for the status quo in southern Africa. In 1972, he left the Nixon Administration to join the Overseas Companies of Portugal "to become a Washington advocate of white colonial rule in Africa," according to the *Wall Street Journal*. [83] Later still, he became involved in a murky effort with Robert Vesco to wrest control of the Azores Islands from Portugal and turn them into a tax-free haven for financial pirates. [84] In March 1981, Allen and Kirkpatrick appeared together at the Conservative Political Action Conference to tell its cheering delegates that the U.S. must develop a new and positive relationship with South Africa, what Allen had once said would constitute a "politically courageous act" on the part of the United States. [85]

Already at this early juncture, the Administration had committed itself to a show of bravado in what it gambled would be an environment amenable to its successful demonstration — Central America. Kirkpatrick took the opportunity at the conservative conclave to drum up support for the test by fire that Reagan and Haig were already loudly proclaiming. Sounding the axial themes of Containment Militarism, Kirkpatrick declared a friendly regime, in the sphere of "vital U.S. interests" no less, to be under attack. Moreover, the forces behind this destabilization were "Soviet proxies," all the more reason for the U.S. to come to the rescue of its beleaguered ally. The country of which she spoke was El Salvador, the unlikely spot the Administration had chosen to "draw the line" on the perceived shift in the world balance of power.

The events that propelled El Salvador to center stage began with the Administration barely in office, when the Revolutionary Democratic Front announced the launching of its so-called final offensive. The Reagan forces seized upon the declaration as opportunity to turn the civil war into an East-West showdown. In this way, they hoped early on to display a bold new American will that would send a message around the world that the Vietnam syndrome had been decisively exorcised by a new Reagan mandate. Accordingly, the Front's "final offensive" against the regime *in El Salvador* was translated for the Administration's purposes into "the decisive battle *for Central America*." Assistant Secretary of State Thomas Enders' justification for $135 million of emergency aid and military equipment was a textbook application of the containment doctrine:

> The dangers are rising fast. . . If, after Nicaragua, El Salvador
> is captured by a violent minority, who in Central America

would not live in fear? How long would it be before major strategic U.S. interests — the (Panama) canal, sea lanes, oil supplies — were at risk? [86]

Haig promised soon a full report that would document outside communist support and use of Cuba and Nicaragua as "proxies" and "supply routes." In the meantime he fanned the flames of Enders' apocalyptic Cold War scenario, adding:

> What we are watching is a four-phased operation of which phase one has already been completed — the seizure of Nicaragua. Next is El Salvador, to be followed by Honduras and Guatemala. . .

Asked on the occasion of this congressional hearing if he was spelling out a new domino theory, Haig replied:

> I wouldn't necessarily call it a domino theory. I would call it a priority target list — a hit list, if you will, for the ultimate takeover of Central America. [87]

Top Salvadorean government officials vehemently disagreed with the new secretary's assessment, one summing up what would become a widespread reaction once the State Department's White Paper on outside involvement in El Salvador was released, exclaiming: "The Secretary of State has an incredible imagination." [88]

Meanwhile White House aide Ed Meese hinted at the wider agenda under consideration when he told reporters it was "entirely possible" that the U.S. would take direct action against Cuba if arms shipments to revolutionaries in El Salvador did not cease. This in reaction to the supposedly "incontrovertible" evidence contained in the White Paper. The possibility of some action against Cuba, Meese explained quite candidly, was part of Reagan's larger foreign policy strategy "to have America's foes go to bed each night uncertain what Washington's next move might be." [89] Thus events seemed to be moving according to the plan outlined in Kirkpatrick's "U.S. Security and Latin America", a sequel to "Dictatorships and Double Standards" that appeared in *Commentary* just as Reagan was assuming power.

In "U.S. Security and Latin America" where she accuses the Carter Administration of having "brought down the Somoza regime," Kirkpatrick lays out the prescription for reversing policy from a managerial to a militaristic course — ignore human rights and support moderately repressive regimes that will uphold order; redefine popular human rights struggles as terrorist campaigns supported by the Soviet Union and its so-called proxies. [90] The CPD had of course been playing the same themes in its policy papers and public pronouncements, reinforced further by its leading figures in their individual speeches and writings. In *Foreign Affairs* just before the election for instance, Nitze made the extraordinary claim that "it appears probable that the Red Brigades in Italy, the assault on the Mosque at Mecca, and the seizure of the American hostages in Iran were supported and perhaps instigated by agents of the Soviet bloc." [91] Now however, with the election behind and the virtual merger of the Committee into government, it could be of little help in rallying public opinion for the next step of carrying the policy out. At the same time, the Administration could not afford to go it alone on its controversial strategy for Central America either, even in this early presidential grace period. Accordingly, a new organization came into existence claiming to have arisen spontaneously to lead the "struggle for freedom" against stepped-up Soviet efforts to take over "democratic societies." [92]

Calling itself The Committee For The Free World the group took out a full-page ad which appeared in the *New York Times* of April 6, 1981. It began by paraphrasing the Administration's dogged claim that the war in El Salvador "depends on weapons supplied by the Soviet Union through such client states as Cuba, Nicaragua, Vietnam and others." If the revolutionary forces should succeed, the ad warned, "El Salvador would be added to Cuba and Nicaragua as instruments of further expansion of the burgeoning Soviet empire." From there it repeats Kirkpatrick's thesis that the end result of a revolution in El Salvador would bring not "progressive change" (their qualification) but "totalitarian regimes" (mine) far more repressive than those it replaced and "much less likely to be liberalized." Finally, responding to the widespread apprehension of another Vietnam in the making, the Committee agreed, providing its own revisionist interpretation of what that would mean:

> There is . . . a sense in which El Salvador could become another Vietnam. If we abdicate and allow the Soviet block to force a communist regime into existence there, El Salvador will suffer the same hideous fate that has befallen Vietnam since that country was unified under totalitarian Communist rule; a new Gulag, thousands upon thousands of refugees driven into the sea, the destruction of any hope for future liberalization, and the creation of another armed instrument of Soviet imperialism. [93]

If all this sounds familiar as the CPD line, a glance at the membership list shows why. The executive director of the Committee was Midge Decter, friend of Kirkpatrick and wife of Podhoretz. Decter had resigned her position as an editor at Basic Books to become fulltime coordinator of the project. Podhoretz was also a member of the group which bore the mark of his broodings, along with such other CPD heavies as Rostow and Zumwalt. General Rowny was also among the signers, as was Nitze's son-in-law Scott Thompson, and Decter's nephew Joshua Maravchik of Warnke memo fame. Like its earlier predecessors in the Carter years, the Committee included among its founders bona fide right-wingers from the Heritage Foundation and the National Strategy Information Center in addition to these neoconservative champions.

Funding for the Free World lobby reflected the new ecumenicalism that distinguished Cold War II, with much of the organization's seed money coming from the Smith Richardson Foundation — long a backer of such hardline militarists as the National Strategy Information Center headed by CPD member Frank Barnett — and the Scaife Family Charitable Trusts which had generously underwritten both the CPD and the New Right. Both foundations have been identified as having extensive ties to the CIA. Moreover, many of Free World's founders were involved in the Congress for Cultural Freedom, a propaganda cabal operating from 1950 to 1966 until it was exposed in the *New York Times* and elsewhere as a front for the CIA. [94] Leading the list of holdovers was Cold War philosopher Sidney Hook. As one observer noted, "The formation of the Committee For The Free World in 1981, is a sign that a new cultural cold war is about to erupt, along with a renewed arms race." [95] Indeed, that they were inextricably linked together under the doctrine of Containment Militarism was apparent in Reagan's campaign pitch for *moral* as well as *military* rearmament. This was the underlying twist of irony that gave linkage its real meaning and explained why El Salvador was suddenly thrust into global prominence.

Arms Control: The Transparent Illusion

In the Carter years, human rights and arms control characterized more the style than the actual substance of foreign policy. Nevertheless, despite their tentative and limited implementation, they remained official aims of that policy. Given Reagan's goals, it was not enough to dismiss these concerns in the everyday conduct of policy: they had to be devalued as desirable ends as well. That is to say, a policy built on the support of repressive dictatorships that suppress human rights, cannot hold up human rights as a worthy benchmark for judging that policy. Similarly, if the cornerstone of foreign policy rests on remilitarization, then arms control must be deemphasized to the same degree. Accordingly, we now turn to the relegitimation of militarism and downgrading of arms control.

Earlier it was pointed out how the initial statements of President Reagan, Secretary of State Haig, and Secretary of Defense Weinberger, stressed in common and unequivocally the notion that military force was the *sine qua non* of foreign policy. In his first trip to Europe, Weinberger reiterated the Administration's thesis with what observers called "some of the toughest rhetoric since the Cold War." [96] He charged that detente had only "reinforced the Soviet prison wall which stretches from the Balkans to the Baltic," calling it a mistaken policy that would not be continued by the Reagan Administration. He also outlined a new policy of "linkage in advance" in which the U.S. would set prior penalties for specified actions so as to deter Soviet moves in designated areas. Weinberger conceded that linking Soviet behavior to arms control was not a popular idea among European allies but remained undeterred nonetheless.

In past administrations such hawkish attitudes were to some extent counterbalanced by more moderate views founded in redoubts like the Arms Control and Disarmament Agency (ACDA). ACDA is a bureau of some importance in that it shapes policy on arms limitation, and generally as one would expect, is regarded as an advocate for control. Reagan, however, elected to change radically ACDA's historic role with his nomination of Eugene Rostow as director. Rostow not only shared Reagan's conviction that a decline of American power could be attributed to diminished military strength but was, of course, one of the most passionate and early spokesmen for a reassertion of U.S. military might. Thus, as Lefever's nomination had similarly demonstrated for human rights, the appointment of Rostow to oversee ACDA was a clear signal of Administration intentions to dismantle arms control for all practical purposes. The cast of characters was complete when General Rowny was named to head the strategic arms negotiations, and Nitze was called upon to preside over intermediate range talks in Europe.

Even as he was under consideration for the arms control post, Rostow made no effort to moderate his views, offering such dire predictions as "anarchy and war will come" unless the U.S. returns to a policy of containment to arrest the "world crisis caused by the surge of Soviet power since the collapse of our policy in Vietnam." [97] Such statements by Rostow during the confirmation process prompted the *New York Times* to editorially wonder, "What Place For Arms Control?"[98]

During the hearings, Rostow served up a steady diet of the CPD's cherished nostrums. He told the Senators that the Administration was correct in its commitment to counter militarily the "Soviet drive for empire." Lecturing them on the wisdom of absolute and total linkage, he admonished that unless the Soviet Union abandoned its "imperial dreams" arms control efforts could not be entertained. Despite Reagan's promise in the final days of the campaign that his Administration would begin negotiations immediately upon assuming office, Rostow quipped: "It may be that a brilliant light will strike our officials. But I don't know anyone who knows what it is yet that we want to negotiate about." [99] Senator Alan Cranston (D-Cal) said to Rostow at the end of the hearings: "I get the feeling that you do not really consider arms control efforts with the Soviet Union a very practical way to spend our time." [100] Nevertheless, Rostow moved smoothly through the Foreign Relations Committee opposed only by Cranston. On June 26, 1981, his nomination was confirmed in the full senate by voice vote without dissent. [101] So much for bureaucratic safeguards against the arms race.

For Containment Militarism, arms control was as pernicious to its aim as human rights. Where human rights undermined the legitimacy of support for repressive regimes, arms control acted as a foil to the nuclear threat that helped keep them in power. As the CPD stressed repeatedly in its analyses, "The strategic deterrent is the fulcrum upon which all other use of military force pivots." The logic of the position was explained as follows: "If Soviet dominance of the strategic nuclear level is allowed to persist, Soviet policymakers may — and almost certainly will — feel freer to use force at lower levels, confident that the United States will shy away from a threat of escalation." [102] In its familiar elliptical style, the barely concealed message was that U.S. policymakers as much as their Soviet counterparts would also be "freer to use force at lower levels" with superior nuclear capabilities at their disposal. The Committee couched the point in "defensive" terms, of course, to make it palatable:

> ... a nuclear balance unfavorable to the West tends to magnify the inadequacies of our general purpose forces. This is particularly so since U.S. and allied strategies for deterring or coping with major conventional conflicts are dependent on a credible threat of nuclear escalation. [103]

Limitations on nuclear arms from the CPD's perspective would therefore, constrain and diminish the credibility of intervention through conventional means in regional and internal conflicts. Conversely, closing the publicly-proclaimed "window of vulnerability" through the continual modernization of nuclear forces would widen the privately-coveted vista of opportunity for intervention. In a very direct sense then, nuclear weapons are to play a central role in dissuading challenges to the present world order. . . if, that is, one can achieve an edge in which their threatened use will be perceived as credible. Accordingly, the "task of American military power for the 1980s", the CPD asserted, "requires overseas general forces of increased mobility and firepower, along with

an improved nuclear balance to insure confident use of such forces." [104]
Arms control, based as it is on the desirability of parity, works against the
achievement of breakthroughs by which such a "state of confidence"
might be realized.

Advances in the technology of weaponry and the concomitant
evolution of strategic doctrine, made the quest for military superiority in
1980 a vastly different proposition than was the case in 1950. To gain
"preponderance" at each level of warfare — from theater to strategic —
would entail an unprecedented buildup of both nuclear and conventional
weapons, as the CPD had warned during the presidential campaign. Just
how costly this would be was revealed in the Administration's early
projections that military spending would double from 1981 to 1986,
reaching a total of $1.6 trillion by the end of that period.

Having inherited the Carter budget for fiscal year 1982, and thus
unable to proceed forward with a full-range buildup in all areas simultaneously, Reagan decided to concentrate on so-called "general purpose
forces" that could most readily "show the flag." What was termed the
new "Weinberger strategy" was presented as a way of preparing the U.S.
for fighting a protracted conventional war with the Soviet Union or *its
proxies*. Moreover, it called for the capability to confront "the Soviets" at
many points *simultaneously*. This represented a departure from the one-
and-a-half war concept — i.e., the U.S. should be able to fight one large
war and one small war at the same time — that had prevailed since
Vietnam. To carry out this mandate, the secretary of defense ordered the
military services to plan their forces, weapons, and equipment to defend
"U.S. vital interests" as far from American shores as their resources
would permit. Coming in for special attention in this regard was the
Persian Gulf. Finally, the Pentagon plan expressed its intent to provide
military assistance to allies "battling subversion" at strategic points
around the world. But in case these regional gendarmes proved inadequate to the task, the Administration indicated by its blueprint that it was
ready to return the U.S. to its former role of global policeman.

The full impact of the Reagan-CPD strategy would not be felt until
the fall when the fiscal year 1983 program began to emerge, the first
Reagan budget. Glimpsing what was to come, Representative Henry
Reuss (D-Wis), Chairman of the Joint Economic Committee remarked,
"Those who believe that the Reagan Administration had already
proposed a dramatic buildup in our military forces may have a surprise
coming." [105] Chairman Reuss' warning was in reference to a report that
the Administration planned to build a military force capable of unilateral
action in the Persian Gulf. According to estimates by the Joint Economic
Committee, such a capability would mean a combat posture far greater
than that projected in Carter's rapid deployment force. Meanwhile, the

Washington Post reported that sale of AWACS radio surveillance planes to Saudi Arabia was only the tip of a grand strategy in the Middle East, at the core of which was an ambitious plan to build surrogate bases in Saudi Arabia, equipped and waiting for American forces. Thus in effect, the account concluded, Saudi Arabia was to become the nerve center for U.S. forces in the Persian Gulf region. This went beyond the Carter doctrine not only in projected capabilities, but in its intended application as well. Where Carter had spoken of repelling outside interests, Reagan indicated that his version of the doctrine would be directed at the threat of internal and local insurgency as well.

Since "preponderance" at the strategic level is, in militarist logic, necessary to "prevail" in lesser theater levels of conflict, there was ample attention to modernization of nuclear weaponry in this first real Reagan budget. Weinberger had already announced that the U.S. had begun assembly of the neutron bomb, and within hours, would be able to deploy the controversial enhanced radiation weapon to arenas of theater conflict. He indicated that its use would be considered in situations where conventional forces were about to be overwhelmed by an enemy force, and not necessarily confined to Europe.* In answer to the controversy surrounding its renewed manufacture, Weinberger sniffed: "There is no particular reason to consult anyone, any more than there would have been to consult on the production of the 155mm conventional artillery bomb." [106]

In addition to the neutron bomb and the continuation of plans to modernize theater nuclear forces in Europe already begun under Carter, Reagan also announced the go-ahead for production and deployment of the M-X, the B-1 and Stealth bombers, Cruise missiles, the Trident II coutersilo missile system, and funds for new antisatellite weapons. Added to that were extra billions earmarked for a command, control, communications, and intelligence system (C^3I) designed to survive nuclear exchanges. All of this taken together led critics to worry that the Reagan Administration was planning a prolonged nuclear war-fighting strategy to back its earlier announced conventional doctrine, a charge that would be confirmed in May 1982 with disclosure of the Department of Defense five-year strategic plan. [107]

But that was later. Returning to the unfolding events of the first year, the Administration produced what was immediately christened "the largest peacetime military buildup in U.S. history." With it, Containment Militarism was back in vogue as the cornerstone of America's foreign

---

*The Carter Administration had introduced the neutron warhead ostensibly for European use but held up its planned deployment in response to public outcry.

policy. Moreover, the establishment elite had apparently regrouped around the militarist strategy of Reagan and the CPD. To announce the occasion, the bellwether Council on Foreign Relations released a report designed to make the Soviet Threat respectable again. Known as the Commission on U.S.-Soviet Relations, the CFR-sponsored panel opened its report emphasizing the "need for the widest possible domestic consensus" on the subject of East-West matters. [108] Observers were quick to note that its assessment and recommendations were "strikingly similar to those espoused by the Reagan Administration." [109] Why this should be so was apparent once turning to the authorship of "The Soviet Challenge: A Policy Framework For The 1980s." Prominent among them was the omnipresent Paul Nitze.

Drawing from the wisdom of NSC-68, the Commission counseled a return to containment in its most primal form, reasoning that "since Soviet capabilities and the ambitions they now serve have a global sweep, so must our response." The exact nature of the *response* followed predictably: "The requirements for contingencies stretching from the Persian Gulf to Northeast Asia dictate a sharp acceleration (in military budget expenditures) over those of the last decade, and almost certainly to the level of 6% of GNP." [110]

The panel's position on arms control also followed in lockstep fashion: "The Commission believes that in the recent past arms control has been the centerpiece of U.S policy toward the Soviet Union and that this was wrong." Taking a favorite line from the CPD, the report read: "We cannot hope to achieve at the negotiating table what we are unwilling or unable to achieve in the wider world of defense policy."[111]

The "moderate" CFR also put its stamp of approval on the Administration's repressive strategy in the Third World. In a section headed "Human Rights", the panel went out of its way to lend support to the Kirkpatrick doctrine even as it gave lip service to managerial concerns:

> It will often be necessary, however, for us to work with some which do not (observe internationally-accepted human rights standards), especially on security matters. This should not mean that we support their repressive practices, and for the sake of their own survival we may at times need to press for internal reforms. [112]

Having once reflected the deep divisions within the Establishment between militarism and managerialism, the new Council stance announced that fifties-style cold war ideology was now back in vogue. Like other artifacts from that period which experienced a renascent popularity in 1980, the effect would be one of caricature its second time around.

Still for the moment, the CPD had every right to bask in the glow of success. Only a few years before the Committee's leaders had been banished to the political wilderness, themselves branded as the clear and present danger. Their triumphant return to Washington at the head of the Reagan parade gave testimony to the CPD's almost alchemic mastery of the netherworld of elite power politics and mass public opinion. The celebration would prove short-lived however once Reagan militarism proved no better at containment than Carter's managerial strategy. How fortunes changed in so short a time is the final matter to be considered.

CHAPTER 8
Containment Militarism in the 1980s

1. The Committee on the Present Danger, *The 1980 Crisis (And What We Should Do About It)*, Washington, D.C.: January, 1980, p. 13.
2. *New York Times*, November 13, 1980, p. 1.
3. Ronald Reagan, addressing the Republican National Committee at a White House reception, June 12, 1981; cited by James Reston in *New York Times*, June 24, 1981, p. A-23.
4. *The 1980 Crisis*, p. 6.
5. *Ibid.*, p. 8.
6. *Ibid.*, p. 7.
7. *Ibid.*, p. 7.
8. *Ibid.*, pp. 7-8.
9. U.S. National Security Council, "NSC-68: A Report to the National Security Council, April 14, 1950," *Naval War College Review*, May-June, 1975, pp. 98-99.
10. *The 1980 Crisis*, p. 9.
11. *Ibid.*, pp. 14-15.
12. *Ibid.*, p. 9.
13. The Committee on the Present Danger, *Countering The Soviet Threat: U.S. Defense Strategy In The 1980s*, Washington, D.C.: May, 1980, p. 8.
14. *Ibid.*, pp. 11, 13.
15. *The 1980 Crisis*, p. 2.
16. "NSC-68," p. 68.
17. Daniel Patrick Moynihan, "A New American Foreign Policy," *The New Republic*, February 9, 1980, p. 20.
18. Morton Kondracke, "Politics: The Neoconservative Dilemma," *The New Republic*, August 2-9, 1980, p. 11.
19. Rowland Evans and Robert Novak, "Human Rights Turnaround," *Washington Post*, December 12, 1980.
20. *Washington Post*, May 13, 1980, p. A-6.
21. "Ex-Defense Aides Ask Big Increase in Arms Outlays," *New York Times*, May 11, 1980, p. 12.
22. "Reagan Meets Foreign Policy Advisors," *New York Times*, July 30, 1980, p. 12.
23. "Reagan On Defense," *Honolulu Advertiser*, August 19, 1980, p. 1.
24. "2nd Reagan Group Raising 'Millions'," *San Francisco Chronicle*, July 10, 1980, p. 5.
25. "Reagan On Defense,"*Honolulu Advertiser*, August 19, 1980, p. 1.
26. Richard Pipes, "Why The Soviet Union Thinks It Could Fight And Win A Nuclear War," *Commentary*, July, 1977, pp. 21-35.
27. "New U.S. Atom War Policy Told," (Richard Burt, *New York Times*), *San Francisco Chronicle*, August 6, 1980; "Administration In Disarray," (Leslie Gelb, *Newsday*), *Honolulu Advertiser and Star-Bulletin*, August 31, 1980, p. 1.
28. "Reagan On Defense," *Honolulu Advertiser*, August 19, 1980, p. 1.
29. Norman Podhoretz, "The Future Danger," *Commentary*, April, 1981, p. 34.

30. "Their Mission Is To Keep 'Strength On the Barricades'," *Boston Globe*, April 28, 1981, p. 1.
31. Podhoretz, "The Future Danger," p. 35.
32. "Reagan Favors Linking Arms Talks To Soviet Behavior," *New York Times*, November 7, 1981, p. 5.
33. Evans and Novak, *Washington Post*, December 13, 1980.
34. "Attack Strongest Since Kennedy's 1961 Blast," (Jack Nelson, *Los Angeles Times*), *Honolulu Advertiser*, January 30, 1981, p. 1.
35. *Ibid.*
36. "Some Things Worth Fighting For, Haig says," (Oswald Johnston, *Los Angeles Times*), *Honolulu Advertiser*, January 10, 1981, p. 1.
37. *Ibid.*
38. "Excerpts From Haig's Remarks At First News Conference As Secretary Of State," *New York Times*, January 19, 1981, p. 1.
39. Cited in Evans and Novak, "The White House Soviet Scholar," *Washington Post*, February 12, 1981, p. A-19.
40. *Ibid.*
41. "Weinberger: We'll Sharpen Combat Readiness", *Honolulu Advertiser*, January 23, 1981, p. 1.
42. *Ibid.*
43. "Military Spending Will Come Before Social Programs," *Honolulu Advertiser*, January 29, 1981, p. B-12.
44. "U.S. Neutron Bombs Eyed For Europe," *Honolulu Advertiser*, February 8, 1981, p. 1.
45. "U.S. To Keep Troops In Korea," *Honolulu Advertiser*, February 8, 1981, p. 1.
46. *Ibid.*
47. Jeane Kirkpatrick, "Dictatorships And Double Standards," *Commentary*, November, 1979, p. 40.
48. *Ibid.*, p. 41.
49. "Reagan's Brain Trust Font Of Varied Ideas," *New York Times*, December 1, 1980, p. A-1.
50. Podhoretz, "The Present Danger," p. 31.
51. Podhoretz, "The Future Danger," p. 39.
52. Cited in Cindy Buhl, "A Disappearing Policy: Human Rights and the Reagan Administration," Coalition For A New Foreign And Military Policy, Policy Analysis, October, 1981, p. 1.
53. "Nominee Toughest On Soviets," *Honolulu Advertiser*, May 19, 1981, p. A-15.
54. *Ibid.*
55. "Behind Lefever's Downfall," (Ellen Hume, *Los Angeles Times*), *Honolulu Advertiser*, May 27, 1981.
56. "Backing Israel in UN, US Says," *Honolulu Advertiser*, May 23, 1981.
57. Richard Allen, "For The Record," op-ed, *Washington Post*, June 4, 1981.
58. "Report Says 750 Million Live In 'Absolute Poverty'," *San Francisco Chronicle*, August 10, 1981.
59. Hobart Rowen, "Reagan Putting Squeeze on World Bank," *Honolulu Advertiser*, p. E-9.
60. "Try Magic Reagan Tells Poor Nations," *Honolulu Advertiser*, September 30, 1981.

61. *Ibid.*
62. *Ibid.*
63. "Reagan to 3rd World: Do Not Lose Faith In Free Market System," *Honolulu Advertiser*, October 16, 1981, p. B-3.
64. "Reagan Firm: Trade, Not Aid," *Honolulu Advertiser*, October 23, 1981, p. A-1.
65. "Delegates Summit Up: Cancun No Big Success," *Honolulu Advertiser*, October 25, 1981, p. A-1.
66. *Ibid.*
67. Walter LaQueur, "Containment For the 80s," *Commentary*, October, 1980, p. 41.
68. "Foreign Aid Falling Victim To Administration Cutbacks," (Newsday), *Honolulu Advertiser*, May 24, 1982.
69. Hobart Rowen, "Reagan Downgrades Third World," *Honolulu Advertiser*, March 5, 1981.
70. "Foreign Aid Falling Victim To Administration Cutbacks," (Newsday), *Honolulu Advertiser*, May 24, 1982.
71. "U.S. Will Sell Arms To 'Friends'," *Honolulu Advertiser*, May 22, 1982, p. D-1.
72. White House press release, July 9, 1981.
73. "U.S. Weapons Sales Expected To Top $30 Billion in '82," *Honolulu Advertiser*, April 20, 1982, p. A-13.
74. "Taxpayers Have Role In Business Of Selling Arms," *Honolulu Advertiser*, September 16, 1981, p. A-15.
75. "Reagan Team Moves To Give Big Boost To Sale Of Weapons," *Honolulu Advertiser*, April 19, 1981, A-15.
76. Ruth Leger Sivard, *World Military and Social Expenditures, 1981*, (Leesburg, Virginia: World Priorities, 1981), p. 7.
77. Buhl, p. 2.
78. Hobart Rowen, "Reagan Putting The Squeeze On World Bank," *Honolulu Advertiser*, March 7, 1982, p. E-9.
79. "U.S. Looks To Dictatorships," *San Francisco Chronicle*, August 9, 1982, p. A-18.
80. Buhl, p. 1.
81. "Doing It Her Way," *Parade*, September 13, 1981, p. 22.
82. Dorothy Gilliam, "We Need To Yell Louder About South African Policy," *Washington Post*, March 30, 1981, p. C-3.
83. "Reagan's Kissinger," *Wall Street Journal*, October 28, 1980, p. 1.
84. *Ibid.*; See also, Fred Strasser and Brian McTigue, "An Azores Tie," *Boston Globe*, October 21, 1980, p. 13; Strasser and McTigue, "Reagan Advisor Linked to Vesco," *Boston Globe*, July 22, 1981, p. 1.
85. "Reagan's All-In-One Ehrlichman, Mitchell and Kissinger," *Mother Jones*, September/October, 1980, p. 42.
86. "Reagan Steps Up Military Aid To El Salvador," *Honolulu Advertiser*, February 2, 1981, p. A-1.
87. "Haig: U.S. To Continue 'Carter Doctrine'," *Honolulu Advertiser*, March 19, 1982, p. A-16.
88. "Salvador Blasts Haig On Soviet Threat Stand," *Honolulu Advertiser*, March 20, 1981, p. B-8.

89. "Action Against Cuba Possible Meese Says," *Honolulu Advertiser*, February 23, 1981, p. 1.
90. Jeane Kirkpatrick, "U.S. Security and Latin America," *Commentary*, January, 1981.
91. Paul H. Nitze, "Strategy In the 1980s," *Foreign Affairs*, Fall 1980, p. 91.
92. *New York Times*, February 19, 1981, p. 19.
93. *New York Times*, April 6, 1981, p. B-7.
94. John S. Friedman, "Culture War II," *The Nation*, April 18, 1981, p. 453.
95. *Ibid.*
96. "Detente Will Give Way To Deterrent," (George Wilson, *Washington Post*), *Honolulu Advertiser*, April 10, 1981, p. A-1.
97. "Rostow Says That U.S. Must Contain Russians," *New York Times*, April 5, 1981, p. A-3.
98. "What Place For Arms Control?", *New York Times*, May 2, 1981, p. A-2.
99. "Arms Talk Called Unlikely Until '82," *San Francisco Chronicle*, June 23, 1981, p. 6.
100. "Rostow's Testimony Illustrates Reagan's Shift On Arms Control," *Washington Post*, June 24, 1981, p. A-12.
101. *New York Times*, June 27, 1981, p. A-3.
102. The Committee On The Present Danger, *Has America Become Number Two?* Washington, D.C.: June 29, 1982, p. 18.
103. *Ibid.*, p. 19.
104. *Ibid.*, p. 20.
105. "Persian Gulf Force In Reagan Doctrine," (David Wood, *Los Angeles Times*), *Honolulu Advertiser*, October 27, 1981, p. 1.
106. "Neutron Force Will Be Ready Soon, U.S. Says," *San Francisco Chronicle*, August 9, 1981, p. 1.
107. "Pentagon Draws Up First Strategy For Fighting A Long Nuclear War," *New York Times*, May 30, 1982, p. 1.
108. The Commission On U.S.-Soviet Relations (Council On Foreign Relations), *The Soviet Challenge: A Policy Framework For The 1980s* (New York, 1981), p. 1.
109. "Stronger Policy To Counter Russia Urged By Blue-Ribbon Study Panel," *Honolulu Advertiser*, May 14, 1981, p. B-4.
110. *The Soviet Challenge*, pp. 10-11.
111. *Ibid.*, p. 14.
112. *Ibid.*, p. 28.

Chapter 9

FOUNDERING ON THE SHOALS OF REALITY

There could be serious arms control negotiations, but only after we have built up our forces — in 10 years.

    Paul Nitze, Chief Negotiator for
    Theater Nuclear Forces [1]

Senator Pell: In the event of a full nuclear exchange between the Soviet Union and the United States, do you envision either country surviving to any substantial degree?
Mr. Rostow: So far as the risk of survival is concerned, I suppose the answer to your question is, it depends on how extensive the nuclear exchange is. Japan, after all, not only survived but flourished after the nuclear attack . . . the human race is very resilient, Senator Pell.

    Eugene V. Rostow, Director, Arms Control and
    Disarmament Agency (ACDA) [2]

Everybody is going to make it if there are enough shovels to go around.

    T.K. Jones, Deputy Undersecretary of Defense
    For Strategic Nuclear Forces (formerly technical
    adviser to the Committee on the Present Danger) [3]

317

A winning electoral strategy is one thing, a mode of governance quite another. Midway through Reagan's term of office the spectacular success of Containment Militarism in *domestic politics* has been matched by the degree to which it has failed as a *foreign policy*. Something was lost in translation from rhetoric to execution. The ringing promise that "peace through strength" and national prestige could be recovered by "rearming America" sounded an increasingly shrill and discordant note — at first abroad, but then at home as well. Having campaigned on fear and made a referendum of presidential leadership, the CPD-laden Reagan Administration has been hoisted on its own petard. The Soviet Threat it turned out, still had magic. But this time the fear it engendered was not of communism, but nuclearism, not just of Moscow but of Washington as well. Moreover, unlike the 1950s, the American public was scared not into paralysis, but mobilization. Similarly, the focus on the presidency as the seat of national decline proved opposite from its intended effect. Once Reagan attempted to beat the world of the 1980s back into a Cold War configuration in the image of the 1950s, his actions were read not as strength by those he wished to lead but as a sign of weakness.

While the legitimation and implementation of Containment Militarism came in stages, the former in the campaign culminating in Reagan's election, and the latter in the new Administration's first year, its disintegration cannot be understood so schematically. On the contrary, no sooner were the policies put into place than they began to come apart at the seams, beginning with El Salvador (at this writing the process of unravelling proceeds apace with the recent Soviet pipeline decision). Reagan's clumsy attempts to stem the decline of America's empire through Containment Militarism has not only reopened the old elite struggle but has also inspired a popular challenge to the larger orthodoxy of containment itself. It is to these developments that we now turn.

The Pax Americana In Disrepair

While detente was declared dead in American politics, it remained very much alive in international economics. This was a sore point about which the CPD was especially rabid. [4] The Cold War thaw had been of particular benefit to Europe where a higher rate of productivity during the 1970s, geographical proximity, and closer cultural ties, led Western Europe to take greater advantage of detente with the Soviet Union and its Eastern counterparts than did the United States. As detente turned back to cold war, the gap in economic practice and diplomatic perception grew ever wider, with Europe largely unaffected by the militarist turn in the domestic political climate of the United States.

The increase in European trade between East and West rested on a natural affinity of interests. Each potentially had much to offer the other. The Soviet Union and Eastern Europe needed western technology and capital, and Western Europe needed the markets, relatively cheap labor, and energy resources of the communist bloc. The latter was especially important given Western Europe's dependency on Mideast oil, a factor which made Siberian reserves of natural gas look especially attractive. Standing in the way of realizing the full potential of a mutually beneficial economic relationship were East-West ideological differences institutionalized in the military alliances of NATO and the Warsaw Pact. As we saw in early chapters, it was this military alliance system that prevented Western Europe from steering a more independent course in the critical period from 1949 to 1952. In a similar fashion, the Soviet Union blocked independent movement in Eastern Europe through the Warsaw Pact. It was not surprising therefore that Soviet hawks were as wary of detente as the CPD, offering their own scenarios of "Finlandization" if a thaw of Cold War tensions were allowed to progress. Hardliners on both sides were committed to traditional militarist-ideological alliances that had served their respective ambitions well, as opposed to economic-interest ties of detente which threatened the further erosion of their belief systems and authority.

Given the long-term underlying shifts in economic relations within the Atlantic alliance — including the increasing strength of the European economies relative to the U.S. — as well as between East and West, the policy struggle pitting militarism against managerialism did not end with Reagan's election. With so many Trilateralists in power in Paris, London, Rome, and especially Bonn, managerialism moved its intellectual capital across the Atlantic, reflecting the widening ideological rift between a militarist America bent on returning to frontier containment and a Europe just as committed to the benefits of trade under a managerial policy of *Ostpolitik*.

The elite struggle for control of containment broke dramatically to the surface once again in American domestic politics with the resignation of Secretary of State Haig. Unlike his predecessor Cyrus Vance who resigned in protest over Carter's election-year militarism, Haig was hardly a Trilateralist. As a former NATO commander and self-styled pragmatist however, Haig had kept a foot in both militarist and managerial worlds until the rift across the Atlantic proved too wide to straddle.

The incident that caused Haig to resign was Reagan's decision in June 1982 to impose controls over foreign as well as U.S. corporations in an all-out effort to block construction of the Siberian natural gas pipeline. The joint European-Soviet effort which when completed would supply Western Europe with lower-cost energy was the largest East-West deal in history. The $250 billion, twenty-five-year pipeline pact had been in the works for some years and was approved in the summer of 1980 under the leadership of West Germany. Although the Carter Administration had not objected to the decision, Reagan expressed his longstanding disapproval of the agreement at the Ottawa summit of western leaders held in June 1981. In lieu of Siberian gas, he offered American coal and nuclear power to discourage the pipeline's completion. The Europeans showed little interest in the Reagan proposal and continued forward with the project. Then in December, the Polish military government jailed the leaders of Solidarity and imposed martial law over the country. The Administration's reaction was, among other measures, to bar American companies from selling oil and gas equipment or participate in any way in furthering the pipeline. Attempts to persuade the Europeans to do likewise, ostensibly in order to punish the Russians for responsibility in the crackdown, fell on deaf ears however. The best Washington was able to wring out of its allies was a verbal condemnation issued through NATO. While this frayed the nerves of an already shaky partnership, it was another six months before the shock that brought Haig's resignation.

At this point Haig was still in control of Administration policy, much to the chagrin of militarist hardliners. While he counseled sensitivity to European concerns and cautioned against unilateralism, Administration hawks led by Weinberger and Kirkpatrick mounted a campaign for a full-scale grain and credit embargo of Poland and the Soviet Union, even though Soviet troops had not crossed the Polish border. The core of this proposed strategy was to drive Poland to the brink of default on its outstanding loans, forcing the USSR to make good on Poland's debts or watch it fall into bankruptcy. Reagan avoided going for the financial jugular however, opting instead for a series of measures which hardliners complained, with considerable justification, were more symbol than substance: High technology exports, for instance, which were banned by Reagan, had already dwindled to a trickle. Future grain negotiations were postponed, but current shipments continued undisturbed. And finally, Soviet commercial aircraft were denied landing rights in the United States. All this a far cry from what the militarists had in mind. The final straw, however, was the Administration's decision to pay $70 million in interest installments falling due on Poland's loans. In the words of Assistant Secretary of the Treasury Marc Leland, "The president had decided that maximum pressure can be put on Poland by insisting on repayment rather than declaring a default now." To do otherwise Haig argued would "bring down the temple of Western unity." [5]

The attack from the various quarters of the Cold War coalition came fast and furiously. Senator Moynihan knew Trilateral managerialism when he saw it and called the Administration's response "near to shameful," announcing that he would soon introduce legislation to declare Poland in default if Reagan would not. Harkening back to the CPD's early assaults on multinational corporations and bankers for their unscrupulous enthusiasm for detente, Lane Kirkland's name appeared over a *Washington Post* article deriding Chamber of Commerce President Richard Lesher's argument that the pipeline would give Western Europe "a degree of leverage over the Soviets rather than vice versa." The AFL-CIO president and CPD executive board member further charged that within the Administration "principled anti-communist ideologues" were being overruled by "commercial and banking interests." [6]

While it was no doubt true, as intimated by the militarists, that the suppression of independent trade unions and adoption of austerity measures were greeted by international bankers with a collective sigh of relief, the hardliners themselves had cynically manipulated the plight of the Polish people for their own ends. The Committee For A Free World was quick to take out another full-page ad in the *New York Times* lamenting Poland's loss of freedom, just as it had done in support of the suppression of freedom in El Salvador. [7] The former was, of course, totalitarian in Kirkpatrick's formula and deserved condemnation, the latter was authoritarian and did not. As one observer noted,

> not once during the 16 months of Solidarity's breathtaking emergence did *Commentary* find space for an article on Poland . . . not once did Jeane Kirkpatrick deliver a speech or write an article about the movement. Nor did Irving Kristol see fit to devote to Solidarity even one of his dozens of *Wall Street Journal* columns on foreign affairs during that period. [8]

Once Solidarity was broken however, these neoconservatives and their right wing friends emerged jackal-like to use the misfortunes of Poland for their own purposes. In the process, they showed themselves to be as short on principle as the managerialists they maligned.

Opportunism permeated the Committee's manifesto which at one telling point declared the Polish crisis to be a splendid chance in which to reveal "the illusions of detente for what they are." The ad went on to argue that the logic of leverage through economic ties fell flat and that policy should be directed instead to denying "Western loans, Western grain, and above all Western technology" to Poland as well as the Soviet Union. Interestingly, these measures were portrayed as merely the means to a larger purpose. Demonstrating once again the easily-traversed line between containment and rollback, the Committee argued that such a policy would "further the process of disintegration from within that may mark the beginning of the end of the Soviet empire." [9]

Richard Allen, speaking out for the first time since his ouster as national security chief, adopted a similar tone of barely concealed glee in the wake of Poland's tragedy. Allen, who continued to serve on the President's Foreign Intelligence Advisory Board, asked: "Are we not now presented with a beautiful opportunity to raise the cost suddenly and dramatically and seize the high ground?" In additional remarks before the Heritage Foundation, Allen suggested in a criticism levelled at his arch-rival Haig, that the Administration had missed a golden opportunity to "cripple, weaken" the Soviet Union. [10] Such talk, both inside and outside the Administration from Reagan's staunch supporters caused many to worry that he would waiver. An Emergency Committee For American Trade representing sixty-three multinational corporations came into being to ward off the growing political fallout. Echoing big business' concern, the U.S. Chamber of Commerce made public a letter to the president which expressed its fears that the Administration appeared to be on the brink of a "profound change (that) could be likened to a strategy of economic warfare." [11] Their sense of unease was well-founded. Even while Reagan adhered to Haig's more moderate approach, he suggested that the Soviets had "strained their economy — to the limit" and might be forced into political concessions to avoid economic disaster. [12]

The successful use of trade and credit as leverage was contingent however on European cooperation. Otherwise, as U.S. firms worried, market sacrifices would simply accrue to their competitors in Japan and West Europe. Since the allies showed little interest in such a scheme, this seemed to be its probable outcome. The Europeans who had firmly and uniformly rejected Reagan's request for economic sanctions had also expressed their concern that such coordinated efforts would constitute an act of war. Indicative of the growing strain within the alliance, Weinberger, shortly before the Versailles summit of western leaders in June 1982, characterized the sale of technology to the Soviet Union as "shortsightedness raised to the level of a crime." [13] Reagan's decision soon after to extend U.S. law over East-West business transactions was intended as the final nail in the coffin of detente.

European leaders were understandably angered by Reagan's cavalier disregard of their economic interests and, of course, of their national sovereignty. Moreover, they were particularly incensed with what they read as U.S. intent to force them to bear the burden of economic warfare. As then West German Prime Minister Helmut Schmidt tirelessly pointed out, Europe was far more dependent on East-West trade than either the U.S. or the USSR, and therefore would suffer most in an economic boycott. European sensibilities were especially piqued that the Reagan Administration found the sale of U.S. grain within the bounds of prudence, while demanding that Europe stop the flow of credit and technology. Reagan's argument that the one forced the Russians to give up hard currency while the other resulted in its accumulation was distinguished only by its lack of persuasiveness. If that were not enough, the Administration's economic policies — especially tight money and high interest rates — had brought on recession in Europe making the profits and jobs coming out of the long-term pipeline commitment even that much more attractive. Taken together with restrictions on the import of European steel into the U.S. and a growing chorus demanding that Europe spend more for NATO defense, many began to consider that perhaps, in the words of French foreign minister Claude Cheysson, the time had come for a "progressive divorce" on the grounds that Europe and the United States "no longer speak the same language."

The imagery was *apropos*, if somewhat overdrawn. Each side of the Atlantic still adhered to the language of containment but spoke in different dialects. Managerialists, who maintained allegiance to detente, believed that the primary crisis facing the West was economic and could be relieved through greater trade with communist nations, a strategy which would at the same time moderate Soviet policy toward the West and lessen the need for military vigilance. Militarists, who had expunged the word detente from their vocabulary, remained steadfast in their opposition to improved economic relations on the grounds that western security would become compromised as a result. Ostensibly this was because of the Soviet's sinister design for world domination, beginning with Western Europe. A darker motivation however has been the American foreign policy establishment's concern throughout the cold war with disintegration of Pax Americana beginning at its European center, irrespective of its driving force.

If the strategy of Containment Militarism was unchanged in thirty years, the world it hoped to redress had undergone profound changes. So much so that its application brought results near opposite from those intended. Whereas the Soviet Union was successfully portrayed as militaristic and isolated from Western Europe in the 1950s, the same tactic applied thirty years later has caused Europeans to distance themselves from Washington. Whereas European neutralism, the great fear of NSC-68 and CPD-I, was averted in the 1950s through military integration in NATO, the attempt by Reagan to strengthen U.S.-European relations through Cold War hostility in the 1980s has driven a wedge in the western partnership. What had changed across this span of time was that the U.S., no longer in such a preeminent position, was unable to guarantee that

European nations would have more to gain than lose by falling in line behind U.S. policy. In fact the costs seemed to outweigh the benefits the more U.S. policy attended to narrow nationalistic interest to stem the decline of its own economic and political power. Nowhere was this more the case than the pipeline decision which in Europe was interpreted as evidence that the United States no longer had the capacity to exercise world leadership, even as Reagan demanded continued fealty to an order fast becoming relegated to the past.

If the Administration's economic warfare strategy rankled Europe's elites, its nuclear war-fighting strategy aroused the ire of the European people. This drama would not be confined to the salons of Versailles however, but instead sweep across the continent in a wave of mass protest that reached American shores by the end of the year. The currency in this case was not profits but survival, the motivation not advantage but community, the challenge not just to containment tactics but to the cold war belief system itself.

European Protest Paves A New Way

Barely a month in office, during the same period in which the Administration was busy drawing lines in El Salvador, Reagan hinted in an interview in the popular conservative French magazine *Le Figaro*, that the U.S. would not hesitate to use nuclear weapons in Europe. [14] Coming from anyone else this might have been accepted, however uneasily, as standard NATO policy. But given the bellicose pronouncements from Reagan and his cabinet in those first days, along with their posturing in El Salvador, Europeans were understandably nervous at this early injunction. Anxieties were hardly allayed when Richard Allen in his first public address as national security adviser levelled the blast that Europe was "beset by a dangerous 'better Red than dead' attitude and outright pacifist sentiments." [15] Allen's remarks had themselves followed fast on the heels of Richard Pipes' assessment that the Soviet Union, to avoid nuclear war, would have to change its system. In the same diatribe, Pipes had also intimated that the West German foreign minister might be susceptible to Soviet influence. [16]

Such virulent rhetoric only confirmed Europe's worst fears of U.S. militarism and widened the breach across the Atlantic. While Washington urged its NATO allies to commit a larger share of their budgets to the military, they in turn reminded the Administration that their agreement to accept the new generation of Pershing II and Cruise missiles on European soil had been made with the understanding that arms negotiations would be conducted in the interim before actual deployment, the so-called two-track agreement. In his talk Allen dismissed the "advocacy of arms control negotiations as a substitute for military strength" as just one more manifestation of the retreatist mood. [17] Weinberger's and Rostow's pronouncements that arms control would be held in abeyance indefinitely only served to further rankle European opinion.

Given the growing climate of distrust, Weinberger's surprise announcement that the neutron bomb might be revived as one of the first orders of business sent shock waves through Europe. The alarm spread across the continent that the U.S. was restructuring NATO not to deter, but to fight a nuclear war in Europe. Those in favor of deploying the U.S. Cruise missile in the Netherlands were shortly defeated. The British Labor Party had already gone on record with its opposition in the event of resuming power. Public disapproval in Belgium also made deployment doubtful there as well. Just before the Administration's first NATO meeting, Prime Minister Schmidt's Social Democratic Party (SDP) voted for a review of the December 1979 deployment decision. Polls commissioned by the U.S. Intèrnational Communications Agency showed 60 percent of Germans opposed to the Pershing II and Cruise. [18] Understandably, Schmidt, who had initially raised the issue of NATO deployment was incensed by the timing of the Weinberger's neutron gaffe and issued a stern rebuke to the defense secretary.

Driven by the swelling tide of domestic protest in their polities, the NATO foreign ministers pressured Reagan to set an opening for negotiations on theater nuclear weapons. The date was to be November although no similar time was set for strategic talks. Whatever meager palliative gained was quickly lost however, when the neutron bomb reached the headlines again, this time with the Administration's decision to start up production in August. In response to this announcement, the Copenhagen daily *Ekstra Bladet* ran a full-page photograph of Reagan with the banner headline: "CRAZY". In Amsterdam, protesters waved placards denouncing "Reagan, the Neutron Cowboy." [19] In Bonn, the movement in the streets carried into the Bundestag where Chancellor Schmidt's SDP formally split with their party chief over his tacit acceptance of the neutron bomb. In early October, on the occasion of a Weinberger visit to Germany, an estimated 250,000 people — the largest demonstration in West Germany's history — poured into Bonn to denounce deployment of U.S. missiles on German soil. Weinberger's response was to assail this dangerous and growing "neutralism" with a studied disdain that only reinforced America's unilateralist cowboy image.

Weinberger's remarks were typical of the Administration's inability to refrain from provocative and alarmist pronouncements at the worst possible time. At the height of the autumn wave of protest, Major General Robert L. Schweitzer came forward with the prediction that the "Soviets are going to strike" and that the U.S. was in the midst of "the greatest danger that the public has ever faced since its founding days." [20] Even while Schweitzer was transferred from his post as head of the National Security Council's defense group for making public his apocalyptic vision, what the President and the Secretary of State themselves said touched off a far greater furor. With Weinberger attending another NATO meeting in Europe, Reagan confirmed the worst fears of the Europeans when he said that he could envision a nuclear war limited to Europe. [21] Attempting to dampen down the controversy but in the process only making it worse, NATO Secretary General Joseph Lun affirmed that Reagan's remarks were consistent with NATO strategy. What had originally been intended as a decision to relink U.S. strategic forces with NATO was now seen as an attempt by the U.S. to keep any conflict limited to Europe.

In Rome and London that weekend nearly one-half million protesters joined their Bonn counterparts in record turnouts against nuclear weapons. The Rome demonstration was of particular importance in that Germany had earlier declared it would not be the only nation on the continent to deploy the new missiles. With Italy added to the "unstable" list, no country was definite in its commitment. These demonstrations in turn were joined by marches of more than a quarter million persons through the streets of Paris, Brussels, Oslo, and Madrid, to name a few of the larger events. In all, several million people had participated in anti-nuclear demonstrations by the end of November. Weinberger responded characteristically saying that he didn't believe the massive outpouring "really signifies anything." [22]

When asked at a news conference whether a limited nuclear exchange would inevitably escalate into an intercontinental showdown, Reagan replied: "I don't honestly know," but then went on to reflect: "I could see where you could have the exchange of tactical (nuclear) weapons against troops in the field without it bringing either one of the major powers to pushing the button." [23] If that were not enough, Haig in defending Reagan's remarks, blurted out the possibility that NATO might set off a "nuclear bomb for demonstration purposes." The former NATO commander told Congress that such a strategy was among NATO's contingency plans and was designed "to demonstrate to the other side they are exceeding the limits of toleration in the conventional areas." [24]

With the mass pressure threatening the stability of governing coalitions in Europe, their attempt to distance themselves from Washington was creating the unthinkable — that the Atlantic alliance itself, the core of the empire, was in danger of breakdown. Swerving to avoid such a course before it was too late, Reagan offered to cancel the new generation of intermediate-range missiles destined for Europe (108 Pershing II's and 464 Cruise missiles) if the Soviets dismantled those they had already deployed (600 SS-4's, SS-5's and SS-20's). This so-called "zero-option" was unveiled in what was billed as Reagan's "first major foreign policy speech." [25] In an extraordinary effort to reach European opinion, the United States paid the costs of televising the President's speech by satellite to Europe.

This move told the story. The proposal was more clearly intended to deflect the European peace movement, than to negotiate a serious arms agreement with the Soviet Union. The Russian reaction was expectedly negative since they were being asked to dismantle weapons already in place for a promise that the U.S. would not deploy missiles of their own in the future. Moreover, from their point of view, the offer was hardly in good faith since it failed to include U.S. forward-based systems already operational on sea and in the air capable of reaching Soviet territory. Nor were British and French nuclear forces included in the equation. The Soviets countered with the position that a freeze of existing forces should be the starting point, with the option of dismantling to be considered after that. Anything less, the Soviets argued, would leave them at a strategic disadvantage.

The date for the opening of negotiations on theater forces was set for November 30, 1981. Underscoring the hardline stance the Administration planned to take into the talks, despite its conciliatory rhetoric, Paul Nitze was named as chief negotiator. When asked by the *Los Angeles Times* about the worth of engaging in arms negotiations, Nitze said it would be first necessary to redress the nuclear balance. Queried as to when that might be, he replied, "possibly ten years." [26] As one observer was quick to note upon the appointment, "In the world of nuclear weaponry, Paul Nitze is not known as Mr. Arms Control. He is Mr. Arms Buildup, and has been for more than 30 years." [27]

On the day the negotiations opened in Geneva, Rostow as the Administration's chief arms control spokesman delivered a speech in London where he reiterated the theme of relentless Soviet expansion in which existing arms treaties "have turned into ashes in our mouths." Downplaying the significance of Nitze's mission, Rostow explained that "negotiations have no magic in themselves." [28] Thus while Reagan and Haig attempted to court public opinion in Europe and recover from their own disastrous gaffes on "warning shots" and "limited nuclear exchanges", the presence of Nitze and the candor of Rostow spoke volumes for the Administration's intentions.

The U.S. and Soviet positions were so far apart they had little to say to one another. On the other hand, given the growing strength of the peace movement in Europe, they were compelled to go through the motions. Neither could afford to appear intransigent under the circumstances. Small wonder that reports from Geneva told of the Soviet and American negotiating teams cruising the placid Swiss lakes and partaking of ballet together. [29] The real driving force was not found at the negotiating table and the splendor of Geneva, but in the cities of Europe sobered by the ravages of two world wars and determined not to play host to a third.

The Movement Spreads Across the Atlantic

The seeds of a new type of Atlantic alliance — between the peoples of America and Europe — were further sown with the eruption of the peace movement in the United States. Its potential appeared earlier in the year not at first in protest against the buildup of nuclear weapons, but in opposition to intervention in Central America. The more the Administration railed against the making of another Cuba in the Americas, the more Americans saw another Vietnam in El Salvador. The white paper Reagan produced entitled "Communist Interference In El Salvador," purporting to demonstrate the guiding hand of the USSR and its Cuban "proxy" in the Salvadorean civil war, created a mood of national *deja vu*. It had been another white paper in 1965 labelled "Aggression From The North" that similarly ignored the political and social dynamics of the Vietnamese conflict, laying the blame instead on outside forces to justify the dispatch of additional arms and troops to Southeast Asia. Just as Vietnam had been promoted in its time as the place "to draw the line" against communism, so now was El Salvador.

Building up to release of the white paper, the Administration promised in a flurry of dramatic news conferences that it would produce "incontrovertible" evidence of Soviet and Cuban involvement. The centerpiece of the Administration's case was its allegation that hundreds of tons of "the most modern weapons and equipment" were smuggled into El Salvador by a cabal consisting of Soviets, Eastern Europeans, Cubans and Nicaraguans. Moreover, the public was assured, missives intercepted from guerrilla channels would provide documentary evidence for the charges. Once exposed to public scrutiny however, they told quite another story, one of little fraternal cooperation from outside sources and heavy reliance on the Salvadorean black market for weapons. Confronted with "incontrovertible" evidence of fraudulent and shoddy analysis the white paper's principal author admitted to the *Wall Street Journal* that its assessment was "full of mistakes" and "guessing" — its conclusions "possibly misleading and overembellished." [30] The same could also be said for Haig's charges of "Soviet hit lists" and "terrorist training camps" for the takeover of Central America since intelligence agencies admitted to having no hard evidence of such conspiracy. [31]

The lowest point in the Administration's showing came when a

Nicaraguan youth upstaged intelligence de-briefers on network television. With a great deal of fanfare the Administration trotted out a lone 19-year-old as proof of outside infiltration into El Salvador. When the cameras turned his way however, the embarrassment of the white paper was revisited. Instead of telling a tale of intrigue beginning with orders from Moscow and training in Havana, he explained with considerable passion how, after having participated in the overthrow of Somoza he walked across the border alone to join the movement in neighboring El Salvador. Once captured and fearing for his life, he participated in the charade that had brought him to this elaborate press conference. [32] A mortified Administration released the youth to Nicaragua, knowing full well the fate that awaited him if returned to El Salvador. After the murders of American Catholic nuns and El Salvador's Archbishop Romero, Reagan did not need to be saddled with further public outcry against his Administration's support of the "moderately repressive" Salvadorean regime.

Far from exorcising "the Vietnam syndrome" as it was supposed to do, the reckless bravado displayed in these early days brought back the ghost of Vietnam to haunt the Administration's interventionist plans. Reagan's decision to dispatch military advisors and increase military aid to El Salvador was met with a chorus of opposition from Congress and the public. They were joined by almost universal condemnation from allies in Europe, led by West Germany, as well as key nations in Latin America such as Venezuela and Mexico. Hobbled by constraints foreign and domestic that surprised them in intensity, the Administration opted to drop the containment hardline in favor of the "political solution" that eventuated in the election stalemate of 1982.

The public relations campaign conducted from Washington for the election also recalled the Vietnam era. And, as was the case there, the exercise had little influence one way or another in the ongoing struggle. Accordingly, the Administration left the door open to covert action in the region when it refused to rule out the use of force in response to congressional demand for approval of any further military aid or CIA activity. [33] In March 1982, the same month as the Salvadorean election, Secretary of Defense Weinberger ordered the beefing up of capabilities for guerrilla operations, sabotage, clandestine assault, and other forms of unconventional warfare. The defense guidance document authorizing these actions read that where instability endangers American interests "special operations forces will be employed to assist United States friends and allies." Under such circumstances, special operations would be undertaken "where the use of conventional forces would be premature, inappropriate, or infeasible, to conduct surgical operations and to control the situation or terminate the crisis on favorable terms." [34] With other avenues closed or ineffective, covert actions of this type have come to play an increasingly central role in the Reagan strategy for Central America. [35] Thus the success of anti-interventionist constraints has been a partial one, delegitimizing intervention but as yet unable to prevent its being carried out by means of duplicitous certifications of progress in human rights and clandestine military operations.

The same qualified achievement in the field of intervention has proven to be the case for the protest against nuclear weapons. The American movement against nuclear militarism had more modest beginnings than its European counterpart. It emerged in one part of the country as a petition drive to halt the production of nuclear weapons, in another as a medical and scientific forum on the horrors of nuclear weapons, or as a religious congregation's witness against the arms race. On Veteran's Day, 1981, the Union of Concerned Scientists along with numerous cosponsoring groups held teach-ins on 151 campuses in 41 states, putting the new antiwar movement on the map in the process. Like the people of Europe, an increasing number of Americans had reached the conclusion that Reagan was preparing to fight a nuclear war — one that would surely involve strategic intercontinental exchanges, as well as theater strikes "limited" to Europe.

The suspicion was brought home quite vividly in the macabre plans unveiled by the Federal Emergency Management Agency for mass evacuations from U.S. cities under the guise of civil defense. The agency declared that "the United States could survive nuclear attack and go on to recovery within a few years". [36] Rostow had expressed the same unsettling opinion during his confirmation hearings when he was asked whether the U.S. could win or survive a nuclear war. His response was that, "Japan, after all, not only survived but flourished." [37] And this from the Administration's caretaker of arms control.

Surreal planning began to filter out of Washington for homemade recreational bomb shelters, evacuation from cities by odd and even numbered auto license plates, and instructions for post-attack mail delivery, convincing more and more people that the Administration had taken leave of its senses. In town forums and teach-ins throughout the spring, those who still needed convincing were treated to devastating presentations by medical experts that made a mockery of Deputy Undersecretary of Defense T.K. Jones' widely quoted remark that, "Everybody is going to make it if there are enough shovels to go around." [38]

By May, a nationwide Ground Zero education week on nuclear war had drawn thousands in every state of the union and a nuclear freeze proposal calling for the immediate halt in the testing, production, and deployment of nuclear weapons, to be followed by major reductions in weapons stockpiles, had the support of a majority of the American public according to opinion surveys. [39] In response to this groundswell, the freeze resolution was introduced in Congress as the Kennedy-Hatfield Amendment, a proposal that drew the backing of 180 lawmakers as well as the endorsement of several state legislatures. The freeze idea was so popular in fact, that its detractors had to cloak their attack as an alternative freeze — in effect, a continuation of the arms buildup until such time that the "Soviet advantage" had been overcome. Introduced as the Jackson-Warner amendment, this competing freeze would ostensibly occur at the point where both sides were deemed equal. In short, arm now, freeze later — if ever.

The breadth and intensity of the freeze movement forced Reagan to respond in a prime time press conference. On this occasion, he branded an immediate freeze "disadvantageous" and "dangerous." Endorsing the Jackson-Warner version he argued that the Soviet Union enjoyed a "definite margin of superiority." The President went on to explain that "the Soviet's great edge is one in which they could absorb our retaliatory blow and hit us again." [40] No president had ever described U.S. vulnerability quite so starkly, at least not to a nationwide audience. The claim that the Soviets had achieved superiority was immediately challenged as irresponsible and untrue by arms experts. It was pointed out for instance that even assuming all U.S. ICBM's were destroyed, there would still be 3000 warheads at sea in submarines and 2000 in bombers, each several times the destructive power of the Hiroshima bomb. [41] Moreover, not only had Reagan confused the facts, but he had also contradicted the Defense Department's annual report that the nuclear equation was one of parity, a view emphasized by the Chairman of the Joint Chiefs of Staff in testimony before Congress. [42] Finally, former Defense Secretaries Harold Brown and James Schlesinger disputed Reagan's claim and pointed out the danger in perception created by such a statement.

In an attempt to head off the withering storm of criticism, Assistant Secretary of State for Politico-Military Affairs Richard Burt, himself a former national security reporter for the *New York Times*, attempted to reconstruct the record explaining: "I think what the President is referring to . . . is that we are concerned that the Soviet Union, with these new large ICBM's, has the capability to destroy a large fraction of our missile systems, and we do not possess and equivalent capability." Furthermore, Burt gamely reported: "The president was reflecting the view that the Soviets have the momentum in the strategic arms competition and we are worried about the trends." [43] Nevertheless, even after Burt's diplomatic editing, Reagan did not back down and worse, was supported in his provocative claim by Weinberger. [44]

The antinuclear movements on both sides of the Atlantic received an added boost when four experts who stood at what news reports termed "the heart of the orthodox foreign policy establishment" urged that the U.S. renounce first-use of nuclear weapons. With strong ties to its managerial wing the four were Robert McNamara, secretary of defense in the Kennedy and Johnson Administrations; McGeorge Bundy, Kennedy's national security adviser; Gerard Smith, chief strategic arms negotiator in the Nixon administration; and George Kennan, Truman's ambassador to Moscow and author of containment. Although while in office each had supported official U.S. doctrine to use nuclear weapons in the event of a Soviet invasion of Western Europe, they now called for a significant departure from this past practice. Speaking for the so-called "gang of four", McNamara argued: "The role of nuclear weapons should be limited solely to the deterrence of nuclear war initiated by an opponent. We believe in a policy of no first use as imperative to the survival not only of this country but of civilization." [45] Citing the fact that the Soviet Union had forsworn first-use a quarter century ago, the four said that a comparable renunciation would permit the U.S. to give up the controversial generation of tactical weapons that threatened to disrupt the Atlantic alliance.

Reagan Counterattacks

Reagan's reaction to the challenge at home was similar to his response when the European movement erupted some six months earlier. On May 9, 1982, addressing the graduating class of his alma mater at Eureka College in Illinois, he suggested an opening date for the much-delayed strategic arms reduction talks (START). Since the creator of the new acronym was Eugene Rostow, one could be forgiven for taking the proposal with a grain of salt.

After castigating the Soviet Union for spreading "violence and suffering" in Central America and elsewhere, and increasing the threat of nuclear war, the President got around to the terms of the START proposal. In substance, once unveiled, START bore striking resemblance to the intermediate-range offer in that it too called for cutbacks in weapons, again with most of the cutting to be done by the Soviet Union. The heart of START was its call for a reduction in the number of warheads to 5000 on each side with no more than half being land-based. Since approximately 70 percent of the Soviet arsenal is land-based in comparison to only about 20 percent of U.S. warheads, the Soviets would be forced to dismantle some 3,260 land-based warheads while the U.S. remained within acceptable limits. Moreover, a second phase of START would seek equal ceilings on megatonnage or throw-weight, a formula that would again disproportionately affect the Soviets because of the heavy weapons on which they rely to offset the U.S. advantage in warheads of greater number and accuracy. Finally, with U.S. plans for modernization left unaffected by START, Soviet land-based missiles would become even more vulnerable to submarine-launched cruise missiles, the B-1 and Stealth bombers, and the M-X, once this new generation of weapons was deployed. In essence, as noted by Leslie Gelb of the *New York Times*, the proposal asked the Soviets "to trade the present for the future: If the USSR made significant cuts now, the U.S. would curtail a major buildup later." [46]

Even as the Eureka speech was heralded as "a major shift" in U.S. thinking, the Administration was in the midst of developing a plan to fight limited nuclear wars. This was revealed in a leak of the Pentagon's five-year posture statement shortly after Reagan's call for arms reductions. In the controversial document in question — *Fiscal Year 1984-1988 Defense Guidance* — what was termed the "first complete defense guidance of this Administration" by Pentagon officials, Weinberger ordered the military to prepare for nuclear war against the Soviet Union "over a protracted period." [47] According to the *New York Times*, the Administration's strategic blueprint read that in the event of war with the Soviet Union, if conventional means "are insufficient to ensure a satisfactory termination of the war, the United States will prepare options for the use of nuclear weapons." Further, the guidance plan stated that "the United States must prevail and be able to force the Soviet Union to seek earliest termination of hostilities on terms favorable to the United States." In order to "prevail" the U.S. would require "forces that will maintain, throughout a protracted conflict period and afterward, the capability to inflict very high levels of damage against the industrial and economic base of the Soviet Union and her allies." Defense Guidance goes on to explain that such attacks must provide Soviet leaders with "a strong incentive to seek conflict termination short of an all-out attack on our cities and economic assets." Finally, U.S. nuclear forces must be capable of "controlled nuclear counterattacks over a protracted period while maintaining a reserve" for later "protection and coercion." [48] What this document represented in effect, was an expansion of the counterforce strategy set forth in skeletal form in PD-59.

In addition to nuclear war fighting the Pentagon plan envisioned an improvement in covert operations over the next five years as well as an even greater emphasis on military aid to "friendly nations." Demonstrating once again the false distinction between containment and rollback, *Fiscal Year 1984-1988 Defense Guidance* revealed also that "particular attention would be given to eroding support within the Soviet sphere of Eastern Europe." Finally, according to the *New York Times*, the planning document asserted that "the United States and its allies should, in effect, declare economic and technical war on the Soviet Union," a strategy that would shortly be put to the test in the Administration's attempts to block construction of the trans-Siberian pipeline. [49]

Understandably, what was viewed as most disturbing was the article of faith that a nuclear exchange could be "protracted," "limited" through command and control, and that in the end the U.S. could "prevail." Upon his retirement from the Joint Chiefs of Staff, General David C. Jones expressed skepticism about such a notion, joining the growing number of arms experts who had already raised serious reservations about how a nuclear exchange, once begun, could be prevented from escalating into an all-out holocaust. Moreover, Jones warned: "If you try to do everything to fight a protracted nuclear war, then you end up with the potential of a bottomless pit." [50]

Reflecting the dominant view within the Administration that the Soviet Union would be unable to match the U.S. in this game of economic brinksmanship, the Pentagon's five-year plan called for weapons which would be "difficult for the Soviets to counter, impose disproportionate costs, open up new areas of military competition and obsolesce (sic) previous Soviet investment." [51] As two arms experts assessed its implications, Weinberger's guidance blueprint for the 1980s came "close to a declaration of war on the Soviet Union and contradicts and may destroy . . . initiatives toward nuclear arms control." [52] So much for a new start, clever acronyms notwithstanding.

Revelations of the Pentagon's plans for nuclear war-fighting dashed whatever hopes the Administration had that the announcement of START talks would quell the mass demonstrations planned for the UN Special Session on Disarmament (SSD II) in New York. On June 12, 1982 the largest demonstration in U.S. history was held outside the United Nations when over 700,000 people gathered to protest the arms race. This was followed by the arrest of 1,691 protestors who conducted sit-ins at the embassies of the world's five nuclear powers. Most took place at the U.S. mission. The response of officialdom to the mass plea was telling. While West German Chancellor Schmidt admonished world leaders not to ignore the global drive for disarmament, Weinberger stubbornly maintained that it would have no effect on U.S. policy.

This was no mere tactical bluff on Weinberger's part. One month after SSD II, the Administration decided to break off negotiations for a Comprehensive Test Ban of nuclear weapons as well as withdraw from Senate consideration the earlier negotiated but unratified Threshold Test Ban and Peaceful Nuclear Explosion treaties. With the Comprehensive Test Ban veto, Reagan spurned an agreement that had virtually reached completion under Carter despite the CPD's best efforts at sabotage. So strong was the Committee in its opposition to the test ban that, like a shadow government-in-waiting, it took upon itself the task of briefing

Britain's Prime Minister Margaret Thatcher on the perils of such a comprehensive agreement before she assumed office. [53]

The outwardly expressed reason for these actions was discovery of alleged inadequacies in test ban verification procedures. One need not look far however for a stronger incentive. In testimony before the Senate Foreign Relations Committee, Rostow explained: "There is a feeling in many parts of the Government that given the uncertainties of the nuclear situation and *the need for new weapon modernizations, we are going to need testing,* and perhaps even testing above the 150 kiloton limit."[54] Since the new generation of first-strike counterforce weapons — the MX, Trident II, Pershing II, and Cruise — were nearing test completion, the Administration's adamant opposition to the test ban was an ominous portent of further escalation in weapons technology. Reagan's subsequent announcement of intentions to develop space-based weapons systems and hints by both Weinberger and Rostow that the MX once deployed might require an antimissile system to protect it only served to confirm these fears.

Under Reagan, the weapons test budget for 1982 was increased 30 percent to $250 million. [55] In the spring, at the height of opposition to the nuclear arms buildup the manager of the Nevada Test Site expressed the opinion that the protests would not even slow the pace of nuclear testing. Mahlon E. Gates, the official in question, took the added stance that the opening of arms talks would have no effect on the testing program either. Lending unwitting support to those who argued that negotiations were no substitute for a freeze in production and testing, Gates revealed that in earlier talks "while the three countries — the United States, the United Kingdom and USSR — were discussing nuclear arms ban treaties, all of them were conducting arms test programs." [56] Underscoring the Administration's fascination with things nuclear, Energy Secretary James B. Edwards standing witness at a nuclear test at the Nevada Site, assured that President Truman had "made the right decision" in exploding the world's first nuclear bomb over Hiroshima. On the eve of the 37th anniversary of that fateful day, Edwards, viewed a test explosion of a magnitude far greater than the one that ushered in the nuclear age and pronounced it "exciting." [57]

Returning to the UN disarmament conference in June, Reagan showed the same contempt for the proceedings inside as Weinberger had expressed for the demonstrations in the street. Fresh from speeches in London and Bonn where he promised in particularly ill-chosen words to "leave Marxism-Leninism on the ash heap of history," Reagan refused to join with the Soviet Union in a pledge to the world body not to be the first to use nuclear weapons again. Dismissing Brezhnev's June 15 pledge as "propaganda," he used the opportunity instead to lash out in standard stump fashion against the USSR's "record of tyranny." On the arms race itself, the subject of the convocation, all Reagan could say was that "the decade of detente witnessed the most massive Soviet military buildup of military power in history . . . While we exercised unilateral restraint, they forged ahead." Finally, in concluding his show of disrespect for the disarmament gathering, Reagan insinuated that the burgeoning peace movement was under the influence of Moscow. [58]

With several states slated to vote on weapons freeze referenda in the midterm elections and some Republican Congressional seats potentially vulnerable to the freeze issue, Reagan repeated his fifties-style redbaiting when he spoke ominously of "a movement that has swept across our country that I think is inspired by not the sincere, honest people who want peace, but by some who want the weakening of America and so are manipulating honest and sincere people." [59] Suspicions were aroused that Reagan's remarks were not a slip of the tongue, but well-rehearsed lines of an orchestrated campaign. The Freeze had after all received the over-whelming endorsement of the House Foreign Affairs Committee and had narrowly lost a vote before the full House in August (204-202) after a seven-hour debate and intense Administration lobbying capped by the President's meeting with ten undecideds. [60] When a proposed Peace Day was put together by Betty Bumpers — wife of Arkansas Senator Dale Bumpers — archconservative Senator Jeremiah Denton of Alabama called its sponsor Peace Links "a sucker deal . . . organized in part by groups that are openly critical of, even hostile to . . . our country." [61] Then came an article in *Readers' Digest* on the Freeze movement entitled, "The KGB's Magical War For 'Peace'." In the boldfaced preface (colored bright red), to this smear piece written by a senior editor of the magazine, lurid charges were made that the Freeze movement "has been penetrated, manipulated and distorted to an amazing degree by people who have but one aim — to promote communist tyranny by weakening the United States." [62] This was then followed by the President's harangue.

Despite their public stance that the Freeze would have no effect on policy, the Administration had to be worried that the movement's remarkable success in delegitimizing nuclear weapons would begin to translate into budgetary constraints on its war-fighting plans. Having themselves conducted a campaign that turned the political climate against SALT II in the Senate, hardliners were acutely aware of Con-gressional sensitivity to public opinion. Here the polls were unequivocal — a clear majority favored a nuclear freeze (87 percent in a *New York Times* survey) and a plurality (43 percent) were in favor of reduced military spending. [63] The latter was the more serious from the Ad-ministration's perspective since cuts in the military budget, unlike lip service endorsement of the idea of a freeze, could not be so easily reconciled with continued remilitarization. While Reagan might be able to get away with an alternative bogus proposal, secure in the knowledge that it would never be accepted by the Soviet Union, he could not portray himself as the champion of military budget cuts without seriously undermining the five-year plan to achieve military superiority. As the tide of protest mounted in the spring, Congress began to cast a critical eye toward military spending, an extraordinary turnaround from that body's lemming-like response to Reagan's first-year march into the nuclear wilderness. [64] So seriously was this challenge taken that, as we shall see, the CPD was called back on active duty.

Alongside growing antinuclear sentiment, the failure of Reaganomics played a critical role in the Congressional challenge to Containment Militarism. Military spending from 1981 to 1986 was slated to double from $162 billion to $343 billion, with the total cost exceeding $1.7 trillion. The Pentagon's share of the federal budget would be increased from 25 percent to nearly 40 percent as a result of Reagan's tenure. All this, the public was told, could be accomplished while corporations and wealthy individuals enjoyed tax cuts in accord with supply-side fantasies of robust growth and gutted social programs, the combination of which was supposed to add up to a balanced budget. Economists and noneconomists alike however predicted yawning federal deficits and tightening pressure on financial markets as government absorbed the available capital necessary for even a partial closure of the gap between revenue and expenditures. George Bush, before he became Vice President, called it voodoo economics. Budget Director David Stockman confirmed the accuracy of Bush's assessment in his insider's revelations in *The Atlantic* on the eve of the Administration's first anniversary.

By spring 1982, as Congress faced the largest military budget and the largest budget deficit in the nation's history, it was clear that the magic wasn't working. The only economic growth in sight was at the Pentagon, where defense spending was due for an 11 percent increase after inflation. [65] The fact that the biggest increase would take place in the purchase of weapons — 28.4 percent — meant that these enormous sums would be locked in to future budgets since the monies already authorized would show up as outlays in future years as the weapons were built and delivered. To make matters worse, these figures did not take into account the huge cost overruns endemic to weapons procurement that would in the end inflate the cost of arms well beyond their contracted price.

The upshot of the Pentagon's increasing monopoly of societal resources portended still a larger deficit, higher interest rates, and further slowdown of the economy. The President's own Council of Economic

Advisers predicted that the proposed increase in military spending would create "adverse economic effects" including "crowding out of private investment." [66] They have been right. This in turn has brought about a further adverse effect in that the decrease in funds available for research and development, and plant and equipment modernization, has only hastened the decline of U.S. ability to compete in international trade with its European and Japanese allies. [67] The final link in this chain of causality was forged in the pressure brought to bear on NATO and Japan to increase their defense spending to offset the negative impact of hyper-active militarism on the U.S. economy, a move itself that has only served to further erode the tenuous supports of the western alliance. [68]

All this taken together, along with mounting unemployment and a social "safety net" scheduled for still further shredding, it began to dawn on all but the most diehard militarists in Congress that the military budget could no longer be considered sacrosanct if the decline in America's economy and society was to be halted. In so doing, they added to the ranks of those alarmed not just by America's relative decline, but with the possibility of its absolute destruction. Together their voices could no longer be ignored by the Administration, whose Congressional allies warned that the ambitious plans for a concerted long-term buildup were in trouble.

The CPD Vigilantes Ride Again

From the early days of the 1980 campaign, the CPD had urged Reagan to adopt the figure of 7 percent in annual real growth to carry out his promise to rearm America. But with the election barely two months away, he had managed to run on such a platform without having to reveal what it might cost. Finally on September 9, during an address in Chicago, candidate Reagan settled on a 5 percent annual increase. The previous two years Carter had increased defense spending by 3 percent, and in his own bid for a second term, adopted a 4 percent figure. William Van Cleave, serving on the executive committee of the CPD and as Reagan's chief defense adviser, strongly recommended that his boss come out for 7 percent in the September speech. In the end however, Reagan was dissuaded from such a pronouncement by his economic advisers who even at this early date were worried that the budgetary projections wouldn't hold up under examination.

Before leaving office however, Carter gave the CPD hardliners on the advisory team an unexpected boost when he matched Reagan's pledge with an increase of 5 percent in the proposed fiscal year 1982 military budget. By this time Van Cleave was Director of Defense Planning on the transition team and, by most accounts, had the inside track on the top Defense post. Van Cleave argued once again for 7 percent, this time as a "signal" to the Soviets of Reagan's resolve to take a harder line than his predecessor. [69] While Van Cleave lost the Secretary position to Reagan's old friend Weinberger, the latter enthusiastically took up the cause for 7 percent growth. After Van Cleave's having stocked the upper reaches of the Pentagon with CPD hardliners, it would have been difficult for the inexperienced Weinberger to have become other than a "seven-percenter," even if he were inclined to challenge the military buildup.

The final figures revealed quite a coup for the militarists. Reagan's original 5 percent pledge in 1980 was based on a $158 billion budget for fiscal year 1981. By the time Reagan took office and the 7 percent figure had been accepted, its baseline was the 1982 budget of $222 billion. In the words of Steven R. Weisman of the *New York Times*: "Reckoned on the basis of the 1981 budget, the new growth rate was actually *11%* after inflation, *more than twice* what Mr. Reagan had promised (emphasis added)." [70]

With momentum behind him, Reagan opened his second year determined to continue the steady climb in military spending. Congress had begun to have other ideas however once its own budget office started to predict annual federal deficits reaching $140 to $160 billion. [71] After long and acrimonious debate, Congress joined by Administration moderates, persuaded Reagan to abandon his dream of supply-side miracles and to increase taxes by $98 billion over a three-year period. As part of the deal for an impolitic tax increase in an election year, Congress insisted upon a reduction of $30 billion in military spending distributed from 1983 to 1985.

Shortly before passage of the compromise measure however Reagan announced that he wasn't bound by the limitations set down in the resolution beyond 1983. Caught off guard by this maneuver, Congress was reported to have felt "betrayed and double-crossed" by the White House, echoing the European reaction to the recently announced pipeline decision after the Versailles summit. [72] Weinberger then reinforced Reagan's announcement, arrogantly dismissing the Congressional resolution as mere "wishful thinking." [73] At the same time, Pentagon officials let it be known that they were close to a budget for 1984 which called for an 11 percent increase in real growth over that of 1983, an estimated 17.3 percent with inflation. Such a jump, they claimed, would put military spending back on track after having been *held down* by Congress in 1983. This despite the fact that when push came to shove Congress passed a budget only slightly less than what the Administration had requested.

One of the major reasons cited by Pentagon officials for the

Administration's success in turning back the Congressional challenge to this record military budget, even as the House came close to endorsing the Freeze, was the aggressive lobbying campaign launched in support of a sustained buildup. At its center, in a cameo performance, was none other than the CPD.

In March, with the Freeze movement gaining ground and Congress beginning to scrutinize the military budget, the Committee issued its first position paper since 1980. This latest report was entitled, "Is the Reagan Defense Program Adequate?" The answer, according to the CPD, was a resounding *no*. Far from excessive as charged by critics, the Reagan program was characterized by the Committee as a "minimal one", inadequate to "halt the unfavorable trends in the U.S.-Soviet military balance."[74] In order to reverse this alleged power shift, the CPD called for a level of spending even greater than that proposed by Reagan, citing "the intrusion of Soviet power into the Western Hemisphere" as,

> all the more reason why any budgetary revision by the Congress cutting the projected levels of defense funding or deferring or stretching-out the proposed five-year program, against the will of the President, would give a dangerous signal to the Soviet Union and to our Allies. [75]

The March report as it turned out, was only a prelude to a larger study released to coincide with Independence Day. Presented as an updated sequel to the earlier "Is America Becoming Number Two?", the claim made in "Has America Become Number Two?" caused the reader no surprise. In effect, the CPD argued, the trends documented in the earlier work had worsened to the point where the Committee could only conclude that "the answer is unequivocally yes. The United States has become second best." [76] As alarming as this might seem, the report noted that it only reinforced what the president and secretary of defense had already admitted.

News stories of the CPD's revival, unwittingly or not, played into the 1982 campaign strategy. Noting that thirty-three of its members including the president himself were on leave serving in the Administration with another eighteen in a part-time capacity, one account marveled that the Committee "demonstrated its non-partisan politics in its attack on the Reagan program." [77] One of the Administration's part-timers was Charls E. Walker, who served on Reagan's economic policy advisory board in addition to acting as chairman of the CPD. Walker had replaced Rostow when the latter became director of the Arms Control and Disarmament Agency. In his capacity as the Committee's chief spokesman, Walker pronounced the Administration's five-year military budget projections too low by $100 billion, calling the increases since 1980 only "modest." [78] The report itself termed it a "most significant defect" that "new guidelines for protracted nuclear conflict and protracted conventional conflict *in several parts of the world at the same time* imply a greater gap between means and ends." [79] The CPD of course, like Reagan and Weinberger, were in longstanding agreement that the only acceptable way to close the gap was to increase the means of violence rather than abandon the interventionist ends for which they were deemed necessary. It should have been perfectly clear by both the wording and timing of these latest CPD releases, if not by their ideological and personal ties to the Administration, that the spring offensive was only obliquely critical of Reagan's program in order to get at those in Congress who would dare to underfund even these "modest" and "inadequate" efforts.

The revival of the CPD in 1982 recalls the campaign of its forbearer some thirty years earlier. At that time the Nitze-led militarists had, in Acheson's unforgettable words, "bludgeoned the mass mind of the elite." This in reference to the purge of early-day managerialists like George Kennan who counseled against the hardline course laid down in NSC-68. Having accomplished their coup within the policy establishment, it was still another matter to convince the public and its representatives in Congress to spend what was then an enormous sum for a military buildup to make the strategy of Containment Militarism credible. This is where Robert Lovett in an equally memorable phrase called for a "vast propaganda machine" — nonpartisan in makeup — to carry out a comparable bludgeoning beyond the rarified chambers of the Council on Foreign Relations and the State Department. CPD-I became the embodiment of Lovett's imagination, working hand-in-glove with Truman, Acheson, and Nitze to legitimize Containment Militarism in the critical months of its infancy.

In a similar fashion, Haig's departure culminated the process of ideological purification in the Reagan Administration. The fact that Haig played this Administration's Kennan was indicative of just how far the drift to the right had proceeded. With the self-proclaimed but never-anointed vicar of foreign policy removed, there remained no one with either the inclination or stature to challenge Nitze and Rostow on arms negotiations, or William Clark (Richard Allen's replacement as National Security chief) and Weinberger in their enthusiasm for economic warfare against the Soviet Union. While Clark and Weinberger were not members of the CPD, neither were they knowledgeable in the field of national security. Those they relied upon to draft the position papers at Defense and the National Security Council had been handpicked from the ranks of the CPD by Allen and Van Cleave before their departures from the Administration. In this group were ambitious hardliners like Richard Perle, who was named to the important post of Assistant

Secretary of Defense for International Security Policy, a position known as the Pentagon's "little State Department" because it encompasses the gamut of policy from relations with the Soviet Union, NATO and Europe, to economic and strategic issues.

Perle, who got his start in government as a protege of Nitze's, gained a ruthless reputation as the man behind Henry Jackson's decade-long, no-holds-barred assault on detente and arms control. Perle's nominal superior at the Pentagon is Fred Iklé, another member of the CPD who became the head of the Arms Control and Disarmament Agency after a Jackson-Perle purge of the agency in revenge for SALT I. Named as Iklé's deputy was John Lehman, who subsequently joined the CPD and now serves as Reagan's secretary of the Navy. Both were appointed on the recommendation of Jackson and Perle. Within the Reagan Administration, Perle is sometimes credited as the mastermind of the economic warfare strategy which led to Haig's resignation. Moreover, his adroit skill in the kind of bureaucratic guerrilla warfare of which Haig complained throughout his ill-fated tenure is legendary.

As the Nitzes, Rostows, and Perles consolidated their hold on the Administration, jettisoning those unwilling "to stay the course" as prescribed by the CPD, a new challenge burst forth in the form of the grassroots peace movement. When its impact began to register in the public opinion polls and make inroads into Congress, the CPD decided to crank up the "propaganda machine" for another bludgeoning of Capitol Hill. Unlike 1950 of course, the target was not Republican conservatives but Democratic liberals uneasy with projections of unprecedented growth in the military budget and strategies for fighting nuclear wars. Even as the actors had traded roles however, the script remained the same. While the CPD Administration insiders argued for a *carte blanche* military budget, the "nonpartisan" CPD outsiders feigned disappointment that Reagan was not moving faster toward his promise to rearm America. In the end, even as Congressional voices were raised over the prudence of the course the Administration had set, when the votes were counted their words had proven far louder than their actions. The insider-outsider lobby, a modus operandi dating back to the Great Debate of 1950-51, had proven its mettle again.

Beyond Containment

Judging from the aftermath of CPD-I's campaign might we conclude that the lattice-work is now in place for another quarter century of Containment Militarism, what some are calling Cold War II? Such a reading I believe, would be both premature and myopic. Not for a lack of success by the present-day CPD — there is no discounting that. If anything, its victory has been more impressive, its imprint more thoroughgoing than its predecessor's. Yet the terrain today is no longer as hospitable to the stark simplicity of Containment Militarism. The more United States foreign policy comes to reflect the uncompromising extremism of the CPD, the more the Reagan Administration appears to be caught in a midcentury time warp, unable to understand, much less control, the careening maelstrom of events unfolding in this decade.

The secret of both Committees lies in the name itself, but here again with a critical difference. Each was able to evoke a mood of impending crisis on which it could draw for support in struggles over policy. Fear is a volatile emotion, however, which when unleashed collectively has a way of breaking out of the harness for which it was manufactured. The anti-communist hysteria of the early fifties turned inward nearly to topple the Europe-oriented strategy of NSC-68 and before it was spent, to cast a pall of suspicion over the loyalties of such dyed-in-the-wool cold warriors as Acheson and Nitze. And yet, virulent anticommunism at home was readily reconciled with Containment Militarism abroad once the Republican rightwing was defeated.

Fear has again gained a momentum of its own in the current epoch, one risen from wellsprings far different, however, than that which inspired the red scare of thirty years ago. The sense of impending crisis today is not the fear of creeping communism but of methodical drift toward nuclear war. This makes the temporary mood far more difficult to manipulate by militarists since its fear is directed at the very symbols of militarized security; as much at "us" as at "them." The anti-nuclear movement grown out of this climate has served to demystify national security ideology, moving beyond the sterile debates between militarists who want to win the arms race regardless of cost and managerialists who want to rationalize the competition but race nonetheless. This, and other imaginative efforts now being born, threaten the arcane preserve of national security which until now has been defined by a priesthood of elites immune from public review. The inchoate and still largely intuitive grasp that the security of East and West is indivisible, that national security is impossible in an insecure world, holds out promise of revolutionizing the concept of defense and in the process leaving behind the obsession with containment.

It would be presumptuous however, to predict such a desired outcome. Whether its potential is realized will depend upon the ability of the peace issue to make the transition from a cultural phenomenon that gains its identity from public opinion polls to a political force possessed of an agenda for social transformation. Failure to take this critical step will leave the movement susceptible to those who counsel a buildup of conventional forces as a tradeoff for breaking the hold of nuclear dependency. Already such a proposal has emerged as the reasoned managerial response to the Administration's nuclear madness and the mass-based nuclear freeze. What it represents, in effect, is a search for a safer form of containment in which intervention can once again be conducted by means of conventional violence free from the specter of nuclear reprisal.

Aside from its narcissistic cynicism, this position's assumption that a conventional buildup is any kind of insurance against crossing the nuclear threshold borders on voodoo security. Strategic specialists are in general agreement that the most likely scenario in which a nuclear exchange might be triggered is not from a bolt-out-of-the-blue surprise strike, but instead from a theater conflict that escalates upward in graduated steps from the conventional to the nuclear level. Moreover, history suggests in too many cases that once war has begun, the momentum of domestic pressure shifts to the militarists who demand that the ante be raised to the point of "victory." If therefore, the peace constituency should settle for a narrow "lifeboat" preoccupation with nuclear militarism, it may well find itself back at point zero — that much closer to ground zero —given the abysmal record of managerial elites in warding off the attacks of their militarist archrivals in time of crisis. A little containment in this regard is not a sufficient substitute for no containment at all.

Yet to abandon the politics of containment is not enough. The peace movement must embrace a politics of transformation to break containment's death grip on our lives. Only by building a just world order that addresses the everyday violence of grinding poverty and routinized repression can we hope to avoid the episodic violence of war. Paradoxically, the striking success of the CPD may prove to be the catalyst for such a paradigm shift. When managerialism surrendered, the best hope for a post-Vietnam policy of containment went with it. Moving into the Reagan Administration with its self-proclaimed mandate for confrontation in hand, the CPD-led hardliners sowed seeds of discord that rocked each axis of international order: renewed Cold War hostility and an arms race between East and West; suppression of human rights and resurgent interventionism in North-South relations; and a protectionist and divisive mood where there was once western unity. Given this undaunted record of belligerence, one might hazard the proposition that the greater the success of Containment Militarism in the elite world of policy, the more precipitous the decline of U.S. stature in the real world beyond.

How long under these circumstances will the fear and smear tactics which have cowered congressmen and toppled presidents continue to hold sway? As should be clear by now, the consummate skill of CPD cold warriors in turning events of crisis to their advantage cannot be underestimated. Recognizing this nonetheless, the fact that Containment Militarism *worked* in the 1950s goes far in explaining its mass appeal during that period. The fact it *no longer works* suggests a way out today. Up until Vietnam an imperial world order — a Pax Americana — was maintained at minimal cost to the nation's material and psychic well-being. Moreover, most Americans in this period experienced an extraordinary improvement in their standard of living due in no small part to military Keynesian spending and a flow of cheap raw materials from the far reaches of the empire. This made the marriage in popular culture between the American way of life and American empire all the easier.

That way of life is now threatened, not from without as the CPD would have it, but from within; not by those opposed to Containment Militarism, but by its defenders in the Reagan Administration. What will "staying the course" entail? Nothing less than an awesome shift of resources from the already ailing civilian economy to the expanding military colossus, a trend which if continued will put to rest speculation as to whether we are in the throes of recession, or of full-fledged depression. All the while, if Reagan's first two years are any indication, the threats of violence which this program of unprecedented militarization is supposed to make credible, will not be able to put Pax Americana back together again. Those days are over. If ever merchants of fear and peddlers of crisis can be challenged, the time is now.

CHAPTER 9
Foundering on the Shoals of Reality

1. Robert Scheer, "ARMS: Caught in the Quicksand of Strategic Thinking," *Los Angeles Times*, October 4, 1981, 11, p. V-3.
2. United States Senate, Hearings Before the Committee on Foreign Relations (97th Congress, First Session), on the Nomination of Eugene V. Rostow to be Director, Arms Control and Disarmament Agency (ACDA), June 22-23, 1981, pp. 48-49.
3. "Reality and Civil Defense," *Honolulu Advertiser*, January 30, 1982, p. A-10.
4. See Chapter 5, especially "Trade: The Calculus of Managerialism."
5. "U.S. Paying Polish Debts for a Year," *Honolulu Advertiser*, February 6, 1982, p. B-3.
6. "Who Runs Foreign Policy? Business," (Lane Kirkland, *Washington Post*), *Honolulu Advertiser*, February 26, 1982, p. A-14.
7. *New York Times*, January 10, 1982, p. IV-24.
8. Jim Sleeper, "Do They Protest Too Much?" *In These Times*, February 23-March 9, 1982, p. 16.
9. *New York Times*, January 10, 1982, p. IV-24.
10. "Allen Rips Reagan Dealing on Poland, Soviet Union," (George de Lama, *Chicago Tribune*), *Honolulu Advertiser*, February 5, 1982, p. A-16.
11. "C of C Splits with Reaganites Over Stalling of Soviet Pipeline," (Dan Morgan, *Washington Post*), *Honolulu Advertiser*, February 18, 1982, p. A-15.
12. Joseph B. Fleming, "Germany, France Criticize Sanctions," *Honolulu Advertiser*, January 30, 1982, p. A-1.
13. Richard Halloran, "Reagan Aide Tells of New Strategy on Soviet Threat," *New York Times*, May 22, 1982, p. 1.
14. "Reagan Gives Nuke Hint," *Honolulu Advertiser*, February 21, 1981, p. A-11.
15. "Reagan Aide Assails Pacifism in Europe," *New York Times*, March 22, 1981, p. 8.
16. *New York Times*, March 19, 1981, p. 8; see also Michael Getler, "Scaled Down National Security Adviser Still a White House Pillar," *Washington Post*, April 7, 1981, p. A-2.
17. "Reagan Aide Assails Pacifism In Europe," *New York Times*, March 22, 1981, p. 8.
18. Cited in Rowland Evans and Robert Novak, "Too Much Elbow Room for Schmidt?" *Washington Post*, May 8, 1981, p. A-19.
19. Cited in *Newsweek*, August 24, 1981, p. 28.
20. "General Schweitzer Fired for Saying 'Soviets to Strike,' " *Honolulu Advertiser*, October 21, 1981, p. A-1.
21. "Reagan Nuke Comment Causes Flap," *Honolulu Advertiser*, October 21, 1981, p. 1.
22. 'We Don't Want Your War," *Honolulu Advertiser*, October 25, 1981, p. 1.
23. *Washington Post*, November 1, 1981, p. 1.

24. "Haig: 'N-demonstration' Possible if the Soviets Invade W. Europe." *Honolulu Advertiser*, November 5, 1981, p. A-14.
25. "Reagan Plan Gets Siberian Reception," *Honolulu Advertiser*, November 19, 1981, p. 1.
26. Robert Scheer, "ARMS: Caught In The Quicksand of Strategic Thinking," *Los Angeles Times*, October 4, 1981, p. V-3.
27. "Godfather of U.S. Arms Buildup Will Lead Talks on Nuclear Control," *Honolulu Advertiser*, November 29, 1981, p. A-23.
28. David Broder, "Just 'Ashes in our Mouths'?" *Honolulu Advertiser*, December 9, 1981, p. 17.
29. John Vinocur, "Two Sets of Arms Talks Gain Civility from Geneva's Grace and Cordial Air," *New York Times*, July 15, 1982, p. A-10.
30. Jonathan Kwitny, "Tarnished Report? Apparent Errors Cloud U.S. 'White Paper' on Reds in El Salvador," *Wall Street Journal*, June 8, 1981, p. 1.
31. "Drawing Battlelines on Terrorism," (Michael Getler, *Washington Post*), *Honolulu Advertiser*, February 8, 1981, p. A-22; see also *New York Times*, February 9, 1981, p. 3.
32. *New York Times*, March 13, 1982, p. 1; *New York Times*, March 14, 1982, p. 1.
33. "U.S. Eyes 'Global Solution' for El Salvador," (Oswald Johnston, *Los Angeles Times*), *Honolulu Advertiser*, March 14, 1982, p. 1.
34. Richard Halloran, "Military Is Quietly Rebuilding its Special Operations Forces," *New York Times*, July 19, 1982, p. A-9.
35. "U.S. Plans Paramilitary Force to Operate Against Nicaragua," (Patrick E. Tyler and Bob Woodward, *Washington Post*), *Honolulu Advertiser*, March 10, 1982, p. 1.
36. "Administration Feels U.S. Can Survive Nuclear War," (Robert Scheer, *Los Angeles Times*), *Honolulu Advertiser*, January 22, 1982.
37. United States Senate, Hearings Before The Committee On Foreign Relations, (97th Congress, First Session), on the Nomination of Eugene V. Rostow, to be Director, Arms Control and Disarmament Agency (ACDA), June 22-23, 1981, pp. 48-49.
38. "Reality and Civil Defense," *Honolulu Advertiser*, January 30, 1982, p. A-10.
39. "NUCLEAR: Grass-Roots Movement Spreading," *Los Angeles Times*, April 17, 1982, p. 10.
40. *New York Times*, March 16, 1982, p. 1.
41. "Ex-CIA Official Says Nuclear Weapons Freeze Could Be Verified," *Los Angeles Times*, April 11, 1982, p. V-1.
42. "Moscow's Supposed N-Superiority 'A Myth'," (Clayton Fritchey, *Newsday*), *Honolulu Advertiser*, April 3, 1982, p. A-11.
43. *Los Angeles Times*, April 2, 1982, p. 1.
44. Weinberger, *Washington Post*, April 30, 1982.
45. "Four VIPs Ask U.S. to Pledge Not to Use N-Arms First," (Robert S. Boyd, Knight-Ridder) *Honolulu Advertiser*, April 8, 1982, p. A-16.
46. Leslie Gelb, "Arms Accord: Stony Path," *New York Times*, May 11, 1982, p. 1.
47. Richard Halloran, "Pentagon Draws Up First Strategy for Fighting a Long

Nuclear War," *New York Times*, May 30, 1982, p. 1.
48. Cited in Richard Halloran, "50 in Congress Protect Policy on Protracted A-War," *New York Times*, July 22, 1982.
49. *New York Times*, May 30, 1982, p. 1.
50. Richard Halloran, "Top General Questions Policy on Prolonged A-War," *New York Times*, June 19, 1982, p. A-1.
51. Quoted in Tom Wicker, "War to the Death," *New York Times*, p. A-23.
52. Hans A. Bethe and Kurt Gottfried, "The 5-Year War Plan — A Loser 2 Ways," *New York Times*, June 10, 1982, p. A-31.
53. Joel S. Wit, "Backing Away from Test Ban Treaties," *The Bulletin of the Atomic Scientists*, October, 1982, p. 9.
54. Cited in David H. McKillop and Nigel J. Collie, "The Test Ban Treaty: A Litmus Test for Reagan," *New York Times*, August 28, 1981, p. 23.
55. "More Defense $$ Means New A-Bomb Tests," (Casey Bukro, *Chicago Tribune*) *Honolulu Advertiser*, April 20, 1982, p. 7.
56. *Ibid.*
57. "Atom Arms Testing Will Be Continued Cabinet Officer Says," *New York Times*, August, 6, 1982, p. 1.
58. "Levels Charges in UN Speech," *Honolulu Star-Bulletin*, June 17, 1982, p. 1.
59. "President Says Foes of U.S. Have Duped Arms Freeze Group," *New York Times*, October 5, 1982.
60. Judith Miller, "House Supports Reagan on Arms, Adopting His Idea of Atom Freeze," *New York Times*, August 6, 1982, p. 1; also, "Nuclear Freeze Vote: Both Sides Term it a Victory," *New York Times*, August 7, 1982, p. 2.
61. Cited in "A-Freeze Backers Accuse Reagan of Smear Tactics," *Washington Post*, October 6, 1982.
62. John Barron, "The KGB's Magical War for 'Peace'," *Reader's Digest*, October 1982, p. 206.
63. Opinion survey conducted in May, 1982, cited in "Back to 'Grass Roots'," *Nuclear Times*, October, 1982, pp. 8-9; the 43% figure is cited in "Foundations Seek End to Arms Race," *New York Times*, May 2, 1982.
64. "Criticism Rises on Reagan's Plan for 5-Year Growth of the Military," *New York Times*, May 22, 1982, p. B-11.
65. *See* Steven R. Weisman, "Reaganomics And The President's Men," *New York Times Magazine*, October 24, 1982, p. 85.
66. "Economic Flaw Seen in Defense Spending," *Honolulu Advertiser*, February 18, 1982, p. A-14.
67. See Council on Economic Priorities, *The Costs and Consequences of Reagan's Military Buildup* (New York, 1982), especially pp. 13-20.
68. "Pentagon Report Says Allies Fail to Bear Share of Military Burden," *New York Times*, August 2, 1982, p. A-5.
69. For an illuminating account of this budgetary decision-making process see Weisman, *New York Times Magazine*, October 24, 1982.
70. *Ibid.*, p. 85.
71. *New York Times*, July 28, 1982, p. D-1.
72. Richard Halloran, "Reagan Cites His Right to Shift Funds to Arms," *New*

York Times, July 29, p. A-19.

73.   Richard Halloran, "New Version Given on Reagan Stand on Arms," *New York Times*, August 11, 1982, p. A-10.

74.   Committee on the Present Danger, "Is the Reagan Defense Program Adequate?" March 1982, p. 34.

75.   *Ibid.*, p. 9.

76.   Committee on the Present Danger, "Has America Become Number Two?" June 29, 1982, pp. 58-59.

77.   Charles W. Corddry, "Group Reagan Helped Found Calls His Military Buildup Inadequate," *Baltimore Sun*, July 4, 1982.

78.   *Ibid.*

79.   "Has America Become Number Two?" p. 16.

BIBLIOGRAPHY

Acheson, Dean
    1957   *A Citizen Looks at Congress*. New York: Harper.
    1969   *Present at the Creation: My Years in the State Department*.
    New York: Norton.

Alger, Chadwick F.
    1962   "The External Bureaucracy in U.S. Foreign Affairs,"
    Administrative Science Quarterly, 7.

Almond, Gabriel
    1950   *The American People and Foreign Policy*. New York:
    Harcourt, Brace.

Alperowitz, Gar
    1967   *Atomic Diplomacy: Hiroshima and Potsdam*. New York:
    Vintage.

Ball, George W.
    1967   "The Promise of the Multinational Corporation," *Fortune*,
    June.

Barnet, Richard J.
    1971   *Roots of War: The Men and the Institutions Behind U.S.
    Foreign Policy*. Baltimore: Penguin.
    1981   *Real Security: Restoring American Power in a Dangerous
    Decade*. New York: Simon and Schuster.

Barraclough, Geoffrey
    1975   "Wealth and Power: The Politics of Food and Oil." *New York
    Review of Books*, August 7.

Bauer, Raymond A.; Pool, Ithiel de Sola, and Dexter, Lewis Anthony
    1963   *American Business and Public Policy*. New York: Atherton.

Berger, Peter
    1976   "The Greening of American Foreign Policy." *Commentary*,
    March 23.

Bergsten, C. Fred
    1975   *Toward a New International Economic Order*. Lexington,
    Massachusetts: Lexington Books.

Block, Fred L.
    1977   *The Origins of International Economic Disorder*. Berkeley:
    University of California.

Blumberg, Paul
    1980   *Inequality in an Age of Decline*. New York: Oxford University
    Press.

Borosage, Robert
    1970   "The Making of the National Security State." *The Pentagon
    Watchers*, Leonard S. Rodberg and Derek Shearer (eds). New
    York: Doubleday.

Brzezinski, Zbigniew
    1974   "The Deceptive Structure of Peace." *Foreign Policy*, 14: 35-
    55.
    1974-75 "Recognizing the Crisis." *Foreign Policy*, 17: 63-74.
    1976   "America in a Hostile World." *Foreign Policy*, 23: 65-96.

Buhl, Cindy
    1981   "A Disappearing Policy: Human Rights and the Reagan Administration," *Policy Analysis*, Washington, D.C.: Coalition for a New Foreign and Military Policy, October.

Cammett, John
    1967   *Antonio Gramsci and the Origins of Italian Communism.* Stanford, California: Stanford University.

Chace, James
    1976   "American Jingoism." *Harper's*, May: 37-44.

Chichilnisky, Graciela
    1980-81 "Basic Needs and Global Models: Resources, Trade and Distribution." *Alternatives: A Journal of World Policy*, VI, 3.

Clausewitz, Karl von
    1943   *On War.* New York: Random House.

Coalition for a Democratic Majority
    1974   *The Quest for Detente.* Foreign Policy Task Force.
    1976   *For an Adequate Defense.* Foreign Policy Task Force.
    1977   Open Letter to President Carter, May 14.

Committee on the Present Danger
    1976   *Common Sense and the Common Danger.* Washington, D.C.: Committee on the Present Danger.
    1976   *How the CPD Will Operate — What It Will Do, and What It Will Not Do.*
    1977   *What Is the Soviet Union Up To?*
    1977   *Where We Stand on SALT.*
    1978   *Is America Becoming Number Two? Current Trends in the U.S.-Soviet Military Balance.*
    1978   "Peace With Freedom: A Discussion by the Committee on the Present Danger." Before the Foreign Policy Association, March 14.
    1979   *Is SALT II a Fair Deal for the United States?*
    1979   *Does the Official SALT II Treaty Hold Up Under Analysis?*
    1979   *Public Attitudes on SALT II.*
    1979   *Why the Soviet Union Wants SALT II.*
    1980   *The 1980 Crisis and What We Should Do About It.*
    1980   *Countering the Soviet Threat: U.S. Defense Strategy in the 1980's.*
    1982   *Has America Become Number Two?*
    1982   *Is the Reagan Defense Program Adequate?*

Conant, James B.
    1970   *My Several Lives.* New York: Harper and Row.

Council on Economic Priorities
    1982   *The Costs and Consequences of Reagan's Military Buildup.* New York: Council on Economic Priorities.

Council on Foreign Relations
    1981   Commission on U.S.-Soviet Relations, *The Soviet Challenge: A Policy Framework for the 1980s.* New York: Council on Foreign Relations.

Crozier, Michel J.; Huntington, Samuel P.; and Watanuki, Joji.
    1975   *The Crisis of Democracy: Report on the Governability of Democracies to the Trilateral Commission*. New York: New York University Press.
Domhoff, G. William
    1967   *Who Rules America?* Englewood Cliffs, N.J.: Prentice-Hall.
    1970   *The Higher Circles*. New York: Random House.
Donovan, John C.
    1974   *The Cold Warriors: A Policy-Making Elite*. Lexington, Massachusetts: D.C. Heath.
Draper, Theodore
    1974   "Detente." *Commentary*, June: 23-47.
Drell, Sidney D. and von Hippel, Frank
    1976   "Limited Nuclear War." *Scientific American*, November.
Eidenberg, Eugene
    1969   "The Presidency: Americanizing the War in Vietnam." *American Political Institutions and Public Policy*, Alan P. Sindler (ed.). Boston: Little, Brown.
Eisenhower, Dwight D.
    1963   *Mandate for Change, 1953-1956*. Garden City, New York: Doubleday.
Ellsberg, Daniel
    1981   "Introduction: Call to Mutiny." *Protest and Survive*, E.P. Thompson and Dan Smith (eds.). New York and London: Monthly Review Press.
Etzold, Thomas H. and Gaddis, John Lewis (eds.)
    1978   *Containment: Documents on American Policy and Strategy, 1945-1950*. New York: Columbia University Press.
Falk, Richard A.
    1976   "Beyond Internationalism." *Foreign Policy*, 24: 65-113.
Filler, Louis
    1964   *The President Speaks: From William McKinley to Lyndon Johnson*. New York: G.P. Putnam.
Fitzgerald, Frances
    1976   "The Warrior Intellectuals." *Harper's*, May: 45-64.
Fleming, Denna D.
    1961   *The Cold War and Its Origins 1917-1960*. 2 vols. Garden City, New York: Doubleday.
Gaddis, John Lewis
    1972   *The United States and the Origins of the Cold War, 1941-47*. New York: Columbia University.
    1978   "The Strategy of Containment." *Containment: Documents on American Policy and Strategy, 1945-1950*: 25-37. Thomas H. Etzold and John Lewis Gaddis (eds). New York: Columbia University.
Galtung, Johan
    1980   *The North/South Debate: Technology, Basic Human Needs and the New International Economic Order*. World Order Models Project, Working Paper #12. New York: Institute for World Order.

Gardner, Richard N.
    1974   "The Hard Road to World Order." *Foreign Affairs*, April: 556-576.
Gelb, Leslie H.
    1977   "National Security and New Foreign Policy." *Parameters, Journal of the United States Army War College,* November 8.
    1980   "Beyond the Carter Doctrine." *The New York Times Magazine*, February 10: 18-24.
Gelb, Leslie H. with Betts, Richard K.
    1979   *The Irony of Vietnam: The System Worked*. Washington, D.C.: Brookings.
Gilpin, Robert
    1975   *U.S. Power and the Multinational Corporation: The Political Economy of Foreign Direct Investment*. New York: Basic Books.
Goldman, Eric
    1960   *The Crucial Decade*. New York: Vintage.
Goldstein, Robert Justin
    1978   *Political Repression in Modern America*. Cambridge: Schenkman.
Goodpaster, Andrew J. and Huntington, Samuel P.
    1977   *Civil-Military Relations*. Washington, D.C.: American Enterprise Institute for Public Policy Research.
Graham, Daniel O., Lt. General (ret.)
    1977   *A New Strategy for the West: NATO after Detente*. Washington, D.C.: The Heritage Foundation.
Gray, Colin S.
    1975   "Hawks and Doves: Values and Policy." *Journal of Political and Military Sociology*, 3: 85-94.
Halberstam, David
    1969   *The Best and the Brightest*. New York: Random House.
Halperin, Morton
    1961   "The Gaither Committee and the Policy Process." *World Politics*, 13.
    1974   *Bureaucratic Politics and Foreign Policy*. Washington, D.C.: Brookings.
Hammond, Paul Y.
    1962   "NSC-68: Prologue to Rearmament." *Strategy, Politics, and Defense Budgets*: 272-374. Warner R. Schilling, Paul Y. Hammond, and Glen H. Snyder. New York: Columbia University.
Henry, John B. II
    1971   "February, 1968." *Foreign Policy*, 4.
Hewlett, R.G. and Anderson, O.E., Jr.
    1962   *The New World, 1939-46*. University Park: Pennsylvania State University.
Hodgson, Godfrey
    1973   "The Establishment." *Foreign Policy*, 10: 3-41.

Hoffman, Paul
 1951 *Peace Can Be Won*. Garden City, New York: Doubleday.
Holbrooke, Richard
 1973-74 "Washington Dateline: The New Battle Lines." *Foreign Policy*, 13: 178.
 1976 "A Sense of Drift, A Time for Calm." *Foreign Policy*, 23: 97.
Hoopes, Townsend
 1969 *The Limits of Intervention: An Inside Account of How the Johnson Policy of Escalation Was Reversed*. New York: McKay.
Hughes, Thomas L.
 1975 "Liberals, Populists, and Foreign Policy." *Foreign Policy*, 20.
Huntington, Samuel P.
 1957 *The Soldier and the State*. Cambridge: Belknap.
 1962 *The Common Defense*. New York: Columbia.
 1962 *Changing Patterns of Military Politics* (ed.). Glencoe: The Free Press.
 1974 "Paradigms of American Politics: Beyond the One, the Two, and the Many." *Political Science Quarterly*, 89: 18-22.
Jones, Joseph M.
 1964 *The Fifteen Weeks*. New York: Harcourt, Brace and World.
Kaplan, Fred
 1980 *Dubious Specter: A Skeptical Look at the Soviet Nuclear Threat*. Washington: Institute for Policy Studies.
Kauffman, William W.
 1964 *The McNamara Strategy*. New York: Harper and Row.
Kennan, George
 1969 *Memoirs 1925-60*. New York: Bantam.
Key, V.O.
 1961 *Public Opinion and American Democracy*. New York: Knopf.
Kirkpatrick, Jeane
 1977 "Why the New Right Lost." *Commentary*, February: 34-39.
 1981 "U.S. Security and Latin America." *Commentary*, January.
Kissinger, Henry

 1957 *Nuclear Weapons and Foreign Policy*. Garden City, New York: Doubleday.
Kistiakowsky, George B.
 1979 "False Alarm: The Story Behind SALT II." *New York Review of Books*, 26, 4: 33-38.
Kolko, Gabriel
 1969 *The Roots of American Foreign Policy*. Boston: Beacon.
Kolko, Gabriel and Kolko, Joyce
 1972 *The Limits of Power: The World and United States Foreign Policy, 1945-1954*. New York: Harper and Row.
Kondracke, Morton
 1977 "The Assault on SALT." *The New Republic*, December 17: 19-21.

　　　　　1978　　"Home for Hardliners." *The New Republic*, February 4: 21-
　　　　　　　　　25.
Kopkind, Andrew
　　　　　1977　　"America's New Right." *New Times*, September 30: 21-33.
　　　　　1978　　"Cold War II." *New Times*, October 30: 29-41.
Kraft, Joseph
　　　　　1966　　*Profiles in Power*. New American Library.
LaFeber, Walter
　　　　　1966　　*America, Russia and the Cold War, 1945-1966*. New York:
　　　　　　　　　John Wiley.
La Queur, Walter
　　　　　1980　　"Containment for the 80s." *Commentary*, October.
Lasswell, H.D.
　　　　　1941　　"The Garrison State." *American Journal of Sociology*, 46.
　　　　　1965　　"The Language of Power." *Language of Politics: Studies in
　　　　　　　　　Quantitative Semantics*. Cambridge: MIT Press.
Lo, Clarence Yin-Hsieh
　　　　　1978　　"The Truman Administration's Military Budgets During the
　　　　　　　　　Korean War." Ph.D. dissertation, University of California,
　　　　　　　　　Berkeley.
Lovell, John P. and Kronenberg, Philip S. (eds.)
　　　　　1974　　*New Civil-Military Relations*. New Brunswick, N.J.: Trans-
　　　　　　　　　action.
Lowi, Theodore
　　　　　1967　　"Making Democracy Safe for the World." *Domestic Sources of
　　　　　　　　　Foreign Policy*. James M. Rosenau (ed.). New York: The Free
　　　　　　　　　Press.
Mandelbaum, Michael and Schneider, William
　　　　　1978　　"The New Internationalisms." *International Security*, winter.
Melman, Seymour
　　　　　1974　　*The Permanent War Economy*. New York: Simon and Schuster.
Mencken, H.L.
　　　　　1956　　*Minority Report*. New York: Knopf.
Meyer, Herbert E.
　　　　　1977　　"The Communist Internationale Has a Capitalist Accent."
　　　　　　　　　Fortune, February.
Millis, Walter (ed.)
　　　　　1951　　*The Forrestal Diaries*. New York: Viking.
Millis, Walter; Mansfield, Harvey C.; and Stein, Harold
　　　　　1958　　*Arms and the State: Civil-Military Elements in National
　　　　　　　　　Policy*. New York: The Twentieth Century Fund.
Mills, C. Wright
　　　　　1956　　*The Power Elite*. New York: Oxford.
Morehouse, Ward
　　　　　1980-81 "Separate, Unequal, But More Autonomous: Technology,
　　　　　　　　　Equity, and World Order in the Millenial Transition." *Alter-
　　　　　　　　　natives: A Journal of World Policy*, VI, 3.
Moynihan, Daniel Patrick
　　　　　1979　　"Reflections: The SALT Process." *The New Yorker*, Novem-
　　　　　　　　　ber 19: 104.

1980   "A New American Foreign Policy." *The New Republic*, February 9: 17-20.

Neal, Fred Warner
1977   *A Survey of Detente — Past, Present, Future*. Washington, D.C.: American Committee on East-West Accord.

Neustadt, Richard E.
1960   *Presidential Power: The Politics of Leadership*. New York: Wiley.

Nitze, Paul H.
1974-75   "The Strategic Balance Between Hope and Skepticism." *Foreign Policy*, 17.
1976-77   "Deterring Our Deterrent." *Foreign Policy*, 25.
1978   "SALT II — The Objective vs. the Results." Washington, D.C.: The Committee on the Present Danger.
1980   "Strategy in the 1980s." *Foreign Affairs*, fall.

Nye, Joseph S., Jr.
1976   "Independence and Interdependence." *Foreign Policy*, 22: 130-147.

Oberdorfer, Don
1971   *Tet!* Garden City, New York: Doubleday.

Owen, Henry
1976   "Peace or War." *Setting National Priorities: The Next Ten Years*. Washington, D.C.: Brookings.

Pentagon Papers
1971   *The Pentagon Papers: The Defense Department History of U.S. Decision-Making on Vietnam*. The Senator Gravel edition. Boston: Beacon.
1971   *The Pentagon Papers: The Defense Department History of U.S. Decision-Making on Vietnam*. The New York Times edition. New York: Bantam.

Phillips, Kevin P.
1979   "The Hype That Roared." *Politics Today*, May-June: 54-58.

Pipes, Richard
1977   "Why the Soviet Union Thinks It Could Fight and Win a Nuclear War." *Commentary*, July: 21-35.

Podhoretz, Norman
1976   "Making the World Safe for Communism." *Commentary*, April: 31-41.
1977   "The Culture of Appeasement." *Harper's*, October: 25-32.
1980   "The Present Danger." *Commentary*, April.
1981   "The Future Danger." *Commentary*, April.

Price, Harry Bayard
1955   *The Marshall Plan and Its Meaning*. Ithaca: Cornell University Press.

Relyea, Harold C.
1972   "The American Security Council." *The Nation*, January 24.

Rosenau, James M.
1963   *National Leadership and Foreign Policy*. Princeton, N.J.: Princeton University Press.

Roskin, Michael
    1974   "From Pearl Harbor to Vietnam: Shifting Generational Para-
                digms and Foreign Policy." *Political Science Quarterly*, vol.
                19, no. 3.
Rostow, Eugene V.
    1976   "Statement on Foreign and Defense Policy before the Platform
                Committee of the Democratic National Convention, May 19."
                Washington, D.C.: Coalition for a Democratic Majority.
    1977   "What Is Our Defense Program For? American Foreign and
                Defense Policy after Vietnam." *Arms, Men, and Military Bud-
                gets, Issues for Fiscal Year 1978*. Francis P. Hoeber and
                William Schneider (eds.). New York: Crane, Russak.
    1978   "Statement to the Committee on the Budget, U.S. Senate,
                March 1." Washington, D.C.: Committee on the Present
                Danger.
    1978   "SALT II — A Soft Bargain, A Hard Sell: An Assessment of
                SALT in Historical Perspective." Washington, D.C.: Com-
                mittee on the Present Danger.
Rothmyer, Karen
    1981   "Citizen Scaife." *Columbia Journalism Review*, July-August.
Sanders, Jerry
    1980   "Shaping the Cold War Consensus: The Soviet Threat, Inter-
                elite Conflict, and Mass Politics in the Korean War Era."
                Berkeley Journal of Sociology, 24.
    1982   "Elites, Public Opinion, and Empire: On Lions, Foxes, and
                Mass Politics in the Post-Vietnam Era." *Alternatives: A Journal
                of World Policy*, 8:1, summer.
Schandler, Herbert Y.
    1977   *The Unmaking of a President: Lyndon Johnson and
                Vietnam*. Princeton, N.J.: Princeton University Press.
Schneider, William
    1974-75   "Public Opinion: The Beginning of Ideology?" *Foreign Policy*,
                17: 88-120.
Schrag, Peter
    1975   "America Needs an Establishment." *Harper's*, December: 51-
                58.
Schuettinger, Robert L.
    1977   "The New Foreign Policy Network." *Policy Review*, summer.
Schultze, Charles L.
    1973   "The Economic Content of National Security Policy." *Foreign
                Affairs*, April.
Schurmann, Franz
    1974   *The Logic of World Power*. New York: Pantheon.
Scoville, Herbert
    1974   "Flexible Madness?" *Foreign Policy*, 14.
Shoup, Laurence H. and Minter, William
    1977   *The Imperial Brain Trust*. New York: Monthly Review.
Sivard, Ruth Leger
    1981   *World Military and Social Expenditures*, Leesburg, VA:
                WMSE.

Sklar, Holly
1980   "Trilateralism: Managing Dependence and Democracy — An Overview." *Trilateralism: The Trilateral Commission and Elite Planning for World Management*. Boston: South End Press.

Smith, Gaddis
1972   *Dean Acheson. The American Secretaries of State and Their Diplomacy*, vol. 16. Robert H. Ferrell (ed.). New York: Cooper Square Publishers.

Spanier, John W.
1959   *The Truman-MacArthur Controversy and the Korean War*. New York: Norton.
1967   *American Foreign Policy Since World War II*. New York: Praeger.

Steinfels, Peter
1979   "The Reasonable Right." *Esquire*, February 13: 24.

Taylor, Maxwell
1959   *The Uncertain Trumpet*. New York: Harper and Brothers.

Thompson, E.P.
1981   "A Letter to America." *The Nation*, January 24.

Tonelson, Alan
1979   "Nitze's World." *Foreign Policy*, 35: 74-91.

Trilateral Commission
1977   *Towards a Renovated International System*. The Triangle Papers, No. 14.
1978   *An Overview of East-West Relations*. The Triangle Papers, No. 15.
1979   *Industrial Policy and the International Economy*. The Triangle Papers, No. 19.

Trout, B. Thomas
1975   "Rhetoric Revisited." *International Studies Quarterly*, vol. 19, no. 3.

Truman, Harry S.
1956   *Memoirs: Years of Trial and Hope*. Garden City, New York: Doubleday.

Ullman, Richard H.
1976   "Trilateralism: Partnership for What?" *Foreign Affairs*, October.

U.S. Congress, Senate, Committee on Foreign Relations
1977   "Hearings, Warnke Nomination. (Ninety-fifth Congress, 1st session, February, 809.) Washington, D.C.: Government Printing Office.

U.S. Department of State
1950   *Foreign Relations of the United States*. Washington, D.C.: Government Printing Office.

U.S. Department of Defense
1977   "Remarks by the Honorable Harold Brown, Secretary of Defense, at the Thirty-Fourth Annual Dinner of the National Security Industrial Association, September 15, 1977." News

Release, Office of the Assistant Secretary of Defense, Public Affairs.

U.S. National Security Council
1950   "NSC-68: A Report to the National Security Council by the Executive Secretary on United States Objectives and Programs for National Security, April 14, 1950." *Naval War College Review*, May-June, 1975: 51-108.

U.S. Senate
1981   Hearings Before the Committee on Foreign Relations. 97th Congress, First Session, on the Nomination of Eugene V. Rostow to be Director, Arms Control and Disarmament Agency (ACDA), June 22-23.

Volk, Steven S.
1979   "The International Competitiveness of the U.S. Economy: A Study of Steel and Electronics." *Capitalism and the State in U.S.-Latin American Relations*. Richard Fagen (ed.). Stanford, CA: Stanford University Press.

von N. Whitman, Marina
1975   "Leadership Without Hegemony: Our Role in the World Economy." *Foreign Policy*, 20: 138-160.

Voorhees, Tracy S.
1968   "The Committee on the Present Danger, 1950-1953." Tracy S. Voorhees Papers, Alexander Library, Rutgers University.

Wallerstein, Immanuel
1980   "Friends as Foes." *Foreign Policy*, Fall: 119-131.

Warnke, Paul
1975   "Apes on a Treadmill." *Foreign Policy*, 18.
1976-77 "We Don't Need a Devil (To Make or Keep Our Friends)." *Foreign Policy*, 25.

Wattenberg, Ben and Scammon, Richard
1970   *The Real Majority*. New York.

Watts, William and Free, Lloyd A.
1976   "Nationalism, Not Isolationism." *Foreign Affairs*, 24: 3-25.

Weisman, Steven R.
1982   "Reaganomics and the President's Men." *New York Times Magazine*, October 24.

Weisskopf, Thomas
1981   "The Current Economic Crisis in Historical Perspective." *Socialist Review*, 11:3, May-June.

Williams, William Appleman
1959   *The Tragedy of American Diplomacy*. Cleveland: World.
1980   *Empire as a Way of Life*. New York: Oxford University Press.

Wolfe, Alan
1979   "National Security and Domestic Politics." Mimeographed.
1980   "Reflections on Trilateralism and the Carter Administration: Changed World Realities vs. Vested Interests." *Trilateralism: The Trilateral Commission and Elite Planning for World Management*. Boston: South End Press.

1980   *The Rise and Fall of the Soviet Threat.* Washington: Institute for Policy Studies.

Wolfe, Alan and Sanders, Jerry
1979   "Resurgent Cold War Ideology: The Case of the Committee on the Present Danger." *Capitalism and the State in U.S.-Latin American Relations.* Richard Fagen (ed.). Stanford, California: Stanford University Press.

Woodhouse, Charles E. and McLellan, David S.
1966   "American Business Leaders and Foreign Policy: A Study in Perspectives." *American Journal of Economics and Sociology*, July.

Yergin, Daniel
1977   *Shattered Peace: The Origins of the Cold War and the National Security State.* Boston: Houghton Mifflin.

PRIVATE PAPERS, UNPUBLISHED LETTERS, AND MEMORANDA

Tracy S. Voorhees Papers, Alexander Library, Rutgers University.

Letter to Eugene V. Rostow from Secretary of State Henry Kissinger, August 19, 1974.

Letter to Secretary of State Henry Kissinger from Eugene V. Rostow, September 4, 1974.

Letter to James Schlesinger from Eugene V. Rostow, May 17, 1976.

Letter to Eugene V. Rostow from Frank Barnett, May 24, 1976.

Letter to Frank Barnett from Eugene V. Rostow, June 1, 1976.

Letter to Jerry W. Sanders from Eugene V. Rostow, July 25, 1977.

Memorandum to the Members of the Committee on the Present Danger from Eugene V. Rostow, Chairman, Executive Committee, August 1, 1979.

Memorandum to Friends and Supporters of the Committee on the Present Danger from Eugene V. Rostow, Chairman Executive Committee, December 5, 1979.

Anonymous Memorandum, RE: Paul Warnke, Staff, Coalition For A Democratic Majority, undated.

INDEX